NE능률 영어교과서

대한민국 고등학생 **10**명 중
4.7 명이 보는 교과서

영어 고등 교과서 점유율 1위
[7차, 2007 개정, 2009 개정, 2015 개정]

KB124617

능률보카

그동안 판매된
능률VOCA 1,100만 부

대한민국 박스오피스
**천만명을 넘은 영화
단 28개**

차곡차곡 쌓으면 19만 미터

**에베레스트
21 배 높이**

190,000m

에베레스트 8,848m

그래머존

그동안 판매된 450만 부의 그래머존을 바닥에 쭉 ~ 깔면
1000km 서울 - 부산 왕복가능

서울

부산

교재 검토에 도움을 주신 선생님들

1316
LISTENING LEVEL 3

지은이	NE능률 영어교육연구소
영문교열	Curtis Thompson, Keeran Murphy, Angela Lan
디자인	닷츠
내지 일러스트	박응식, 윤병철
맥편집	김재민

NE능률이
미래를
창조합니다.

건강한 배움의 고객가치를 제공하겠다는 꿈을 실현하기 위해
40년이 넘는 시간 동안 열심히 달려왔습니다.

앞으로도 끊임없는 연구와 노력을 통해
당연한 것을 멈추지 않고

고객, 기업, 직원 모두가 함께 성장하는 NE능률이 되겠습니다.

기초부터 실전까지 중학 듣기 완성

1316

1316 LISTENING

LEVEL
3

STRUCTURE & FEATURES

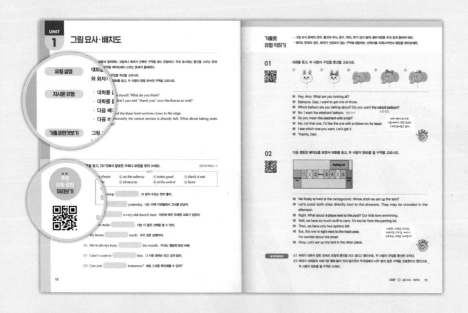

기출로 유형 익히기

기출 문제를 들어보면서 최신 출제 경향을 알 수 있습니다. 내용 파악에 도움이 되는 듣기 전략, 정답의 결정적인 근거가 되는 '정답 단서'와 오답을 유도하는 '오답 함정'을 통해 해당 유형에 대한 적응력을 키울 수 있습니다.

유형 설명 & 지시문 유형 & 기출 표현 맛보기

해당 기출 문제 유형의 전반적인 특징과 대표 지시문을 확인할 수 있습니다.
유형별 실제 기출 문장을 제시하여 해당 문제의 정답과 직결된 표현을 익힐 수 있습니다.

주요 어휘·표현 미리보기

본격적인 문제 풀이에 앞서 해당 단원에 등장할 중요한 어휘와 표현을 미리 학습할 수 있습니다.

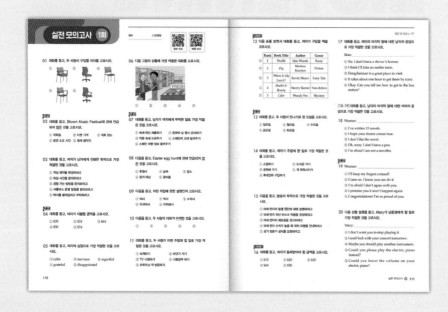

실전 모의고사

실제 중학 영어듣기 능력평가 유형을 충실히 반영한 실전 모의고사 6회분으로 문제 풀이 능력을 향상할 수 있습니다.

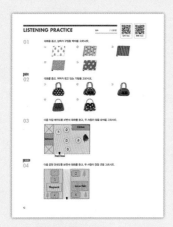

LISTENING PRACTICE

다양한 소재와 상황으로 구성된
대화 및 담화를 통해 해당 유형을
집중적으로 훈련할 수 있습니다.
단원마다 고난도 문제와 영국식
발음으로 녹음한 문제가 포함되어
있어 실전에 대한 자신감을 키울
수 있습니다.

DICTATION

주요 표현을 받아쓰면서 시험에
자주 나오는 구문을 익힐 수
있습니다. 또한, '정답 단서'와
'오답 함정'을 참고하여 학습한
내용을 확실히 점검할 수 있습니다.

어휘·표현 다지기

듣기에 등장한 어휘와 표현을
정리하고 복습할 수 있습니다.

시험 직전 모의고사

실제 시험 형식으로 구성된 2회분의
모의고사로, 중학 영어듣기 능력평가
직전에 활용할 수 있습니다.
듣기 MP3 파일, Dictation,
어휘·표현 테스트지는 www.
nebooks.co.kr에서 내려받을 수
있습니다.

CONTENTS

SECTION

2

실전 모의고사 &
시험 직전 모의고사

1316 LISTENING

LEVEL 3

중3 기출 문제 유형 분석

	유형	형태	단어 수 (words)	페어 수 (pairs)	2020 2회	2021 1회	2021 2회	2022 1회	2022 2회	2023 1회	계
1	그림 묘사	대화	81~110	4~4.5	1	1	1	1	1	1	6
2	언급되지 않은 내용	대화	80~93	4~5.5	1	1	1	1	1	1	6
		담화	58~87		1	1	1	1	1	1	6
3	목적	대화	81~102	4~5	1	1	1	1	1	1	6
		담화	54~83		1	1	1	1	1	1	6
4	숫자 정보	대화	83~110	3.5~5.5	2	3	3	3	2	2	15
5	심정	대화	66~104	3~5	1		1	1	1	1	5
6	대화 장소	대화	108	4.5		1					1
7	그림 상황에 적절한 대화	대화			1	1	1	1	1	1	6
8	부탁한 일	대화	70~96	3.5~4.5	1	1	1	1	1	1	6
9	주제/화제	담화	58~77		1		1	1	1	1	5
10	직업	담화	55			1					1
11	어색한 대화	대화			1	1	1	1	1	1	6
12	할 일 · 한 일	대화	80~96	4~5	2	2	2	2	2	2	12
13	도표	대화	84~100	4~4.5	1			1	1	1	4
14	배치도	대화	114	4~4.5		1	1				2
15	세부 정보	대화	75~101	3.5~4.5	1				1	1	3
16	마지막 말에 대한 응답	대화	70~105	3~5	3	3	3	3	3	3	18
17	상황에 적절한 말	담화	53~83		1	1	1	1	1	1	6
	계				20	20	20	20	20	20	

www.nebooks.co.kr

Section

1

유형 설명
UNIT 1·12

그림 묘사·배치도

유형 설명

대화를 듣고, 내용과 일치하는 그림이나 화자가 선택한 구역을 찾는 유형이다. 주로 묘사하는 물건을 고르는 문제와 화자가 선택한 구역을 배치도에서 고르는 문제가 출제된다.

지시문 유형

· 대화를 듣고, 여자가 구입할 쿠션을 고르시오.
· 다음 배치도를 보면서 대화를 듣고, 두 사람이 앉을 좌석의 구역을 고르시오.

기출 표현 맛보기

그림 묘사

W I drew the carnation myself. What do you think?

M It's beautiful. Why don't you add "thank you" over the flower as well?

배치도

M I want to sit in one of the three front sections closer to the stage.

W I agree, but unfortunately the central section is already full. What about taking seats near the entrance?

**주요
어휘·표현
미리보기**

다음을 듣고, [보기]에서 알맞은 어휘나 표현을 찾아 쓰세요.

정답 및 해설 p. 2

보기
ⓐ a better choice ⓑ on the subway ⓒ tastes good ⓓ check it out
ⓔ used to be ⓕ sit next to ⓖ at the end of ⓗ faces

01 This potato soup _____ . 이 감자 수프는 맛이 좋아.

02 I met her _____ yesterday. 나는 어제 지하철에서 그녀를 만났어.

03 There _____ a very old church here. 이곳에 매우 오래된 교회가 있었어.

04 You can make _____ . 너는 더 좋은 선택을 할 수 있어.

05 My home _____ south. 우리 집은 남향이야.

06 We're always busy _____ the month. 우리는 월말에 항상 바빠.

07 I don't want to _____ him. 그 사람 옆에는 앉고 싶지 않아.

08 Can you _____ tomorrow? 내일 그것을 확인해줄 수 있어?

기출로 유형 익히기

- 그림 묘사 문제의 경우, 물건의 무늬, 문구, 위치, 추가 장식 등의 세부사항을 주의 깊게 들어야 해요.
- 배치도 문제의 경우, 화자가 선호하지 않는 구역에 해당하는 선택지를 지워나가면서 정답을 찾아보세요.

01

대화를 듣고, 두 사람이 구입할 풍선을 고르시오.

① ② ③ ④ ⑤

M   Hey, Amy. What are you looking at?

W   Balloons. Dad, I want to get one of those.

M   Which balloon are you talking about? Do you want the rabbit balloon?

W   No. I want the elephant balloon. 정답 단서   오답 함정

M   Do you mean the elephant with a hat?

W   No, not that one. I'd like the one with a ribbon on its head.

M   I see which one you want. Let's get it.

W   Thanks, Dad.

> 세부사항이 하나씩 나올 때마다 정답 후보도 2개씩 줄어들고 있어.

02

다음 캠핑장 배치도를 보면서 대화를 듣고, 두 사람이 텐트를 칠 구역을 고르시오.

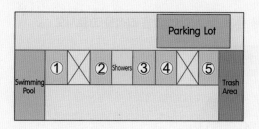

Parking Lot

① ② Showers ③ ④ ⑤

Swimming Pool   Trash Area

M   We finally arrived at the campground. Where shall we set up the tent?

W   Let's avoid both sites directly next to the showers. They may be crowded in the afternoon.

M   Right. What about a place next to the pool? Our kids love swimming.

W   Well, we have so much stuff to carry. It's too far from the parking lot.

M   Then, we have only two options left.

W   But, this one is right next to the trash area. I'm worried about the smell.

M   Okay. Let's set up the tent in the other place.

> 샤워장, 수영장, 주차장, 쓰레기장 근처 중, 여자가 선호하는 구역은 어디일까?

ANSWER

01 여자가 리본이 달린 코끼리 모양의 풍선을 사고 싶다고 했으므로, 두 사람이 구입할 풍선은 ④이다.

02 여자가 샤워장과 쓰레기장 옆에 붙어 있지 않으면서 주차장에서 너무 멀지 않은 구역을 선호한다고 했으므로, 두 사람이 텐트를 칠 구역은 ④이다.

LISTENING PRACTICE

일반 속도

빠른 속도

01 대화를 듣고, 남자가 구입할 벽지를 고르시오.

①   ②   ③

④   ⑤

02 대화를 듣고, 여자가 찾고 있는 가방을 고르시오.

①   ②   ③

④   ⑤

03 다음 식당 배치도를 보면서 대화를 듣고, 두 사람이 앉을 좌석을 고르시오.

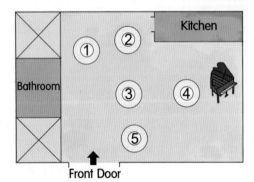

04 고난도
다음 공원 안내도를 보면서 대화를 듣고, 두 사람이 앉을 곳을 고르시오.

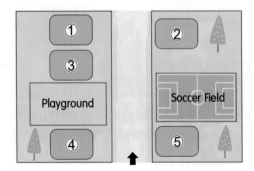

05 대화를 듣고, 남자가 구입할 옷을 고르시오.

①    ②    ③

④

06 대화를 듣고, 여자가 설명하는 텐트를 고르시오.

①    ②    ③

④   ⑤

07 다음 교실 좌석 배치도를 보면서 대화를 듣고, 남자가 앉는 좌석을 고르시오.

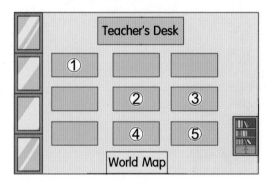

08 다음 경기장 주차 안내도를 보면서 대화를 듣고, 두 사람이 주차할 구역을 고르시오.

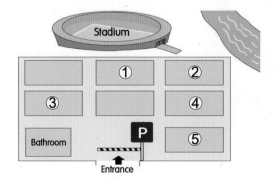

09 대화를 듣고, 여자가 목격한 용의자를 고르시오.

10 대화를 듣고, 여자의 사촌을 고르시오.

11 다음 가구 배치도를 보면서 대화를 듣고, 두 사람이 꽃병을 놓을 장소를 고르시오.

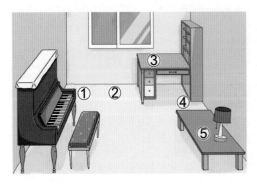

12 다음 객실 배치도를 보면서 대화를 듣고, 여자가 선택한 객실을 고르시오.

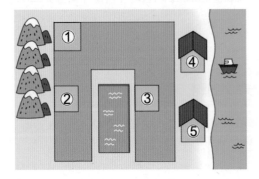

DICTATION

정답 단서 오답 함정
일반 속도   빠른 속도

01

대화를 듣고, 남자가 구입할 벽지를 고르시오.

① 　②

③ 　④

⑤

M What do you think of this wallpaper?

W I like it. The pattern of pine trees is really nice.

M They also have wallpaper with stars. But I think stripes might be _____ _____ _____.

W Stars and stripes together?

M No, I like the one that just has stripes. I think I'm going to buy it.

W I _____ _____ _____ with wavy stripes. It would look great in your kitchen.

M I disagree. It _____ _____ _____ _____. I'll stick with straight stripes.

02

대화를 듣고, 여자가 찾고 있는 가방을 고르시오.

① 　②

③ 　④

⑤

W Excuse me. I left my bag _____ _____ _____ yesterday. Have you found it?

M Maybe. We found several bags yesterday. What does it look like?

W It's a black-and-white bag with _____ _____ _____ _____.

M How many pockets does it have on the front?

W It doesn't have any.

M Is your bag checkered?

W No. It is black _____ _____ _____.

M Aha! Here it is!

03

다음 식당 배치도를 보면서 대화를 듣고, 두 사람이 앉을 좌석을 고르시오.

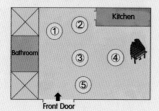

M Where should we sit?

W Well, I don't want to sit _____.

M Okay. But that table over there is too close to the piano.

W Yes, someone will be playing it soon. It will be _____.

M How about over there, near the door to the kitchen?

W Okay, that _____ _____.

M Great. I just need to use the bathroom. Sit down, and I'll be right back.

W All right. I'll _____ _____ _____ the menu while you're gone.

04

다음 공원 안내도를 보면서 대화를 듣고, 두 사람이 앉을 곳을 고르시오.

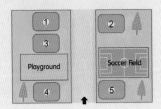

W It's a perfect day for a picnic!

M Yes, it is. Which side of the jogging path should we put the blanket on?

W The playground is always noisy. Let's have our picnic _____ _____ _____ _____.

M Okay. We should have our picnic under a tree.

W Yes. It will be cooler if we're not _____ _____ _____.

M How about there?

W It's too _____ _____ _____ _____. What if a ball lands on our blanket?

M Good point. Let's go over there instead.

W It looks perfect. The grass is soft, and the view is lovely.

M And hopefully the _____ _____ _____! This will be a great picnic.

05

대화를 듣고, 남자가 구입할 옷을 고르시오.

① ② ③ ④ ⑤

W What do you think of this shirt? You should get it for your dad _____ _____ _____ _____.

M That's a good idea. But he doesn't really like _____ _____ _____.

W Well, does he like patterned shirts or plain ones?

M Actually, he _____ _____ _____ _____.

W How about this one?

M Yes, it's nice, but do they have one with long sleeves?

W Yes, but the color is different. _____ _____ _____.

M Oh, yes. He'd love that one!

06

대화를 듣고, 여자가 설명하는 텐트를 고르시오.

① ② ③ ④ ⑤

W Wow, look at all these tents!

M A lot of people _____ _____ this weekend! Which one is your brother's tent?

W It's over there. It has black circles _____ _____ _____.

M Is it one of the triangular ones with a pointed top?

W No, it is round. And the _____ _____ _____ _____.

M I see it. There's a picnic table behind it.

W Yes. We all can sit there when we have dinner together.

07

다음 교실 좌석 배치도를 보면서 대화를 듣고, 남자가 앉는 좌석을 고르시오.

M This is my classroom for Chinese class, Mom. That's my teacher's desk at the front of the room.

W Yes, I see. But where is your desk?

M It _____ _____ _____ in the middle of the room. But now it's in the back.

W Is it ～～～～～～～～～～～～～～～～～～～～～～～？

M No, I don't like to sit by the window. It's too cold in the winter.

W _____ _____ _____. Is it next to the bookshelf?

M Yes! And my best friend Carl _____ _____ _____ _____, in front of the map of the world.

고난도

08

다음 경기장 주차 안내도를 보면서 대화를 듣고, 두 사람이 주차할 구역을 고르시오.

M We're finally here.

W Right. Where should we park the car?

M Let's park ～～～～～～～～～～～～～～～～～～～～～～～～～～～～～～.

W But what if someone hits a home run? The ball could hit my new car!

M I didn't think of that. Then let's park near the river. It will be a short walk to the stadium.

W But many cars will be leaving at the same time _____ _____ _____ _____ _____ _____.

M That's true. So we should park near the parking lot entrance.

W Yes. Do you need to use the bathroom? There's one ～～～～～～～～～～～～～～～～～～～～ the entrance.

M No, that's okay. Let's just park on the other side.

W Sounds good.

09

대화를 듣고, 여자가 목격한 용의자를 고르시오.

W Officer! I saw the man who _____ _____ _____! He ran out and got into a van!

M Excellent. I need a description of him. What did he look like?

W He had black, curly hair.

M Did you see his face?

W No, I didn't. He was _____ ～～～～～～～～～～～～～～～～ _____ over his face.

M Do you remember anything else?

W He was _____ ～～～～～～～～～ _____.

M Thank you for your help, ma'am.

10

대화를 듣고, 여자의 사촌을 고르시오.

W This is a really exciting tennis match. Which side are you _____ _____?

M I'm cheering for the team that's winning.

W I'm cheering for the other team. My cousin is one of the players.

M Really? Which one is she?

W She's the one _____ _____ _____ _____.

M But they're both wearing striped skirts.

W Oh, right. She's the one _____ _____ _____ the net.

M I see her! She looks a lot like you!

11

다음 가구 배치도를 보면서 대화를 듣고, 두 사람이 꽃병을 놓을 장소를 고르시오.

W Where is _____ _____ _____ for the big vase?

M How about under the window?

W I'm going to put the fan there.

M How about putting the vase _____ _____ _____ _____?

W No, I don't think that's the right place.

M Why not? There's _____ _____ _____.

W Yeah, but I'm going to put a bookshelf there.

M How about _____ _____ _____? You can move the lamp somewhere else.

W That's a good idea! I'll put the lamp on the desk.

12

다음 객실 배치도를 보면서 대화를 듣고, 여자가 선택한 객실을 고르시오.

M Welcome to the Tropical Resort!

W Thank you! Do you have _____ _____ _____?

M Yes. We have several rooms in the main building. We also have some rooms _____ _____ _____ _____.

W I'd prefer to be in the main building.

M Certainly. We have rooms that _____ _____ _____ and others that have a view of the mountain.

W Oh, I'd like to have a nice view of the mountain!

M Okay. If you _____ _____ _____ _____, you can have a corner room. They're a bit bigger.

W No, a regular room is fine.

A 다음 영어 어휘나 표현의 뜻을 우리말로 쓰세요.

01 wallpaper	**02** several
03 pattern	**04** stripe
05 bookshelf	**06** blanket
07 plenty of	**08** vase
09 retirement	**10** sleeve
11 parking lot	**12** entrance
13 cheer for	**14** curly
15 match	**16** rob

B 우리말에 맞는 영어 어휘나 표현을 [보기]에서 찾아 쓰세요.

	보기	view	by the window	triangular	stick with	make sense
		plain	in the middle of	pointed	available	take a look at

01 ~을 보다	**02** 무늬가 없는
03 이용할 수 있는	**04** 전망
05 삼각형의	**06** 끝이 뾰족한
07 창가에	**08** ~의 중앙에
09 ~을 계속하다	**10** 이해가 되다, 의미가 통하다

언급되지 않은 내용

유형 설명 대화나 담화를 듣고 언급되지 않은 내용을 찾는 유형이다. 주로 특정 제품이나 행사 등에 대한 두 사람의 대화나 소개 내용에서 언급되지 않은 사항을 고르는 문제가 출제된다.

지시문 유형
- 대화를 듣고, 스키 강습에 관해 언급되지 <u>않은</u> 것을 고르시오.
- 다음을 듣고, Korean Wave Day에 관해 언급되지 <u>않은</u> 것을 고르시오.

기출 표현 맛보기
- The winner will get a trophy and a 50-dollar gift card. (우승 상품)
- Are you ready for the 2016 International Fireworks Festival sponsored by the Max Company? (후원사)
- This event includes various programs such as a K-pop contest, a dance competition, and a Korean food fair. (행사 프로그램)

주요 어휘·표현 미리보기

다음을 듣고, [보기]에서 알맞은 어휘나 표현을 찾아 쓰세요. 　　　　　정답 및 해설 p. 5

보기
ⓐ located on　　ⓑ was founded　　ⓒ former　　ⓓ took notes ⓔ a variety of　　ⓕ participate in　　ⓖ world-famous　　ⓗ graduate from

01 I'm planning to _____ the cooking competition. 나는 요리 대회에 참가할 예정이야.

02 This church _____ 100 years ago. 이 교회는 100년 전에 세워졌어.

03 When did you _____ university? 너는 대학을 언제 졸업했니?

04 I _____ to remember the important points. 나는 요점을 기억하기 위해 메모했어.

05 She is a _____ artist from Spain. 그녀는 스페인 출신의 세계적으로 유명한 화가야.

06 My house is _____ Fourth Street. 우리 집은 4번 가에 있어.

07 _____ animals live together here. 이곳에 여러 동물이 함께 살아.

08 That man is the _____ mayor of Seoul. 저분은 전 서울 시장이야.

기출로
유형 익히기

- 먼저 지시문과 선택지를 읽고 주의해서 들어야 할 내용이 무엇인지 파악하세요.
- 선택지 순서대로 내용이 언급되므로, 들려주는 내용과 선택지를 비교하며 오답을 지워나가세요.

01

대화를 듣고, 배우에 관해 언급되지 <u>않은</u> 것을 고르시오.

① 이름　　　② 출연작　　　③ 외모　　　④ 성격　　　⑤ 연기 경력

W Jiho, what are you looking at?
M I'm looking at pictures of my favorite actor, Daniel Parker.
W Doesn't he play the main character in the movie, *The Great World*?
M Yes, he does. He's a really handsome guy.
W I agree with you. His dark eyes are so lovely.
M Yeah, and he's also an excellent actor. He has 20 years of acting experience.
W Maybe I should watch one of his movies soon.
M Yes, you should.

두 사람은 남자가
좋아하는 영화배우에
관해 이야기하고 있어.

02

다음을 듣고, Book Fair에 관해 언급되지 <u>않은</u> 것을 고르시오.

① 시작 연도　　　② 행사 기간　　　③ 활동 내용
④ 신청 방법　　　⑤ 참가 선물

M Hi, students. I'm Andrew from the book club. Our Book Fair is coming soon. It has been 12 years since it first started in 2008. This year's event will be held next week from Monday to Friday in the library. You can exchange books with each other and have a talk with famous writers through this event. All participants will be given a bookmark as a gift. Come and enjoy!

도서 전시회에 관한 안내
사항이야. 먼저 선택지를
읽고 흐름을 추측해 보자.

ANSWER

01 배우의 이름(Daniel Parker), 출연작(The Great World), 외모(매우 잘생김), 연기 경력(20년)은 언급되었지만, 성격에 관한 언급은 없으므로 정답은 ④이다.

02 Book Fair의 시작 연도(2008년), 행사 기간(다음 주 월요일부터 금요일), 활동 내용(책 교환, 유명 작가와의 대화), 참가 선물(북마크)은 언급되었지만, 신청 방법에 관한 언급은 없으므로 정답은 ④이다.

LISTENING PRACTICE

점수   / 10문항

일반 속도   빠른 속도

01 대화를 듣고, 지갑에 관해 언급되지 <u>않은</u> 것을 고르시오.

① 크기   ② 디자이너   ③ 소재
④ 가격   ⑤ 색상

02 대화를 듣고, Walk across the Country에 관해 언급되지 <u>않은</u> 것을 고르시오.

① 거리   ② 출발지   ③ 예상 일정
④ 참가 인원   ⑤ 참가비

03 대화를 듣고, Your Next Baker에 관해 언급되지 <u>않은</u> 것을 고르시오.

① 방영 채널   ② 방영 시간   ③ 참가자 수
④ 우승 상금   ⑤ 진행자

04 다음을 듣고, Oceanview Resort에 관해 언급되지 <u>않은</u> 것을 고르시오.

① 위치   ② 객실 수   ③ 객실 요금
④ 부대시설   ⑤ 주변 관광지

05 다음을 듣고, Miller Memorial Hospital에 관해 언급되지 <u>않은</u> 것을 고르시오.

① 병실 수   ② 편의시설   ③ 설립연도
④ 현 위치   ⑤ 병원명의 유래

고난도
06 대화를 듣고, Eugene Williams에 관해 언급되지 <u>않은</u> 것을 고르시오.
① 국적   ② 수상 경력   ③ 학력
④ 별명   ⑤ 연주회 일정

07 대화를 듣고, City Garden Project에 관해 언급되지 <u>않은</u> 것을 고르시오.
① 장소   ② 참가 대상   ③ 신청 방법
④ 참가비   ⑤ 마감 일자

고난도
08 다음을 듣고, Barrington National Park에 관해 언급되지 <u>않은</u> 것을 고르시오.
① 연간 방문객   ② 위치   ③ 규모
④ 서식 동물   ⑤ 편의시설

09 다음을 듣고, Littleton High School의 신입 교사에 관해 언급되지 <u>않은</u> 것을 고르시오.
① 이름   ② 담당 교과목   ③ 담당 학년
④ 학력   ⑤ 거주지

10 다음을 듣고, 불국사 현장 학습에 관해 언급되지 <u>않은</u> 것을 고르시오.
① 요일   ② 참가 인원   ③ 복장
④ 준비물   ⑤ 우천 시 유의 사항

DICTATION

일반 속도   빠른 속도

01

대화를 듣고, 지갑에 관해 언급되지
않은 것을 고르시오.
① 크기   ② 디자이너
③ 소재   ④ 가격
⑤ 색상

M Excuse me, I'd like to buy a wallet for my mom.

W How wonderful! What type of wallet are you looking for?

M My mom usually carries a long wallet, so I _____ _____ _____ _____.

W How about this wallet? _____ _____ _____ _____ Victoria Lee.

M Oh, Victoria Lee? I know her. She's a world-famous designer.

W You're right. Also, it is on sale now, so it's only 100 dollars.

M Sounds like a good deal. What colors do you have?

W It _____ _____ _____ _____: red, brown, and black.

M Then I'll take a brown one. I hope my mom will like it.

02

대화를 듣고, Walk across the
Country에 관해 언급되지 않은 것을
고르시오.
① 거리   ② 출발지
③ 예상 일정   ④ 참가 인원
⑤ 참가비

W I heard you _____ _____ _____ Walk across the Country.

M Right. I'm going to walk from one end of the country to the other.

W That's amazing. How long will it be?

M It's around 400 kilometers. We're planning to arrive in Seoul in 20 days.

W 400 kilometers in 20 days? I can't imagine walking _____ _____ _____ _____.

M I probably wouldn't be able to do it alone. But there are 200 other students, and we can help each other.

W True. How much is the participation fee?

M It's _____ _____ several companies, so students don't need to pay any money.

W That's good. I hope you finish the walk _____ _____ _____.

03

대화를 듣고, Your Next Baker에 관
해 언급되지 않은 것을 고르시오.
① 방영 채널   ② 방영 시간
③ 참가자 수   ④ 우승 상금
⑤ 진행자

M Hey, Kate, have you ever seen the show called *Your Next Baker*?

W No, I haven't. _____ _____ _____ _____?

M It is on Friday at 11:00 p.m. It started just two weeks ago.

W Oh, I see. Is it a competition for making creative desserts?

M Yep. There are 16 participants and the winner will receive 10,000 dollars.

W Sounds like fun.

M Also, Sandra Park hosts the show. She's really _____ _____ _____ how the desserts taste.

W Oh, I like her too. I'd like to watch the show _____ _____ _____ _____ _____.

24

04

다음을 듣고, Oceanview Resort에 관해 언급되지 <u>않은</u> 것을 고르시오.

① 위치　　　② 객실 수
③ 객실 요금　④ 부대시설
⑤ 주변 관광지

W Come to the Oceanview Resort! _____ _____ sunny Panna Island, our resort features 15 double rooms and 5 single rooms. _____ _____ _____ _____ have air conditioning and ocean views. We also have a large swimming pool and one of the best restaurants on the island. There's a beautiful beach _____ _____ _____. And you can walk to a popular museum and a traditional market. _____ _____ _____ today!

05

다음을 듣고, Miller Memorial Hospital에 관해 언급되지 <u>않은</u> 것을 고르시오.

① 병실 수　　② 편의시설
③ 설립연도　　④ 현 위치
⑤ 병원명의 유래

W Miller Memorial Hospital is the largest hospital in the New City area, with more than 1,000 rooms _____ _____. There are approximately 2,500 employees on the hospital's staff, _____ _____ _____ _____. It was founded in 1931. At that time, it was located downtown. Later, it moved to _____ _____ _____ on Maple Street. It was _____ _____ Brian Miller, the former mayor of New City.

고난도

06

대화를 듣고, Eugene Williams에 관해 언급되지 <u>않은</u> 것을 고르시오.

① 국적　　　② 수상 경력
③ 학력　　　④ 별명
⑤ 연주회 일정

M Sally, have you _____ _____ _____ _____ for the research project?
W Yes. I want to write about a rising pianist, Eugene Williams.
M Eugene Williams?
W He's from Australia. He _____ _____ _____ at the Chopin Competition when he was 16. He also _____ _____ _____ in other competitions after that.
M Amazing. Why is his music so loved?
W His music has the power _____ _____ _____ _____. That's why many fans call him a ray of sunshine.
M I'm curious about his music now.
W He's going to have a recital this December in Korea. _____ _____ _____ go with me?
M Sounds great!

대화를 듣고, City Garden Project 에 관해 언급되지 <u>않은</u> 것을 고르시오.

① 장소　　② 참가 대상
③ 신청 방법　④ 참가비
⑤ 마감 일자

W Look at this advertisement. Our city is going to start the City Garden Project.
M What is the City Garden Project?
W The city _____ _____ _____ a piece of land, and then we can plant flowers there.
M I see. It's like _____ _____ _____ _____! Where is the land located?
W It _____ _____ _____ Grand Park.
M Oh, it's close to my house. Are there any requirements to participate in the project?
W This project is only for teenagers. _____ _____ _____ _____, we should send an application via email.
M Okay. I want to plant roses and daisies. When is the deadline?
W It's next Monday, so we should apply soon.

고난도
08

다음을 듣고, Barrington National Park에 관해 언급되지 <u>않은</u> 것을 고르시오.

① 연간 방문객　② 위치
③ 규모　　④ 서식 동물
⑤ 편의시설

W Barrington National Park, the country's newest national park, attracts more than 200,000 visitors each year. It is located on a triangular piece of land next to beautiful Barrington Lake. _____ _____ _____ _____ wildlife can be found there, including elk, bears, and mountain lions. The park's visitor facilities include _____ _____ _____, several hiking trails, and three campsites. You can find more information at the visitor center _____ _____ _____ _____ _____ or by visiting the national park website.

09

다음을 듣고, Littleton High School 의 신입 교사에 관해 언급되지 <u>않은</u> 것을 고르시오.

① 이름　　② 담당 교과목
③ 담당 학년　④ 학력
⑤ 거주지

M Littleton High School would like to _____ _____ _____ _____. Her name is Victoria Choi, and she'll be teaching English classes. Victoria graduated from Duke University with a _____ _____ _____ in 2007. She worked at St. Mary's Middle School for seven years before joining our staff. Victoria now lives in Littleton with her husband and daughter. _____ _____ _____ _____ _____ if you see her!

10

다음을 듣고, 불국사 현장 학습에 관해 언급되지 <u>않은</u> 것을 고르시오.

① 요일　　② 참가 인원
③ 복장　　④ 준비물
⑤ 우천 시 유의 사항

W May I have your attention, please? This Friday, we will _____ _____ _____ _____ _____ to Bulguksa. You must be at school by 8:30 a.m., and you have to wear your school uniform. I _____ _____ _____ _____ because we will walk a lot. Please bring a pen _____ _____ _____, as well as a lunch. We will return to school by 3:00 p.m. If it rains, the trip _____ _____ _____, and we'll have classes as usual. Thank you.

A

다음 영어 어휘나 표현의 뜻을 우리말로 쓰세요.

01 patient

02 air conditioning

03 mayor

04 approximately

05 distance

06 employee

07 sneakers

08 downtown

09 recital

10 current

11 introduce

12 rising

13 field trip

14 facility

15 school uniform

16 main entrance

B

우리말에 맞는 영어 어휘나 표현을 [보기]에서 찾아 쓰세요.

보기	sponsor	air	as well as	participant	deadline
	degree	feature	name after	requirement	as usual

01 특별히 포함하다

02 참가자

03 늘 그렇듯이, 평상시처럼

04 자격 요건, 요구 조건

05 후원하다

06 학위

07 기한, 마감 일자

08 방송되다

09 ~의 이름을 따서 명명하다

10 ~뿐만 아니라

| 유형 설명 | 대화를 듣고 전화한 목적을 파악하는 문제와, 담화를 듣고 방송의 목적을 파악하는 문제가 출제된다. |

지시문 유형
- 대화를 듣고, 여자가 남자에게 전화한 목적으로 가장 적절한 것을 고르시오.
- 다음을 듣고, 방송의 목적으로 가장 적절한 것을 고르시오.

기출 표현 맛보기

전화 목적
- He broke his leg. Why don't we go visit him this afternoon?
- My car suddenly stopped at 702 Main Street. Could you send somebody to help?

방송 목적
- There will be a special event.
- Your participation is important, so please start today.

주요
어휘·표현
미리보기

다음을 듣고, [보기]에서 알맞은 어휘나 표현을 찾아 쓰세요.   정답 및 해설 p. 9

| 보기 |
| ⓐ was supposed to | ⓑ at least | ⓒ at the last minute | ⓓ fully booked |
| ⓔ hand over | ⓕ deal with | ⓖ feel stressed | ⓗ come with |

01 I had to _____ a difficult situation at work. 난 직장에서 힘든 상황을 해결해야 했어.

02 She changed her plans _____. 그녀는 마지막 순간에 계획을 변경했어.

03 We're _____ on that day. 그날은 예약이 꽉 찼습니다.

04 He _____ come at five o'clock. 그가 5시 정각에 오기로 했었어.

05 You have to _____ your cell phone to Ms. Kim. 네 휴대전화를 김 선생님께 내야 해.

06 Cut the grass _____ once a week. 최소한 일주일에 한 번은 잔디를 깎아주세요.

07 I _____ by exams these days. 나는 요즘 시험 때문에 스트레스를 받아.

08 Would you like to _____ me? 나와 함께 가고 싶니?

- 전화한 목적을 파악하는 문제의 경우, 전화를 건 사람이 초반에 하는 말을 유념해서 들으세요.
- 방송의 첫 부분과 마지막 부분에 방송의 목적을 직접적으로 언급하는 경우가 많으므로 이 부분에 유의하세요.

01

대화를 듣고, 남자가 여자에게 전화한 목적으로 가장 적절한 것을 고르시오.

① 입상 소식을 통보하려고
② 대회 장소 변경을 안내하려고
③ 작품 제출 여부를 확인하려고
④ 제출된 미술 작품을 돌려주려고
⑤ 전시회 개최 날짜를 공지하려고

[Cell phone rings.]

W Hello.

M Hello. This is Vision Art Center. Is this Emma Taylor?

W Yes, speaking.

M Oh, I want to inform you that the location of the 2020 art contest has been changed.   정답 단서

W It was supposed to be in auditorium A at your center, wasn't it?

M Yes, it was. But it'll be held in auditorium D instead.

W Oh, I see. Is there any change to the date or time?   오답 함정

M No. Those are the same. Thank you for understanding.

W No problem.

바뀐 대회 장소에 대해 이야기하고 있어.

02

다음을 듣고, 방송의 목적으로 가장 적절한 것을 고르시오.

① 플라스틱 사용량 줄이기를 촉구하려고
② 쓰레기 분리수거 방법을 알리려고
③ 친환경 물품 구매를 권유하려고
④ 재활용 제품의 성분을 안내하려고
⑤ 플라스틱의 재활용 과정을 설명하려고

W Hello, *Green Earth* listeners. Plastic pollution is a serious problem. So we need to take some personal actions to reduce the amount of plastic we use. First, use a reusable bag when you go shopping. Also, bring your own container when you get take-out food. Keep these in mind. Your participation is important, so please start today.

청취자들에게 플라스틱 사용량 줄이기에 동참하자고 말하고 있어.

ANSWER

01 남자가 여자에게 미술 대회의 장소가 변경되었음을 알려 주고 있으므로, 전화한 목적으로 ②가 알맞다.

02 플라스틱 사용량을 줄이기 위해 개인적으로 해야 하는 일에 대해 말하고 있으므로, 방송의 목적으로 ①이 알맞다.

LISTENING PRACTICE

점수 _____ / 10문항

일반 속도

빠른 속도

01 대화를 듣고, 남자가 여자에게 전화한 목적으로 가장 적절한 것을 고르시오.

① 분실물에 대해 문의하려고
② 병원 위치를 문의하려고
③ 진료 예약 시간을 변경하려고
④ 분실물 센터 운영 시간을 확인하려고
⑤ 진료를 예약하려고

02 대화를 듣고, 여자가 남자에게 전화한 목적으로 가장 적절한 것을 고르시오.

① 저녁 식사에 초대하려고
② 생일 파티 참석 여부를 확인하려고
③ 수업 시간을 확인하려고
④ 수업을 취소하려고
⑤ 외식할 만한 장소를 알아보려고

고난도

03 대화를 듣고, 남자가 여자에게 전화한 목적으로 가장 적절한 것을 고르시오.

① 함께 병문안을 가려고
② 수업에 결석할 것을 알리려고
③ 숙제를 물어보려고
④ 함께 축구 연습을 하려고
⑤ 수술 결과에 대해 물어보려고

04 다음을 듣고, 방송의 목적으로 가장 적절한 것을 고르시오.

① 새로운 주민 환영 행사를 알리려고
② 대형 폐기물 처리 방법을 안내하려고
③ 이사 시 엘리베이터 이용 협조를 요청하려고
④ 쓰레기장 위치 이동을 공지하려고
⑤ 쓰레기장 이용 규정을 안내하려고

05 다음을 듣고, 방송의 목적으로 가장 적절한 것을 고르시오.

① 폭우에 대비할 것을 경고하려고
② 우산 구매 및 대여 방법을 안내하려고
③ 지하철역 내 시설을 안내하려고
④ 분실물 센터 이용 방법을 설명하려고
⑤ 분실 우산 습득 사실을 알리려고

06 대화를 듣고, 여자가 남자에게 전화한 목적으로 가장 적절한 것을 고르시오.

① 귀가 예정 시간을 알리려고　　　　② 데리러 와달라고 부탁하려고
③ 자동차 사고를 신고하려고　　　　④ 귀가가 늦는 이유를 물어보려고
⑤ 자동차 정비소의 위치를 물어보려고

07 대화를 듣고, 남자가 여자에게 전화한 목적으로 가장 적절한 것을 고르시오.

① 미용실 예약을 확인하려고　　　　② 제품 정보를 문의하려고
③ 분실물을 찾으려고　　　　　　　④ 서비스 불만 사항을 말하려고
⑤ 제품을 홍보하려고

08 대화를 듣고, 여자가 남자에게 전화한 목적으로 가장 적절한 것을 고르시오.

① 뉴욕행 항공권을 취소하려고　　　　② 뉴욕에 도착한 것을 알리려고
③ 뉴욕의 날씨를 물어보려고　　　　　④ 회의 시간을 조정하려고
⑤ 회의 장소를 변경하려고

09 다음을 듣고, 방송의 목적으로 가장 적절한 것을 고르시오.

① 교내 상담 센터 이용을 안내하려고
② 새로 오신 상담 선생님을 소개하려고
③ 청소년 우울증의 위험성을 경고하려고
④ 올바른 스트레스 해소 방법을 설명하려고
⑤ 학교 폭력 방지 위원회의 설립을 알리려고

고난도
10 다음을 듣고, 방송의 목적으로 가장 적절한 것을 고르시오.

① 올바른 자외선 차단제 사용 방법을 알려주려고
② 피부 타입에 따른 세안법을 안내하려고
③ 새로 출시된 청소년용 화장품을 홍보하려고
④ 청소년을 위한 피부 관리법을 소개하려고
⑤ 청소년 여드름의 다양한 원인을 설명하려고

DICTATION

정답 단서 　 오답 함정

 일반 속도　 빠른 속도

01

대화를 듣고, 남자가 여자에게 전화한 목적으로 가장 적절한 것을 고르시오.

① 분실물에 대해 문의하려고
② 병원 위치를 문의하려고
③ 진료 예약 시간을 변경하려고
④ 분실물 센터 운영 시간을 확인하려고
⑤ 진료를 예약하려고

[Telephone rings.]

W Dr. Hwang's clinic. May I help you?

M Yes. This is Dan Lee. I _____ _____ _____ in an hour.

W All right.

M Well, I was wondering _____ _____ _____ _____ _____ _____. I lost my wallet, so I have to go to the lost and found office at the subway station.

W I see. What time would you like to come in?

M How about five o'clock?

W I'm sorry. We're _____ _____ at that time. How about 5:30?

M That's fine. Thank you.

02

대화를 듣고, 여자가 남자에게 전화한 목적으로 가장 적절한 것을 고르시오.

① 저녁 식사에 초대하려고
② 생일 파티 참석 여부를 확인하려고
③ 수업 시간을 확인하려고
④ 수업을 취소하려고
⑤ 외식할 만한 장소를 알아보려고

[Cell phone rings.]

M Hello?

W Hello, Mr. Phillips? This is Kate.

M Hi, Kate. We're supposed to meet in an hour, aren't we? Why are you calling?

W I'm sorry, but I can't _____ _____ _____. It's my father's birthday, so I have to go out to dinner with my family.

M I see. We can _____ _____ _____ _____ for next week.

W Thank you for understanding. I'm sorry to cancel _____ _____ _____ _____.

M It's okay. Have a good time with your family.

고난도

03

대화를 듣고, 남자가 여자에게 전화한 목적으로 가장 적절한 것을 고르시오.

① 함께 병문안을 가려고
② 수업에 결석할 것을 알리려고
③ 숙제를 물어보려고
④ 함께 축구 연습을 하려고
⑤ 수술 결과에 대해 물어보려고

[Cell phone rings.]

W Hello?

M Hi, Hyejin. This is Seungmin.

W Hi, Seungmin. Are you calling about our Spanish homework?

M No. I'm calling about Sohyun. She was _____ _____ _____ yesterday.

W Oh no! I noticed she wasn't at school today, but I assumed she was sick. Is she okay?

M Yes, but she _____ _____ _____. She's in the hospital.

W We should visit her!

M That's why I called. I'm going to the hospital tomorrow after soccer practice. Do you want to come with me?

W Sure. _____ _____ _____ _____?

M Let's meet at 3:00 in front of your house.

04

다음을 듣고, 방송의 목적으로 가장
적절한 것을 고르시오.
① 새로운 주민 환영 행사를 알리려고
② 대형 폐기물 처리 방법을 안내하려
  고
③ 이사 시 엘리베이터 이용 협조를
  요청하려고
④ 쓰레기장 위치 이동을 공지하려고
⑤ 쓰레기장 이용 규정을 안내하려고

W Good morning, residents! This is an announcement from the apartment management office. Recently, new residents have moved into our building. So we would like to remind you about the _____ _____ _____ _____ _____ _____. You can only access the garbage area _____ _____ _____ _____ _____. For large waste items such as desks, closets, and sofas, you have to _____ _____ _____ to our office. You can find the form in the elevator. Please be considerate when taking out your trash. Thank you.

05

다음을 듣고, 방송의 목적으로 가장
적절한 것을 고르시오.
① 폭우에 대비할 것을 경고하려고
② 우산 구매 및 대여 방법을 안내하
  려고
③ 지하철역 내 시설을 안내하려고
④ 분실물 센터 이용 방법을 설명하려
  고
⑤ 분실 우산 습득 사실을 알리려고

M Hello, passengers! It's raining heavily outside right now. It doesn't seem like it will stop raining soon. If you _____ _____ _____, you can buy one at the convenience store or the vending machine at the station. The convenience store is located at exit 1, and the _____ _____ _____ right next to the ticket gate. You can also _____ _____ at the station office on the second floor. However, you must hand over your ID and return the umbrella within three days. We hope everyone gets home safely. Thank you.

06

대화를 듣고, 여자가 남자에게 전화한
목적으로 가장 적절한 것을 고르시오.
① 귀가 예정 시간을 알리려고
② 데리러 와달라고 부탁하려고
③ 자동차 사고를 신고하려고
④ 귀가가 늦는 이유를 물어보려고
⑤ 자동차 정비소의 위치를 물어보려
  고

[Telephone rings.]

M Hello?

W Hi, Dad. It's Jinhee.

M Where are you? You _____ _____ _____ _____ half an hour ago! .

W Sorry. _____ _____ _____ _____ _____. I'm at the auto repair shop on Oxford Avenue, near the library.

M I see. What's wrong with your car?

W I'm not sure, but I think it'll _____ _____ _____ _____ _____ it. Could you pick me up?

M Okay. I'll be there in ten minutes.

07

대화를 듣고, 남자가 여자에게 전화한
목적으로 가장 적절한 것을 고르시오.
① 미용실 예약을 확인하려고
② 제품 정보를 문의하려고
③ 분실물을 찾으려고
④ 서비스 불만 사항을 말하려고
⑤ 제품을 홍보하려고

[Telephone rings.]

W Thank you for calling Happy Hair. How may I help you?

M Hi, this is Carl. I had an appointment at eleven o'clock this morning.

W I remember. Don't you _____ _____ _____ _____ _____?

M Actually, I love it!

W Good! Then _____ _____ _____ _____ for you?

M I think I left my wallet at the salon. Can you please _____ _____ _____ _____ it's there?

W Of course. One moment, please. [pause] Someone left a green wallet here.

M Oh! That's mine!

대화를 듣고, 여자가 남자에게 전화한 목적으로 가장 적절한 것을 고르시오.

① 뉴욕행 항공권을 취소하려고
② 뉴욕에 도착한 것을 알리려고
③ 뉴욕의 날씨를 물어보려고
④ 회의 시간을 조정하려고
⑤ 회의 장소를 변경하려고

[Cell phone rings.]

M Hello, Susan.

W Hi, Dan. I'm afraid I might be _____ _____ _____ _____ today.

M What is wrong?

W My flight to New York _____ _____ _____ due to bad weather conditions.

M Oh, I see. Then what time will you arrive?

W I will arrive around 2:00 p.m. So I need you to change the meeting time.

M I understand. I'll let the team know, and we'll _____ _____ _____ _____ .

W Thank you for your _____ _____ _____ .

M No problem, Susan. Safe travels and see you soon.

09

다음을 듣고, 방송의 목적으로 가장 적절한 것을 고르시오.

① 교내 상담 센터 이용을 안내하려고
② 새로 오신 상담 선생님을 소개하려고
③ 청소년 우울증의 위험성을 경고하려고
④ 올바른 스트레스 해소 방법을 설명하려고
⑤ 학교 폭력 방지 위원회의 설립을 알리려고

W Hello, students! I'm Ms. Smith, the school counselor. Sometimes you may feel worried or stressed. We want to remind you that _____ _____ _____ _____ at our school. We can help you with any personal, social, or academic issues that you may be facing. Everything will be _____ _____ and we won't share them with anyone else. You can _____ _____ _____ by phone, text, or email. Remember, it's okay to _____ _____ _____ when you need it. Our counselors are here to support you. Thank you.

10

다음을 듣고, 방송의 목적으로 가장 적절한 것을 고르시오.

① 올바른 자외선 차단제 사용 방법을 알려주려고
② 피부 타입에 따른 세안법을 안내하려고
③ 새로 출시된 청소년용 화장품을 홍보하려고
④ 청소년을 위한 피부 관리법을 소개하려고
⑤ 청소년 여드름의 다양한 원인을 설명하려고

M Hello, this is *Today's Health*! Many teenage listeners have asked about their various skin problems. Here are some tips for _____ _____ them. First, wash your face _____ _____ _____ _____ — once in the morning, and once before you go to bed. Second, use a gentle, oil-free cleanser. When you apply it, use your hands or a soft washcloth. Third, use sunscreen every day, even on cloudy days. It's _____ _____ _____ your skin from the sun. Last, _____ _____ _____ and eat a balanced diet. If you follow these tips, then you can _____ _____ _____ _____ !

A 다음 영어 어휘나 표현의 뜻을 우리말로 쓰세요.

01 considerate

02 clinic

03 car accident

04 management office

05 remind

06 vending machine

07 social

08 heavily

09 extra

10 balanced

11 passenger

12 convenience store

13 teenage

14 condition

15 submit

16 auto repair shop

B 우리말에 맞는 영어 어휘나 표현을 [보기]에서 찾아 쓰세요.

	보기		notice	assume	apply	appointment	schedule
			form	resident	access	accordingly	personal

01 예약, 약속

02 알아채다, 눈치채다

03 주민

04 (사실로) 생각하다, 추정하다

05 일정을 잡다

06 바르다

07 개인적인

08 양식, 신청서

09 이용하다

10 그에 맞춰

숫자 정보

유형 설명
대화를 듣고 금액이나 시각/시간 등의 숫자 정보를 파악하는 유형이다. 주로 지불할 금액이나 거스름돈, 특정한 시각을 묻는 문제가 출제된다.

지시문 유형
· 대화를 듣고, 여자가 지불할 금액을 고르시오.
· 대화를 듣고, 두 사람이 만나기로 한 시각을 고르시오.

기출 표현 맛보기
· W Hi. I'd like to have a cheeseburger, please.
  M That will be five dollars. If you pay two dollars more, you can get a drink and fries.

· M So, the 7 a.m. class is not a great idea.
  W Right. 4 p.m. is better for me because my school finishes at 3 p.m. So, I can go to the soccer class after school.

주요 어휘·표현 미리보기

다음을 듣고, [보기]에서 알맞은 어휘나 표현을 찾아 쓰세요.   정답 및 해설 p. 12

┌─────────────────────── | 보기 | ───────────────────────┐
│ ⓐ would you like   ⓑ attend   ⓒ gain   ⓓ end   │
│ ⓔ per hour   ⓕ get a discount ⓖ speaker   ⓗ on sale │
└──┘

01 How can I _____ ? 어떻게 하면 할인받을 수 있나요?

02 This job pays 10,000 won _____ . 이 일은 시간당 만 원을 지급합니다.

03 _____ some coffee? 커피 좀 드시겠어요?

04 How does the story _____ ? 그 이야기는 어떻게 끝나?

05 He didn't _____ my wedding. 그는 내 결혼식에 참석하지 않았어.

06 Let me introduce today's _____ . 오늘의 연사를 소개하겠습니다.

07 Why did I _____ weight? 나는 왜 몸무게가 늘었을까?

08 All clothes are _____ today. 오늘 모든 의류가 할인 판매 중입니다.

기출로 유형 익히기

- 금액을 묻는 문제의 경우, 구입할 물건의 개수, 정가, 할인율, 쿠폰 여부 등의 정보를 메모하며 들으세요.
- 시각을 묻는 문제의 경우, 대화 중에 시각이 변경되는 때가 많으므로 주의 깊게 들어야 해요.

01

대화를 듣고, 남자가 지불할 금액을 고르시오.

① $35　　　　② $45　　　　③ $70　　　　④ $75　　　　⑤ $85

M Excuse me. How much does it cost a month to take swimming lessons here?

W It's $30 a month, but if you sign up for three months, it's only $70. 정답 단서

M Oh, it's much cheaper if I sign up for three months. How about the cost of lockers? 오답 함정

W They are $5 a month each.

M So, $15 for 3 months, right? Okay. I'll take three months of lessons and one locker for that time.

W You got it.

수영 강습을 등록하는 내용이야.

02

대화를 듣고, 어머니가 아들을 깨울 시각을 고르시오.

① 6 a.m.　　　　② 7 a.m.　　　　③ 8 a.m.　　　　④ 9 a.m.　　　　⑤ 10 a.m.

M Mom, can you wake me up early tomorrow morning?

W Why? Tomorrow is Saturday. You don't need to go to school.

M Yeah, but I'm going to watch a movie with my friends.

W When does the movie begin?

M It starts at 9 a.m.

W Okay. Then, I will wake you up at 7.

M It only takes 10 minutes to go there. Please wake me up at 8.

W Okay. Good night, son.

남자가 엄마에게 아침에 깨워달라고 부탁하고 있어.

ANSWER

01 남자가 3개월치 수영 강습($70)을 등록하며 개인 사물함($15)도 이용하겠다고 했으므로, 남자가 지불할 금액은 ⑤이다.

02 아들이 깨워달라고 한 시각은 어머니가 말한 7시가 아니라 8시이므로, 정답은 ③이다.

LISTENING PRACTICE

점수   / 10문항

01 대화를 듣고, 남자가 지불할 금액을 고르시오.

① $4.50   ② $5.00   ③ $5.50   ④ $6.00   ⑤ $6.50

고난도
02 대화를 듣고, 두 사람이 만날 시각을 고르시오.

① 10:00 a.m.   ② 12:00 p.m.   ③ 12:30 p.m.   ④ 1:00 p.m.   ⑤ 1:30 p.m.

03 대화를 듣고, 남자가 지불할 금액을 고르시오.

① $10   ② $12   ③ $14   ④ $16   ⑤ $20

04 대화를 듣고, 남자의 현재 몸무게를 고르시오.

① 68 kg   ② 70 kg   ③ 72 kg   ④ 82 kg   ⑤ 92 kg

05 대화를 듣고, 여자가 지불할 금액을 고르시오.

Menu			
Hamburger	$3.00	French Fries	$1.00
Cheeseburger	$3.50	Coffee	$1.00
Chicken Sandwich	$4.00	Orange Juice	$1.00

① $9.50   ② $10.00   ③ $10.50   ④ $11.00   ⑤ $11.50

06 대화를 듣고, 강연 시간이 얼마나 되는지 고르시오.

① 1시간　　　　② 1시간 30분　　　③ 2시간　　　　④ 2시간 30분　　　⑤ 3시간

07 대화를 듣고, 여자가 지불할 금액을 고르시오.

① $2.70　　　　② $3.60　　　③ $4.00　　　　④ $4.50　　　⑤ $5.00

고난도
08 대화를 듣고, 남자가 지불할 금액을 고르시오.

① $20　　　　② $28　　　③ $30　　　　④ $46　　　⑤ $48

09 대화를 듣고, 두 사람이 만날 시각을 고르시오.

① 1:10 p.m.　　　② 1:45 p.m.　　　③ 2:00 p.m.　　　④ 2:15 p.m.　　　⑤ 2:30 p.m.

10 대화를 듣고, 여자가 음식점을 예약한 시각을 고르시오.

① 5:00 p.m.　　　② 5:30 p.m.　　　③ 6:00 p.m.　　　④ 6:30 p.m.　　　⑤ 7:00 p.m.

DICTATION

정답 단서 오답 함정

일반 속도

빠른 속도

01

대화를 듣고, 남자가 지불할 금액을
고르시오.

① $4.50　　② $5.00
③ $5.50　　④ $6.00
⑤ $6.50

M How much is a medium soda and a medium popcorn?

W A medium soda is $2, and a medium popcorn is $3. But _____ _____ _____ _____.

M What is it?

W You can get a large soda and a large popcorn _____ _____ _____ _____ as a medium.

M Great. I'll have that with caramel syrup.

W Okay. Caramel syrup is 50 cents extra. If you _____ _____ _____ _____, you get $1 off.

M I don't have one.

고난도

02 ·

대화를 듣고, 두 사람이 만날 시각을
고르시오.

① 10:00 a.m.　　② 12:00 p.m.
③ 12:30 p.m.　　④ 1:00 p.m.
⑤ 1:30 p.m.

M Hi, Yuram. Do you have plans for tomorrow?

W _____ _____ _____ _____ with some classmates.

M I'm going to Changdeokgung with my American friends. Do you want to come?

W You have American friends?

M Yes, I met them at summer camp.

W _____ _____ _____ _____ _____. What time are you going?

M They have Korean class from ten o'clock until noon. After that, it'll _____ _____ _____ _____ to get here.

W My meeting will be ending around then. Could you wait for me for thirty minutes?

M Sure. _____ _____ _____ _____ _____.

W Great!

03

대화를 듣고, 남자가 지불할 금액을
고르시오.

① $10　　② $12
③ $14　　④ $16
⑤ $20

W Welcome to Smithfield Concert Hall. How can I help you?

M How much are your concert tickets?

W We have afternoon concerts and evening concerts. _____ _____ _____ _____ _____?

M I'd like to attend an evening concert.

W All right. Tickets for our evening shows are $6 for adults and $4 for children.

M Okay. _____ _____ _____ _____ this evening's concert for two adults and one child.

W Certainly, sir. _____ _____ _____, and enjoy the concert.

04

대화를 듣고, 남자의 현재 몸무게를
고르시오.

① 68 kg   ② 70 kg
③ 72 kg   ④ 82 kg
⑤ 92 kg

W Hi, Paul. _____ _____ _____ _____. You look great. Have you been exercising?

M Yes. I ride my bicycle every day after school. Also, I've stopped eating fast food.

W Wow! _____ _____ _____ did you lose?

M When I started in March, I weighed 80 kg. I lost 10 kg in six months.

W That's a lot.

M Unfortunately, I gained 2 kg this month.

W Don't worry. It's natural _____ _____ _____ a little weight.

05

대화를 듣고, 여자가 지불할 금액을
고르시오.

Menu			
Hamburger	$3.00	French Fries	$1.00
Cheeseburger	$3.50	Coffee	$1.00
Chicken Sandwich	$4.00	Orange Juice	$1.00

① $9.50   ② $10.00
③ $10.50   ④ $11.00
⑤ $11.50

M May I _____ _____ _____?

W Yes, please. I'd like a cheeseburger for myself and a chicken sandwich for my son.

M _____ _____ _____ french fries with that?

W Yes, two orders of fries. And I'll have a coffee, and my son will have an orange juice.

M Okay, that's one cheeseburger, one chicken sandwich, one order of fries, one coffee, and one orange juice, right?

W No, _____ _____ _____ _____.

M Okay.

06

대화를 듣고, 강연 시간이 얼마나 되
는지 고르시오.

① 1시간   ② 1시간 30분
③ 2시간   ④ 2시간 30분
⑤ 3시간

W Would you like to _____ _____ _____ _____ with me this evening? It'll be interesting.

M I'd like to go, but I'm not sure I can. _____ _____ _____ _____ _____?

W It starts at 6:30. The speaker is a famous scientist. He studies global warming.

M It sounds great, but I have to _____ _____ _____ _____ at the airport at 9:00. How long will it be?

W It ends at 7:30.

M Okay. Then I can go.

07

대화를 듣고, 여자가 지불할 금액을
고르시오.

① $2.70   ② $3.60
③ $4.00   ④ $4.50
⑤ $5.00

W I'm _____ _____ _____ _____. I'd like to pay now.

M All right. Which computer were you using?

W I was using number eight. It costs $1 per hour, doesn't it?

M Yes. You used the computer for five hours, right?

W No, I only _____ _____ _____ _____ _____. I started at eleven, and now it's three.

M That's right. I'm sorry.

W It's okay. I also _____ _____ _____.

M Okay. Then you get a 10% discount.

08

대화를 듣고, 남자가 지불할 금액을
고르시오.

① $20   ② $28
③ $30   ④ $46
⑤ $48

W Can I help you?

M Yes. Does your spring sale _____ _____ _____ _____ _____?

W No. Only our books are on sale. Magazines are still _____ _____.

M And all of these books are 50% off?

W That's right. They're usually $10 each, but they're _____ _____ _____ $5.

M I'll take these four books and these two magazines.

W Okay. The magazines are $4 each.

M Great.

09

대화를 듣고, 두 사람이 만날 시각을
고르시오.

① 1:10 p.m.   ② 1:45 p.m.
③ 2:00 p.m.   ④ 2:15 p.m.
⑤ 2:30 p.m.

[Cell phone rings.]

W Hey, Derek! Why don't we have lunch together this weekend?

M Hi, Emily. Sure! What day works for you?

W How about Saturday? I have a swimming lesson _____ _____ _____ on Saturdays. Let's meet after the lesson.

M What time does your lesson end?

W Around 2 p.m. I think we can meet at 2:30.

M I'm afraid that's too late. Most of the restaurants near here _____ _____ _____ _____ at 2:30.

W Oh, I didn't know that. I _____ _____ _____ 15 minutes earlier then.

M Okay. That should give us enough time. See you then.

W Good. See you.

10

대화를 듣고, 여자가 음식점을 예약한
시각을 고르시오.

① 5:00 p.m.   ② 5:30 p.m.
③ 6:00 p.m.   ④ 6:30 p.m.
⑤ 7:00 p.m.

[Telephone rings.]

M Amy's Kitchen. May I help you?

W I'd like to _____ _____ _____ for five people at six o'clock this evening.

M I'm sorry. There are no tables for five _____ _____ _____ _____. How about an hour later?

W We're going to a show at the theater next door. It ends at five, so that's _____ _____ _____ _____.

M Well, I can get you a table _____ _____ _____ _____ your show ends.

W Thank you!

A

다음 영어 어휘나 표현의 뜻을 우리말로 쓰세요.

01 lecture

02 adult

03 global warming

04 ride a bicycle

05 join

06 classmate

07 include

08 weigh

09 soda

10 next door

11 magazine

12 full price

13 lose

14 exercise

15 half an hour

16 later

B

우리말에 맞는 영어 어휘나 표현을 [보기]에서 찾아 쓰세요.

| 보기 | each | off | at that time | take an order | medium |
| | cost | pay | certainly | special offer | natural |

01 당연한, 자연스러운

02 (크기 등이) 중간의

03 할인하여

04 지불하다, 계산하다

05 주문을 받다

06 그럼, 물론이지

07 특가 판매, 특별 할인

08 (값이) ~이다[들다]

09 각각, 한 개에

10 그때에(는)

심정·장소

정답 및 해설 p. 16

| 유형 설명 | 대화를 듣고 화자가 느끼는 심정을 파악하는 문제가 출제된다. 대화를 듣고 대화가 이루어지는 장소를 고르는 문제와 두 사람이 만나기로 한 장소를 고르는 문제도 출제된다. |

지시문 유형
- 대화를 듣고, 여자의 심정으로 가장 적절한 것을 고르시오.
- 대화를 듣고, 두 사람이 대화하는 장소로 가장 적절한 곳을 고르시오.

기출 표현 맛보기

심정
- The screen is fixed, but now I can't hear any sound. (annoyed)
- Oh, no! I can't believe that I made such a big mistake. (frustrated)

장소
- I can't believe I'm seeing the artworks of the great masters so closely! (미술관)
- This place offers services such as mail delivery and the sale of stamps. (우체국)

주요 어휘·표현 미리보기

다음을 듣고, [보기]에서 알맞은 어휘나 표현을 찾아 쓰세요.

| 보기 |
| ⓐ do well | ⓑ bring back | ⓒ in a few minutes | ⓓ won first prize |
| ⓔ around the corner | ⓕ have trouble | ⓖ making a mistake | ⓗ run out of |

01 The shop will _____ supplies soon. 상점에서 곧 재고가 없어질 것입니다.

02 If you study hard, you will _____ on the exam. 열심히 공부하면, 시험에서 잘할 거야.

03 You can learn from _____. 실수하는 것으로부터 배울 수 있어.

04 Please _____ the book you borrowed. 빌린 책을 돌려주세요.

05 He _____ in the piano competition. 그가 피아노 콩쿠르에서 일등 상을 탔어.

06 Could you come back _____? 몇 분 후에 다시 와주시겠어요?

07 The post office is just _____. 길모퉁이만 돌면 우체국이 있어요.

08 I _____ falling asleep at night. 나는 밤에 잠드는 데 문제를 겪고 있어.

- 심정을 추론하는 문제의 경우, 먼저 지시문을 읽고 누구의 심정을 묻는지 파악하세요. 선택지가 영어로 출제되므로 심정과 관련된 어휘를 미리 익혀두는 것이 좋아요.
- 기쁨, 슬픔, 놀람, 긴장, 분노 등 감정을 나타내는 어구나 감탄사, 대화자의 어조에 유의하며 들어보세요.
- 장소를 묻는 문제의 경우, 장소 파악에 중요한 단서가 되는 대화의 주제나 화제를 파악하며 들으세요.

01

대화를 듣고, 남자의 심정으로 가장 적절한 것을 고르시오.

① upset　　　　② regretful　　　　③ satisfied
④ bored　　　　⑤ embarrassed

W　Welcome to Wendy's Flower Shop.
M　Hello. I'm here to pick up the flowers I ordered.
W　Okay. What's your name?
M　Brian Anderson. I ordered them yesterday for my wife's birthday.
W　Alright. Hold on, please. *[pause]* Here you are.
M　Wow! I love how you put all of the flowers together.
W　I'm glad you like them.　　정답 단서
M　They're perfect. Thank you so much. My wife is going to love them.
W　Have a nice day.

> 남자가 꽃집에 주문해
> 놓은 꽃을 찾으러 온
> 상황이야.

02

대화를 듣고, 두 사람이 대화하는 장소로 가장 적절한 곳을 고르시오.

① 식당　　② 약국　　③ 카페　　④ 은행　　⑤ 보건실

W　Hello. May I have your prescription?
M　Here it is.
W　Okay. I'll be with you shortly. *[pause]* Mr. Choi, here is your medicine. Take these pills three times a day, 30 minutes after meals.
M　But the doctor said I can take them twice a day if I feel better. Is it okay?
W　Sure. In that case, you can skip the medicine after lunch. But make sure you don't take it with milk or coffee.　　오답 함정
M　I'll keep that in mind. Thank you.
W　You're welcome. Is there anything else you need?
M　No, I'm good. How much is it?
W　It'll be five dollars.

> 약을 복용하는
> 방법에 대해 이야기하는
> 상황이야.

ANSWER

01 남자는 자신의 아내를 위해 주문한 꽃이 예뻐서 만족하고 있으므로, 남자의 심정으로 ③이 알맞다.

02 여자가 남자의 처방전을 확인하고 약 복용법을 안내하고 있으므로, 두 사람이 대화하는 장소로 ②가 알맞다.

LISTENING PRACTICE

점수 _____ / 10문항

01

대화를 듣고, 여자의 심정으로 가장 적절한 것을 고르시오.

① grateful   ② excited   ③ regretful
④ concerned   ⑤ embarrassed

02

대화를 듣고, 여자의 심정으로 가장 적절한 것을 고르시오.

① bored   ② proud   ③ regretful
④ relieved   ⑤ embarrassed

고난도

03

대화를 듣고, 남자의 심정으로 가장 적절한 것을 고르시오.

① excited   ② angry   ③ satisfied
④ sorry   ⑤ jealous

04

대화를 듣고, 여자의 심정으로 가장 적절한 것을 고르시오.

① jealous   ② calm   ③ excited
④ surprised   ⑤ worried

05

대화를 듣고, 두 사람이 대화하는 장소로 가장 적절한 곳을 고르시오.

① 기차역   ② 공항   ③ 지하철역
④ 버스 정거장   ⑤ 택시 승강장

06 대화를 듣고, 남자의 심정으로 가장 적절한 것을 고르시오.

① jealous   ② regretful   ③ annoyed
④ nervous   ⑤ thankful

07 대화를 듣고, 여자의 심정으로 가장 적절한 것을 고르시오.

① shy   ② thankful   ③ annoyed
④ bored   ⑤ scared

08 대화를 듣고, 남자의 심정으로 가장 적절한 것을 고르시오.

① annoyed   ② satisfied   ③ proud
④ sorry   ⑤ delighted

09 대화를 듣고, 남자의 심정으로 가장 적절한 것을 고르시오.

① relaxed   ② nervous   ③ hopeful
④ excited   ⑤ disappointed

고난도
10 대화를 듣고, 두 사람이 대화하는 장소로 가장 적절한 곳을 고르시오.

① 영화관   ② 안과   ③ 사진관
④ 방송국   ⑤ 안경원

DICTATION

01

대화를 듣고, 여자의 심정으로 가장 적절한 것을 고르시오.

① grateful ② excited
③ regretful ④ concerned
⑤ embarrassed

W Hi! Long time no see! How have you been?

M I'm sorry, but _____ _____ _____ _____?

W What? Come on, it's Stacey. Stacey Black. Don't you remember me?

M Stacey Black? Umm... I don't think I know you.

W I can't believe this. _____ _____ _____ _____ me? We met at the Student Leaders' Camp in Seoul last year.

M Student Leaders' Camp? I've never been there before.

W Oh, my gosh! Aren't you Owen?

M No, I'm Harry, Harry Wilson.

W I'm so sorry. I thought you were my friend Owen. I've _____ _____ _____ _____.

M That's fine. Don't worry about it.

02

대화를 듣고, 여자의 심정으로 가장 적절한 것을 고르시오.

① bored ② proud
③ regretful ④ relieved
⑤ embarrassed

M Mom, I'm home.

W Alex, you _____ _____ _____ _____ _____ by seven, but it's already nine o'clock.

M Well, I lost my bag. Unfortunately, my wallet was in the bag, so I couldn't take the bus.

W Oh no! Why didn't you call me?

M I couldn't use my phone because it ran out of battery. So I just walked home.

W I see. I was afraid _____ _____ _____ _____ _____.

M I'm sorry for making you worry.

W No, it's okay. You _____ _____ _____ _____, so that's enough.

03

대화를 듣고, 남자의 심정으로 가장 적절한 것을 고르시오.

① excited ② angry
③ satisfied ④ sorry
⑤ jealous

W I'm excited to see this musical! The show starts _____ _____ _____ _____. We should hurry.

M Hmm... Wait a minute.

W What's wrong?

M Oh no! I think I _____ _____ _____ at home!

W Are you sure? Check your bag. What about your pockets?

M Nope, I can't find them. I put them on the table last night. They must still be there.

W Well, I guess we can't go to the show tonight then.

M You _____ _____ very angry at me.

W No. Everybody makes mistakes. Let's _____ _____ _____ _____ to do!

04

대화를 듣고, 여자의 심정으로 가장 적절한 것을 고르시오.

① jealous　② calm
③ excited　④ surprised
⑤ worried

M Mina! I just heard the good news. I'm really jealous.

W _____ _____ _____ was a great honor. It was hard work, but I earned it.

M You must have spent a lot of time on your essay.

W Yes, I _____ _____ _____ every night for two weeks.

M Well, congratulations! What did you write about?

W I _____ _____ _____ _____ _____, *Me Before You*. It's a sad story, but you should read it.

05

대화를 듣고, 두 사람이 대화하는 장소로 가장 적절한 곳을 고르시오.

① 기차역　② 공항
③ 지하철역　④ 버스 정거장
⑤ 택시 승강장

W I'd like to go to Grand Central Station. Does _____ _____ _____ _____ stop here?

M Yes. You should take bus number 71. But you've just missed it.

W _____ _____ _____ _____ _____?

M It comes every 25 minutes.

W I see. But I need to be there in 20 minutes! Is there another bus that goes there?

M Not directly. I _____ _____ _____ _____ _____. The subway station is just around the corner.

W How long does it take by subway?

M It only takes 10 minutes. Grand Central Station is just _____ _____ _____.

06

대화를 듣고, 남자의 심정으로 가장 적절한 것을 고르시오.

① jealous　② regretful
③ annoyed　④ nervous
⑤ thankful

W Are you okay? You don't look well.

M I _____ _____ _____.

W What's wrong? Are you cold?

M No. You don't remember? The Spanish speech contest is tonight. I really want to _____ _____.

W Don't worry. Everything will be fine. You did great last year. Remember?

M I don't know, though. I'm sure I will _____ _____ _____.

W Don't think that way. You practiced a lot. I know you can win this contest.

07

대화를 듣고, 여자의 심정으로 가장 적절한 것을 고르시오.

① shy　② thankful
③ annoyed　④ bored
⑤ scared

[Cell phone rings.]

W Hello?

M Hello. Is this Mrs. Wilson?

W Yes, this is she.

M You were just in my taxi. You _____ _____ _____ on the seat. Luckily, I found your number in it.

W Oh, I'm so glad you found it. I wasn't sure what to do.

M Well, I can bring it back to you. Let's meet at the spot where I _____ _____ _____.

W That would be wonderful. I can't _____ _____ _____.

대화를 듣고, 남자의 심정으로 가장 적절한 것을 고르시오.

① annoyed ② satisfied
③ proud ④ sorry
⑤ delighted

[Telephone rings.]

W Hello, AT Internet Services.

M Hi, I've been _____ _____ _____ to the internet all day.

W I'm sorry to hear that. Can I _____ _____ _____ and address?

M My name is Brian Kim, and my address is 100 Main Street.

W Let me check. [pause] It seems that there are some network problems in your area.

M Network problems again? I don't know why this happens so often.

W Repair work is already underway, so it should be okay _____ _____ _____ _____ _____.

M What? I couldn't work at all today. Now I have to wait even longer?

W I apologize again for the inconvenience.

09

대화를 듣고, 남자의 심정으로 가장 적절한 것을 고르시오.

① relaxed ② nervous
③ hopeful ④ excited
⑤ disappointed

W Look at all those boxes! Did you _____ _____ _____?

M Yes. I got the clothes I ordered online.

W You must have ordered a lot.

M I did. Everything looked great and the prices were low, so I bought _____ _____ _____ _____ and three shirts.

W I see. But why do you look so upset?

M The clothes _____ _____ _____ _____ _____. They're cheap and ugly.

W Really? I guess you have to be careful when you find good deals online.

고난도

10

대화를 듣고, 두 사람이 대화하는 장소로 가장 적절한 곳을 고르시오.

① 영화관 ② 안과
③ 사진관 ④ 방송국
⑤ 안경원

M Good morning. How can I help you?

W I'm trying to decide between _____ _____ _____ and switching to contact lenses.

M Have you ever worn contact lenses before?

W I tried them when I was a student, but they weren't comfortable.

M In that case, it's probably _____ _____ _____ to continue wearing glasses.

W Okay. Can you show me some new styles?

M Sure. Here are some of our _____ _____ _____.

W Wow! These look nice. My favorite movie actress has a similar pair.

M Why don't you _____ _____ _____?

W Okay. [pause] Oh, they look good. I'll take them.

A

다음 영어 어휘나 표현의 뜻을 우리말로 쓰세요.

01 similar

02 away

03 regretful

04 suggest

05 repair

06 nervous

07 delighted

08 comfortable

09 honor

10 forget

11 decide

12 purse

13 earn

14 embarrassed

15 apologize

16 continue v-ing

B

우리말에 맞는 영어 어휘나 표현을 [보기]에서 찾아 쓰세요.

| 보기 | else | directly | wait a minute | unfortunately | switch to |
| | spot | leave | stay up late | inconvenience | drop off |

01 두고 오다

02 잠깐 기다리다

03 그 밖의, 다른

04 늦게까지 자지 않다

05 곧장, 똑바로

06 불행히도, 안타깝게도

07 (특정한) 곳, 장소

08 ~로 바꾸다

09 불편

10 ~을 (탈것에서) 내려주다

그림 상황에 적절한 대화·어색한 대화

유형 설명

다섯 개의 짧은 대화를 듣고, 그림의 상황에 적합한 대화나 대화의 흐름이 어색한 대화를 고르는 유형이다. 주로 제시된 그림 상황에 어울리는 대화를 찾거나 상대의 말에 대한 대답이 자연스럽지 않은 대화를 찾는 문제가 출제된다.

지시문 유형

· 다음 그림의 상황에 가장 적절한 대화를 고르시오.
· 다음을 듣고, 두 사람의 대화가 <u>어색한</u> 것을 고르시오.

기출 표현 맛보기

그림 상황에 적절한 대화

· **W** May I have the Wi-Fi password?
  M Sure. It's written on the wall over here.

어색한 대화

· **M** Which bag do you prefer, the red one or the black one?
  W ~~I'll pay by credit card.~~

**주요
어휘·표현
미리보기**

다음을 듣고, [보기]에서 알맞은 어휘나 표현을 찾아 쓰세요.   정답 및 해설 p. 20

| 보기 |
ⓐ ready to   ⓑ got a perfect score   ⓒ cool off   ⓓ wash the dishes
ⓔ wait in line   ⓕ make sure   ⓖ scary   ⓗ dying for

01 I put the soup in the fridge to let it _____. 나는 수프를 식히려고 냉장고에 넣었어.

02 I _____ on my English test. 나는 영어 시험에서 만점을 받았어.

03 Would you help me _____? 설거지하는 것 좀 도와줄래?

04 You have to _____. 줄 서서 기다리셔야 합니다.

05 _____ that you read the article. 반드시 그 기사 읽어봐.

06 Are you _____ be a parent? 부모 될 준비가 되셨나요?

07 I'm _____ a cup of coffee! 나는 커피 한 잔 마시고 싶어 죽겠어!

08 The movie was a little _____. 그 영화는 약간 무서웠어.

- 그림 상황에 적절한 대화를 고르는 문제의 경우, 그림을 미리 살펴보고 이에 어울리는 대화나 말을 추측해 보세요.
- 어색한 대화를 고르는 문제의 경우, 동일한 어휘나 유사한 표현을 이용한 오답 선택지가 있을 수 있으므로 주의하세요.

01

다음 그림의 상황에 가장 적절한 대화를 고르시오.

① ② ③ ④ ⑤

① W You're not allowed to take pictures here.
   M I'm sorry. I didn't know that.
② W Wow! I like your painting. It's really good.
   M Thank you. I've been practicing a lot.
③ W David, why don't you sit down and get some rest?
   M Thanks, but I prefer standing.
④ W Hey, what are you watching?
   M I'm watching this new action movie.
⑤ W Oh, why are you taking down the picture?
   M It was sold to an art gallery.

그림과 관련된 어휘를
이용한 오답이 있으니,
어휘보다는 상황에 집중해!

02

다음을 듣고, 두 사람의 대화가 <u>어색한</u> 것을 고르시오.

① ② ③ ④ ⑤

① W What happened to your bag?
   M I'm sorry to hear that you lost the bag.
② W Dad, I'm going hiking with my friend.
   M Be careful and make sure to bring water with you.
③ W Do you have a minute?
   M Yes, I do. What's up?
④ W Do you mind if I turn on the television?
   M Not at all. I'd like to watch something, too.
⑤ W What time do you go to sleep?
   M I usually go to bed at 11 p.m.

질문에 나온 어휘를
사용하였더라도 자연스러운
대답이 아닐 수 있어.

ANSWER
01 여자가 남자의 그림을 보고 놀라워하는 상황이므로, 그림의 상황에 가장 적절한 대화는 ②이다.
02 가방이 어떻게 된 거냐고 묻는 질문에 상대방이 가방을 잃어버린 데 대한 유감을 나타내는 ①은 어색하다.

LISTENING PRACTICE

점수 _____ / 9문항

일반 속도

빠른 속도

01 다음 그림의 상황에 가장 적절한 대화를 고르시오.

①   ②   ③   ④   ⑤

02 다음 그림의 상황에 가장 적절한 대화를 고르시오.

①   ②   ③   ④   ⑤

03 다음을 듣고, 두 사람의 대화가 <u>어색한</u> 것을 고르시오.

①   ②   ③   ④   ⑤

04 다음을 듣고, 두 사람의 대화가 <u>어색한</u> 것을 고르시오.

①   ②   ③   ④   ⑤

05 다음 그림의 상황에 가장 적절한 대화를 고르시오.

①   ②   ③   ④   ⑤

고난도

06 다음 그림의 상황에 가장 적절한 대화를 고르시오.

①   ②   ③   ④   ⑤

07 다음을 듣고, 두 사림의 대회가 <u>어색한</u> 것을 고르시오.

①   ②   ③   ④   ⑤

고난도

08 다음을 듣고, 두 사람의 대화가 <u>어색한</u> 것을 고르시오.

①   ②   ③   ④   ⑤

09 다음을 듣고, 두 사람의 대화가 <u>어색한</u> 것을 고르시오.

①   ②   ③   ④   ⑤

DICTATION

 일반 속도 빠른 속도

01

다음 그림의 상황에 가장 적절한 대화
를 고르시오.

① ② ③ ④ ⑤

① **W** Which camera _____ _____ _____?

   M That one on your right is 20% off this week.

② **W** My photo exhibition is next week. Would you like to come?

   M Sure. I really like your photos of nature.

③ **W** Would you please _____ _____ _____ _____ _____?

   M Sure. Go stand in front of the waterfall.

④ **W** _____ _____ _____ _____ I borrowed your phone?

   M No, not at all. Here you are.

⑤ **W** How about going to the movies tomorrow?

   M I can't. I'm _____ _____ in the woods.

02

다음 그림의 상황에 가장 적절한 대화
를 고르시오.

① ② ③ ④ ⑤

① **M** Can you _____ _____ _____ _____ _____, Mom?

   W Okay, but you need to start your homework soon.

② **M** I'm going to the library to study math.

   W Okay. Can you _____ _____ _____ for me?

③ **M** Be careful. This tea is very hot.

   W I won't drink it until it _____ _____.

④ **M** Oh, no. I spilled milk all over my textbook.

   W Here! Clean it up with this towel.

⑤ **M** What happened? You look upset!

   W I broke a glass while _____ _____ _____.

03

다음을 듣고, 두 사람의 대화가 <u>어색</u>
한 것을 고르시오.

① ② ③ ④ ⑤

① **W** _____ _____ _____ _____ _____?

   M Sure, I'm free now. What's up?

② **W** I _____ _____ _____ a slice of pizza!

   M That's just what I was thinking!

③ **W** Are there any more buses going to Seoul today?

   M No. The last one just left a few minutes ago.

④ **W** _____ _____ _____ _____ your new middle school?

   M I like it a lot. I've made many new friends.

⑤ **W** I've never seen _____ _____ _____ _____!

   M I agree. I couldn't understand the story!

04

다음을 듣고, 두 사람의 대화가 <u>어색</u>한 것을 고르시오.

① ② ③ ④ ⑤

① W We are _____ _____ _____ and vegetables.

　 M Then let's go grocery shopping.

② W Would you like _____ _____ _____?

　 M Yes, I'd like an orange juice, please.

③ W Did you _____ _____ _____ with you?

　 M Yes, they're at home.

④ W I'm going to visit my sister this weekend.

　 M I hope you have fun together.

⑤ W _____ _____ _____ _____ in this blouse?

　 M You look wonderful!

05

다음 그림의 상황에 가장 적절한 대화를 고르시오.

① ② ③ ④ ⑤

① M Can you help me _____ _____ _____ _____?

　 W Sure, I'd be happy to help you.

② M Did you enjoy the movie yesterday?

　 W Yes, I thought it was a wonderful film.

③ M Have you been _____ _____ _____ for a long time?

　 W No, I just arrived a few minutes ago.

④ M _____ _____ _____ that heavy chair for you.

　 W Oh, that's very nice of you.

⑤ M Excuse me, but _____ _____ _____ _____?

　 W No, nobody is sitting there.

06

다음 그림의 상황에 가장 적절한 대화를 고르시오.

① ② ③ ④ ⑤

① M Did you see any tigers on your trip to India?

　 W Yes, I saw one or two _____ _____ _____.

② M Does this zoo have any lions or tigers?

　 W Yes. All of our big cats _____ _____ over there.

③ M The tiger is one of Africa's most dangerous animals.

　 W Actually, it is only found in parts of Asia.

④ M This is going to be _____ _____ _____.

　 W Make sure you include the little tiger in the picture.

⑤ M Look at this picture of a baby tiger!

　 W It's cute, but its mother _____ _____ _____.

① **M** _____ _____ _____ _____ _____ ?

W Yes, thank you. I'd like shrimp fried rice.

② **M** I forgot my umbrella today.

W Here, we can share mine.

③ **M** You shouldn't bring _____ _____ _____ _____ on the subway.

W I should've brought my dog.

④ **M** I _____ _____ _____ _____ on the math test.

W That's wonderful! I'm proud of you.

⑤ **M** What do you like to do _____ _____ _____ _____ ?

W I play basketball with my friends.

① **W** I wish I could _____ _____ more quickly.

M It would help if you exercised regularly.

② **W** I'm _____ _____ _____ _____ _____ you provided.

M We were glad to be _____ _____ .

③ **W** How was the concert you saw yesterday?

M Terrific. You should have joined us.

④ **W** My car has been _____ _____ a lot.

M Why don't you buy a new one?

⑤ **W** Do you know how to get to the highway?

M Yes, it was built more than twenty years ago.

① **M** The traffic is terrible.

W Yeah, it's always like this _____ _____ _____ .

② **M** Excuse me. Do you mind if I sit here?

W Yes. The seat is empty.

③ **M** I'm thinking about _____ _____ _____ _____ .

W Oh really? What kind are you considering?

④ **M** When is the deadline for this project?

W We should _____ _____ _____ _____ .

⑤ **M** Do you want to go to the concert with me?

W I'm not sure. Who's performing?

A

다음 영어 어휘나 표현의 뜻을 우리말로 쓰세요.

01 fix _____

02 terrific _____

03 consider _____

04 waterfall _____

05 go grocery shopping _____

06 wood _____

07 make friends _____

08 film _____

09 lose weight _____

10 exhibition _____

11 recommend _____

12 break down _____

13 go hiking _____

14 highway _____

15 have fun _____

16 spill _____

B

우리말에 맞는 영어 어휘나 표현을 [보기]에서 찾아 쓰세요.

보기	return	upset	rush hour	a slice of	share
	empty	regularly	assistance	be grateful for	nature

01 속상한 _____

02 함께 쓰다 _____

03 비어 있는, 빈 _____

04 ~의 한 조각 _____

05 도움 _____

06 ~에 감사하다 _____

07 (출퇴근) 혼잡 시간대 _____

08 (책을) 반납하다 _____

09 규칙적으로 _____

10 자연 _____

유형 설명   대화를 듣고 남자 또는 여자가 상대에게 부탁한 일을 고르는 유형이다.

지시문 유형   대화를 듣고, 여자가 남자에게 부탁한 일로 가장 적절한 것을 고르시오.

기출 표현 맛보기
- Could you choose the clothes for the play?
- Can you book them(= tickets) for us? Then, I'll buy some popcorn.
- **W**   Should I bring it(= the English book) to your house later?
  M   You don't have to do that. Could you just bring it to school tomorrow?

주요 어휘·표현 미리보기

다음을 듣고, [보기]에서 알맞은 어휘나 표현을 찾아 쓰세요.

정답 및 해설 p. 23

| 보기 |
| ⓐ appreciate | ⓑ whole | ⓒ seldom | ⓓ relax |
| ⓔ due | ⓕ mind | ⓖ lie down | ⓗ mostly |

01   Don't ⬚⬚⬚ right after you have a meal.   식사한 직후에 눕지 마.

02   Thanks for your help. I really ⬚⬚⬚ it.   도와주셔서 고마워요. 정말 감사합니다.

03   Would you ⬚⬚⬚ opening the door?   문 좀 열어주시겠어요?

04   We lived together for a ⬚⬚⬚ month.   우리는 한 달 내내 함께 살았어.

05   This paper is ⬚⬚⬚ today.   이 과제물의 마감일은 오늘이야.

06   It ⬚⬚⬚ rains in this region.   이 지역은 좀처럼 비가 오지 않아.

07   He ⬚⬚⬚ works with artists.   그는 주로 예술가들과 일해.

08   You need to ⬚⬚⬚ for a while.   너는 잠시 쉴 필요가 있어.

기출로 유형 익히기

- 'Can I / Can you / Could you / Will you / Would you / Please'로 시작하는 표현에 집중하세요.
- 대화 상대가 하겠다고 제안하는 일이 함정일 수 있으니 주의해야 해요.

01

대화를 듣고, 여자가 남자에게 부탁한 일로 가장 적절한 것을 고르시오.

① 아침 차려주기　　② 과제 도와주기　　③ 아이들 깨우기
④ 자명종 수리하기　　⑤ 차로 자녀 등교시키기

M　Honey, you look worried.
W　Yeah, I'm going on a business trip for the next three days.
M　Well, what's the matter, then?
W　Our kids! They usually get up early, but mid-term exams start tomorrow.
M　Right. They're really tired these days since they're staying up so late.
W　I know. So, will you give them a ride to school for the next three days? 정답 단서
M　All right, I will. Should I make them breakfast as well? 오답 함정
W　No. They can get sandwiches near the school.

출장을 앞둔 여자가 남자에게 무엇을 부탁하고 있을까?

02

대화를 듣고, 남자가 여자에게 부탁한 일로 가장 적절한 것을 고르시오.

① 응원 도구 제작　　② 경기 규칙 설명　　③ 참가자 명단 작성
④ 학급 티셔츠 디자인　　⑤ 체육대회 일정 안내

W　Hello, Mr. Han. Did you want to see me?
M　Yes. Sports Day is around the corner. How's it going?
W　We got our group T-shirts yesterday. Also, we're almost done with cheering practice.
M　Good. Can you make a list of participants for each game?
W　I can. I'll make sure that every student plays in at least one game.
M　Great. Thank you.

남자가 체육대회 준비 상황을 점검하면서 여자에게 무엇을 부탁했지?

ANSWER

01 여자가 남자에게 3일 동안 차로 자녀를 등교시켜줄 수 있냐고 했으므로 여자가 남자에게 부탁한 일은 ⑤이다.

02 남자가 여자에게 참가자 명단을 작성해줄 수 있냐고 했으므로 남자가 여자에게 부탁한 일은 ③이다.

LISTENING PRACTICE

점수 _____ / 10문항

일반 속도   빠른 속도

01 대화를 듣고, 남자가 여자에게 부탁한 일로 가장 적절한 것을 고르시오.

① 음식점 정보 알려주기   ② 할머니께 전화 드리기
③ 요리법 알려주기   ④ 음식 주문하기
⑤ 이메일 주소 알려주기

02 대화를 듣고, 여자가 남자에게 부탁한 일로 가장 적절한 것을 고르시오.

① 휴대전화 빌려주기   ② 수리점 위치 알려주기
③ 휴대전화 골라주기   ④ 전화번호 알려주기
⑤ 휴대전화 수리 맡기기

고난도
03 대화를 듣고, 남자가 여자에게 부탁한 일로 가장 적절한 것을 고르시오.

① 작가 추천해주기   ② 책 빌려주기
③ 수강 신청 도와주기   ④ 강의 시간표 알려주기
⑤ 책 대신 반납하기

04 대화를 듣고, 여자가 남자에게 부탁한 일로 가장 적절한 것을 고르시오.

① 신발장 정리하기   ② 휴대전화 가져다주기
③ 자동차 시트 청소하기   ④ 옷 교환하기
⑤ 짐 들어주기

고난도
05 대화를 듣고, 남자가 여자에게 부탁한 일로 가장 적절한 것을 고르시오.

① 안경테 골라주기   ② 발표 자료 만들기
③ 보고서 복사하기   ④ 보고서 작성 돕기
⑤ 아침에 깨워주기

06 대화를 듣고, 여자가 남자에게 부탁한 일로 가장 적절한 것을 고르시오.

① 음료 사다 주기　　　　　② 점심 사 주기
③ 주유소 위치 알려주기　　④ 간식 준비하기
⑤ 화장실 청소하기

07 대화를 듣고, 남자가 여자에게 부탁한 일로 가장 적절한 것을 고르시오.

① 자리 바꿔주기　　　　　② 분실물 보관소에 전화하기
③ 숙제 알려주기　　　　　④ 공책 빌려주기
⑤ 시험 일정 알려주기

08 대화를 듣고, 여자가 남자에게 부탁한 일로 가장 적절한 것을 고르시오.

① 뒷마당 청소하기　　　　② 집 구경시켜 주기
③ 개 내보내기　　　　　　④ 집들이 음식 준비하기
⑤ 개 돌봐주기

09 대화를 듣고, 남자가 여자에게 부탁한 일로 가장 적절한 것을 고르시오.

① 파티에서 노래 부르기　　② 파티용 노래 선곡하기
③ 합창단 가입하기　　　　④ 파티에 함께 참석하기
⑤ 노래 가르쳐주기

10 대화를 듣고, 여자가 남자에게 부탁한 일로 가장 적절한 것을 고르시오.

① 샐러드 만들기　　　　　② 손 씻기
③ 소스 구입하기　　　　　④ 병뚜껑 열기
⑤ 수건 가져다주기

DICTATION

정답 및 해설 pp. 23-25

정답 단서 오답 함정

일반 속도

빠른 속도

01

대화를 듣고, 남자가 여자에게 부탁한
일로 가장 적절한 것을 고르시오.

① 음식점 정보 알려주기
② 할머니께 전화 드리기
③ 요리법 알려주기
④ 음식 주문하기
⑤ 이메일 주소 알려주기

M What restaurant did you order this chicken from?

W Actually, I _____ _____ _____. Would you like some more?

M Yes, please! I can't stop eating it. It's delicious.

W Thanks. I got the recipe from my grandmother.

M Would you _____ _____ _____ _____? I'd like to make it myself.

W I'd be happy to. I'll email it to you later.

M Thanks. I _____ _____ _____.

02

대화를 듣고, 여자가 남자에게 부탁한
일로 가장 적절한 것을 고르시오.

① 휴대전화 빌려주기
② 수리점 위치 알려주기
③ 휴대전화 골라주기
④ 전화번호 알려주기
⑤ 휴대전화 수리 맡기기

W _____ _____ _____ my cell phone again.

M What happened this time?

W It deleted some of my saved phone numbers, including yours.

M You should get a new one. There are some great new models.

W I know, but they're too expensive. Can you just _____ _____ _____ _____ again?

M Sure. But you should at least _____ _____ _____ before it happens again.

고난도
03

대화를 듣고, 남자가 여자에게 부탁한
일로 가장 적절한 것을 고르시오.

① 작가 추천해주기
② 책 빌려주기
③ 수강 신청 도와주기
④ 강의 시간표 알려주기
⑤ 책 대신 반납하기

M It's finally summer vacation! I'm going to relax and do nothing _____ _____ _____ _____.

W You'll get bored. You need to _____ _____ _____ _____.

M I guess you're right. What are your plans? Are you taking a class?

W No, I'm going to relax too. But I'm also going to read some good books.

M Really? I like to read, but _____ _____ _____.

W Why is that?

M I don't know any good authors. Do you think you could suggest a few?

W I'd be happy to. I know some _____ _____ _____ _____.

M Excellent! Thanks, Michelle.

64

04

대화를 듣고, 여자가 남자에게 부탁한
일로 가장 적절한 것을 고르시오.

① 신발장 정리하기
② 휴대전화 가져다주기
③ 자동차 시트 청소하기
④ 옷 교환하기
⑤ 짐 들어주기

W I can't believe I bought so much stuff. There were a lot of good sales.
M Wow, you have so many shopping bags! _____ _____ _____ a few for you.
W No, that's okay. They're not heavy. But can you get my cell phone? It's _____ _____.
M Sure, no problem. So, did you mostly buy clothes?
W Yes, and a pair of shoes. I'll show you everything later.
M All right. I'm _____ _____ _____ _____.

고난도

05

대화를 듣고, 남자가 여자에게 부탁한
일로 가장 적절한 것을 고르시오.

① 안경테 골라주기
② 발표 자료 만들기
③ 보고서 복사하기
④ 보고서 작성 돕기
⑤ 아침에 깨워주기

M Ellen, have you seen my glasses? I need my glasses!
W They're _____ _____, on your desk.
M Oh! I can't find anything right now!
W Calm down, Justin. Are you all right?
M Yes. But I _____ _____ _____ _____ working on my report.
W Oh, that's right. It's _____ _____. Did you finish it?
M Yes, but I still need to make copies. Would you mind doing that for me?
W Of course not. Why don't you _____ _____ and rest for a while?
M Thank you, Ellen. That's a good idea.

06

대화를 듣고, 여자가 남자에게 부탁한
일로 가장 적절한 것을 고르시오.

① 음료 사다 주기
② 점심 사 주기
③ 주유소 위치 알려주기
④ 간식 준비하기
⑤ 화장실 청소하기

W We need some gas. I'm going to stop at that gas station up ahead.
M Oh, good idea. I really need to use the bathroom.
W It looks like they have a store. Could you _____ _____ _____ _____? I'm really thirsty.
M Sure. I'll _____ _____ _____, too. Do you need some money for the gas?
W No, that's okay. You bought me lunch yesterday.
M That's right, I did. Okay, I'll _____ _____ _____ _____.

07

대화를 듣고, 남자가 여자에게 부탁한
일로 가장 적절한 것을 고르시오.

① 자리 바꿔주기
② 분실물 보관소에 전화하기
③ 숙제 알려주기
④ 공책 빌려주기
⑤ 시험 일정 알려주기

M Hanna, you took notes in yesterday's science class, didn't you?
W Of course I did. Didn't you? You _____ _____ _____. You sat right next to me.
M I took notes, but I lost my notebook. I think I _____ _____ _____ _____ _____.
W Oh, no! Did you check the lost and found office?
M Not yet. But _____ _____ _____ _____ _____ for a short time? I just want to review them.
W Of course. You'll need that information for Friday's test.

대화를 듣고, 여자가 남자에게 부탁한
일로 가장 적절한 것을 고르시오.

① 뒷마당 청소하기
② 집 구경시켜 주기
③ 개 내보내기
④ 집들이 음식 준비하기
⑤ 개 돌봐주기

M Welcome to my house, Maria! Come in!

W Thanks! _____ _____ _____ _____! [pause] Oh! You have a dog…

M Yes. He's big, but he's very friendly. Don't be afraid.

W Sorry, but dogs _____ _____ _____. Could you put him in the yard while I'm here?

M Oh, of course. He _____ _____. He actually prefers playing in the backyard.

W I apologize. I'm sure he's well-behaved.

M It's my fault. I _____ _____ _____ you about him. Anyway, have a seat!

09

대화를 듣고, 남자가 여자에게 부탁한
일로 가장 적절한 것을 고르시오.

① 파티에서 노래 부르기
② 파티용 노래 선곡하기
③ 합창단 가입하기
④ 파티에 함께 참석하기
⑤ 노래 가르쳐주기

M I really enjoyed listening to you sing at the party. You have _____ _____ _____ _____.

W Thank you. Why didn't you sing along? It was fun.

M It looked fun. Unfortunately, I can't sing.

W _____ _____ _____. Everyone can sing!

M Yes, that's true. But I can't sing well. Can you teach me how?

W Sure, I'd be glad to _____ _____ _____. It's easier than you think!

10

대화를 듣고, 여자가 남자에게 부탁한
일로 가장 적절한 것을 고르시오.

① 샐러드 만들기
② 손 씻기
③ 소스 구입하기
④ 병뚜껑 열기
⑤ 수건 가져다주기

M Do you need any help _____ _____?

W No, it's just a simple meal. I'm making pasta and a salad.

M Are you making your own tomato sauce?

W No, I bought some at the store. But I can't _____ _____ _____ _____.

M It's because your hands are wet. Do you want a towel?

W No, but can you open the jar for me?

M Sure. I'm always _____ _____ _____ _____ _____.

A

다음 영어 어휘나 표현의 뜻을 우리말로 쓰세요.

01 recipe

02 save

03 delete

04 calm down

05 silly

06 expensive

07 active

08 fault

09 wet

10 author

11 get bored

12 make a copy

13 thirsty

14 stuff

15 gas station

16 warn

B

우리말에 맞는 영어 어휘나 표현을 [보기]에서 찾아 쓰세요.

보기	friendly	review	up ahead	sing along	lost and found office
	help out	miss	have a seat	work on	well-behaved

01 놓치다, 빠지다

02 앉다, 착석하다

03 우호적인

04 그 앞쪽에

05 복습하다

06 얌전한, 예의 바른

07 분실물 보관소

08 노래를 따라 부르다

09 ~에 노력을 들이다, 착수하다

10 ~을 도와주다

주제/화제 · 직업

담화에서 설명하는 대상이 무엇인지 고르는 문제가 출제된다. 설명하는 직업이 무엇인지 묻는 문제도 출제된다.

지시문 유형
· 다음을 듣고, 무엇에 관한 설명인지 고르시오.
· 다음을 듣고, 어떤 직업에 관한 설명인지 고르시오.

기출 표현 맛보기

주제/화제
· It has many wheels but it can only run on rails. (기차)
· When people want to go to different floors, it is used to carry them. (엘리베이터)

직업
· People who have this job check animals' health conditions and give them proper care.
  (수의사)

주요
어휘·표현
미리보기

다음을 듣고, [보기]에서 알맞은 어휘나 표현을 찾아 쓰세요.   정답 및 해설 p. 26

| 보기 |
| ⓐ peel off | ⓑ is made of | ⓒ overall | ⓓ customer's needs |
| ⓔ atmosphere | ⓕ depends on | ⓖ motion | ⓗ is responsible for |

01 The price _____ the quality. 가격은 품질에 달려 있어.

02 You need to _____ the skin of an orange. 오렌지의 껍질을 벗겨야 해.

03 He made a _____ with his hand to stop me. 그는 나를 멈추게 하기 위해 손짓을 했어.

04 The chair in the living room _____ wood. 거실에 있는 의자는 나무로 만들어졌어.

05 The _____ at the concert was energetic. 콘서트의 분위기는 에너지가 넘쳤어.

06 A team leader _____ managing a team. 팀 리더는 팀을 관리할 책임이 있어.

07 The company understands their _____. 그 회사는 고객의 요구를 이해해.

08 The _____ experience of the trip was fantastic. 여행의 전체적 경험은 굉장했어.

기출로 유형 익히기

· 먼저 선택지를 보고, 어떤 내용이 나올지 예상해 보세요.
· 담화의 일부 내용이 아닌 내용 전체를 포함할 수 있는 선택지를 고르세요.

01

다음을 듣고, 어떤 동물에 관한 설명인지 고르시오.

① 토끼　　　② 사슴　　　③ 원숭이　　　④ 코알라　　　⑤ 캥거루

W　This animal can jump very high and run very fast. It moves by jumping on its back legs. It has a long and thin tail to help its balance when it walks. It gives birth to only one baby a year and carries the baby in a pocket on its stomach. This animal usually eats grass and leaves. It's common in Australia. 정답 단서

> 내용을 들으면서 설명에 해당하지 않는 선택지를 지우는 것도 도움이 돼.

02

다음을 듣고, 어떤 직업에 관한 설명인지 고르시오.

① 교사　　　② 기자　　　③ 의사　　　④ 건축가　　　⑤ 소방관

W　People who have this job tell us about what's happening in the world. When an event happens, they go to the site right away and find out facts about the event. They also interview people about events. Then they write articles for the Internet and newspapers, and report on TV.

> 해당 직업을 가진 사람의 핵심적인 역할이나 일이 무엇인지를 생각해.

ANSWER

01 뒷다리로 뛰어서 움직이고, 길고 가는 꼬리가 있으며, 배에 있는 주머니에 새끼를 넣고 다닌다고 했으므로, 정답은 ⑤이다.

02 세상에서 일어나는 일에 대해 인터넷과 신문에 기사를 쓰거나 TV에 보도를 한다고 했으므로 정답은 ②이다.

LISTENING PRACTICE

점수 _____ / 10문항

일반 속도　빠른 속도

01 다음을 듣고, 무엇에 관한 설명인지 고르시오.

① 스마트 TV　　　② 보조 배터리　　　③ 스마트폰
④ 컴퓨터 모니터　　⑤ 태블릿 PC

02 다음을 듣고, 무엇에 관한 설명인지 고르시오.

① 하키　　　　② 골프　　　　③ 야구
④ 당구　　　　⑤ 게이트볼

03 다음을 듣고, 무엇에 관한 설명인지 고르시오.

① 피아노　　　② 바이올린　　　③ 플루트
④ 첼로　　　　⑤ 기타

04 다음을 듣고, 어떤 직업에 관한 설명인지 고르시오.

① 교사　　　　② 수의사　　　③ 탐험가
④ 카메라 감독　　⑤ 동물 훈련사

고난도
05 다음을 듣고, 어떤 직업에 관한 설명인지 고르시오.

① 의사　　　　② 경호원　　　③ 경찰관
④ 구조 대원　　⑤ 헬스 트레이너

06 다음을 듣고, 무엇에 관한 설명인지 고르시오.

① 망고   ② 레몬   ③ 바나나
④ 파인애플   ⑤ 오렌지

07 다음을 듣고, 무엇에 관한 설명인지 고르시오.

① 숟가락   ② 포크   ③ 젓가락
④ 나이프   ⑤ 국자

08 다음을 듣고, 어떤 직업에 관한 설명인지 고르시오.

① 정비사   ② 기자   ③ 조종사
④ 경비원   ⑤ 승무원

09 다음을 듣고, 어떤 직업에 관한 설명인지 고르시오.

① 작가   ② 아나운서   ③ 기상 캐스터
④ 쇼핑 호스트   ⑤ 패션 디자이너

고난도
10 다음을 듣고, 어떤 직업에 관한 설명인지 고르시오.

① 화가   ② 건축가   ③ 사진사
④ 호텔 지배인   ⑤ 인테리어 디자이너

DICTATION

정답 단서 오답 함정

일반 속도

빠른 속도

01

다음을 듣고, 무엇에 관한 설명인지
고르시오.

① 스마트 TV　　② 보조 배터리
③ 스마트폰　　④ 컴퓨터 모니터
⑤ 태블릿 PC

W This is an electronic device that is popular nowadays. It _____
_____ ~~_____~~, but it is larger. It has many of the same
functions as a laptop. Instead of a keyboard and a mouse, however, it has
a touchscreen. As it is _____ _____ _____, a lot of people
own one. People like this because it is easy to carry around. It also allows
them to _____ _____ _____ _____ _____.

02

다음을 듣고, 무엇에 관한 설명인지
고르시오.

① 하키　　　② 골프
③ 야구　　　④ 당구
⑤ 게이트볼

W This is a team sport. It started in America, but it is now _____
_____ _____ _____. It is played on a field called a diamond.
There are nine positions to play. _____ _____ _____
_____ _____ is to hit a white ball with a bat and then run around
the bases. If a batter hits the ball over the wall on the far side of the field, it's
_____ _____ _____ _____.

03

다음을 듣고, 무엇에 관한 설명인지
고르시오.

① 피아노　　② 바이올린
③ 플루트　　④ 첼로
⑤ 기타

M This is a musical instrument _____ _____ _____
_____. When you play it, you sit down and hold it between your legs.
You also need a _____ _____ _____ _____. You move
the bow across the strings with a smooth motion to create a sound. It is often
used in classical music, and it has a _____ _____ _____
_____.

04

다음을 듣고, 어떤 직업에 관한 설명
인지 고르시오.

① 교사　　　　② 수의사
③ 탐험가　　　④ 카메라 감독
⑤ 동물 훈련사

W People who have this job work with animals, such as dogs, horses, birds, and dolphins. They study _____ _____ _____ and develop ways of training them. What they teach an animal depends on the owner's needs. For example, they might teach pets good behaviors and _____ _____ _____. Or, they might _____ _____ _____ to animals for shows in zoos and aquariums.

고난도

05

다음을 듣고, 어떤 직업에 관한 설명
인지 고르시오.

① 의사　　　　② 경호원
③ 경찰관　　　④ 구조 대원
⑤ 헬스 트레이너

M People who have this job work to keep their clients safe. Their usual clients are well-known people, including singers, actors, and politicians. They _____ _____ to their clients and escort them in their everyday life. They check their surroundings carefully to _____ _____ _____ from any possible danger. When something dangerous happens, they help their clients get out of the situation. To have this job, it is important to be healthy and strong, and you have to go through a lot of _____ _____.

06

다음을 듣고, 무엇에 관한 설명인지
고르시오.

① 망고　　　　② 레몬
③ 바나나　　　④ 파인애플
⑤ 오렌지

W This is a popular fruit that grows on trees. It is grown _____ _____ _____ _____ around the world. It is usually long and yellow, and has _____, _____ _____ _____ inside. To eat it, you need to _____ _____ _____ _____. It is a good source of vitamins and minerals. It is also great for making smoothies.

07

다음을 듣고, 무엇에 관한 설명인지
고르시오.

① 숟가락　　　② 포크
③ 젓가락　　　④ 나이프
⑤ 국자

M This is a tool for eating food. It has one handle and two or more points at the end of it. It is often made of _____, _____, _____ _____. To use it, you just hold its handle and pick up food _____ _____ _____ _____. You usually use it when you eat something like pasta or vegetables. But you don't use it for eating soup or ice cream. It is an important tool that is commonly _____ _____ _____ _____ around the world.

08

다음을 듣고, 어떤 직업에 관한 설명
인지 고르시오.

① 정비사　　② 기자
③ 조종사　　④ 경비원
⑤ 승무원

W People who have this job work with airplanes. They are responsible for making sure that an _____ _____ _____, flies, and lands safely. Before takeoff, they check the weather and the airplane. _____ _____ _____, they communicate with air traffic control and the plane crew. They also _____ _____ _____ for passengers. After landing, they do some paperwork and prepare for the next flight. Having this job requires a lot of _____ _____ _____, but it can be a very meaningful job.

09

다음을 듣고, 어떤 직업에 관한 설명
인지 고르시오.

① 작가　　　　② 아나운서
③ 기상 캐스터　④ 쇼핑 호스트
⑤ 패션 디자이너

W People who have this job appear in special kinds of television shows. Together with one or more guests, they _____ _____ _____ to viewers during a live show. They try the product and explain its various features. They usually focus on _____ _____ _____ _____. They want viewers to make a phone call and purchase the product before the show ends. To do this job, people should have good public speaking skills and creative marketing strategies that _____ _____.

10

다음을 듣고, 어떤 직업에 관한 설명
인지 고르시오.

① 화가　　　　② 건축가
③ 사진사　　　④ 호텔 지배인
⑤ 인테리어 디자이너

M People who have this job _____ _____ _____ in buildings. These spaces could be rooms in a house or larger spaces like hotel lobbies. Typically, they start by discussing the customer's needs, the budget, and the purpose of the space. Then, they decide on the _____ _____ _____. This may include colors, materials, furniture, and even lighting. They consider every _____ _____ _____ _____ to create the atmosphere the customer wants. Their goal is to make the space both functional and beautiful.

A

다음 영어 어휘나 표현의 뜻을 우리말로 쓰세요.

01 element

02 wirelessly

03 behave

04 function

05 position

06 tropical

07 commonly

08 take off

09 appear

10 trick

11 source

12 connect

13 nowadays

14 hit

15 electronic device

16 typically

B

우리말에 맞는 영어 어휘나 표현을 [보기]에서 찾아 쓰세요.

보기	object	surroundings	field	in-flight	go through
	tool	budget	own	carry around	pick up

01 주변 환경

02 도구

03 소유하다

04 ~을 거치다

05 예산

06 ~을 집다

07 기내의

08 목적, 목표

09 경기장, 운동장

10 들고 다니다, 휴대하다

할 일·한 일

유형 설명
대화를 듣고 화자가 앞으로 할 일이나 과거에 한 일을 파악하는 유형이다. 주로 대화 직후에 할 일, 주말이나 어제 한 일을 고르는 문제가 출제된다.

지시문 유형
· 대화를 듣고, 여자가 대화 직후에 할 일로 가장 적절한 것을 고르시오.
· 대화를 듣고, 남자가 어제 한 일로 가장 적절한 것을 고르시오.

기출표현맛보기

할 일

· W Then, why don't you go get the laptop computer from the teachers' office? I'll get the magnets for you.
  M Thank you. I'll do that right away.

한 일

· W I went to the school library two days ago, but the book was already checked out.
  M So, you still haven't got the book.
  W Right. But, I did order it online yesterday.

주요 어휘·표현 미리보기

다음을 듣고, [보기]에서 알맞은 어휘나 표현을 찾아 쓰세요.

정답 및 해설 p. 29

| 보기 |
| ⓐ have a fever | ⓑ a big fan | ⓒ rest | ⓓ absent from |
| ⓔ take the medicine | ⓕ sign up | ⓖ put on | ⓗ a close game |

01 I used to _____ and enjoy the sunshine. 나는 쉬면서 햇빛을 즐기곤 했어.

02 If you _____, you should stay home. 열이 나면 집에 있어야 해.

03 She is _____ of superhero movies. 그녀는 슈퍼히어로 영화 열혈 팬이야.

04 It's cold outside. _____ your coat, please. 밖이 추워요. 코트를 입으세요.

05 The two teams played _____. 두 팀은 막상막하의 경기를 펼쳤어.

06 I think I'll _____ for a dance class. 나는 댄스 수업에 등록할까 생각 중이야.

07 Why were you _____ school yesterday? 어제 왜 학교에 결석했어?

08 The doctor told me to _____. 의사는 내게 약을 먹으라고 말했어.

- 먼저 지시문을 읽고, 누가 할 일이나 한 일을 파악해야 하는지 확인한 후 들으세요.
- 지시문과 다른 시점의 일, 상대방이 할 일이나 한 일이 함정으로 등장하므로 주의하세요.

01

대화를 듣고, 남자가 할 일로 가장 적절한 것을 고르시오.

① 음식 만들기　　　　② 케이크 사기　　　　③ 물건 환불하기
④ 선물 포장하기　　　　⑤ 식당 예약하기

W Hi, Jiho! What did you buy?

M Hi, Kate! I bought some tomatoes and mushrooms to make spaghetti.

W You really like spaghetti, don't you?

M Actually, this time, it's not just for me. I'm going to cook for my mom. 정답 단서

W Is it a special day for her?

M Yes, today is her birthday and I'll cook for her this evening.

W I hope she likes your food.

> 선택지를 미리 보고 남자의 말을 잘 들으면 답을 쉽게 알 수 있어.

02

대화를 듣고, 여자가 지난 주말에 한 일로 가장 적절한 것을 고르시오.

① 밤 줍기　　　　② 사과 따기　　　　③ 고구마 캐기
④ 나무 심기　　　　⑤ 블루베리 따기

M Charlotte, how was your weekend? Did you go blueberry picking like you'd planned? 오답 함정

W No. I couldn't because the blueberry picking season ended a couple of weeks ago. I didn't know that.

M Then what did you do last weekend?

W I went apple picking.

M Cool. How many apples did you pick?

W A lot. I filled up a big basket.

M It sounds like it was fun.

W Yeah, it was. You should try it someday.

> 하려고 계획했지만 하지 못한 일이 오답 함정으로 나올 수 있어.

ANSWER

01 남자는 어머니의 생일을 위해 스파게티를 만들겠다고 했으므로, 정답은 ①이다.

02 여자는 지난 주말에 블루베리를 따러 갈 계획이었으나 수확철이 끝나서 사과를 따러 갔다고 했으므로, 정답은 ②이다.

LISTENING PRACTICE

점수 _____ / 9문항

 일반 속도 빠른 속도

01 대화를 듣고, 남자가 대화 직후에 할 일로 가장 적절한 것을 고르시오.

① 스웨터 입기 ② 전열기 켜기 ③ 전열기 사기
④ 담요 가져오기 ⑤ 티셔츠 입어보기

02 대화를 듣고, 남자가 방과 후에 할 일로 가장 적절한 것을 고르시오.

① 문구점 가기 ② 미술 학원 가기 ③ 책 주문하기
④ 온라인 쇼핑하기 ⑤ 미술 과제 하기

03 대화를 듣고, 여자가 어제 한 일로 가장 적절한 것을 고르시오.

① 친구 만나기 ② 바다에서 수영하기 ③ 병원 진료받기
④ 방 정리하기 ⑤ 집에서 쉬기

04 대화를 듣고, 남자가 어제 한 일로 가장 적절한 것을 고르시오.

① 축구 연습하기 ② 골프 레슨 등록하기 ③ 운동복 쇼핑하기
④ 산책하기 ⑤ 배구 경기 관람하기

05

대화를 듣고, 남자가 대화 직후에 할 일로 가장 적절한 것을 고르시오.

① 아이스크림 사 오기　　② 물 가져다주기　　③ 약국 가기
④ 냉장고 청소하기　　　⑤ 병원에 전화하기

06

대화를 듣고, 남자가 대화 직후에 할 일로 가장 적절한 것을 고르시오.

① 수업 등록하기　　　② 저녁 식사하기　　③ 축구하기
④ 첼로 연주하기　　　⑤ 미술 수업 가기

07

대화를 듣고, 여자가 지난 크리스마스 연휴에 한 일로 가장 적절한 것을 고르시오.

① 귤 따기 체험하기　　② 보드게임 하기　　③ 해외 여행 가기
④ 조부모님댁 방문하기　⑤ 항공박물관 관람하기

고난도
08

대화를 듣고, 여자가 지난 금요일에 한 일로 가장 적절한 것을 고르시오.

① 아르바이트 하기　　② 영화 관람하기　　③ 수리 센터 방문하기
④ 휴대전화 구입하기　⑤ 댄스 대회 출전하기

고난도
09

대화를 듣고, 남자가 지난 주말에 한 일로 가장 적절한 것을 고르시오.

① 친구와 게임하기　　② 여행 계획 짜기　　③ 영어 공부하기
④ 온라인 수업 듣기　　⑤ 박물관 관람하기

DICTATION

정답 단서 ～～ 오답 함정

 일반 속도

 빠른 속도

01

대화를 듣고, 남자가 대화 직후에 할
일로 가장 적절한 것을 고르시오.

① 스웨터 입기
② 전열기 켜기
③ 전열기 사기
④ 담요 가져오기
⑤ 티셔츠 입어보기

W What's that, William?

M It's an electric heater. I bought it on sale yesterday.

W Oh. Are you going to ～～～～～～～～～～～～ now?

M Yes. It's cold in here, isn't it?

W A little. But you're only wearing a T-shirt. Why don't you _____ _____ _____ _____?

M All right. I have a sweater. I'll put it on instead.

W Great. Electric heaters _____ _____ _____ _____.

M That's a good point.

02

대화를 듣고, 남자가 방과 후에 할 일
로 가장 적절한 것을 고르시오.

① 문구점 가기
② 미술 학원 가기
③ 책 주문하기
④ 온라인 쇼핑하기
⑤ 미술 과제 하기

W What are you going to do after school?

M I'm going to buy some art supplies _____ _____ _____.

W Why don't you buy them online? It's cheaper and more convenient.

M I've ～～～～～～～～ _____ before, but not art supplies. How long does it take?

W You can get your order the next day.

M That's great. Do you know _____ _____ _____?

W Yes, the website called Joe's Art Stuff is good.

M Oh, thanks. I'll do that at home after school.

03

대화를 듣고, 여자가 어제 한 일로 가
장 적절한 것을 고르시오.

① 친구 만나기
② 바다에서 수영하기
③ 병원 진료받기
④ 방 정리하기
⑤ 집에서 쉬기

M Hey, how have you been? Why _____ _____ _____ _____ _____ yesterday?

W Well, do you remember that I went to the sea on Saturday?

M Of course, you said you were going swimming with Jessi.

W It was fun, but I started _____ _____ _____ on Sunday.

M Oh, poor you! Did you go to the hospital yesterday?

W No, I just _____ _____ _____ all day long.

M Are you feeling okay now?

W Yes, I _____ _____ _____ today. Thanks.

04

대화를 듣고, 남자가 어제 한 일로 가
장 적절한 것을 고르시오.

① 축구 연습하기
② 골프 레슨 등록하기
③ 운동복 쇼핑하기
④ 산책하기
⑤ 배구 경기 관람하기

W Ryan, I heard you are a big fan of sports.

M Yes, I am. I love both playing sports and _____ _____ . _____
_____ .

W What sports do you like to play?

M I usually play soccer in my free time. I also enjoy playing basketball, tennis,
and golf.

W Wow, you can _____ _____ _____ _____ _____ .
That's amazing.

M Yesterday, I went to a stadium to watch a volleyball game for the first time.

W How was it? Did you enjoy it?

M It was incredible! It was a close game, so it was _____ _____
_____ .

05

대화를 듣고, 남자가 대화 직후에 할
일로 가장 적절한 것을 고르시오.

① 아이스크림 사 오기
② 물 가져다주기
③ 약국 가기
④ 냉장고 청소하기
⑤ 병원에 전화하기

W Can you _____ _____ _____ _____ , Martin?

M Sure. You don't look like you're feeling well.

W I'm not. So could you get me some ice cream at the supermarket?

M Oh, _____ _____ _____ _____ in the refrigerator.
Why do you want ice cream?

W My throat hurts. Eating ice cream _____ _____ _____
_____ .

M That's not good. You need to take some medicine. I'll get some at the
pharmacy.

W No, it's okay. You don't have to.

M It's not a problem. I'll be back soon.

06

대화를 듣고, 남자가 대화 직후에 할
일로 가장 적절한 것을 고르시오.

① 수업 등록하기
② 저녁 식사하기
③ 축구하기
④ 첼로 연주하기
⑤ 미술 수업 가기

W Hey, Ian. What do you usually do on Saturday afternoons?

M Well, I used to play soccer in the park. But it's too cold now.

W Then how about ~~~~~~~~~~~~~~~~~~~~~~~~~~~~~~ with me?

M Oh, that sounds fun. Do you have one in mind?

W Yes, it starts next week. Today is _____ _____ _____
_____ _____ _____ .

M Oh! Let's go sign up together right now!

W Actually, I've already signed up. And I have to go to my cello lesson now.

M Okay. Then I'll go alone. This _____ _____ _____
_____ _____ .

W Yes. And we can have dinner together after our classes.

M That sounds great!

대화를 듣고, 여자가 지난 크리스마스 연휴에 한 일로 가장 적절한 것을 고르시오.

① 귤 따기 체험하기
② 보드게임 하기
③ 해외 여행 가기
④ 조부모님댁 방문하기
⑤ 항공박물관 관람하기

M How was your Christmas holiday? Did you _____ _____ _____ _____ with your grandparents?

W No, we couldn't visit their house.

M What happened?

W They live on Jeju Island, so we were going to ~~~~~~~~~~ ~~~~~~~~~~ _____ _____ _____.

M Oh, I remember. You were so excited about going tangerine picking there.

W Right. But _____ _____ _____ _____ _____, all the flights were canceled during the holidays.

M No way! You must be very disappointed.

W Yes, my brother and I just played some board games at home.

M Well, at least you still had fun!

08

대화를 듣고, 여자가 지난 금요일에 한 일로 가장 적절한 것을 고르시오.

① 아르바이트 하기
② 영화 관람하기
③ 수리 센터 방문하기
④ 휴대전화 구입하기
⑤ 댄스 대회 출전하기

M Minji, look at this. There will be a K-pop dance contest in May.

W That's perfect for me. You know I'm a good dancer.

M Of course, I know. And the winner will _____ _____ _____ _____ _____!

W A cell phone? You know what? I _____ _____ _____ a week ago and the screen cracked!

M Are you serious? And you weren't able to _____ _____ _____?

W I went to a service center last Friday, but it was _____ _____ _____ _____ the screen.

M Oh, I see. Doesn't it cost about 200 dollars?

W Right. So I should just participate in the contest to get a new phone.

M I'm sure you can do it!

09

대화를 듣고, 남자가 지난 주말에 한 일로 가장 적절한 것을 고르시오.

① 친구와 게임하기
② 여행 계획 짜기
③ 영어 공부하기
④ 온라인 수업 듣기
⑤ 박물관 관람하기

W Taemin, what did you do last weekend?

M I met James to ~~~~~~~~~~ ~~~~~~~~~~ _____ to New York this summer vacation.

W Are you going on a trip with him?

M No. James _____ _____ New York, so he helped me plan the trip.

W Oh, I see. Have you _____ _____ _____ _____ _____?

M Almost. I'm going to visit an art museum, take a walk in Central Park, and go to a famous restaurant.

W Sounds great. _____ _____ _____ ~~~~~~~~~~ English before traveling.

M Of course. I'm taking an English class online these days.

A 다음 영어 어휘나 표현의 뜻을 우리말로 쓰세요.

01 throat

02 convenient

03 winner

04 take a class

05 due to

06 holiday

07 stadium

08 alone

09 electricity

10 lesson

11 free time

12 pharmacy

13 volleyball

14 cancel

15 cheap

16 electric heater

B 우리말에 맞는 영어 어휘나 표현을 [보기]에서 찾아 쓰세요.

	보기		hurt	do ~ a favor	disappointed	drop	container
			crack	refrigerator	remember	already	brand-new

01 냉장고

02 아프다

03 금이 가다

04 아주 새로운

05 이미, 벌써

06 떨어뜨리다

07 실망한

08 기억하다

09 그릇, 용기

10 ~의 부탁을 들어주다

UNIT 10 세부 정보·도표

유형 설명
대화를 듣고 화자가 방문하거나 예약할 날짜, 만나기로 한 요일 등 특정 일이 일어나는 때를 묻는 문제가 출제된다. 화자가 선택하는 것을 표에서 고르는 문제도 출제된다.

지시문 유형
· 대화를 듣고, 두 사람이 만나기로 한 요일을 고르시오.
· 다음 표를 보면서 대화를 듣고, 두 사람이 주문할 텔레비전을 고르시오.

기출 표현 맛보기

세부 정보
· W   The 22nd? It's Saturday. I have to volunteer for the elderly on that day. Does April 21st work for you?
  M   Yes. I like that day. Let's make a reservation. (날짜)

도표
· W   What's your budget?
  M   I don't want to spend over 1,000 dollars.

주요 어휘·표현 미리보기

다음을 듣고, [보기]에서 알맞은 어휘나 표현을 찾아 쓰세요.   정답 및 해설 p. 32

| 보기 |
ⓐ looking for   ⓑ make a reservation   ⓒ go for   ⓓ after school
ⓔ was sold out   ⓕ looking forward to   ⓖ come soon   ⓗ a trial class

01   What do you usually do _____? 너는 보통 방과 후에 뭐 해?

02   You can take _____ for free. 무료로 시범 수업을 들을 수 있어요.

03   The video game _____ at the store. 그 비디오 게임은 그 상점에서 품절되었어.

04   My family is _____ a new apartment. 우리 가족은 새 아파트를 찾고 있어.

05   I'll _____ the blue shirt instead of the red one. 빨간 것 대신 파란 셔츠를 택할게요.

06   We should _____ at the restaurant this weekend. 이번 주말에 식당에 예약해야 해.

07   The weather report said the rain would _____. 일기 예보는 비가 곧 올 거라고 했어.

08   We are all _____ summer vacation. 우리는 모두 여름 방학을 고대하고 있어.

기출로 유형 익히기

• 먼저 지시문과 선택지를 읽고, 파악해야 하는 정보가 무엇인지 알아두세요.
• 대화의 마지막 부분에서 정답이 결정되는 경우가 많으므로 끝까지 집중해서 들어야 해요.

01

대화를 듣고, 두 사람이 로봇 박물관에 가기로 한 날짜를 고르시오.

① 9월 15일 ② 9월 17일 ③ 9월 24일
④ 9월 25일 ⑤ 9월 26일

W Hey, Leo. What are you doing?

M Hi, Iris. I'm reading an article about a new robot museum. It's opening in Seoul.

W Oh, cool. I love robots. When will it open?

M On September 17th. 오답 함정

W Do you want to go there together?

M Sure. How about going on September 24th? I think it'll be crowded the first week.

W Hmm. My family is visiting my grandparents on the 24th. How about September 25th?

M Sounds great.

정답 단서

> 문제에서 요구하는 것과 무관한 정보나, 중간에 변동된 정보 등을 혼동하지 마.

02

다음 표를 보면서 대화를 듣고, 두 사람이 빌릴 자동차를 고르시오.

	Model	Number of Seats	Baby Seat	Price (a day)
①	A	5	×	$10
②	B	5	○	$15
③	C	7	×	$20
④	D	7	○	$25
⑤	E	7	○	$30

M Honey, which car do you want to rent?

W How about renting a bigger car? We have a lot of things to carry.

M I agree. Let's get a car with seven seats.

W Okay. Do we need a baby seat?

M Of course. We need one for our son.

W Then, we have two options left.

M Let's choose the cheaper one since we're renting it for a month.

W I agree. Then, we can save some money. Let's rent that one.

> 내용을 들으면서 표의 항목별로 화자의 선택과 일치하는 것을 추려 나가자.

ANSWER

01 대화의 마지막 부분에서 여자가 9월 25일에 가자고 제안하자 남자가 동의했으므로, 정답은 ④이다.

02 좌석 7개에 아기용 좌석이 있고 더 저렴한 차를 빌리기로 했으므로, 정답은 ④이다.

LISTENING PRACTICE

점수 _____ / 9문항

일반 속도   빠른 속도

01

대화를 듣고, 두 사람이 Seoul Jazz Festival에 가기로 한 날짜를 고르시오.

① 6월 1일　　　　　　② 6월 3일　　　　　　③ 6월 4일
④ 6월 5일　　　　　　⑤ 6월 6일

02

대화를 듣고, 두 사람이 무료 수업을 듣기로 한 요일을 고르시오.

① 월요일　　　　　　② 화요일　　　　　　③ 수요일
④ 목요일　　　　　　⑤ 금요일

03

대화를 듣고, 두 사람이 만나기로 한 요일을 고르시오.

① 월요일　　　　　　② 화요일　　　　　　③ 수요일
④ 목요일　　　　　　⑤ 금요일

고난도
04

다음 표를 보면서 대화를 듣고, 남자가 예약한 캠핑장을 고르시오.

	Campsite	Date	Site Type	Firewood Ordered
①	A	July 4	tent camping	○
②	B	July 4	tent camping	×
③	C	July 4	glamping	×
④	D	July 5	tent camping	×
⑤	E	July 5	glamping	○

05

다음 표를 보면서 대화를 듣고, 남자가 주문한 컵케이크를 고르시오.

	Cupcakes	Quantity	Flavor(s)	Toppings
①	A	6	chocolate	○
②	B	6	chocolate & vanilla	×
③	C	12	chocolate	×
④	D	12	chocolate & vanilla	○
⑤	E	12	chocolate & vanilla	×

06 대화를 듣고, 남자가 가구를 배달받기로 한 날짜를 고르시오.

① 4월 10일   ② 4월 11일   ③ 4월 12일

④ 4월 13일   ⑤ 4월 14일

07 다음 표를 보면서 대화를 듣고, 두 사람이 예약할 관광 열차를 고르시오.

	Tourist Train	Destination	Price (per person)	Departure Time
①	A	ocean	$50	9:00 a.m.
②	B	ocean	$50	11:00 a.m.
③	C	mountain valley	$100	9:00 a.m.
④	D	mountain valley	$50	10:00 a.m.
⑤	E	mountain valley	$100	11:00 a.m.

고난도

08 다음 표를 보면서 대화를 듣고, 여자가 구입할 노트북 컴퓨터를 고르시오.

	Model	Price	Weight	Screen Size
①	A	$1,300	1.5 kg	15 inches
②	B	$1,500	1.25 kg	13 inches
③	C	$1,500	1.75 kg	15 inches
④	D	$1,800	1.5 kg	13 inches
⑤	E	$1,800	1.75 kg	15 inches

09 다음 표를 보면서 대화를 듣고, 여자가 주문할 열쇠고리를 고르시오.

	Key Rings	Shape	Color	Size
①	A	puppy	pink	small
②	B	puppy	white	big
③	C	bunny	pink	big
④	D	bunny	white	small
⑤	E	bunny	white	big

DICTATION

정답 단서 오답 함정

일반 속도

빠른 속도

01

대화를 듣고, 두 사람이 Seoul Jazz Festival에 가기로 한 날짜를 고르시오.

① 6월 1일　② 6월 3일
③ 6월 4일　④ 6월 5일
⑤ 6월 6일

W Hey, David! You love jazz, don't you?

M Yes, I absolutely do. Why do you ask?

W Well, the Seoul Jazz Festival is coming soon.

M Oh, that sounds like fun. When is it?

W It starts on June 4 and _____ _____ _____ _____. Do you want to go with me?

M Yeah, I'd love to! But I'm not available on the first day.

W How about June 6?

M That day works for me.

W Let me check… Ah, the tickets for June 6 _____ _____ _____ _____.

M I guess we only have one option, then.

W Right. Let's buy _____ _____ _____ _____.

02

대화를 듣고, 두 사람이 무료 수업을 듣기로 한 요일을 고르시오.

① 월요일　② 화요일
③ 수요일　④ 목요일
⑤ 금요일

W Daniel, look at this advertisement. A newly-opened sports center is _____ _____ _____ _____.

M Sounds great. What class do you want to take?

W How about tennis? The trial class is this Thursday afternoon.

M Oh no. I _____ _____ _____ _____ on Thursday.

W Umm, then we can take a golf class on Wednesday or a K-pop dance class on Friday.

M I love K-pop dances! Let's _____ _____ _____. I'll show you my dancing skills.

W Okay, I look forward to it. See you on Friday!

03

대화를 듣고, 두 사람이 만나기로 한 요일을 고르시오.

① 월요일　② 화요일
③ 수요일　④ 목요일
⑤ 금요일

M Are we going to study history together this week?

W Sure! _____ _____ _____ after school?

M Tomorrow is Tuesday. I have baseball practice _____ _____.

W Oh, I forgot that you play baseball.

M Is Thursday okay? Or _____ _____ _____ _____ on Thursdays?

W No, it's fine. I only work on Wednesdays and Fridays.

M Great. I'll see you at the library.

04

다음 표를 보면서 대화를 듣고, 남자가 예약한 캠핑장을 고르시오.

	Campsite	Date	Site Type	Firewood Ordered
①	A	July 4	tent camping	○
②	B	July 4	tent camping	×
③	C	July 4	glamping	×
④	D	July 5	tent camping	×
⑤	E	July 5	glamping	○

[Cell phone rings.]

W Hello, this is Best Campers. How can I help you?

M Hi, I'd like to _____ _____ _____ for a campsite for next Saturday, July 5.

W Let me check. *[pause]* Sorry, we're _____ _____ on that day.

M How about July 4? I want to stay for one night.

W We have a few sites available on July 4. Would you like a tent camping site or a glamping one?

M This is our first time camping, so using a tent would be _____ _____.

W Then glamping will be a better option. Do you need us to order any firewood?

M No, we'll _____ _____ _____ _____. Thanks.

W Okay, you're all set! See you next weekend.

05

다음 표를 보면서 대화를 듣고, 남자가 주문한 컵케이크를 고르시오.

	Cupcakes	Quantity	Flavor(s)	Toppings
①	A	6	chocolate	○
②	B	6	chocolate & vanilla	×
③	C	12	chocolate	×
④	D	12	chocolate & vanilla	○
⑤	E	12	chocolate & vanilla	×

W Hi, how can I help you?

M Hello, I'd like to order some cupcakes for my party.

W How many cupcakes do you need? You can order them _____ _____ _____ _____.

M I need twelve cupcakes. _____ _____ _____ _____ _____?

W You can choose chocolate or vanilla.

M Can I get _____ _____ _____ chocolate and half of them vanilla?

W Sure. Would you like any toppings on the cupcakes?

M No, I don't want any toppings.

W Okay. Thank you for your order.

06

대화를 듣고, 남자가 가구를 배달받기로 한 날짜를 고르시오.

① 4월 10일　　② 4월 11일
③ 4월 12일　　④ 4월 13일
⑤ 4월 14일

[Cell phone rings.]

M Hello?

W Hello. This is Galaxy Furniture Delivery Center. _____ _____ _____ Mr. Brown.

M Speaking.

W Your bookcase order is ready now. _____ _____ _____ _____ on April 10?

M April 10? Well, I'm not sure about my schedule that day. How about April 12 or 14?

W Wait a moment, please. *[pause]* We have a delivery slot _____ _____ _____ _____ on April 12. Does that work for you?

M Yes, that's perfect. Thank you very much.

07

다음 표를 보면서 대화를 듣고, 두 사람이 예약할 관광 열차를 고르시오.

	Tourist Train	Destination	Price (per person)	Departure Time
①	A	ocean	$50	9:00 a.m.
②	B	ocean	$50	11:00 a.m.
③	C	mountain valley	$100	9:00 a.m.
④	D	mountain valley	$50	10:00 a.m.
⑤	E	mountain valley	$100	11:00 a.m.

M Honey, how about taking a tourist train this weekend?

W A tourist train? Sounds interesting.

M We can choose our destination: the ocean or a mountain valley.

W I _____ _____ _____ to the mountains. It'll be really amazing to travel along the coast.

M Absolutely. The Ocean Train _____ _____ _____ _____, at 9:00 a.m. and 11:00 a.m.

W Is there a price difference?

M No, the price is the same: $50. There are _____ _____ _____, so we have to pay $100 total.

W Let's leave and come back early.

M Yes, that sounds good to me. Let's make a reservation now.

고난도

08

다음 표를 보면서 대화를 듣고, 여자가 구입할 노트북 컴퓨터를 고르시오.

	Model	Price	Weight	Screen Size
①	A	$1,300	1.5 kg	15 inches
②	B	$1,500	1.25 kg	13 inches
③	C	$1,500	1.75 kg	15 inches
④	D	$1,800	1.5 kg	13 inches
⑤	E	$1,800	1.75 kg	15 inches

W Steve, can you help me choose a new laptop?

M Sure. What is your budget?

W I'm _____ _____, and I'll have $1,500 to spend by next month.

M Okay, so your budget is $1,500. What will the laptop _____ _____ _____?

W I'm planning to _____ _____ _____ with me so I can do my homework.

M Then it shouldn't be too heavy. Hmm… A weight from 1 kg to 1.5 kg would be great.

W How about the screen size? Lightweight means a small-sized screen, doesn't it?

M Usually. But you can still get one with a 13-inch screen or a 15-inch screen. The bigger one _____ _____, though.

W I think a 13-inch screen is fine. This one looks good! I'll buy it.

09

다음 표를 보면서 대화를 듣고, 여자가 주문할 열쇠고리를 고르시오.

	Key Rings	Shape	Color	Size
①	A	puppy	pink	small
②	B	puppy	white	big
③	C	bunny	pink	big
④	D	bunny	white	small
⑤	E	bunny	white	big

W Dad, I'm looking for key rings for my friends. Any ideas?

M These animal-shaped ones look nice. Puppy-shaped or bunny-shaped ones should _____ _____ _____ among girls.

W We were all born in the year of the rabbit, so I'll go for the bunny-shaped ones.

M Oh, good thinking. What about the color?

W Well, we _____ _____ _____ _____, but not anymore. Everybody will like the white ones, though.

M Okay. And you need to choose the size, too.

W I think small ones are better than big ones. They're _____ _____ _____.

M I agree. Then let's order the small ones.

A

다음 영어 어휘나 표현의 뜻을 우리말로 쓰세요.

01 option

02 absolutely

03 delivery

04 campsite

05 slot

06 lightweight

07 departure

08 valley

09 flavor

10 be a hit

11 offer

12 skill

13 difference

14 challenging

15 practice

16 supply

B

우리말에 맞는 영어 어휘나 표현을 [보기]에서 찾아 쓰세요.

	보기	firewood	half	quantity	bookcase	coast
		advertisement	run	mainly	destination	prefer

01 광고

02 책장

03 장작

04 목적지

05 절반

06 주로

07 운행하다

08 더 좋아하다

09 해안

10 양, 수량

마지막 말에 대한 응답

유형 설명 대화를 듣고 화자의 마지막 말에 대한 알맞은 응답을 고르는 유형이다. 내용의 흐름을 파악하여 대화의 마지막 말에 이어질 응답으로 적절한 것을 묻는 문제가 출제된다.

지시문 유형 대화를 듣고, 여자의 마지막 말에 대한 남자의 응답으로 가장 적절한 것을 고르시오.

기출 표현 맛보기 W Everyone is welcome to join. We meet every Wednesday at 3 p.m. in the library.
M Okay. I'll be there at that time.

주요 어휘·표현 미리보기

다음을 듣고, [보기]에서 알맞은 어휘나 표현을 찾아 쓰세요.   정답 및 해설 p. 35

| 보기 |
| @ in fact | ⓑ for dessert | ⓒ gave me a ride | ⓓ come in |
| ⓔ motion sickness | ⓕ out of stock | ⓖ delayed | ⓗ lately |

01 What colors does this jacket ⬚⬚⬚⬚⬚? 이 자켓은 어떤 색깔들로 나와요?

02 I get ⬚⬚⬚⬚⬚ when I read in a car. 나는 차 안에서 책을 읽으면 멀미가 나.

03 The flight is ⬚⬚⬚⬚⬚ due to bad weather. 악천후로 항공편이 지연되고 있습니다.

04 ⬚⬚⬚⬚⬚, he's older than me. 사실, 그는 나보다 나이가 많아.

05 Those shoes are ⬚⬚⬚⬚⬚ right now. 저 신발은 지금 품절입니다.

06 Try this strawberry pudding ⬚⬚⬚⬚⬚. 후식으로 이 딸기 푸딩을 먹어 봐.

07 Sorry for replying late. I've been busy ⬚⬚⬚⬚⬚. 답장이 늦어서 미안해. 최근에 바빴어.

08 He ⬚⬚⬚⬚⬚ home. 그가 집까지 나를 태워주었어.

기출로 유형 익히기

- 전반적인 대화 내용을 이해하는 것이 중요하므로, 전체 흐름을 파악하며 들으세요.
- 대화의 마지막 말을 주의 깊게 들으세요. 특히 대화의 마지막 말이 질문인 경우 의문사를 놓쳐서는 안 돼요.

01

대화를 듣고, 남자의 마지막 말에 대한 여자의 응답으로 가장 적절한 것을 고르시오.

Woman: _____

① Sorry, but I've already had enough food.
② All right, we'll prepare one tomorrow.
③ The smell of food makes me hungry.
④ Don't forget to take out the trash.
⑤ I'd like to have a beef steak.

[Cell phone rings.]

M Hello.

W Hi. This is Hugo's French Food. Is this Alan Kim?

M Yes, speaking.

W I'm calling to check your reservation. You're having dinner for five at 6 p.m. tomorrow, correct?

M That's right. Thank you for reminding me. Is the table by the window?

W Yes, it is. Is there anything else that I can help you with?

M We're coming with a baby. So please prepare a baby chair for him.

W _____

> 식당의 저녁 식사 예약 사항을 확인하고 있는 상황이야.

02

대화를 듣고, 남자의 마지막 말에 대한 여자의 응답으로 가장 적절한 것을 고르시오.

Woman: _____

① I wish you could come to the show with me.
② I really enjoyed watching that movie.
③ I'm glad you can come with me.
④ I'm sorry you couldn't go on a family trip.
⑤ I'm disappointed that the show is canceled.

M Hey, you look very excited today. What's up?

W Yeah, I got two tickets for the 2017 World Motor Show.

M Wow, that's great. I heard there will be a lot of nice cars.

W I heard that, too. Would you like to go with me?

M I'd love to. When is it?

W The show is from July 4 to the 11.

M Oh, no. I already have a plan to go on a family trip at that time.

W _____

> 남자가 가족 여행과 모터쇼 개최 기간이 겹친다고 말했어.

ANSWER

01 남자가 아기용 의자를 요청했으므로, 여자의 응답으로는 이를 준비하겠다는 ②가 알맞다.

02 남자가 가족 여행 계획이 있어 모터쇼에 함께 갈 수 없다고 했으므로, 여자의 응답으로는 이에 대한 아쉬움을 나타내는 ①이 알맞다.

[01-02] 대화를 듣고, 여자의 마지막 말에 대한 남자의 응답으로 가장 적절한 것을 고르시오.

01

Man: _____

① It's on sale now.

② I'll pay by credit card.

③ No, I'll take it with me.

④ Sure. When can I pick up my item?

⑤ Sorry, but we don't have a delivery service.

고난도

02

Man: _____

① No, they don't have a website.

② You can call me anytime you want.

③ I can't believe you don't know my number.

④ Wait a moment. I'll look it up on my phone.

⑤ No problem. I can help you move your items.

[03-04] 대화를 듣고, 남자의 마지막 말에 대한 여자의 응답으로 가장 적절한 것을 고르시오.

03

Woman: _____

① I'd better start soon.

② Six hours is a lot of time.

③ I have lots of things to do.

④ I think it's better if it's longer.

⑤ But it's not for my English class.

04

Woman: _____

① Sorry, I don't like fruit.

② I think I missed the last bus.

③ How can I get to the station?

④ It takes thirty minutes by subway.

⑤ Thanks, but my brother is waiting for me.

[05-06] 대화를 듣고, 여자의 마지막 말에 대한 남자의 응답으로 가장 적절한 것을 고르시오.

05

Man: _____

① I can't seem to find your information.

② It was delivered to your home yesterday.

③ The book is very interesting and easy.

④ You must return the book in two weeks.

⑤ I'm afraid the book is temporarily out of stock.

06

Man: _____

① I was too busy studying to watch the game.

② I think Brazil has a better chance of winning.

③ I'm going to watch it at my house with my family.

④ I saw a soccer game with my classmates last year.

⑤ If I were you, I'd take the subway to City Hall station.

[07-08] 대화를 듣고, 남자의 마지막 말에 대한 여자의 응답으로 가장 적절한 것을 고르시오.

07

Woman: _____

① I'd like to sit by a window.

② The ticket price is 25,000 won.

③ Let me bring some snacks for you.

④ It will take two hours to get there.

⑤ I didn't know that you had motion sickness.

고난도

08

Woman: _____

① You can make a reservation online.

② I work every Wednesday and Saturday.

③ My favorite Mexican food is beef fajitas.

④ Why don't we cook Italian food instead?

⑤ The restaurant is located on the second floor.

DICTATION

정답 단서 오답 함정

 일반 속도   빠른 속도

01

대화를 듣고, 여자의 마지막 말에 대한 남자의 응답으로 가장 적절한 것을 고르시오.

Man: _____

① It's on sale now.
② I'll pay by credit card.
③ No, I'll take it with me.
④ Sure. When can I pick up my item?
⑤ Sorry, but we don't have a delivery service.

W Good afternoon. How can I help you?
M Hello, _____ _____ _____ a chair for my seven-year-old daughter.
W Okay. How about this pink one? It's one of the best-selling products in the store.
M I love its design, but do you have it in any other colors?
W _____ _____ _____ _____ green, brown, and white.
M Then I'll take the white one. How much is it?
W It's $50. Do you _____ _____ _____ _____ _____?
M _____

고난도
02

대화를 듣고, 여자의 마지막 말에 대한 남자의 응답으로 가장 적절한 것을 고르시오.

Man: _____

① No, they don't have a website.
② You can call me anytime you want.
③ I can't believe you don't know my number.
④ Wait a moment. I'll look it up on my phone.
⑤ No problem. I can help you move your items.

M I heard that you're going to _____ _____ _____ _____ _____ soon.
W Right. I'm trying to organize my things, but there's one problem.
M What is it?
W I have so many things that I don't use anymore. But most of them are almost new, so I don't want to just _____ _____ _____.
M Here's a solution: Why don't you donate them to the nearby shelter?
W Are they _____ _____?
M You should call the shelter first. They will _____ _____ _____ what they need.
W Oh, I see. Do you know their phone number?
M _____

03

대화를 듣고, 남자의 마지막 말에 대한 여자의 응답으로 가장 적절한 것을 고르시오.

Woman: _____

① I'd better start soon.
② Six hours is a lot of time.
③ I have lots of things to do.
④ I think it's better if it's longer.
⑤ But it's not for my English class.

M Have you _____ _____ _____ for English class yet?
W Yes. In fact, I'm almost finished.
M Wow, you _____ _____ _____ really hard!
W I guess so. English is my favorite subject, so it was kind of fun for me.
M That's good. And _____ _____ _____ _____ _____ when it's finished?
W It'll be about six pages long.
M I thought it only had to be three or four pages. That's too long!
W _____

04

대화를 듣고, 남자의 마지막 말에 대한 여자의 응답으로 가장 적절한 것을 고르시오.

Woman: _____

① Sorry, I don't like fruit.
② I think I missed the last bus.
③ How can I get to the station?
④ It takes thirty minutes by subway.
⑤ Thanks, but my brother is waiting for me.

M Did you like the dinner?
W Yes, thank you. But I think I _____ _____ _____.
M Would you like a kiwi _____ _____? They're really good.
W No, thanks. I'm so full.
M Oh, I see. Then maybe you can have one later.
W Actually, I think I have to go now.
M Can't you stay one more hour? My dad will _____ _____ _____ _____ when he gets home.
W _____

05

대화를 듣고, 여자의 마지막 말에 대한 남자의 응답으로 가장 적절한 것을 고르시오.

Man: _____

① I can't seem to find your information.
② It was delivered to your home yesterday.
③ The book is very interesting and easy.
④ You must return the book in two weeks.
⑤ I'm afraid the book is temporarily out of stock.

[Telephone rings.]

M Thank you for calling Riverside Bookstore. How can I help you?
W Hello. I ordered a book about a week ago, but it _____ _____ _____ yet.
M I see. Can you tell me the order number? I'll _____ _____ _____ for you.
W Okay. It's SQ14732.
M Let me see. *[pause]* Oh, I'm really sorry. Your delivery _____ _____ _____.
W Really? What's the problem?
M _____

06

대화를 듣고, 여자의 마지막 말에 대한 남자의 응답으로 가장 적절한 것을 고르시오.

Man: _____

① I was too busy studying to watch the game.
② I think Brazil has a better chance of winning.
③ I'm going to watch it at my house with my family.
④ I saw a soccer game with my classmates last year.
⑤ If I were you, I'd take the subway to City Hall station.

W Hi, Patrick. _____ _____ _____ _____ the World Cup finals tomorrow?
M Of course. I can't believe our national team _____ _____ _____ _____! I'm sure they'll win. They've been playing very well lately.
W I agree. They have a good _____ even though they're playing Brazil.
M Where are you going to watch the game?
W At Seoul Plaza with some friends. How about you?
M _____

07

대화를 듣고, 남자의 마지막 말에 대한 여자의 응답으로 가장 적절한 것을 고르시오.

Woman: _____

① I'd like to sit by a window.
② The ticket price is 25,000 won.
③ Let me bring some snacks for you.
④ It will take two hours to get there.
⑤ I didn't know that you had motion sickness.

M Emily, _____ _____ that we're going to Busan next weekend!

W Of course I won't! _____ _____ _____ _____ Busan, so I'm very excited.

M Me too. Do you want to go by car or train?

W I _____ _____ _____ _____. I get motion sickness in cars.

M I see. Let's check the train schedule. *[pause]* There are trains leaving at eleven and two.

W The eleven o'clock train would be better. We can have lunch _____ _____ _____ Busan.

M That's a good idea. Do you have a seat preference?

W _____

고난도

08

대화를 듣고, 남자의 마지막 말에 대한 여자의 응답으로 가장 적절한 것을 고르시오.

Woman: _____

① You can make a reservation online.
② I work every Wednesday and Saturday.
③ My favorite Mexican food is beef fajitas.
④ Why don't we cook Italian food instead?
⑤ The restaurant is located on the second floor.

M Christina, what's up? Why are you so busy these days?

W Well, I recently _____ _____ _____.

M I didn't know that. Where are you working?

W I _____ _____ a Mexican restaurant in a shopping mall.

M Isn't that really tiring?

W A little bit. But I'm enjoying my work because I can have lots of Mexican food. It's really delicious.

M _____ _____ _____, I've never tried Mexican food before.

W Why don't you visit the restaurant _____ _____ _____? I can recommend some dishes for you to try.

M Sounds great! When should I visit the restaurant?

W _____

A 다음 영어 어휘나 표현의 뜻을 우리말로 쓰세요.

01 organize

02 shelter

03 solution

04 full

05 tiring

06 credit card

07 agree

08 almost

09 hard

10 station

11 chance

12 wait for

13 national

14 look up

15 stay

16 throw away

B 우리말에 맞는 영어 어휘나 표현을 [보기]에서 찾아 쓰세요.

	보기		final	best-selling	temporarily	to be honest	recently
		donate	advance to	nearby	preference	be excited about

01 기부하다

02 인근의, 가까운 곳의

03 일시적으로

04 선호(하는 것)

05 결승전

06 가장 많이 팔리는

07 ~에 진출하다

08 ~에 신이 나다

09 최근에

10 솔직히 말하면

UNIT 12 상황에 적절한 말

유형 설명
담화를 듣고 주어진 상황에서 할 수 있는 말을 고르는 유형이다. 담화를 다 듣고 난 후 그 상황에서 할 수 있는 적절한 말을 묻는 문제가 출제된다.

지시문 유형
· 다음 상황 설명을 듣고, Angela가 남자에게 할 말로 가장 적절한 것을 고르시오.
· 다음 상황 설명을 듣고, Michael이 Jenny에게 할 말로 가장 적절한 것을 고르시오.

기출 표현 맛보기
· Mr. Kim would like to tell her that she has to trust herself.
  → Yeji, you should believe in yourself.
· So, she wants to ask him to stop kicking her seat.
  → Can you stop kicking my seat?

주요 어휘·표현 미리보기

다음을 듣고, [보기]에서 알맞은 어휘나 표현을 찾아 쓰세요.   정답 및 해설 p. 39

| 보기 |
| ⓐ not long after | ⓑ encouraged | ⓒ look back on | ⓓ have an idea |
| ⓔ make a plan | ⓕ dozed off | ⓖ get off | ⓗ take part in |

01 Are you going to _____? 너 계획을 짤 거니?

02 Does anyone _____? 누구 좋은 생각 있나요?

03 He will _____ the marathon next month. 그는 다음 달에 마라톤에 참가할 거야.

04 _____ I left, it started to rain. 내가 떠난 지 오래지 않아 비가 오기 시작했어.

05 When I _____ my childhood, I feel happy. 나는 어린 시절을 되돌아보면 행복해.

06 We have to _____ the bus at the next stop. 우리는 다음 정거장에 버스에서 내려야 해.

07 The baby _____ in his mother's arms. 그 아기는 엄마의 품 안에서 잠이 들었어.

08 My dad _____ me to study hard. 아빠는 내가 열심히 공부하도록 격려해 주셨어.

- 담화에서 설명하는 상황 전반을 이해하는 것이 중요하므로 전체 흐름을 파악하며 들으세요.
- 담화의 문제는 후반부에 상황을 요약하는 문장이 나오기도 하므로, 후반부 내용에 특히 집중해요.

01

다음 상황 설명을 듣고, Tiffany가 Austin에게 할 말로 가장 적절한 것을 고르시오.

Tiffany: Austin, _____

① you're really good at playing the guitar.
② would you like to take piano lessons together?
③ you should exchange your guitar for a new one.
④ why don't you watch video clips on the Internet?
⑤ watching videos is one of my favorite things to do.

> 온라인 동영상을 통해 기타 연주법을 배운 자신의 경험을 토대로 친구에게 조언하려는 상황이야.

M Tiffany is learning to play the guitar. She started a few weeks ago, and she's already learned some basic guitar skills by watching online videos. Austin, her classmate, also wants to learn to play the guitar. But he has no idea where to start. So he asks Tiffany what he should do to learn some basic guitar skills. Tiffany would like to suggest to him that he watch video clips online. In this situation, what would Tiffany most likely say to Austin?　　정답 단서

02

다음 상황 설명을 듣고, Tina가 Mr. Duncan에게 할 말로 가장 적절한 것을 고르시오.

Tina: Mr. Duncan, _____

① I heard that the competition is delayed.
② I'm sorry, but I don't know where the gym is.
③ I think I'm almost recovered from my leg injury.
④ I believe there's something wrong with my skate.
⑤ I'm afraid I can't take part in the competition this time.

> 담화에 나온 단어나 표현이 포함된 오답을 고르지 않도록 주의해.

M Tina is a speed skater. She is preparing for the local speed skating championship. One week before the competition, she twisted her ankle while exercising alone. She thought she would recover soon, but it got worse. So, she decides to tell her coach, Mr. Duncan, that she cannot participate in the competition. In this situation, what would Tina most likely say to Mr. Duncan?　　오답 함정

ANSWER

01 Tiffany는 기본적인 기타 연주법을 어떻게 배워야 할지 묻는 Austin에게 온라인 동영상을 시청해 보라고 조언하고 싶다고 했으므로, 정답은 ④이다.

02 Tina는 발목 부상으로 이번 대회에 참여할 수 없다는 의사를 밝혀야 하므로, 정답은 ⑤이다.

LISTENING PRACTICE

점수 _____ / 9문항

01

다음 상황 설명을 듣고, Peter가 여자에게 할 말로 가장 적절한 것을 고르시오.

Peter: _____

① May I sit here?

② Which station are you getting off at?

③ Could you tell me what the next station is?

④ How long does it take to go to school by subway?

⑤ Can you give me a wake-up call tomorrow morning?

02

다음 상황 설명을 듣고, Mr. Wilson이 Mina에게 할 말로 가장 적절한 것을 고르시오.

Mr. Wilson: Mina, _____

① you should have practiced more.

② don't be afraid of making mistakes.

③ I'm sure you will do better next time.

④ how about trying a new skating technique?

⑤ why don't you go skating with me tomorrow?

03

다음 상황 설명을 듣고, Daniel이 Colin에게 할 말로 가장 적절한 것을 고르시오.

Daniel: Colin, _____

① how about learning first aid?

② don't forget to put on sunscreen.

③ let's go surfing early in the morning.

④ the sun won't come out tomorrow.

⑤ why don't you wear a long-sleeved swimsuit?

고난도

04

다음 상황 설명을 듣고, Alice가 Irene에게 할 말로 가장 적절한 것을 고르시오.

Alice: Irene, _____

① I'm glad to be your friend.

② you should not lie to me.

③ why don't you stop talking for a while?

④ don't share my secrets with anyone else again.

⑤ I can help you if you want to make new friends.

고난도

05 다음 상황 설명을 듣고, Ryan이 남동생에게 할 말로 가장 적절한 것을 고르시오.

Ryan: _____

① We can eat the pie on the train.
② There isn't enough time to do that.
③ I think that is an excellent idea.
④ Why don't we bake one ourselves?
⑤ We need to visit our grandfather first.

06 다음 상황 설명을 듣고, Katie가 Emily에게 할 말로 가장 적절한 것을 고르시오.

Katie: Emily, _____

① can I borrow your charger?
② do you know where my phone is?
③ what time do you usually go to bed?
④ what would you like to do tomorrow?
⑤ could you turn off your cell phone, please?

07 다음 상황 설명을 듣고, Alex가 사람들에게 할 말로 가장 적절한 것을 고르시오.

Alex: _____

① Excuse me. I need to get off.
② Can you tell me which floor we're on?
③ What can I do for you today?
④ That's right. It's on the ninth floor.
⑤ I'm sorry that I kept you waiting.

08 다음 상황 설명을 듣고, Bruce가 Jenny에게 할 말로 가장 적절한 것을 고르시오.

Bruce: Jenny, _____

① let's study for it tomorrow night.
② what time shall we meet today?
③ I'm sorry. I will try to be quieter.
④ I think we should study together.
⑤ why don't you come to my house instead?

09 다음 상황 설명을 듣고, Mason이 도서관 사서에게 할 말로 가장 적절한 것을 고르시오.

Mason: _____

① What are the library hours?
② Could you help me find this book?
③ I'd like to sign up for a membership.
④ I forgot to bring my membership card.
⑤ How many days can I borrow a book for?

DICTATION

정답 단서 오답 함정

 일반 속도   빠른 속도

01

다음 상황 설명을 듣고, Peter가 여자에게 할 말로 가장 적절한 것을 고르시오.

Peter: _____

① May I sit here?
② Which station are you getting off at?
③ Could you tell me what the next station is?
④ How long does it take to go to school by subway?
⑤ Can you give me a wake-up call tomorrow morning?

W Peter is sitting on a subway train to go to school. Yesterday, he was working on his homework _____ _____ _____ _____. Feeling tired, he soon _____ _____. After some time, he suddenly wakes up. He looks around, but he has no idea _____ _____ _____. So he decides to ask the woman _____ _____ _____ _____ if she knows what the next station is. In this situation, what would Peter most likely say to the woman?

Peter _____

02

다음 상황 설명을 듣고, Mr. Wilson이 Mina에게 할 말로 가장 적절한 것을 고르시오.

Mr. Wilson: Mina, _____

① you should have practiced more.
② don't be afraid of making mistakes.
③ I'm sure you will do better next time.
④ how about trying a new skating technique?
⑤ why don't you go skating with me tomorrow?

W Mr. Wilson is a figure skating coach at Woori Middle School. Mina, one of his students, is _____ _____ _____ the national competition for figure skating. She is a good figure skater, but she _____ _____ _____ _____ _____ during her performance and fails to win any prizes. Mina _____ _____ _____ _____ the results. Mr. Wilson wants to encourage her by telling her that her performance will _____ _____ _____ _____. In this situation, what would Mr. Wilson most likely say to Mina?

Mr. Wilson Mina, _____

03

다음 상황 설명을 듣고, Daniel이 Colin에게 할 말로 가장 적절한 것을 고르시오.

Daniel: Colin, _____

① how about learning first aid?
② don't forget to put on sunscreen.
③ let's go surfing early in the morning.
④ the sun won't come out tomorrow.
⑤ why don't you wear a long-sleeved swimsuit?

M Daniel plans to go to the sea tomorrow with his friend Colin. Daniel is an experienced surfer, and he will teach Colin _____ _____ _____. He checks to make sure he has all the items he will need. Now he thinks that he is fully prepared. _____ _____ _____ _____ his last time surfing, he remembers that he _____ _____ _____ _____. So, he decides to call Colin to suggest that he _____ _____. In this situation, what would Daniel most likely say to Colin?

Daniel Colin, _____

다음 상황 설명을 듣고, Alice가 Irene 에게 할 말로 가장 적절한 것을 고르 시오.

Alice: Irene, _____

① I'm glad to be your friend.
② you should not lie to me.
③ why don't you stop talking for a while?
④ don't share my secrets with anyone else again.
⑤ I can help you if you want to make new friends.

다음 상황 설명을 듣고, Ryan이 남동 생에게 할 말로 가장 적절한 것을 고 르시오.

Ryan: _____

① We can eat the pie on the train.
② There isn't enough time to do that.
③ I think that is an excellent idea.
④ Why don't we bake one ourselves?
⑤ We need to visit our grandfather first.

06

다음 상황 설명을 듣고, Katie가 Emily에게 할 말로 가장 적절한 것을 고르시오.

Katie: Emily, _____

① can I borrow your charger?
② do you know where my phone is?
③ what time do you usually go to bed?
④ what would you like to do tomorrow?
⑤ could you turn off your cell phone, please?

M Alice and Irene _____ _____ _____ _____ since they were young. They trust each other, and there are _____ _____ _____ _____. One day, Alice finds out that Irene told Alice's secret to their other friends. Alice _____ _____ _____. She doesn't want to _____ _____ _____, but she worries it might happen again. So Alice wants to tell Irene never to talk about her secrets with others again. In this situation, what would Alice most likely say to Irene?

Alice Irene, _____

W Ryan and his little brother are going to ~~_____ _____ _____~~. He lives in another city, so they will take the train there. When Ryan gets to the train station, his brother ~~_____ _____ _____~~. There is a famous bakery near the train station that makes delicious apple pies. Their grandfather loves apple pie. So his brother _____ _____ _____ for their grandfather. However, their train _____ _____ in five minutes. In this situation, what would Ryan most likely say to his brother?

Ryan _____

W Katie _____ _____ _____ _____ with her best friend, Emily. It is nighttime, and after a great day of fun activities, Katie feels very tired. _____ _____ _____ _____ _____ on their beds, Emily starts playing games on her phone. Katie tries to _____ _____, but the light from Emily's phone is _____ _____ _____. Katie would like to ask if Emily could stop using her phone. In this situation, what would Katie most likely say to Emily?

Katie Emily, _____

07

다음 상황 설명을 듣고, Alex가 사람들에게 할 말로 가장 적절한 것을 고르시오.

Alex: _____

① Excuse me. I need to get off.
② Can you tell me which floor we're on?
③ What can I do for you today?
④ That's right. It's on the ninth floor.
⑤ I'm sorry that I kept you waiting.

M Alex _____ _____ _____ _____ _____ on the first floor and presses the button for the ninth floor. On the next floor, a large group of people get on the elevator and _____ _____ _____ _____ him. They are all going to the eleventh floor. When the elevator reaches the ninth floor, _____ _____ _____ that he is trying to get off. In this situation, what would Alex most likely say to the people?

Alex _____

08

다음 상황 설명을 듣고, Bruce가 Jenny에게 할 말로 가장 적절한 것을 고르시오.

Bruce: Jenny, _____

① let's study for it tomorrow night.
② what time shall we meet today?
③ I'm sorry. I will try to be quieter.
④ I think we should study together.
⑤ why don't you come to my house instead?

M Bruce has an important English test tomorrow. So he _____ _____ _____ to study with Jenny, one of his classmates tonight. She invited him to come to her house, and he agreed. But now she is calling Bruce to tell him _____ _____ _____ _____. Her brother's friends are at her house, and they are very noisy. However, Bruce's house is _____ _____ _____ _____. In this situation, what would Bruce most likely say to Jenny?

Bruce Jenny, _____

09

다음 상황 설명을 듣고, Mason이 도서관 사서에게 할 말로 가장 적절한 것을 고르시오.

Mason: _____

① What are the library hours?
② Could you help me find this book?
③ I'd like to sign up for a membership.
④ I forgot to bring my membership card.
⑤ How many days can I borrow a book for?

M Mason is in a new public library that opened just _____ _____ _____ _____. While looking around the library, he finds _____ _____ _____ that he really wants to read. But only members can borrow books from the library. He would like to tell the librarian that he wants to _____ _____ _____ _____ _____ _____. In this situation, what would Mason most likely say to the librarian?

Mason _____

A

다음 영어 어휘나 표현의 뜻을 우리말로 쓰세요.

01 result

02 press

03 librarian

04 situation

05 important

06 activity

07 trust

08 experienced

09 first aid

10 noisy

11 long-sleeved

12 enough

13 public

14 invite

15 fail to-v

16 keep ~ up

B

우리말에 맞는 영어 어휘나 표현을 [보기]에서 찾아 쓰세요.

	보기		sunburn	friendship	on a trip	charger	win a prize
		reach	suddenly	get on	annoyed	a group of

01 갑자기

02 한 무리의

03 충전기

04 이르다, 도달하다

05 (탈것을) 타다

06 짜증이 난

07 햇볕에 탐

08 여행 중인

09 우정

10 상을 타다

www.nebooks.co.kr

Section

2

실전 모의고사
1-6 회

시험 직전 모의고사
1-2 회

01 대화를 듣고, 두 사람이 구입할 의자를 고르시오.

🇬🇧
02 대화를 듣고, Bloom Music Festival에 관해 언급되지 <u>않은</u> 것을 고르시오.

① 개최일   ② 티켓 가격   ③ 개최 장소
④ 공연 소요 시간   ⑤ 참여 음악인

03 대화를 듣고, 여자가 남자에게 전화한 목적으로 가장 적절한 것을 고르시오.

① 객실 예약을 변경하려고
② 퇴실 시간을 문의하려고
③ 공항 가는 방법을 문의하려고
④ 셔틀버스 운행 일정을 알아보려고
⑤ 택시를 불러달라고 부탁하려고

🇬🇧
04 대화를 듣고, 여자가 지불할 금액을 고르시오.

① $20   ② $24   ③ $44
④ $50   ⑤ $54

05 대화를 듣고, 여자의 심정으로 가장 적절한 것을 고르시오.

① calm   ② nervous   ③ regretful
④ grateful   ⑤ disappointed

06 다음 그림의 상황에 가장 적절한 대화를 고르시오.

①   ②   ③   ④   ⑤

🇬🇧
07 대화를 듣고, 남자가 여자에게 부탁한 일로 가장 적절한 것을 고르시오.

① 숙제 대신 제출하기   ② 문화의 날 행사 준비하기
③ 작문 숙제 도와주기   ④ 스페인어 교재 빌려주기
⑤ 스페인 여행 정보 알려주기

08 다음을 듣고, Easter egg hunt에 관해 언급되지 <u>않은</u> 것을 고르시오.

① 후원사   ② 날짜   ③ 장소
④ 참가 대상   ⑤ 준비물

09 다음을 듣고, 어떤 직업에 관한 설명인지 고르시오.

① 의사   ② 약사   ③ 수의사
④ 치과의사   ⑤ 치위생사

10 다음을 듣고, 두 사람의 대화가 <u>어색한</u> 것을 고르시오.

①   ②   ③   ④   ⑤

11 대화를 듣고, 두 사람이 이번 주말에 할 일로 가장 적절한 것을 고르시오.

① 숙제하기   ② 바닷가 가기
③ TV 시청하기   ④ 시험공부 하기
⑤ 조부모님 댁 방문하기

고난도

12 다음 표를 보면서 대화를 듣고, 여자가 구입할 책을 고르시오.

	Rank	Book Title	Author	Genre
①	1	*Wealth*	Mac Woods	Essay
②	2	*Dig*	Marissa Kawkes	Fiction
③	3	*Where Is My Lunch?*	Kevin Meyer	Fairy Tale
④	4	*Health & Beauty*	Sherry Barnet	Non-fiction
⑤	5	*Cider*	Wendy Fox	Mystery

🇬🇧

13 대화를 듣고, 두 사람이 만나기로 한 요일을 고르시오.

① 일요일   ② 월요일   ③ 수요일
④ 금요일   ⑤ 토요일

14 대화를 듣고, 여자가 주말에 한 일로 가장 적절한 것을 고르시오.

① 쇼핑하기   ② 도서관 가기
③ 공원에 가기   ④ 개 목욕시키기
⑤ 휴대전화 구입하기

15 다음을 듣고, 방송의 목적으로 가장 적절한 것을 고르시오.

① 미세 먼지의 발생 원인에 대해 설명하려고
② 미세 먼지 차단 마스크 착용을 권장하려고
③ 미세 먼지의 해로움을 경고하려고
④ 미세 먼지 수치가 높을 때 대처 요령을 안내하려고
⑤ 공기 정화기 설치를 요청하려고

고난도

16 대화를 듣고, 여자가 돌려받아야 할 금액을 고르시오.

① $10   ② $20   ③ $30
④ $40   ⑤ $50

17 대화를 듣고, 여자의 마지막 말에 대한 남자의 응답으로 가장 적절한 것을 고르시오.

Man: _____

① No. I don't have a driver's license.
② I think I'll take an earlier train.
③ Dongdaemun is a great place to visit.
④ It takes about one hour to get there by train.
⑤ Okay. Can you tell me how to get to the bus station?

[18-19] 대화를 듣고, 남자의 마지막 말에 대한 여자의 응답으로 가장 적절한 것을 고르시오.

18 Woman: _____

① I've written 15 novels.
② I hope your dream comes true.
③ I don't like the novel.
④ Oh, sorry. I don't have a pen.
⑤ I'm afraid I am not a novelist.

🇬🇧

19 Woman: _____

① I'll keep my fingers crossed!
② Come on. I know you can do it.
③ I'm afraid I don't agree with you.
④ I promise you it won't happen again.
⑤ Congratulations! I'm so proud of you.

20 다음 상황 설명을 듣고, Mary가 남동생에게 할 말로 가장 적절한 것을 고르시오.

Mary: _____

① I don't want you to stop playing it.
② Good luck with your concert tomorrow.
③ Maybe you should play another instrument.
④ Could you please play the electric piano instead?
⑤ Could you lower the volume on your electric piano?

DICTATION

01 ◀ 그림 묘사

대화를 듣고, 두 사람이 구입할 의자를 고르시오.

① 　②

③　④

⑤

W Which desk chair do you like, Kurt?

M I like the one with wheels. The chairs without wheels will _____ _____ _____.

W I agree. I like that one over there with the soft cushion seat.

M But that one doesn't have any arms. I think it _____ _____ _____.

W You're probably right. How about this chair? It has arms and _____ _____ _____ tomorrow.

M I really like that one. Let's get it!

02 ◀ 언급되지 않은 내용

대화를 듣고, Bloom Music Festival에 관해 언급되지 <u>않은</u> 것을 고르시오.

① 개최일　② 티켓 가격
③ 개최 장소　④ 공연 소요 시간
⑤ 참여 음악인

M Kate, did you see the poster for the Bloom Music Festival?

W No, I didn't. It sounds interesting. When will it be?

M _____ _____ _____. Why don't you come with me?

W I'd love to. How much are the tickets for the festival?

M The tickets are usually twenty dollars, but they're _____ _____ _____ for teenagers like us.

W That's nice! Where is the event taking place?

M It _____ _____ _____ at Central Park.

W Wonderful! Then we can go there on foot. Who will be playing?

M Famous musicians like Thomas and Nathan will perform.

W Wow! I can't wait to see their show.

03 ◀ 전화 목적

대화를 듣고, 여자가 남자에게 전화한 목적으로 가장 적절한 것을 고르시오.

① 객실 예약을 변경하려고
② 퇴실 시간을 문의하려고
③ 공항 가는 방법을 문의하려고
④ 셔틀버스 운행 일정을 알아보려고
⑤ 택시를 불러달라고 부탁하려고

[Telephone rings.]

M Hello, Wallace Hotel. How may I help you?

W Good morning. This is Susan Collins in room 102. I'm _____ _____ tomorrow.

M Yes, I remember. Should I call a taxi to _____ _____ _____?

W No, I'm going to take the shuttle bus. How often does it come?

M It _____ _____ _____ _____.

W I see. Thank you.

04 ◀ 숫자 정보

대화를 듣고, 여자가 지불할 금액을
고르시오.

① $20 ② $24
③ $44 ④ $50
⑤ $54

W Excuse me. How much is this shirt?

M It was originally $25, but now _____ _____ _____ _____ $20.

W Oh! Do you have the same shirt in any other colors?

M Yes, _____ _____ _____ _____ blue, white, red, and green.

W Okay. I'll take one green one and one blue one.

M Certainly. Would you also like some wool socks? They're $2 per pair.

W _____ _____ _____ _____! I'll take two pairs.

05 ◀ 심정

대화를 듣고, 여자의 심정으로 가장
적절한 것을 고르시오.

① calm ② nervous
③ regretful ④ grateful
⑤ disappointed

M Minji, what are you doing?

W Tickets to a K-pop concert are _____ _____ _____ at two o'clock. I'm on standby.

M Oh, I see. Are they difficult to get?

W Of course. I've tried several times, but I've _____ _____.

M Really? Wow, it seems almost impossible.

W Right. Oh, I feel like _____ _____ _____ _____.

M Calm down. Just click the button right away at two o'clock. I'm sure _____ _____ _____ _____ this time.

W Thanks. Oh my gosh, there are only five minutes left!

06 ◀ 그림 상황에 적절한 대화

다음 그림의 상황에 가장 적절한 대화
를 고르시오.

① ② ③ ④ ⑤

① **W** Can I use this coupon to _____ _____ _____?
 M No, I'm afraid not. It expired two days ago.

② **W** How much are these strawberries?
 M They're _____ _____ for $5.

③ **W** Where are the cookies? I can't find them.
 M They're in aisle 12. _____ _____ _____ _____.

④ **W** Do you like watermelons?
 M Yes, they are my favorite fruit.

⑤ **W** A new grocery store opened last week.
 M Really? I'll have to go there.

대화를 듣고, 남자가 여자에게 부탁한
일로 가장 적절한 것을 고르시오.

① 숙제 대신 제출하기
② 문화의 날 행사 준비하기
③ 작문 숙제 도와주기
④ 스페인어 교재 빌려주기
⑤ 스페인 여행 정보 알려주기

M Would you _____ _____ _____ _____, Susie?

W Sure. What can I do for you?

M Can you help me with my Spanish homework? I heard you lived in Spain _____ _____ _____ _____.

W Okay. What's the assignment?

M I need to _____ _____ _____ about Spanish culture.

W That should be easy. I'd be happy to help you.

M Thanks a lot. How about meeting at the library at 7:00 p.m.?

W That sounds good. I'll see you then.

W Attention, parents and children! Our town is having an Easter egg hunt this Saturday, April 12. The event _____ _____ _____ at the Prairie Grove baseball field from 11:00 a.m. to 3:00 p.m. Children under the age of ten _____ _____ _____ the egg hunt. They should bring a small basket for collecting eggs. After the egg hunt, _____ _____ _____ _____ in the blue tent in the parking lot.

M A person with this job _____ _____ _____ _____ and provides any necessary treatment. People visit this person when there is something _____ _____ _____ _____. They may need anything from a simple cleaning to a major surgery. To get this job, you have to have extensive medical knowledge about teeth and _____ _____ _____.

10 ◀ 어색한 대화

다음을 듣고, 두 사람의 대화가 <u>어색</u>한 것을 고르시오.
① ② ③ ④ ⑤

① **M** ＿＿＿＿ ＿＿＿＿ ＿＿＿＿ ＿＿＿＿ ＿＿＿＿ to finish your homework?

    W I was on the bus for three hours.

② **M** This is the best meal I've had ＿＿＿＿ ＿＿＿＿ ＿＿＿＿ ＿＿＿＿.

    W Thanks. I'm glad you like it.

③ **M** ＿＿＿＿ ＿＿＿＿ ＿＿＿＿ ＿＿＿＿ about this shirt. It has a hole in it.

    W I'm sorry about that. Let me get you a new one.

④ **M** I haven't seen you since last year. What have you been doing?

    W I've been traveling.

⑤ **M** Why don't you join the dance club ＿＿＿＿ ＿＿＿＿ ＿＿＿＿?

    W I'll think about it.

11 ◀ 할 일

대화를 듣고, 두 사람이 이번 주말에 할 일로 가장 적절한 것을 고르시오.

① 숙제하기
② 바닷가 가기
③ TV 시청하기
④ 시험공부 하기
⑤ 조부모님 댁 방문하기

W Hey! ＿＿＿＿ ＿＿＿＿ ＿＿＿＿ ＿＿＿＿! I'm doing my homework.

M Why? Tomorrow is Saturday. There's no school.

W Yes, but we're going to the beach this weekend. So I have to ＿＿＿＿ ＿＿＿＿ ＿＿＿＿ now.

M I thought we were going to ＿＿＿＿ ＿＿＿＿ ＿＿＿＿.

W No, that's next weekend.

M Oh! Then I need to cancel my plans for next Saturday.

12 ◀ 도표

다음 표를 보면서 대화를 듣고, 여자가 구입할 책을 고르시오.

	Rank	Book Title	Author	Genre
①	1	Wealth	Mac Woods	Essay
②	2	Dig	Marissa Kawkes	Fiction
③	3	Where Is My Lunch?	Kevin Meyer	Fairy Tale
④	4	Health & Beauty	Sherry Barnet	Non-fiction
⑤	5	Cider	Wendy Fox	Mystery

M Sally, what are you doing?

W Hi, Anthony. I'm trying to buy a book for my cousin.

M Let me help you. I have many cousins. How old is your cousin?

W He is fifteen years old.

M Then he won't like a fairy tale book. How about this book? It ＿＿＿＿ ＿＿＿＿ ＿＿＿＿ in a competition.

W He doesn't seem to like essays. He ＿＿＿＿ ＿＿＿＿.

M Then there are two options left. Which will you choose?

W I will buy the book that's ＿＿＿＿ ＿＿＿＿.

M Nice choice.

13 ◀ 세부 정보

대화를 듣고, 두 사람이 만나기로 한
요일을 고르시오.

① 일요일   ② 월요일
③ 수요일   ④ 금요일
⑤ 토요일

W   Trevor! Is that you?

M   Molly! I haven't seen you in ages! What are you doing in Seoul?

W   I'm _____ _____ _____ _____. I'll be here until next Monday.

M   That's great! Are you free for lunch this weekend? Saturday _____ _____ _____.

W   No, I already have plans on that day. How about noon on Sunday?

M   Sure. I have your phone number. I'll text you tonight _____ _____ _____.

14 ◀ 한 일

대화를 듣고, 여자가 주말에 한 일로
가장 적절한 것을 고르시오.

① 쇼핑하기
② 도서관 가기
③ 공원에 가기
④ 개 목욕시키기
⑤ 휴대전화 구입하기

M   Good morning, Monica. Did you _____ _____ _____ _____?

W   Yes, Eric. I had a wonderful weekend.

M   Oh, what did you do?

W   Originally, I was going to go buy a new phone with my mom, but the cell phone store was closed.

M   So you _____ _____ _____ _____.

W   Exactly. Instead, I went to the park with my mom and my dog.

M   That sounds like fun. The _____ _____ _____ on the weekend.

W   Right. I had a great time.

15 ◀ 방송 목적

다음을 듣고, 방송의 목적으로 가장
적절한 것을 고르시오.

① 미세 먼지의 발생 원인에 대해 설
명하려고
② 미세 먼지 차단 마스크 착용을 권
장하려고
③ 미세 먼지의 해로움을 경고하려고
④ 미세 먼지 수치가 높을 때 대처 요
령을 안내하려고
⑤ 공기 정화기 설치를 요청하려고

W   Good afternoon, students! This is Principal Wilkins speaking. These days, the fine dust problem _____ _____ _____. So I'd like to explain what you should do when the fine dust level is high. First, _____ _____ _____ _____. Second, turn on the air purifier in your classroom. Third, wash your hands frequently. Last, _____ _____ when you are outside. Let's all follow these tips to stay healthy. Thank you.

16 ◀ 숫자 정보

대화를 듣고, 여자가 돌려받아야 할 금액을 고르시오.

① $10   ② $20
③ $30   ④ $40
⑤ $50

W I think the cashier _____ _____ _____ _____ for the shirt I just bought.
M Really? What does the receipt say?
W Well, it says that the shirt costs $50. But _____ _____ _____ _____.
M Oh. How much was it on sale for?
W It was 20% off, so it should have cost $40. I don't think the cashier knew it was on sale.
M You should go back and _____ _____ _____.
W I will.

17 ◀ 마지막 말에 대한 응답

대화를 듣고, 여자의 마지막 말에 대한 남자의 응답으로 가장 적절한 것을 고르시오.

Man: _____

① No. I don't have a driver's license.
② I think I'll take an earlier train.
③ Dongdaemun is a great place to visit.
④ It takes about one hour to get there by train.
⑤ Okay. Can you tell me how to get to the bus station?

W Do you _____ _____ _____? You look lost.
M Yes, I am. I'm trying to get to Dongdaemun, but I'm not sure _____ _____ _____.
W I'm sorry to tell you this, but the last train just left ten minutes ago.
M Oh no! What am I going to do now?
W You could take a night bus. It _____ _____ _____ _____.
M _____

18 ◀ 마지막 말에 대한 응답

대화를 듣고, 남자의 마지막 말에 대한 여자의 응답으로 가장 적절한 것을 고르시오.

Woman: _____

① I've written 15 novels.
② I hope your dream comes true.
③ I don't like the novel.
④ Oh, sorry. I don't have a pen.
⑤ I'm afraid I am not a novelist.

M Hi. Are you Christine Smith?
W Yes, I am. Do I know you?
M No, but I am a _____ _____ _____ _____. Your novels are wonderful.
W Thank you very much.
M I have _____ _____ _____ _____ with me right now. Could you _____ _____ _____ _____?
W Sure. Do you have a pen?
M Yes. Here it is. Thank you. I want to be a novelist like you someday.
W _____

19 ◀ 마지막 말에 대한 응답

대화를 듣고, 남자의 마지막 말에 대한 여자의 응답으로 가장 적절한 것을 고르시오.

Woman: _____

① I'll keep my fingers crossed!
② Come on. I know you can do it.
③ I'm afraid I don't agree with you.
④ I promise you it won't happen again.
⑤ Congratulations! I'm so proud of you.

W James. You look happy. What's up?

M I am. Guess what happened.

W What? You _____ _____ _____ _____ _____ to tell me.

M I do! You're not going to believe it.

W Did you get an A _____ _____ _____ _____?

M No, that's not it. Do you remember when I was practicing for the English speech contest?

W I sure do! Did you win a prize?

M Yes. I _____ _____ _____.

W _____

20 ◀ 상황에 적절한 말

다음 상황 설명을 듣고, Mary가 남동생에게 할 말로 가장 적절한 것을 고르시오.

Mary: _____

① I don't want you to stop playing it.
② Good luck with your concert tomorrow.
③ Maybe you should play another instrument.
④ Could you please play the electric piano instead?
⑤ Could you lower the volume on your electric piano?

M Mary and her brother are spending a weekend together at home. Her brother plays the electric piano in a band, and he has been _____ _____ _____ _____. She understands that he needs to practice, but she is studying for a test. She _____ _____ _____ _____ _____ at all when his music is so loud. She wants him to _____ _____ _____ _____. In this situation, what would Mary most likely say to her brother?

Mary _____

A

다음 영어 어휘나 표현의 뜻을 우리말로 쓰세요.

01 wheel

02 perform

03 uncomfortable

04 assignment

05 expire

06 extensive

07 charge

08 lower

09 license

10 take place

11 frequently

12 on a business trip

13 complaint

14 originally

15 receipt

16 keep one's fingers crossed

B

우리말에 맞는 영어 어휘나 표현을 [보기]에서 찾아 쓰세요.

| 보기 | upcoming | principal | treatment | aisle | regarding |
| | concentrate on | explain | in a long time | text | turn down |

01 (소리를) 줄이다

02 교장

03 통로, 복도

04 ~에 집중하다

05 설명하다

06 오랜만에

07 문자 메시지를 보내다

08 치료, 처치

09 ~에 관해서

10 다가오는, 곧 있을

01 대화를 듣고, 두 사람이 하고 있는 동작을 고르시오.

① ② ③ ④ ⑤

02 대화를 듣고, Global Museum에 관해 언급되지 않은 것을 고르시오.

① 규모　　② 개관 연도　　③ 입장료
④ 휴관일　　⑤ 운영 시간

03 대화를 듣고, 남자가 여자에게 전화한 목적으로 가장 적절한 것을 고르시오.

① 진료 예약을 취소하려고
② 입원 절차를 문의하려고
③ 진료 시간을 확인하려고
④ 예약 시간을 변경하려고
⑤ 주치의를 변경하려고

04 대화를 듣고, 두 사람이 만나기로 한 시각을 고르시오.

① 11:00 a.m.　② 12:00 p.m.　③ 1:00 p.m.
④ 2:00 p.m.　⑤ 3:00 p.m.

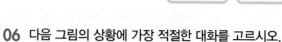

05 대화를 듣고, 두 사람이 대화하는 장소로 가장 적절한 곳을 고르시오.

① 미술관　　② 도서관　　③ 자동차 정비소
④ 극장　　⑤ 자동차 전시장

06 다음 그림의 상황에 가장 적절한 대화를 고르시오.

① ② ③ ④ ⑤

07 대화를 듣고, 남자가 여자에게 부탁한 일로 가장 적절한 것을 고르시오.

① 교과서 빌려주기　　② 숙제 알려주기
③ 숙제 대신 제출하기　　④ 책 가지러 함께 가기
⑤ 교과서 사진 찍어 보내기

08 다음을 듣고, Hawaiian Surfboards의 서핑보드에 관해 언급되지 않은 것을 고르시오.

① 디자이너　　② 소재　　③ 가격대
④ 장점　　⑤ 상품 종류

09 다음을 듣고, 무엇에 관한 설명인지 고르시오.

① 지진　　② 번개　　③ 태풍
④ 폭우　　⑤ 산불

고난도
10 다음을 듣고, 두 사람의 대화가 어색한 것을 고르시오.

① ② ③ ④ ⑤

11 대화를 듣고, 여자가 대화 직후에 할 일로 가장 적절한 것을 고르시오.

① 콘서트 표 양도받기　　② 치과 예약 변경하기
③ 콘서트 홍보하기　　④ 콘서트 표 예매하기
⑤ 공연 시간 확인하기

🇬🇧

12 다음 도서관 컴퓨터실의 좌석 배치도를 보면서 대화를 듣고, 두 사람이 앉을 좌석의 구역을 고르시오.

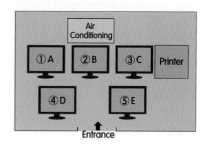

13 대화를 듣고, 현재 시각을 고르시오.

① 6:00 p.m.　　② 6:30 p.m.　　③ 7:00 p.m.

④ 7:30 p.m.　　⑤ 8:00 p.m.

14 대화를 듣고, 남자가 대화 직후에 할 일로 가장 적절한 것을 고르시오.

① 손 씻기　　　　　② 숙제하기

③ 책가방 챙기기　　④ 교복 세탁하기

⑤ 친구에게 전화하기

🇬🇧

15 다음을 듣고, 방송의 목적으로 가장 적절한 것을 고르시오.

① 학교 체육대회 일정을 안내하려고

② 학교 체육대회 시 협조를 부탁하려고

③ 학교 체육대회 안전요원을 모집하려고

④ 학교 체육대회 장소 변경을 공지하려고

⑤ 학교 체육대회 준비물을 안내하려고

고난도

16 대화를 듣고, 여자가 지불할 금액을 고르시오.

① $10　　　② $14　　　③ $15

④ $17　　　⑤ $19

17 대화를 듣고, 남자의 마지막 말에 대한 여자의 응답으로 가장 적절한 것을 고르시오.

Woman: _____

① Okay. Then I will pick Emily up.

② It is hard to fix a computer.

③ You should go shopping first.

④ We need some eggs from the grocery store.

⑤ The store is ten minutes away from here.

[18-19] 대화를 듣고, 여자의 마지막 말에 대한 남자의 응답으로 가장 적절한 것을 고르시오.

18 Man: _____

① Yes, I really enjoyed it.

② No, I didn't have any.

③ Thanks, that would be great.

④ I'll have a piece of cake, please.

⑤ I don't like sweet things.

19 Man: _____

① You are really outgoing.

② I haven't met them yet.

③ You will go to a new school next month.

④ You'd better go see a doctor as soon as possible.

⑤ Don't worry. I'm sure you'll make lots of friends soon.

20 다음 상황 설명을 듣고, Mr. Smith가 아내에게 할 말로 가장 적절한 것을 고르시오.

Mr. Smith: _____

① It's hard to have meetings on the weekend.

② I'm excited to go camping this weekend.

③ I postponed the meeting to another day.

④ I think we should change the meeting date.

⑤ I'm sorry, but we need to postpone our camping trip.

DICTATION

01 ◀ 그림 묘사

대화를 듣고, 두 사람이 하고 있는 동작을 고르시오.

① ② ③ ④ ⑤

M Tiffany, this exercise will _____ _____ _____ _____.

W Oh, can you show me how to do it?

M Sure. First, _____ _____ _____ and spread your legs. There should be some space between your feet.

W Like this?

M Yes. Then _____ _____ _____ out to the sides.

W Okay. What's next?

M Balance on your left leg. Your right foot should be _____ _____ _____.

W I can already feel my muscles getting stronger!

02 ◀ 언급되지 않은 내용

대화를 듣고, Global Museum에 관해 언급되지 않은 것을 고르시오.

① 규모 　② 개관 연도
③ 입장료 　④ 휴관일
⑤ 운영 시간

W Sam, do you have any special plans for this weekend?

M Yes, my history club will _____ _____ _____ _____ _____ to the Global Museum on Saturday.

W I heard that the Global Museum is the largest museum in Korea.

M Right. It opened in 1920 and _____ _____ _____ City Hall.

W Interesting. Do you have to _____ _____ _____ _____?

M No, it's free.

W That's great. _____ _____ _____ _____ _____ on Saturdays?

M The operating hours are from 9:00 a.m. to 5:00 p.m., so we'll have lots of time to look around.

W Nice! I hope you enjoy it!

03 ◀ 전화 목적

대화를 듣고, 남자가 여자에게 전화한 목적으로 가장 적절한 것을 고르시오.

① 진료 예약을 취소하려고
② 입원 절차를 문의하려고
③ 진료 시간을 확인하려고
④ 예약 시간을 변경하려고
⑤ 주치의를 변경하려고

[Telephone rings.]

W Thank you for calling Happy Clinic. How may I help you?

M Hello, I'm going to be late for my four o'clock appointment today.

W What is your name?

M Jason Wilson. _____ _____ _____ at five thirty instead?

W Unfortunately, Dr. Herman _____ _____ _____ then.

M Oh no. I really need to see him today.

W If it is urgent, I can _____ _____ _____ _____ at six with Dr. Thomas. Is that okay?

M Yes, Dr. Thomas would be fine.

04 ◂ 숫자 정보

대화를 듣고, 두 사람이 만나기로 한 시각을 고르시오.

① 11:00 a.m.　② 12:00 p.m.
③ 1:00 p.m.　④ 2:00 p.m.
⑤ 3:00 p.m.

[Cell phone rings.]

M Hey, Megan.

W Hi, James. I was thinking of going to the library tomorrow. _____ _____ _____ _____ ?

M Sure. I have to borrow some books. When are you going?

W I am thinking about going at 11:00 a.m. Would that be okay?

M Unfortunately, I have to _____ _____ _____ _____ _____ at twelve o'clock. What about 1:00 p.m.?

W I'm having lunch with Linda at that time. Is _____ _____ _____ _____ ?

M Yeah, that will work. I'll meet you in front of the library.

05 ◂ 장소

대화를 듣고, 두 사람이 대화하는 장소로 가장 적절한 곳을 고르시오.

① 미술관　② 도서관
③ 자동차 정비소　④ 극장
⑤ 자동차 전시장

W Wow, these cars all look really nice.

M Look! That's _____ _____ _____. I saw advertisements for it on television.

W A superhero was driving _____ _____ _____ _____ in the new action movie I saw yesterday.

M That must be why everyone is taking pictures of it.

W _____ _____ _____ _____ _____ that car.

M You already have a really nice car.

W But my car is too old. I have to take it to the repair shop all the time to _____ _____ _____ .

06 ◂ 그림 상황에 적절한 대화

다음 그림의 상황에 가장 적절한 대화를 고르시오.

①　②　③　④　⑤

① **M** How much is the _____ _____ _____ the pool?

　W It's $10.

② **M** Don't run by the pool! It's dangerous.

　W I'm sorry. I _____ _____ _____ _____ .

③ **M** Would you like to go to the pool today?

　W Sure! That sounds like a great idea.

④ **M** Only people who are more than 150 cm tall can swim here.

　W Oh, that's too bad. The pool _____ _____ _____ .

⑤ **M** You shouldn't swim right after you eat.

　W Okay. I'll wait for thirty minutes, then.

대화를 듣고, 남자가 여자에게 부탁한
일로 가장 적절한 것을 고르시오.

① 교과서 빌려주기
② 숙제 알려주기
③ 숙제 대신 제출하기
④ 책 가지러 함께 가기
⑤ 교과서 사진 찍어 보내기

[Cell phone rings.]

W Hello?

M Hi, Heather. It's Jason.

W Hi, Jason. What's going on?

M Well, I need to _____ _____ _____. I just realized that I left my science textbook at school.

W Did you? You'll need it to _____ _____ ~~~~~~~~~~~~~~~~~ this weekend. I can lend you my book when I'm finished with it tomorrow.

M _____ _____ _____ _____ until tomorrow. Could you send me pictures of the pages we should study?

W No problem. I'll send them right away.

M Thanks a lot, Heather!

다음을 듣고, Hawaiian Surfboards
의 서핑보드에 관해 언급되지 않은 것
을 고르시오.

① 디자이너   ② 소재
③ 가격대   ④ 장점
⑤ 상품 종류

M At Hawaiian Surfboards, all of our surfboards _____ _____ _____ the famous Hawaiian surfer Akamai Kalani. They _____ _____ _____ _____ special wood, so they are lighter, stronger, and more environmentally friendly than plastic boards. We mostly sell longboards, but we also have a _____ _____ of shortboards. Our salespeople help customers find the perfect surfboard. So please stop by!

W You can sometimes see this _____ ~~~~~~~~. It is a very bright light that flashes in the sky. It is often _____ _____ _____ _____ _____ that sounds like an explosion. It can be dangerous because it ~~~~~~ and sometimes hits the earth. Every year, many forest fires are started by this. If a person is _____ _____ _____, he or she can be killed or seriously injured.

10 ◀ 어색한 대화

다음을 듣고, 두 사람의 대화가 어색한 것을 고르시오.

① ② ③ ④ ⑤

① **W** Where can I find the milk and cheese?

　M They're at the end of aisle 6.

② **W** Do you want some more cake?

　M No, thanks. I'm full.

③ **W** _____ _____ _____ _____ _____ with these bags?

　M Yes, how may I help you?

④ **W** _____ _____ _____ _____ your meal?

　M It's very good, thanks.

⑤ **W** _____ _____ _____ _____ by bus?

　M It'll take about five hours.

11 ◀ 할 일

대화를 듣고, 여자가 대화 직후에 할 일로 가장 적절한 것을 고르시오.

① 콘서트 표 양도받기
② 치과 예약 변경하기
③ 콘서트 홍보하기
④ 콘서트 표 예매하기
⑤ 공연 시간 확인하기

M There is going to be a _____ _____ _____ _____.

W Wow! What time does it start?

M It starts at four.

W Really? I'd like to go. How can I get a ticket?

M You can _____ _____ _____.

W I have a dentist appointment at four on Saturday. I'll _____ _____ _____ after I reschedule it.

M The tickets will be gone soon, so you should reserve one now. You can _____ _____ _____ afterwards.

W Okay.

12 ◀ 배치도

다음 도서관 컴퓨터실의 좌석 배치도를 보면서 대화를 듣고, 두 사람이 앉을 좌석의 구역을 고르시오.

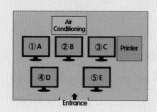

M This library is so big!

W It really is. Where is the computer room?

M It's over there. There are five sections. Which one do you want to sit in?

W Hmm. I don't want to sit by the entrance. There would be _____ _____ _____ _____.

M I agree. What about section C?

W It's _____ _____ _____ _____. I think section B would be better.

M But that's where the air conditioning is. I think it _____ _____ _____ _____.

W Okay. Let's sit in the section next to it instead.

13 ◀ 숫자 정보

대화를 듣고, 현재 시각을 고르시오.
① 6:00 p.m.　　② 6:30 p.m.
③ 7:00 p.m.　　④ 7:30 p.m.
⑤ 8:00 p.m.

W _____ _____ _____ _____ go to the concert. But let's have dinner before we leave. I'm starving.

M I'm not sure if we have time. When does the concert start?

W It _____ ～～～～～～～～.

M We need to leave _____ _____ _____ _____ _____ the concert starts. So we only have thirty minutes to eat now.

W That's not much time. Why don't we go to a fast-food restaurant?

M Oh, I don't like fast food. But I guess there's no other choice.

14 ◀ 할 일

대화를 듣고, 남자가 대화 직후에 할 일로 가장 적절한 것을 고르시오.
① 손 씻기
② 숙제하기
③ 책가방 챙기기
④ 교복 세탁하기
⑤ 친구에게 전화하기

M Mom, can I go to Ben's house now? We want to play computer games.

W Did you finish your homework?

M Yes, I finished it an hour ago, and I also ～～～～～～～～ ～～～～～～.

W What about your school uniform? Have you washed it yet?

M Oh, I forgot. It's _____ _____ _____.

W You _____ _____ _____ _____ before you go to Ben's house.

M Okay, Mom. I will.

15 ◀ 방송 목적

다음을 듣고, 방송의 목적으로 가장 적절한 것을 고르시오.
① 학교 체육대회 일정을 안내하려고
② 학교 체육대회 시 협조를 부탁하려고
③ 학교 체육대회 안전요원을 모집하려고
④ 학교 체육대회 장소 변경을 공지하려고
⑤ 학교 체육대회 준비물을 안내하려고

W Hello, students. This is Vice Principal Sarah Park. It is great to see all of the excitement for today's sports day. But please remember to _____ _____ _____ _____ throughout the day. All of the events will be held at our school playground. If you need to _____ _____ _____ _____ for any reason, you must get permission from your teacher. We want to _____ _____ _____ _____. Please cooperate so that we can all have a safe and fun day. Thank you.

16 ◀ 숫자 정보

대화를 듣고, 여자가 지불할 금액을
고르시오.

① $10   ② $14
③ $15   ④ $17
⑤ $19

M Welcome to John's Hamburgers. How may I help you?

W Hello. I'd like to buy some chicken burger sets.

M Okay. The chicken burger set is _____ _____. How many would you like?

W I_____ _____ _____. And do you sell ice cream too?

M Yes, there is chocolate ice cream and vanilla ice cream. Chocolate is two dollars each and vanilla is one dollar each.

W Then please _____ _____ _____ and one vanilla to my order.

M Okay. Do you need anything else?

W No. Here's my credit card.

M Okay. I'll call your number when the food is ready.

W Thank you.

17 ◀ 마지막 말에 대한 응답

대화를 듣고, 남자의 마지막 말에 대
한 여자의 응답으로 가장 적절한 것을
고르시오.

Woman: _____

① Okay. Then I will pick Emily up.
② It is hard to fix a computer.
③ You should go shopping first.
④ We need some eggs from the grocery store.
⑤ The store is ten minutes away from here.

M Hey, are you busy?

W I'm fixing our computer right now. Why?

M Emily _____ _____ _____, but I need to go to the grocery store before it closes.

W When does it close?

M It closes at 5:00, and it's already four o'clock.

W How about picking up Emily _____ _____ _____ _____?

M That will be too late. I don't _____ _____ _____ _____ at the school that long.

W _____

18 ◀ 마지막 말에 대한 응답

대화를 듣고, 여자의 마지막 말에 대
한 남자의 응답으로 가장 적절한 것을
고르시오.

Man: _____

① Yes, I really enjoyed it.
② No, I didn't have any.
③ Thanks, that would be great.
④ I'll have a piece of cake, please.
⑤ I don't like sweet things.

M The food was delicious. Thanks for _____ _____ _____ _____ _____.

W My pleasure. I'm glad you enjoyed it. _____ _____ _____ _____ _____?

M Thanks, but I'm full.

W Okay. But how about dessert? I have some apple pie and some chocolate cake.

M Oh, I always _____ _____ _____ _____!

W Which would you prefer?

M _____

대화를 듣고, 여자의 마지막 말에 대한 남자의 응답으로 가장 적절한 것을 고르시오.

Man: _____

① You are really outgoing.
② I haven't met them yet.
③ You will go to a new school next month.
④ You'd better go see a doctor as soon as possible.
⑤ Don't worry. I'm sure you'll make lots of friends soon.

M I don't think I've seen you before. _____ _____ _____ _____?

W Yes, I am. This is my first day at this school.

M Well, _____ _____ _____ _____ our school so far?

W So far, I really like it. Everyone seems very nice.

M That's great. But moving to a new school must be hard.

W It is. Actually, I'm _____ _____ _____.

M _____

다음 상황 설명을 듣고, Mr. Smith가 아내에게 할 말로 가장 적절한 것을 고르시오.

Mr. Smith: _____

① It's hard to have meetings on the weekend.
② I'm excited to go camping this weekend.
③ I postponed the meeting to another day.
④ I think we should change the meeting date.
⑤ I'm sorry, but we need to postpone our camping trip.

W Mr. Smith and his wife _____ _____ _____ _____ this weekend. They have already prepared all of the food and supplies they need. Today, however, Mr. Smith found out that he needs to _____ _____ _____ _____ this Saturday. He checked if the meeting could be moved to another day, but it was impossible to _____ _____ _____. In this situation, what would Mr. Smith most likely say to his wife?

Mr. Smith _____

A 다음 영어 어휘나 표현의 뜻을 우리말로 쓰세요.

01 injured

02 textbook

03 muscle

04 as soon as possible

05 lots of

06 operating hour

07 afterwards

08 cooperate

09 urgent

10 closet

11 find out

12 explosion

13 newest

14 strengthen

15 postpone

16 outgoing

B 우리말에 맞는 영어 어휘나 표현을 [보기]에서 찾아 쓰세요.

| 보기 | homesick | starving | reserve | realize | entrance fee | so far |
| | spread | ask a favor | seriously | | environmentally friendly |

01 예약하다

02 부탁하다

03 벌리다, 펴다

04 몹시 배고픈

05 지금까지

06 입장료

07 깨닫다

08 심하게

09 향수병에 걸린

10 환경친화적인

일반 속도

빠른 속도

01 대화를 듣고, 여자가 구입할 티셔츠를 고르시오.

① ② ③ ④ ⑤

02 대화를 듣고, Junior Summer Camp에 관해 언급되지 <u>않은</u> 것을 고르시오.

① 장소　　　　② 활동 내용
③ 참가비　　　④ 준비물
⑤ 참여 가능 인원

03 대화를 듣고, 남자가 전화한 목적으로 가장 적절한 것을 고르시오.

① 함께 스키를 타러 가자고 제안하려고
② 약속을 취소하려고
③ 여동생을 돌봐달라고 부탁하려고
④ 약속 시각을 변경하려고
⑤ 문자에 답장하지 않는 이유를 물어보려고

04 대화를 듣고, 남자가 선택한 수업의 시작 시각을 고르시오.

① 4:00　　　② 4:30　　　③ 5:00
④ 6:00　　　⑤ 6:30

05 대화를 듣고, 두 사람이 대화하는 장소로 가장 적절한 곳을 고르시오.

① 주차장　　　② 수영장　　　③ 공항
④ 주유소　　　⑤ 세탁소

06 다음 그림의 상황에 가장 적절한 대화를 고르시오.

① ② ③ ④ ⑤

07 대화를 듣고, 여자가 남자에게 부탁한 일로 가장 적절한 것을 고르시오.

① 약 사 오기　　　　② 장 보기
③ 음식점 예약하기　④ 샌드위치 사 오기
⑤ 자외선 차단제 빌려주기

08 다음을 듣고, 수학여행에 관해 언급되지 <u>않은</u> 것을 고르시오.

① 장소　　　② 이동 수단　　　③ 기간
④ 신청 방법　⑤ 신청 기한

09 다음을 듣고, 무엇에 관한 설명인지 고르시오.

① 하키　　　② 테니스　　　③ 탁구
④ 야구　　　⑤ 배드민턴

10 다음을 듣고, 두 사람의 대화가 <u>어색한</u> 것을 고르시오.

① ② ③ ④ ⑤

11 대화를 듣고, 남자가 대화 직후에 할 일로 가장 적절한 것을 고르시오.

① 학원에 전화하기　　　② 시험 보기
③ 수업 등록하기　　　　④ 안내 책자 가져가기
⑤ 영어 회화 수업 듣기

12 다음 학교 주변 지도를 보면서 대화를 듣고, 두 사람이 선택한 벼룩시장 개최 구역을 고르시오.

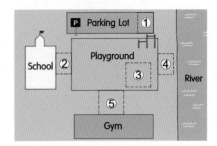

🇬🇧
13 대화를 듣고, 두 사람이 만나기로 한 날짜를 고르시오.

① 7월 6일   ② 7월 8일   ③ 7월 11일
④ 7월 12일   ⑤ 7월 14일

14 대화를 듣고, 여자가 이번 휴가에 한 일로 가장 적절한 것을 고르시오.

① 재택근무하기   ② 요리 배우기
③ 여행 영상 찍기   ④ 요리 책 집필하기
⑤ 노래 배우기

15 다음을 듣고, 방송의 목적으로 가장 적절한 것을 고르시오.

① 공연 출연진을 소개하려고
② 무료 공연을 홍보하려고
③ 공연이 지연되었음을 알리려고
④ 공연 관람 시 따라야 하는 규칙을 설명하려고
⑤ 공연 티켓 구매법을 안내하려고

🇬🇧
16 대화를 듣고, 여자가 지불할 금액을 고르시오.

① $250   ② $275   ③ $300
④ $325   ⑤ $400

17 대화를 듣고, 여자의 마지막 말에 대한 남자의 응답으로 가장 적절한 것을 고르시오.

Man: _____

① A fountain pen is what I really need at school.
② It's very hard to recommend something for you.
③ You have to choose your father's present today.
④ That's a good idea! I will buy a shaver for him.
⑤ It would be too expensive to get a nice one. Can you think of something else?

[18-19] 대화를 듣고, 남자의 마지막 말에 대한 여자의 응답으로 가장 적절한 것을 고르시오.

18 Woman: _____

① I already have one.
② I highly recommend it.
③ Did you make a reservation?
④ Sorry, I'm really not interested.
⑤ He's not at home. Can I take a message?

19 Woman: _____

① She seems to like mystery novels.
② I think she is really kind.
③ Yes, she is a great writer.
④ I forgot that it is Hyejin's birthday.
⑤ I can't make it to the party tonight.

20 다음 상황 설명을 듣고, Peter가 Carrie에게 할 말로 가장 적절한 것을 고르시오.

Peter: _____

① I'm fine, and you?
② Sorry, I have a class on that day.
③ Oh, I have to go to a birthday party on Friday.
④ Great! Can you pick me up on Friday morning?
⑤ Why don't we go on Wednesday instead?

DICTATION

01 ◀ 그림 묘사

대화를 듣고, 여자가 구입할 티셔츠를 고르시오.

①   ②

③   ④

⑤

M Are you going to buy one of those shirts?

W I think so. I like this one. The neck is _____ _____ a V.

M But the sleeves are short. Won't you _____ _____?

W No, I'll wear it in the summer.

M It doesn't have a pocket _____ _____ _____. Is that okay?

W Yes, that isn't a problem. I'll buy this one!

02 ◀ 언급되지 않은 내용

대화를 듣고, Junior Summer Camp에 관해 언급되지 <u>않은</u> 것을 고르시오.

① 장소 ② 활동 내용
③ 참가비 ④ 준비물
⑤ 참여 가능 인원

M Ann, did you hear about Junior Summer Camp for this summer?

W No. Can you tell me about it in detail?

M The camp is held in Mount Westwood and fosters student leadership.

W What activities can you do at the camp?

M You _____ _____ _____ such as exploring the forest, setting traps, and grilling meat.

W That sounds great. How much is the _____ _____?

M Eighty dollars a week.

W That's not that bad. How many people can _____ _____ _____ _____?

M Only 20 people can participate, so we should apply quickly.

03 ◀ 전화 목적

대화를 듣고, 남자가 전화한 목적으로 가장 적절한 것을 고르시오.

① 함께 스키를 타러 가자고 제안하려고
② 약속을 취소하려고
③ 여동생을 돌봐달라고 부탁하려고
④ 약속 시각을 변경하려고
⑤ 문자에 답장하지 않는 이유를 물어보려고

[Telephone rings.]

W Hello?

M Hi. This is Jaeho. May I speak to Yunsu, please? He _____ _____ _____ _____ _____.

W Yunsu isn't here. He went skiing with his classmates.

M Oh, he _____ _____ _____ _____ _____. When is he coming back?

W Tonight. Can I take a message?

M Yes, Yunsu and I were going to play badminton tomorrow, but I can't make it because I have to _____ _____ _____ _____.

W Okay. I'll let him know.

M Thanks. I'll send him a text message too.

04 ◀ 숫자 정보

대화를 듣고, 남자가 선택한 수업의 시작 시각을 고르시오.

① 4:00　　② 4:30
③ 5:00　　④ 6:00
⑤ 6:30

W Welcome to Welton's Swimming Center. How may I help you?

M Hello. I'm here to sign up for a swimming class.

W Okay. Which level would you like to be in a beginner, intermediate, or advanced class?

M I want to be in an _____ _____.

W There are two intermediate classes. One starts at 4:30 and the other starts at 6:00.

M I'll have to take the class that _____ _____ _____. I think the class at 6:00 will end too late.

W So you would like to _____ _____ _____ _____ _____?

M Yes. Here's my credit card.

05 ◀ 장소

대화를 듣고, 두 사람이 대화하는 장소로 가장 적절한 곳을 고르시오.

① 주차장　　② 수영장
③ 공항　　④ 주유소
⑤ 세탁소

M How can I help you?

W Can you _____ _____ _____ _____, please?

M Sure. Can you just _____ _____ a little bit forward?

W Okay. [pause] How's that?

M Perfect. Is there anything else I can do for you?

W Well, can I _____ _____ _____ _____ here for free?

M No. It costs $8. But you get a coupon for 50% off for filling up your tank.

06 ◀ 그림 상황에 적절한 대화

다음 그림의 상황에 가장 적절한 대화를 고르시오.

① ② ③ ④ ⑤

① M Excuse me. How much is this desk?

　 W _____ _____ _____ this week for $50.

② M Is there a bank _____ _____ _____?

　 W Yes. There's one next to the train station.

③ M I don't have much money these days.

　 W You can _____ _____ _____ _____.

④ M We should get tickets to the concert.

　 W Is that a good idea? They're very expensive.

⑤ M I'd like to change $50 to Korean won.

　 W Certainly. May I _____ _____ _____ _____, please?

대화를 듣고, 여자가 남자에게 부탁한
일로 가장 적절한 것을 고르시오.
① 약 사 오기
② 장 보기
③ 음식점 예약하기
④ 샌드위치 사 오기
⑤ 자외선 차단제 빌려주기

M How are you feeling, Hillary?

W Terrible. My sunburn _____ _____.

M I told you that you needed to put on more sunscreen.

W I know. You were right. Anyway, could you _____ _____ _____ _____ at the convenience store?

M Sure. Didn't you have lunch?

W No. There's no food in the house, and I _____ _____ _____ _____ _____.

M Yes, you need to keep out of the sun. Wait there, and I'll be back soon.

W Good morning. This is a reminder about _____ _____ _____ _____ Sokcho. We'll be leaving on July 8 and traveling to the beach by bus. The trip will _____ _____ _____ _____ and two nights. If you're interested in going on the trip, please pick up a permission form at the main office. The form _____ _____ _____ by your parents and returned to the office. Thank you.

M This game is played by two or four people. They stand _____ _____ _____ of a big table. In the middle of the table, there's a net. Each player has a racket. The players _____ _____ _____ over the net with their rackets. The ball must _____ _____ _____ _____. If a player doesn't hit the ball back over the net before it bounces twice, the other team gets a point.

---

10 ◀ 어색한 대화

다음을 듣고, 두 사람의 대화가 어색한 것을 고르시오.

① ② ③ ④ ⑤

① M I'd like you to meet my mother tonight. Can you come to dinner?
　 W Sure. I'm ＿＿＿ ＿＿＿ ＿＿＿ ＿＿＿ her.
② M How do you get to school?
　 W I usually take the subway and then walk.
③ M Do you want some more pizza?
　 W Sure. ＿＿＿ ＿＿＿.
④ M Would you like to go out this evening?
　 W ＿＿＿ ＿＿＿ ＿＿＿ ＿＿＿. I'm busy.
⑤ M Where did you get that jacket?
　 W I don't know. My mother bought it for me.

11 ◀ 할 일

대화를 듣고, 남자가 대화 직후에 할 일로 가장 적절한 것을 고르시오.

① 학원에 전화하기
② 시험 보기
③ 수업 등록하기
④ 안내 책자 가져가기
⑤ 영어 회화 수업 듣기

W Welcome to Kim's English Academy. How can I help you?
M I'd like to take an English conversation class.
W Have you ever taken a class here before?
M No. This will ＿＿＿ ＿＿＿ ＿＿＿ ＿＿＿.
W Then you need to ＿＿＿ ＿＿＿ ＿＿＿ so we can find the right level for you.
M Sure. Can I take it now?
W Yes. You can take it ＿＿＿ ＿＿＿ ＿＿＿ ＿＿＿.
M All right. How long will it take?
W About thirty minutes. After you finish, I'll tell you more about our classes.

고난도

12 ◀ 배치도

다음 학교 주변 지도를 보면서 대화를 듣고, 두 사람이 선택한 벼룩시장 개최 구역을 고르시오.

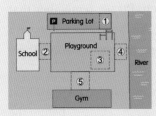

W Will the school flea market be held inside the gym this year?
M No. The weather will be nice, so I want to ＿＿＿ ＿＿＿ ＿＿＿.
W How about on the playground?
M No, the playground is ＿＿＿ ＿＿＿. We could have it between the river and the playground.
W There's ＿＿＿ ＿＿＿ ＿＿＿. And the parking lot will be full of cars.
M How about in front of the gym?
W That's a good idea. Let's have the flea market there.
M All right. I'll tell the principal.

13 ◀ 세부 정보

대화를 듣고, 두 사람이 만나기로 한 날짜를 고르시오.

① 7월 6일 ② 7월 8일
③ 7월 11일 ④ 7월 12일
⑤ 7월 14일

W Welcome to Seoul! It's been such a long time since I saw you! When did you get here?

M Two days ago, on July 8.

W I see. Do you have _____ _____ _____ _____ _____? I know a restaurant that makes great hamburgers.

M Sure. But I _____ _____ _____ on July 11 and 14.

W Are you free the day _____ _____ _____ _____?

M I am. Let's have dinner then!

14 ◀ 한 일

대화를 듣고, 여자가 이번 휴가에 한 일로 가장 적절한 것을 고르시오.

① 재택근무하기
② 요리 배우기
③ 여행 영상 찍기
④ 요리 책 집필하기
⑤ 노래 배우기

M Hello, Carol. Did you have a good vacation?

W Hi, Darrin. I _____ _____ _____ _____.

M Really? Did you finish a lot of work at home?

W No, not really. But I learned to cook this vacation.

M _____ _____ _____ _____ did you learn to cook?

W I learned to cook Western dishes such as pasta and pizza.

M You must have worked very hard. I should try to learn to cook too.

W You should. It's _____ _____ _____ _____ than you think.

15 ◀ 방송 목적

다음을 듣고, 방송의 목적으로 가장 적절한 것을 고르시오.

① 공연 출연진을 소개하려고
② 무료 공연을 홍보하려고
③ 공연이 지연되었음을 알리려고
④ 공연 관람 시 따라야 하는 규칙을 설명하려고
⑤ 공연 티켓 구매법을 안내하려고

W Ladies and gentlemen, welcome to our Sunflower Circus. We promise to show you the best performance you've ever seen. Please remember that _____ _____ _____ _____ these rules when you watch the performance. First, never stand up during the performance. There are flying acts in our performance, so _____ _____ _____ _____. Second, taking pictures and videos is not allowed. We ask you to _____ _____ _____ _____ _____ before the performance starts. If you follow these rules, everyone will be able to enjoy the performance. Thank you.

16 ◀ 숫자 정보

대화를 듣고, 여자가 지불할 금액을 고르시오.

① $250   ② $275
③ $300   ④ $325
⑤ $400

M Can I help you?

W Yes. How much is this guitar?

M That one is $400. But _____ _____ _____ _____ $300. It's one of our best guitars.

W Do you have anything cheaper?

M This one is $250. It's _____ _____ _____.

W I'll take it. And how much is a pack of strings?

M It's $25. But the guitar _____ _____ _____.

W Oh. Then I don't need to buy more. Great!

고난도

17 ◀ 마지막 말에 대한 응답

대화를 듣고, 여자의 마지막 말에 대한 남자의 응답으로 가장 적절한 것을 고르시오.

Man: _____

① A fountain pen is what I really need at school.
② It's very hard to recommend something for you.
③ You have to choose your father's present today.
④ That's a good idea! I will buy a shaver for him.
⑤ It would be too expensive to get a nice one. Can you think of something else?

W Parker, what are you doing on your smartphone?

M I'm looking for my dad's birthday present, but I can't _____ _____ _____.

W Let me help you. _____ _____ _____ do you have in mind?

M I'm thinking between twenty and forty dollars.

W Then how about an electric shaver?

M That's a great idea, but he _____ _____ _____.

W Hmm… What about a fountain pen? He'd be able to use it at work.

M _____

---

18 ◀ 마지막 말에 대한 응답

대화를 듣고, 남자의 마지막 말에 대한 여자의 응답으로 가장 적절한 것을 고르시오.

Woman: _____

① I already have one.
② I highly recommend it.
③ Did you make a reservation?
④ Sorry, I'm really not interested.
⑤ He's not at home. Can I take a message?

M Hi, I'm Sam Jones with NC Insurance Company.

W Hi. What can I do for you?

M Well, I'd like to know if you _____ _____ _____ _____.

W No, I don't. But I don't want to buy any either.

M What will your family do _____ _____ _____ _____? Everyone has to think about that.

W My husband has excellent life insurance.

M But you should have some too. Our company has the _____ _____ _____ life insurance.

W _____

19 ◀ 마지막 말에 대한 응답

대화를 듣고, 남자의 마지막 말에 대한 여자의 응답으로 가장 적절한 것을 고르시오.

Woman: _____

① She seems to like mystery novels.
② I think she is really kind.
③ Yes, she is a great writer.
④ I forgot that it is Hyejin's birthday.
⑤ I can't make it to the party tonight.

W Hi, Jihun. Are you going to Hyejin's birthday party tonight?

M Yes, I am. I'm really looking forward to it. Did you get her a present yet?

W Yes, I _____ _____ _____ _____ after school yesterday and bought her a scarf. What about you?

M Not yet. I'm not sure what she would like.

W Whenever I see her, she's always reading a book. Maybe you could _____ _____ _____ _____ _____.

M Do you know _____ _____ _____ _____?

W _____

20 ◀ 상황에 적절한 말

다음 상황 설명을 듣고, Peter가 Carrie에게 할 말로 가장 적절한 것을 고르시오.

Peter: _____

① I'm fine, and you?
② Sorry, I have a class on that day.
③ Oh, I have to go to a birthday party on Friday.
④ Great! Can you pick me up on Friday morning?
⑤ Why don't we go on Wednesday instead?

M Carrie is going to the lake _____ _____ _____ next week. She asks Peter if he can join her. He wants to, but he has classes on Monday and Wednesday. Also, his cousin's birthday party is on Friday, so he's _____ _____ _____ Tuesday and Thursday. He asks Carrie when she is going. She says she _____ _____ _____ on Friday morning. In this situation, what would Peter most likely say to Carrie?

Peter _____

A

다음 영어 어휘나 표현의 뜻을 우리말로 쓰세요.

01 playground

02 conversation

03 space

04 in detail

05 allow

06 advanced

07 trusted

08 get a point

09 sunscreen

10 permission

11 these days

12 flea market

13 productive

14 insurance

15 beginner

16 look after

B

우리말에 맞는 영어 어휘나 표현을 [보기]에서 찾아 쓰세요.

보기	make it	last	highly	forward	have in mind
	bounce	string	fill up	reminder	neighborhood

01 상기시키는 것

02 앞으로

03 (모임 등에) 가다[참석하다]

04 매우, 크게

05 지속되다

06 근처, 인근

07 줄

08 튀다

09 ~을 가득 채우다

10 ~을 생각하다[염두에 두다]

점수   / 20문항

 일반 속도
 빠른 속도

01 대화를 듣고, 남자가 구입할 마카롱을 고르시오.

`고난도`

02 대화를 듣고, Andy Lee에 관해 언급되지 않은 것을 고르시오.

① 저서   ② 성장 환경   ③ 대학 전공
④ 수상 경력   ⑤ 취미

03 대화를 듣고, 여자가 남자에게 전화한 목적으로 가장 적절한 것을 고르시오.

① 안부를 물으려고
② 약속 시각을 변경하려고
③ 영어 숙제를 물어보려고
④ 함께 영화를 보러 가려고
⑤ 빌린 휴대전화를 돌려주려고

04 대화를 듣고, 여자가 식당을 예약한 시각을 고르시오.

① 2:00   ② 3:00   ③ 5:00
④ 6:00   ⑤ 7:00

05 대화를 듣고, 남자의 심정으로 가장 적절한 것을 고르시오.

① satisfied   ② angry   ③ thankful
④ relieved   ⑤ embarrassed

06 다음 그림의 상황에 가장 적절한 대화를 고르시오.

①   ②   ③   ④   ⑤

07 대화를 듣고, 남자가 여자에게 부탁한 일로 가장 적절한 것을 고르시오.

① 음식점 위치 알려주기   ② 음식 포장해오기
③ 대기 줄 서기   ④ 음식점 예약하기
⑤ 역에 데려다주기

08 다음을 듣고, Networking Event에 관해 언급되지 않은 것을 고르시오.

① 개최 날짜   ② 참가 대상   ③ 행사 목적
④ 참가 신청 방법   ⑤ 복장

09 다음을 듣고, 어떤 직업에 관한 설명인지 고르시오.

① 사서   ② 고고학자   ③ 큐레이터
④ 골동품 수집가   ⑤ 공연 기획자

10 다음을 듣고, 두 사람의 대화가 어색한 것을 고르시오.

①   ②   ③   ④   ⑤

11 대화를 듣고, 여자가 대화 직후에 할 일로 가장 적절한 것을 고르시오.

① 스케이트화 구입하기   ② 병원 진료받기
③ 스케이트화 대여하기   ④ 여동생에게 전화하기
⑤ 스케이트 강습 등록하기

고난도

12 다음 표를 보면서 대화를 듣고, 남자가 구입할 휴대전화를 고르시오.

	Phone	Weight	Color	Storage Space
①	A	150 g	White	128 GB
②	B	170 g	Black	128 GB
③	C	190 g	White	256 GB
④	D	210 g	White	256 GB
⑤	E	220 g	Black	512 GB

13 대화를 듣고, 두 사람이 만나기로 한 시각을 고르시오.

① 4:00 p.m.   ② 4:30 p.m.   ③ 5:00 p.m.
④ 5:30 p.m.   ⑤ 6:00 p.m.

14 대화를 듣고, 남자가 할 일로 가장 적절한 것을 고르시오.

① 집안일 하기   ② 죽 사 오기   ③ 병원 가기
④ 약국 가기   ⑤ 숙제하기

15 다음을 듣고, 방송의 목적으로 가장 적절한 것을 고르시오.

① 교통사고의 원인 규명을 촉구하려고
② 횡단보도 안전 수칙을 설명하려고
③ 학교 앞 신호등 추가 설치를 요청하려고
④ 안전 교육의 필요성을 알리려고
⑤ 무단 횡단 처벌 규정을 공지하려고

고난도

16 대화를 듣고, 여자가 지불할 금액을 고르시오.

① $10   ② $13   ③ $15
④ $18   ⑤ $20

17 대화를 듣고, 여자의 마지막 말에 대한 남자의 응답으로 가장 적절한 것을 고르시오.

Man: _____

① The drama teacher is a great person.
② You shouldn't bring a bicycle to school.
③ Theater class will help you a lot in your career.
④ I'm thinking about changing my after-school class.
⑤ Yes. But don't forget to wear comfortable clothes.

[18-19] 대화를 듣고, 남자의 마지막 말에 대한 여자의 응답으로 가장 적절한 것을 고르시오.

18 Woman: _____

① Great. That will be $10.
② Okay, you need a new ID card now.
③ Can I see your driver's license, please?
④ It is unfair for students to get a discount.
⑤ Sorry, but children under the age of six can't go inside.

19 Woman: _____

① Great! I like horror movies best.
② I heard that movie is really good.
③ Okay, let's watch this movie again.
④ Sorry. I can't go to the movies tonight.
⑤ Okay, next time we'll see a different kind of movie.

20 다음 상황 설명을 듣고, Amanda가 신발 가게 점원에게 할 말로 가장 적절한 것을 고르시오.

Amanda: _____

① I would like to sign up for golf lessons.
② Can I get a refund, please?
③ Which golf shoes do you recommend?
④ Do you have these shoes in a larger size?
⑤ These shoes are damaged. Can I get a new pair?

DICTATION

01 ◀ 그림 묘사

대화를 듣고, 남자가 구입할 마카롱을 고르시오.

①   ②
③   ④
⑤

M Hello, I'm looking for some macarons for my daughter.

W Okay. We have several options. What about our animal-shaped macarons?

M Well, I don't like the chocolate bear macarons, but the _____ _____ _____.

W Oh, actually _____ _____ _____ _____ those to be picked up later.

M That's too bad. What about the macarons _____ _____ _____?

W Those are our most popular ones. It's $20 for a box of six.

M I'll take it!

고난도

02 ◀ 언급되지 않은 내용

대화를 듣고, Andy Lee에 관해 언급되지 <u>않은</u> 것을 고르시오.

① 저서 ② 성장 환경
③ 대학 전공 ④ 수상 경력
⑤ 취미

M Good morning, Megan. Did you have a good weekend?

W Hi, Tyler. I did! I went to my favorite writer's book signing.

M Really? Who did you go to see?

W I saw Andy Lee. He is a famous writer _____ _____ _____ HOPE.

M What do you like about him?

W He _____ _____ _____ _____ _____ _____, but he wasn't discouraged. He expresses his journey through life beautifully in his book.

M That's amazing. Did he major in literature in college?

W No, he _____ _____ _____. He said he has a hobby of reading books related to psychology.

M He sounds cool. I should try reading one of his books.

---

03 ◀ 전화 목적

대화를 듣고, 여자가 남자에게 전화한 목적으로 가장 적절한 것을 고르시오.

① 안부를 물으려고
② 약속 시각을 변경하려고
③ 영어 숙제를 물어보려고
④ 함께 영화를 보러 가려고
⑤ 빌린 휴대전화를 돌려주려고

[Cell phone rings.]

M Hello?

W Hi, Michael, this is Julie. Is everything all right? _____ _____ _____ you several times this morning.

M Sorry, I just _____ _____ _____ _____.

W Were you sleeping?

M No, I was watching a movie at the theater this morning.

W Oh, I see. I was just hoping you could tell me _____ _____ _____ _____ _____.

M You have to write a two-page essay on your favorite celebrity.

W Okay. Thanks, Michael.

04 ◀ 숫자 정보

대화를 듣고, 여자가 식당을 예약한 시각을 고르시오.

① 2:00 ② 3:00
③ 5:00 ④ 6:00
⑤ 7:00

[Telephone rings.]

M Hello, this is Tom's Kitchen. How may I help you?

W Hello. I'd like to _____ _____ _____. Is there a separate room for meetings?

M Yes, there is. How many people is the reservation for?

W Thirteen people. I'd like to make the reservation for October 15. _____ _____ _____ _____?

M Two, five, and seven are available.

W We're going to have dinner, so two o'clock is too early.

M Then would you like to make a reservation for _____ _____ _____?

W Yes. Please make the reservation for Anne Hoult.

05 ◀ 심정

대화를 듣고, 남자의 심정으로 가장 적절한 것을 고르시오.

① satisfied ② angry
③ thankful ④ relieved
⑤ embarrassed

[Cell phone rings.]

W Hello?

M Marie, I have some bad news. I _____ _____ _____.

W What? You usually get to the airport so early.

M I was three hours early. _____ _____ _____ _____, I looked around the duty free shops.

W So you didn't go to the gate on time?

M That's right. I was _____ _____ _____ _____ new bags and sunglasses.

W Didn't they call your name over the loudspeaker?

M I don't know. I was listening to music on my earphones.

06 ◀ 그림 상황에 적절한 대화

다음 그림의 상황에 가장 적절한 대화를 고르시오.

① ② ③ ④ ⑤

① **M** Excuse me! You _____ _____ _____.

   W Oh, thank you very much.

② **M** You're over your credit limit.

   W Oh, am I? I guess I'll _____ _____ _____.

③ **M** Do I have to _____ _____ _____ _____?

   W No, you don't have to.

④ **M** Are you hungry? Let's get dinner!

   W I'm starving. How about burgers?

⑤ **M** I don't have any money right now. Can you _____ _____ _____?

   W Sure, how much do you need?

대화를 듣고, 남자가 여자에게 부탁한
일로 가장 적절한 것을 고르시오.

① 음식점 위치 알려주기
② 음식 포장해오기
③ 대기 줄 서기
④ 음식점 예약하기
⑤ 역에 데려다주기

[Cell phone rings.]

W Hello?

M Hi, Laura. This is Adam. Where are you?

W I'm almost there. The next stop is Sinchon station. What about you?

M I'm actually _____ _____. Could you go to the restaurant and _____ _____ _____ _____?

W Okay. I heard that people have to wait in line for at least forty minutes on weekends.

M All right. Then I should be there by the time you _____ _____ _____.

다음을 듣고, Networking Event에
관해 언급되지 않은 것을 고르시오.

① 개최 날짜   ② 참가 대상
③ 행사 목적   ④ 참가 신청 방법
⑤ 복장

W Attention, everyone. Pinewood College is having a networking event next Saturday, October 4 from 12:00 to 6:00 p.m. The event is open to _____ _____ and recent graduates. The _____ _____ _____ _____ is to help current and former students build professional relationships with employers. We will start the afternoon _____ _____ _____ in the cafeteria. After that, you will have time to talk with various business professionals. Please _____ _____.

다음을 듣고, 어떤 직업에 관한 설명
인지 고르시오.

① 사서   ② 고고학자
③ 큐레이터   ④ 골동품 수집가
⑤ 공연 기획자

M People who have this job _____ _____ _____. They study ancient books or objects. They have usually graduated from a university with a history degree and have _____ _____ _____ _____ _____. They not only introduce artifacts to people, but also plan and _____ _____ in museums.

10 ◀ 어색한 대화

다음을 듣고, 두 사람의 대화가 어색한 것을 고르시오.
① ② ③ ④ ⑤

① **W** How did you like the musical?

M We went there _____ _____.

② **W** Please _____ _____. This is a school zone.

M Oh, is it? I didn't see the sign.

③ **W** _____ _____ _____ to chew gum during class.

M Okay. I'm sorry I broke the rules.

④ **W** This newspaper review says the movie is great.

M Let's go see it.

⑤ **W** When do I have to _____ _____ _____ _____ ?

M By this Friday.

11 ◀ 할 일

대화를 듣고, 여자가 대화 직후에 할 일로 가장 적절한 것을 고르시오.

① 스케이트화 구입하기
② 병원 진료받기
③ 스케이트화 대여하기
④ 여동생에게 전화하기
⑤ 스케이트 강습 등록하기

M Molly, is there something wrong with your foot?

W Yes, it really hurts. I think _____ _____.

M Can you take off your skates? *[pause]* Wow, they're _____ _____ _____.

W I know. They're my sister's. She let me borrow them because I lost mine.

M You shouldn't wear these. Please go to the rental shop and _____ _____ _____ _____.

W Okay. Where is the shop?

M Over there!

고난도
12 ◀ 도표

다음 표를 보면서 대화를 듣고, 남자가 구입할 휴대전화를 고르시오.

	Phone	Weight	Color	Storage Space
①	A	150 g	White	128 GB
②	B	170 g	Black	128 GB
③	C	190 g	White	256 GB
④	D	210 g	White	256 GB
⑤	E	220 g	Black	512 GB

M Hey, Julie. I'm looking for a new phone, but it's hard to choose one.

W Let me help you. Is there anything inconvenient about your current phone?

M Yes. My phone is _____ _____ _____ _____.

W I see. Then you _____ _____ _____ _____.

M Right. I want my new cell phone to be under 200 g.

W Good thinking. Weight is an important factor in choosing a cell phone.

M Also, my phone color is too dark right now. I want to _____ _____ _____ _____ this time.

W Sounds good. Now what about the phone's storage space?

M I like taking pictures, so I hope it _____ _____ _____ _____ _____.

W Then I think this cell phone would be best for you.

M It looks great! I'll take it.

대화를 듣고, 두 사람이 만나기로 한 시각을 고르시오.

① 4:00 p.m.　② 4:30 p.m.
③ 5:00 p.m.　④ 5:30 p.m.
⑤ 6:00 p.m.

W The musical starts at 6:00 p.m., doesn't it?

M Yes. Do you want to meet at the concert hall?

W How about _____ _____ _____ _____ _____?

M That's a good idea. What do you want to eat?

W I want to eat Mexican food.

M Sounds great. Then shall we meet at 5:00 p.m.?

W Isn't that too late? _____ _____ _____ _____ instead?

M That would be _____ _____. Let's meet at 4:30 p.m.

W Okay. See you then!

W Michael, you look sad. What's the matter?

M Hi, Emily. My mom is sick.

W I'm so sorry. Do you know what's wrong?

M She _____ _____ _____. I should do something for her.

W Why don't you _____ _____ _____ _____?

M She got medicine from the hospital yesterday.

W Then why don't you _____ _____ _____ _____?

M Great idea! I think she'd really appreciate that.

다음을 듣고, 방송의 목적으로 가장 적절한 것을 고르시오.

① 교통사고의 원인 규명을 촉구하려고
② 횡단보도 안전 수칙을 설명하려고
③ 학교 앞 신호등 추가 설치를 요청하려고
④ 안전 교육의 필요성을 알리려고
⑤ 무단 횡단 처벌 규정을 공지하려고

M May I have your attention, please? This is your principal, Mr. James. Unfortunately, last week, a student was injured while crossing a crosswalk. Running across the street _____ _____ _____ _____ _____ was the cause of the accident. I strongly recommend that you check the light _____ _____ _____ _____. Also, wait for at least three seconds once the signal changes. This simple act will _____ _____ _____ _____. Our teachers will also do their best to keep you safe. Thank you.

16 ◀ 숫자 정보

대화를 듣고, 여자가 지불할 금액을 고르시오.

① $10 ② $13
③ $15 ④ $18
⑤ $20

W I'd like to _____ _____ _____ _____.
M Okay. What do you have?
W I have two dresses and _____ _____ _____ _____. How much will that be?
M It's $5 for each dress and $3 for the pants.
W Okay. But can you shorten these pants by 2 cm?
M I can do that. It'll _____ _____ _____.
W Oh, really? That's expensive.
M The pants are made of an unusual fabric. That will _____ _____ _____ _____.
W All right. I'll come back next weekend to pick them up.

17 ◀ 마지막 말에 대한 응답

대화를 듣고, 여자의 마지막 말에 대한 남자의 응답으로 가장 적절한 것을 고르시오.

Man: _____

① The drama teacher is a great person.
② You shouldn't bring a bicycle to school.
③ Theater class will help you a lot in your career.
④ I'm thinking about changing my after-school class.
⑤ Yes. But don't forget to wear comfortable clothes.

M Hannah, which after-school class did you sign up for?
W I _____ _____ _____ _____ _____. How about you?
M I did too! I thought I would be alone in the theater class, so I'm glad you'll be there.
W I'm glad too. So, what do we have to bring on the first day of class?
M We need to bring our notebooks and _____ _____ _____ _____.
W Is that all we _____ _____ _____?
M _____

18 ◀ 마지막 말에 대한 응답

대화를 듣고, 남자의 마지막 말에 대한 여자의 응답으로 가장 적절한 것을 고르시오.

Woman: _____

① Great. That will be $10.
② Okay, you need a new ID card now.
③ Can I see your driver's license, please?
④ It is unfair for students to get a discount.
⑤ Sorry, but children under the age of six can't go inside.

M Hello, _____ _____ _____ _____ for the gallery's new exhibition?
W Yes. How many tickets would you like?
M Just one, please. How much are the tickets?
W The weekend price is $15 for adults.
M Is there a _____?
W Yes, the ticket price for students is $10. But you need to show a current student ID to _____ _____ _____.
M I have my student ID card right here.
W _____

19 ◀ 마지막 말에 대한 응답

대화를 듣고, 남자의 마지막 말에 대한 여자의 응답으로 가장 적절한 것을 고르시오.

Woman: _____

① Great! I like horror movies best.
② I heard that movie is really good.
③ Okay, let's watch this movie again.
④ Sorry. I can't go to the movies tonight.
⑤ Okay, next time we'll see a different kind of movie.

M Thanks for _____ _____ _____ _____ _____.

W It's my pleasure. The movie was exciting, wasn't it?

M I guess so...

W What's wrong? Didn't you like it?

M It was _____ _____ _____ _____ for me.

W I see. You must not like horror movies very much.

M No, I don't. I prefer _____ _____ _____ _____ such as romantic comedies and animated movies.

W _____

20 ◀ 상황에 적절한 말

다음 상황 설명을 듣고, Amanda가 신발 가게 점원에게 할 말로 가장 적절한 것을 고르시오.

Amanda: _____

① I would like to sign up for golf lessons.
② Can I get a refund, please?
③ Which golf shoes do you recommend?
④ Do you have these shoes in a larger size?
⑤ These shoes are damaged. Can I get a new pair?

M Amanda bought a pair of hiking shoes as a present for her brother, but he is _____ _____ _____ _____ anymore. He recently _____ _____ _____, so he asked Amanda to return the shoes and _____ _____ _____ _____ _____ instead. In this situation, what would Amanda most likely say to the clerk at the shoe store?

Amanda _____

148

A

다음 영어 어휘나 표현의 뜻을 우리말로 쓰세요.

01 on time

02 late fee

03 unfair

04 journey

05 unusual

06 miss

07 decorate

08 swollen

09 literature

10 satisfied

11 celebrity

12 chew

13 discourage

14 clerk

15 separate

16 shorten

B

우리말에 맞는 영어 어휘나 표현을 [보기]에서 찾아 쓰세요.

| 보기 | lend | sign | break a rule | career | be busy v-ing |
| | weight | hand in | related to | relieved | look around |

01 빌려주다

02 둘러보다

03 ~하느라 바쁘다

04 규칙을 어기다

05 안도하는

06 무게

07 표지판

08 ~을 제출하다

09 진로

10 ~와 관련된

일반 속도

빠른 속도

01 대화를 듣고, 여자가 구입할 스마트폰 케이스를 고르시오.

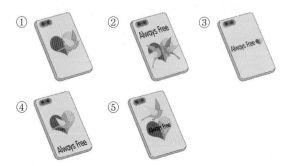

① ② ③ ④ ⑤

🇬🇧
02 대화를 듣고, 바자회에 관해 언급되지 <u>않은</u> 것을 고르시오.

① 개최 목적   ② 시작 시간
③ 개최 장소   ④ 참여 가능 부스 개수
⑤ 판매품 종류

03 대화를 듣고, 남자가 여자에게 전화한 목적으로 가장 적절한 것을 고르시오.

① 여행 경비를 문의하려고
② 예약을 확인하려고
③ 특별 기내식을 주문하려고
④ 여행 상품을 예약하려고
⑤ 비행기 좌석을 변경하려고

고난도
04 대화를 듣고, 두 사람이 출발할 시각을 고르시오.

① 5:00 p.m.   ② 6:00 p.m.   ③ 6:15 p.m.
④ 6:30 p.m.   ⑤ 7:00 p.m.

05 대화를 듣고, 두 사람이 대화하는 장소로 가장 적절한 곳을 고르시오.

① 문구점   ② 백화점   ③ 도서관
④ 버스 정류장   ⑤ 분실물 보관소

06 다음 그림의 상황에 가장 적절한 대화를 고르시오.

① ② ③ ④ ⑤

🇬🇧
07 대화를 듣고, 남자가 여자에게 부탁한 일로 가장 적절한 것을 고르시오.

① 화이트보드 지우기   ② 창문 청소하기
③ 쓰레기통 비우기   ④ 책상 줄 맞추기
⑤ 바닥 쓸기

08 다음을 듣고, 체육대회에 관해 언급되지 <u>않은</u> 것을 고르시오.

① 개최 장소   ② 행사 시간   ③ 종목
④ 복장   ⑤ 예상 날씨

09 다음을 듣고, 무엇에 관한 설명인지 고르시오.

① 벽난로   ② 스탠드   ③ 향수
④ 양초   ⑤ 손전등

10 다음을 듣고, 두 사람의 대화가 <u>어색한</u> 것을 고르시오.

① ② ③ ④ ⑤

🇬🇧
11 대화를 듣고, 남자가 대화 직후에 할 일로 가장 적절한 것을 고르시오.

① 동물원 방문하기   ② 프로젝트 발표하기
③ 도서관 가기   ④ 동물 사진 찾기
⑤ 사진 부가설명 작성하기

고난도

12 다음 표를 보면서 대화를 듣고, 남자가 구입할 밥솥을 고르시오.

	Model	Color	Size	Price
①	Rice King	White	Medium	$70
②	E-670	Black	Large	$150
③	Fast Cooker	Red	Small	$80
④	Kitchen Pal	Black	Small	$95
⑤	Perfect Rice	White	Medium	$100

13 대화를 듣고, 두 사람이 만나기로 한 요일을 고르시오.

① 화요일   ② 수요일   ③ 목요일
④ 금요일   ⑤ 토요일

14 대화를 듣고, 남자가 오전에 한 일로 가장 적절한 것을 고르시오.

① 회의하기   ② 다른 회사 방문하기
③ 안전 교육 듣기   ④ 건설 현장 방문하기
⑤ 건축 자재 확인하기

15 다음을 듣고, 방송의 목적으로 가장 적절한 것을 고르시오.

① 지역 사회 대회 장소를 변경하려고
② 새 지역 센터 개관을 알리려고
③ 지역 사회 문제점을 비판하려고
④ 지역 사회 대회에 참여를 독려하려고
⑤ 반려동물 복지 개선을 요청하려고

16 대화를 듣고, 여자가 지불할 금액을 고르시오.

① $30   ② $40   ③ $60
④ $70   ⑤ $100

고난도

17 대화를 듣고, 여자의 마지막 말에 대한 남자의 응답으로 가장 적절한 것을 고르시오.

Man: _____

① You're lucky to have relatives who live there!
② You should have reserved a hotel room earlier.
③ I think you'd like Hawaii if you ever went there.
④ That's too bad, but you can visit your sister next time.
⑤ You should tell them that you want some time alone.

[18-19] 대화를 듣고, 남자의 마지막 말에 대한 여자의 응답으로 가장 적절한 것을 고르시오.

18 Woman: _____

① I'll adopt one next month.
② I got my dog from my cousin.
③ My parents won't let me.
④ I really enjoy taking care of my dog.
⑤ Ralph needs to find a good home.

19 Woman: _____

① It's a small world, isn't it?
② I was really happy to see her.
③ Congratulations! You did a good job.
④ There were about 150 people at the wedding.
⑤ They were the most beautiful couple.

20 다음 상황 설명을 듣고, Tony가 Olivia에게 할 말로 가장 적절한 것을 고르시오.

Tony: Olivia, _____

① can you give me a ride to my office?
② would you bring my spare car key to me?
③ don't worry. I'll bring your key to you soon.
④ I'll pick you up at your office.
⑤ you need to be careful when you drive.

DICTATION

정답 단서 오답 함정

일반 속도

빠른 속도

01 ◀ 그림 묘사

대화를 듣고, 여자가 구입할 스마트폰 케이스를 고르시오.

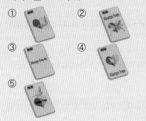

① ② ③ ④ ⑤

M What are you doing?
W _____ _____ _____ a new smartphone case online. What do you think of this one?
M It's okay. I like the big heart _____ _____ _____.
W Yes. And there's a bird flying in front of the heart.
M What does it say _____ _____ _____?
W It says "Always Free." So, do you like it?
M Yes. I think it's cute.
W Okay. I'll buy this one!

02 ◀ 언급되지 않은 내용

대화를 듣고, 바자회에 관해 언급되지 않은 것을 고르시오.
① 개최 목적
② 시작 시간
③ 개최 장소
④ 참여 가능 부스 개수
⑤ 판매품 종류

W John, what are you doing this Saturday?
M Nothing special. Why?
W My school club is holding a bazaar to _____ _____ _____ _____. Why don't you come?
M I should. What time does it start?
W It starts at 9:00 a.m. and closes at 5:00 p.m.
M Sounds good. Where will it be held?
W We decided to do it _____ _____ _____ _____.
M How many booths will there be?
W We have enough room for _____ _____ _____ in the gym. There will be a lot of stuff to look at!
M Great! I'll see you on Saturday.

03 ◀ 전화 목적

대화를 듣고, 남자가 여자에게 전화한 목적으로 가장 적절한 것을 고르시오.
① 여행 경비를 문의하려고
② 예약을 확인하려고
③ 특별 기내식을 주문하려고
④ 여행 상품을 예약하려고
⑤ 비행기 좌석을 변경하려고

[Telephone rings.]
W Go Travel. Can I help you?
M Yes, I'd like to _____ _____ _____. My name is Eric Roberts.
W Let's see... You have a reservation for the 8:00 p.m. flight to Tokyo on Friday.
M That's right. Will a meal be served on that flight?
W Yes, a _____ _____ _____ _____ _____. And you're checking just one bag?
M Yes. Do I have a window seat?
W Yes. And _____ _____ _____, so your reservation is all set.

152

고난도

04 ◀ 숫자 정보

대화를 듣고, 두 사람이 출발할 시각을 고르시오.

① 5:00 p.m. ② 6:00 p.m.
③ 6:15 p.m. ④ 6:30 p.m.
⑤ 7:00 p.m.

W Let's go see the fireworks show at Central Park tonight!

M Sure! What time does it start?

W It _____ _____ _____ p.m.

M Okay. It will take about forty-five minutes to drive there. So let's _____ _____ _____ _____ the show starts.

W Well, there will be lots of traffic today because of the show. Two hours would be better.

M All right. Or we could take the subway. It _____ _____ _____ _____.

W The subway will be too crowded. Let's drive there.

05 ◀ 장소

대화를 듣고, 두 사람이 대화하는 장소로 가장 적절한 곳을 고르시오.

① 문구점   ② 백화점
③ 도서관   ④ 버스 정류장
⑤ 분실물 보관소

W Hello. Can I help you with something?

M Yes. I'm looking for a briefcase. I think I _____ _____ _____ _____ _____ this morning.

W I see. Well, we have several briefcases. Is this one yours?

M No, mine is brown _____ _____ _____ _____ down the center.

W Hmm, let's see... I think this might be it.

M Yes, that's it!

W Great. Here you go. Please _____ _____ _____ _____ to see if everything is there.

M Oh, everything is here! This is very important to me. Thank you.

06 ◀ 그림 상황에 적절한 대화

다음 그림의 상황에 가장 적절한 대화를 고르시오.

① ② ③ ④ ⑤

① W Excuse me, sir. Where can I find tomato sauce?

   M Our tomato sauce is in aisle three.

② W Which of these _____ _____ _____?

   M Let's get the one on the right. It's cheaper.

③ W We need to _____ _____ _____ _____ _____.

   M Why don't we go to the supermarket?

④ W Look what I bought at the store this morning!

   M Oh, great! That's my favorite snack.

⑤ W Can you _____ _____ _____ _____ for me?

   M Sure. I'd be happy to help you.

07 ◀ 부탁한 일

대화를 듣고, 남자가 여자에게 부탁한 일로 가장 적절한 것을 고르시오.

① 화이트보드 지우기
② 창문 청소하기
③ 쓰레기통 비우기
④ 책상 줄 맞추기
⑤ 바닥 쓸기

W What are you doing, Ronald?
M It's my turn to _____ _____ this week.
W Would you like some help?
M Well, I've _____ _____ _____. Could you empty the trash can?
W Sure! No problem.
M Thanks a lot. I just need to _____ _____, and then I'll be finished!
W Great. Then we can walk home together.

08 ◀ 언급되지 않은 내용

다음을 듣고, 체육대회에 관해 언급되지 않은 것을 고르시오.

① 개최 장소   ② 행사 시간
③ 종목   ④ 복장
⑤ 예상 날씨

M Roosevelt Middle School will hold its annual Sports Day on Friday, May 3. It will take place _____ _____ _____ _____ _____.
Games will include soccer, badminton, baseball, and more. First-year and second-year _____ _____ _____ red T-shirts, while third-year students should wear blue T-shirts. It's supposed to be _____ _____ _____ on Friday, so be sure to bring plenty of water.

09 ◀ 주제/화제

다음을 듣고, 무엇에 관한 설명인지 고르시오.

① 벽난로   ② 스탠드
③ 향수   ④ 양초
⑤ 손전등

W You can find these in romantic restaurants. People light them. They _____ _____ _____ _____ that makes the dinner feel special. They are found in many shapes, sizes, and colors. Some even _____. Traditionally, they were used to light rooms. These days, they are usually found on birthday cakes. The number of these on a birthday cake often shows the _____ _____ _____ _____ _____.

10 ◀ 어색한 대화

다음을 듣고, 두 사람의 대화가 <u>어색</u><u>한</u> 것을 고르시오.

①   ②   ③   ④   ⑤

① **M**   I'm not feeling well.

    W   Is there anything I can do to help?

② **M**   I can't believe that you broke my Bluetooth speakers!

    W   I _____ _____ _____ _____.

③ **M**   It was the best game I've ever seen!

    W   I _____ _____ _____.

④ **M**   Wow! Look at all those clouds. I think _____ _____ _____ _____.

    W   Yes, it looks like it will.

⑤ **M**   Can you guess how old I am?

    W   I _____ _____ _____ _____ _____.

11 ◀ 할 일

대화를 듣고, 남자가 대화 직후에 할 일로 가장 적절한 것을 고르시오.

① 동물원 방문하기
② 프로젝트 발표하기
③ 도서관 가기
④ 동물 사진 찾기
⑤ 사진 부가설명 작성하기

M   This research project is very difficult.

W   It's about endangered animals, isn't it?

M   Yes. I _____ _____ _____ in the library and went to a few zoos.

W   Why did you go to the zoos?

M   I _____ _____ _____ for the presentation. Now I _____ _____ _____ _____ of them.

W   What will you do after that?

M   Nothing. After that, I'll be finished. I'm going to start now.

W   Good luck!

고난도

12 ◀ 도표

다음 표를 보면서 대화를 듣고, 남자가 구입할 밥솥을 고르시오.

	Model	Color	Size	Price
①	Rice King	White	Medium	$70
②	E-670	Black	Large	$150
③	Fast Cooker	Red	Small	$80
④	Kitchen Pal	Black	Small	$95
⑤	Perfect Rice	White	Medium	$100

M   I need to buy a rice cooker. Can you help me choose one?

W   Sure! I'd be happy to help.

M   Here's a list of rice cookers.

W   Okay. How much money can you spend?

M   I can only _____ _____ _____ _____.

W   That's enough. Do you need a medium or large rice cooker?

M   Actually, I _____ _____ _____ _____. I don't have much space in my kitchen.

W   All right. And does _____ _____ _____?

M   Any color is fine, except red.

W   In that case, you should buy this one!

대화를 듣고, 두 사람이 만나기로 한 요일을 고르시오.

① 화요일　　② 수요일
③ 목요일　　④ 금요일
⑤ 토요일

M Hi, Chloe. Are we still going to meet on Wednesday night?

W Oh, I _____ _____ _____ _____! I have a soccer game that night.

M That's okay. How about meeting on Tuesday instead?

W _____ _____ _____ on Tuesdays and Thursdays.

M And I have to work on Friday night. How about Saturday then?

W _____ _____ _____ _____. I'll see you then!

14 ◀ 한 일

대화를 듣고, 남자가 오전에 한 일로 가장 적절한 것을 고르시오.

① 회의하기
② 다른 회사 방문하기
③ 안전 교육 듣기
④ 건설 현장 방문하기
⑤ 건축 자재 확인하기

W Hello, Mr. Park. My name is Amy, and I _____ _____ _____ _____ this construction project.

M Nice to meet you, Amy.

W Did you _____ this morning?

M No. I went to check out the building supplies this morning.

W I see. Then do you have any time in the afternoon?

M I have a meeting in the afternoon, but I _____ _____ _____ to another day. Let's visit the construction site.

W All right. Meet me here at one o'clock.

15 ◀ 방송 목적

다음을 듣고, 방송의 목적으로 가장 적절한 것을 고르시오.

① 지역 사회 대회 장소를 변경하려고
② 새 지역 센터 개관을 알리려고
③ 지역 사회 문제점을 비판하려고
④ 지역 사회 대회에 참여를 독려하려고
⑤ 반려동물 복지 개선을 요청하려고

M Good afternoon, listeners. This is James, the manager of our community center. I'd like to tell you about _____ _____ _____ _____, Pawsitively Fantastic Pets. This is a big contest that anyone can participate in. It will _____ _____ _____ _____ and the prize is $100. The person who _____ _____ _____ _____ with their pet will win the prize. If you are interested in this contest, please visit our website.

16 ◀ 숫자 정보

대화를 듣고, 여자가 지불할 금액을 고르시오.

① $30   ② $40
③ $60   ④ $70
⑤ $100

W Hello. I'd like to buy a purse.

M Okay. Do you prefer _____ _____ _____ _____ _____?

W I'm looking for a large one.

M How about this one? It's $100.

W That's too expensive. Can I get a discount?

M No. I'm sorry. It's a new item, so I can't _____ _____ _____ _____.

W That's too bad.

M This one is on sale. It's also $100, but it's 30% off. If you buy it today, I'll _____ _____ _____ _____ _____.

W I can get 40% off? I'll take it.

17 ◀ 마지막 말에 대한 응답

대화를 듣고, 여자의 마지막 말에 대한 남자의 응답으로 가장 적절한 것을 고르시오.

Man: _____

① You're lucky to have relatives who live there!
② You should have reserved a hotel room earlier.
③ I think you'd like Hawaii if you ever went there.
④ That's too bad, but you can visit your sister next time.
⑤ You should tell them that you want some time alone.

W I _____ _____ _____ _____ on Monday. I'm going to Hawaii for a week.

M You've been there before, haven't you? Why do you like it so much?

W Because I really like beaches and warm weather.

M That's a good reason. But there are _____ _____ _____ with beautiful beaches.

W Yes, but my sister's family lives in Hawaii. So I don't have to _____ _____ _____ _____ when I go there.

M _____

18 ◀ 마지막 말에 대한 응답

대화를 듣고, 남자의 마지막 말에 대한 여자의 응답으로 가장 적절한 것을 고르시오.

Woman: _____

① I'll adopt one next month.
② I got my dog from my cousin.
③ My parents won't let me.
④ I really enjoy taking care of my dog.
⑤ Ralph needs to find a good home.

M This is my new dog, Ralph. He's a three-month-old poodle.

W Oh! He's so cute! Where did you get him?

M He didn't have a home, so _____ _____ _____.

W That's great. I want to get a dog too.

M Then _____ _____ _____ _____ _____? There are many dogs that need homes.

W I'd love to, but _____ _____ _____ _____.

M What is it?

W _____

19 ◀ 마지막 말에 대한 응답

대화를 듣고, 남자의 마지막 말에 대한 여자의 응답으로 가장 적절한 것을 고르시오.

Woman: _____

① It's a small world, isn't it?
② I was really happy to see her.
③ Congratulations! You did a good job.
④ There were about 150 people at the wedding.
⑤ They were the most beautiful couple.

W Hi, Peter. What did you do yesterday?

M My classmates and I _____ _____ _____ _____ _____. I saw Eunjae there.

W Really? What was she doing there? She doesn't go to your school, does she?

M No, she doesn't. Actually, I _____ _____ _____ for a long time.

W So why was she there?

M The man _____ _____ _____ _____ is her cousin!

W _____

20 ◀ 상황에 적절한 말

다음 상황 설명을 듣고, Tony가 Olivia에게 할 말로 가장 적절한 것을 고르시오.

Tony: Olivia, _____

① can you give me a ride to my office?
② would you bring my spare car key to me?
③ don't worry. I'll bring your key to you soon.
④ I'll pick you up at your office.
⑤ you need to be careful when you drive.

W Tony _____ _____ _____ every day. One day, he accidentally _____ _____ _____ in his car. He has an extra key, but it's on his desk at home. He knows his sister Olivia is home. He really wants her to _____ _____ _____ _____ to his office so he can drive home. He picks up his phone and calls her. In this situation, what would Tony most likely say to Olivia?

Tony Olivia, _____

158

A

다음 영어 어휘나 표현의 뜻을 우리말로 쓰세요.

01 construction

02 crowded

03 bazaar

04 trash can

05 neighbor

06 additional

07 underneath

08 carry

09 sweep

10 relative

11 in charge of

12 give a discount

13 except

14 description

15 adopt

16 annual

B

우리말에 맞는 영어 어휘나 표현을 [보기]에서 찾아 쓰세요.

	보기				
	accidentally	be all set	in need	be about to-v	in ages
	pick out	endangered	briefcase	be sure to-v	matter

01 어려움에 처한

02 우연히, 뜻하지 않게

03 오랫동안

04 (여러 개 중에서 신중히) 고르다

05 서류 가방

06 막 ~하려고 하다

07 준비가 되어 있다

08 반드시 ~하다

09 중요하다, 문제 되다

10 (동식물이) 멸종 위기에 처한

점수   / 20문항

일반 속도

빠른 속도

01 대화를 듣고, 여자가 만든 연극 포스터를 고르시오.

02 대화를 듣고, 호텔 이용에 관해 언급되지 **않은** 것을 고르시오.

① 귀중품 보관 서비스   ② 운동 시설 위치
③ 수영장 위치   ④ 식당 위치
⑤ 체크아웃 시간

03 대화를 듣고, 남자가 여자에게 전화한 목적으로 가장 적절한 것을 고르시오.

① 아기를 더 오래 돌봐달라고 부탁하려고
② 아기 식사 준비를 요청하려고
③ 저녁 약속을 취소하려고
④ 베이비시터를 고용하려고
⑤ 아기를 집에 데려올 것을 부탁하려고

04 대화를 듣고, 두 사람이 만나기로 한 시각을 고르시오.

① 5:00 a.m.   ② 6:00 a.m.   ③ 7:00 a.m.
④ 8:00 a.m.   ⑤ 9:30 a.m.

05 대화를 듣고, 두 사람이 대화하는 장소로 가장 적절한 곳을 고르시오.

① 꽃집   ② 백화점   ③ 예식장
④ 미용실   ⑤ 문구점

06 다음 그림의 상황에 가장 적절한 대화를 고르시오.

①   ②   ③   ④   ⑤

07 대화를 듣고, 남자가 여자에게 부탁한 일로 가장 적절한 것을 고르시오.

① 집들이 준비 돕기   ② 이사할 집 알아보기
③ 이사업체 알아보기   ④ 이삿짐 싸는 것 돕기
⑤ 송별회 계획하기

08 다음을 듣고, 학급 견학에 관해 언급되지 **않은** 것을 고르시오.

① 견학 날짜   ② 견학 장소
③ 참가 비용   ④ 준비물
⑤ 견학 허가서 제출 기한

09 다음을 듣고, 무엇에 관한 설명인지 고르시오.

① 빗자루   ② 휴지통
③ 진공청소기   ④ 헤어드라이어
⑤ 먼지떨이

10 다음을 듣고, 두 사람의 대화가 <u>어색한</u> 것을 고르시오.

①   ②   ③   ④   ⑤

11 대화를 듣고, 여자가 대화 직후에 할 일로 가장 적절한 것을 고르시오.

① 차고 청소하기   ② 잔디 심기
③ 삽 가져다주기   ④ 모자 찾기
⑤ 잡초 뽑기

고난도

12 다음 비행기 좌석 배치도를 보면서 대화를 듣고, 남자가 앉을 좌석을 고르시오.

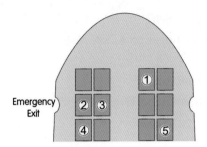

Emergency Exit

고난도

13 대화를 듣고, 여자가 병원에 방문할 날짜를 고르시오.

① 13일   ② 15일   ③ 17일
④ 20일   ⑤ 24일

14 대화를 듣고, 남자가 대화 직후에 할 일로 가장 적절한 것을 고르시오.

① 호텔에 전화하기   ② 휴대전화 충전하기
③ 길 물어보기   ④ 손님 마중 나가기
⑤ 택시 타기

15 다음을 듣고, 방송의 목적으로 가장 적절한 것을 고르시오.

① 아파트 출입 제한 시간을 공지하려고
② 아파트 출입 차단기 설치를 위해 동의를 얻으려고
③ 아파트 출입을 위한 앱 이용을 안내하려고
④ 아파트의 주차 문제 해결을 촉구하려고
⑤ 아파트 앱 이름을 공모하려고

고난도

16 대화를 듣고, 여자가 지불할 금액을 고르시오.

① $17   ② $21   ③ $26
④ $31   ⑤ $33

17 대화를 듣고, 남자의 마지막 말에 대한 여자의 응답으로 가장 적절한 것을 고르시오.

Woman: _____

① All right. I'll call a taxi for you. It can seat four people.
② No, this ticket is not available. Can you pick another one?
③ Yes. Please wait here for a moment while I go check.
④ Yes, the performance will start in a minute. You can enter now.
⑤ No. Cancellation on the day of the performance is not possible.

[18-19] 대화를 듣고, 여자의 마지막 말에 대한 남자의 응답으로 가장 적절한 것을 고르시오.

18 Man: _____

① I donated it to the library.
② Okay. I'll ask him and let you know.
③ Okay, don't forget to return the book.
④ Ethan doesn't have a library card.
⑤ I don't know much about fairytales.

19 Man: _____

① You don't feel like talking, right?
② How did you do on your test?
③ I hope you learned your lesson.
④ What should I do to speak Spanish well?
⑤ I'd rather not swim today.

20 다음 상황 설명을 듣고, Samantha가 집 주인에게 할 말로 가장 적절한 것을 고르시오.

Samantha: _____

① It rains too much here.
② I think one of the pipes is leaking.
③ I don't like the color of the wallpaper.
④ The apartment is flooded.
⑤ There is a stain on the door.

DICTATION

일반 속도   빠른 속도

01 ◀ 그림 묘사

대화를 듣고, 여자가 만든 연극 포스터를 고르시오.

①   ②
③   ④
⑤

M Hey, Bonnie. Did you make this poster yourself?

W Yes, I designed this for the school play. Its title is *Long Time No See*.

M I like that you put the title _____ _____ _____.

W Me too. I also put a clock in the bottom left corner.

M That's great. Why didn't you add "Goodland High School" _____ _____?

W I didn't think it was necessary. Instead, I _____ _____ _____ under the title.

M I see. The tickets are five dollars?

W Yes, they are. You should come!

02 ◀ 언급되지 않은 내용

대화를 듣고, 호텔 이용에 관해 언급되지 않은 것을 고르시오.

① 귀중품 보관 서비스
② 운동 시설 위치
③ 수영장 위치
④ 식당 위치
⑤ 체크아웃 시간

W Good morning. This is the Fantastic Hotel.

M Hello. My name is Lucas Barton, and I'd like to check in.

W All right. This is the room key. Also, our hotel offers a _____ _____ _____ _____, so please let us know if you need to use it.

M Thank you. _____ _____ _____ _____ _____ in the hotel?

W It's on the 2nd floor. If you want to use the swimming pool, it is _____ _____ _____ _____ _____.

M Thank you. Is my checkout time eleven o'clock?

W Yes, that's right. Enjoy your stay!

03 ◀ 전화 목적

대화를 듣고, 남자가 여자에게 전화한 목적으로 가장 적절한 것을 고르시오.

① 아기를 더 오래 돌봐달라고 부탁하려고
② 아기 식사 준비를 요청하려고
③ 저녁 약속을 취소하려고
④ 베이비시터를 고용하려고
⑤ 아기를 집에 데려올 것을 부탁하려고

[Cell phone rings.]

W Hello?

M Hi, Cindy.

W Hi, Mr. Johnson. I'm just feeding Jason now.

M Good. I have to _____ _____ _____ _____ today. I still have a lot of work to do.

W Oh, I'm sorry to hear that.

M If you're free this evening, _____ _____ Jason a little longer? My wife also has to work late.

W Sure, no problem. How long do you _____ _____ _____?

M For two or three more hours. Is that okay?

W That's fine.

04 ◀ 숫자 정보

대화를 듣고, 두 사람이 만나기로 한
시각을 고르시오.

① 5:00 a.m.   ② 6:00 a.m.
③ 7:00 a.m.   ④ 8:00 a.m.
⑤ 9:30 a.m.

W Oliver, I'm really _____ _____ _____ _____ _____.

M Me too. It's been a long time since we traveled abroad. What time is our flight?

W It's at nine thirty in the morning.

M Then shall we meet at the bus stop at seven o'clock?

W I think _____ _____ _____. We have to arrive at the airport at least _____ _____ _____ _____.

M Then should we meet at the bus stop at six o'clock?

W Okay. Are you going to _____ _____ _____ _____?

M No. I don't have anything to buy.

W Then I'll see you in front of the bus stop.

05 ◀ 장소

대화를 듣고, 두 사람이 대화하는 장소
로 가장 적절한 곳을 고르시오.

① 꽃집   ② 백화점
③ 예식장   ④ 미용실
⑤ 문구점

W How may I help you?

M I would like to _____ _____ _____ for my wife for our 10th wedding anniversary.

W Okay. Which ones would you like?

M Do you have any pink roses? My wife _____ _____ _____ of them at our wedding. Pink is her favorite.

W I'm afraid not. We only have red ones now.

M Hmm… Then _____ _____ _____ _____ in pink paper?

W No problem! We have many different kinds of pink paper.

06 ◀ 그림 상황에 적절한 대화

다음 그림의 상황에 가장 적절한 대화
를 고르시오.

①   ②   ③   ④   ⑤

① **M** _____ _____, Sally?

　 W I have a sore throat and a fever.

② **M** Can you tell me _____ _____ _____ _____ the post office?

　 W It's five minutes from here. I'll _____ _____ _____ _____.

③ **M** What a big box!

　 W We need two more boxes to pack all those clothes.

④ **M** Do you need help carrying that? It looks heavy.

　 W Thank you! That would be great.

⑤ **M** _____ _____ _____ would you like?

　 W The largest one, please.

대화를 듣고, 남자가 여자에게 부탁한
일로 가장 적절한 것을 고르시오.

① 집들이 준비 돕기
② 이사할 집 알아보기
③ 이사업체 알아보기
④ 이삿짐 싸는 것 돕기
⑤ 송별회 계획하기

W Hi, Frank! I heard that _____ _____ _____ _____.

M I am! The apartment I found is much closer to my office.

W That's great! Are you going to have a housewarming party?

M I'm not sure. I'm just _____ _____ _____ right now.

W Oh, I see. Do you have a lot to do?

M Yes. If you're not busy this weekend, _____ _____ _____ _____ _____?

W Sure!

다음을 듣고, 학급 견학에 관해 언급
되지 않은 것을 고르시오.

① 견학 날짜   ② 견학 장소
③ 참가 비용   ④ 준비물
⑤ 견학 허가서 제출 기한

M Good morning, students. Don't forget that our class field trip is on Friday, March 4. We will visit a jellybean factory. The CEO of the company will _____ _____ _____ _____, and she will also teach us how to make jellybeans. The _____ _____ _____ _____ is $50. Please ask your parents to _____ _____ _____. I would like it back by this Wednesday.

다음을 듣고, 무엇에 관한 설명인지
고르시오.

① 빗자루   ② 휴지통
③ 진공청소기   ④ 헤어드라이어
⑤ 먼지떨이

W You can find this in your house. _____ _____ _____ and is pushed across the floor. It _____ _____ _____ _____ of food and dirt, so it helps _____ _____ _____ _____. It can be used on almost any kind of surface, from hardwood to carpet. It can even clean hard-to-reach areas like corners!

10 ◀ 어색한 대화

다음을 듣고, 두 사람의 대화가 <u>어색</u>한 것을 고르시오.

① ② ③ ④ ⑤

① M What do you want to be when you grow up?

W _____ _____ _____ _____, so I want to be an astronaut.

② M When did you get up this morning?

W I will get up _____ _____ _____ 7:00 a.m.

③ M Are you afraid of spiders?

W I was afraid of them when I was younger, but not anymore.

④ M I love your new dress!

W _____ _____ _____ _____!

⑤ M What's the matter?

W I lost my favorite cap on the subway this morning.

11 ◀ 할 일

대화를 듣고, 여자가 대화 직후에 할 일로 가장 적절한 것을 고르시오.

① 차고 청소하기
② 잔디 심기
③ 삽 가져다주기
④ 모자 찾기
⑤ 잡초 뽑기

M What is Mr. Grey doing? Why is he _____ _____ _____ _____ in this hot weather?

W Hmm… I think he is pulling weeds out of his garden.

M It looks like it will take a long time _____ _____ _____. I'll go over there and ask him _____ _____ _____ _____.

W Good idea!

M Do you have a hat?

W Yes. It's in the garage. I'll go find it now.

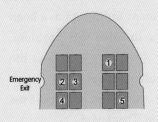

고난도

12 ◀ 배치도

다음 비행기 좌석 배치도를 보면서 대화를 듣고, 남자가 앉을 좌석을 고르시오.

M I'm here to check in.

W Okay. We have three window seats and two aisle seats left.

M I _____ _____ _____ _____ _____ _____.

W Two of them are _____ _____ _____. Is that okay?

M No, I don't like sitting in the back. Where is the other window seat?

W It's in the middle, but it's _____ _____ _____ _____ _____.

M I don't want to sit next to an emergency exit. Where are the two aisle seats?

W One is on the left side of the plane in the middle. The other one is on the right side near the front.

M I _____ _____ _____.

13 ◀ 세부 정보

대화를 듣고, 여자가 병원에 방문할 날짜를 고르시오.

① 13일   ② 15일
③ 17일   ④ 20일
⑤ 24일

M Hey Subin, how do you like my smile? I just _____ _____ _____ _____ at the dentist.

W Hi, Josh. It looks good! I should go to the dentist too. It's been more than a year since I've been to one.

M More than a year? You need to get your teeth checked more often than that.

W I know, but I'm always so busy.

M Even though you're busy, you still need to take care of yourself. I recommend going to my dentist. [pause] How about going on the _____ _____ _____ _____? That's the earliest you can make a reservation for.

W I have a meeting on the afternoon of the thirteenth. How about the seventeenth?

M The clinic _____ _____ _____ then. Would a week from the seventeenth work?

W Yes. I'll make a reservation right now.

14 ◀ 할 일

대화를 듣고, 남자가 대화 직후에 할 일로 가장 적절한 것을 고르시오.

① 호텔에 전화하기
② 휴대전화 충전하기
③ 길 물어보기
④ 손님 마중 나가기
⑤ 택시 타기

W Do you know where we are? _____ _____ _____ to me.

M I thought we were close to the hotel, but I don't see it.

W Maybe we should call the front desk and _____ _____ _____.

M That's a good idea, but I don't know the number.

W Well, there's a taxi over there.

M Oh! I will _____ _____ _____ _____ for directions.

15 ◀ 방송 목적

다음을 듣고, 방송의 목적으로 가장 적절한 것을 고르시오.

① 아파트 출입 제한 시간을 공지하려고
② 아파트 출입 차단기 설치를 위해 동의를 얻으려고
③ 아파트 출입을 위한 앱 이용을 안내하려고
④ 아파트의 주차 문제 해결을 촉구하려고
⑤ 아파트 앱 이름을 공모하려고

M Good afternoon, residents. I'm Mike Wilson, the resident representative. Recently, people who do not live in our apartment building have been frequently _____ _____ _____. To solve this problem, we would like to _____ _____ _____ at the front of the building. Starting next week, all residents should _____ _____ _____ _____ to enter the apartment. I will post the name of the app on the noticeboard of the apartment. Thank you.

고난도

16 ◀ 숫자 정보

대화를 듣고, 여자가 지불할 금액을
고르시오.

① $17   ② $21
③ $26   ④ $31
⑤ $33

W I'd like to _____ _____ _____ _____ _____. I'm here with my husband and kids.
M Okay. We have regular bikes and two-seater bikes.
W How much is it to rent a regular bike?
M It's $5 for thirty minutes and $10 for an hour.
W Okay. I'd like to _____ _____ _____ _____ for an hour for my kids.
M Sure. Would you and your husband like a two-seater bike? They're $7 for thirty minutes and _____ _____ _____ _____.
W Yes. I would like to rent one for an hour.

17 ◀ 마지막 말에 대한 응답

대화를 듣고, 남자의 마지막 말에 대한 여자의 응답으로 가장 적절한 것을 고르시오.

Woman: _____

① All right. I'll call a taxi for you. It can seat four people.
② No, this ticket is not available. Can you pick another one?
③ Yes. Please wait here for a moment while I go check.
④ Yes, the performance will start in a minute. You can enter now.
⑤ No. Cancellation on the day of the performance is not possible.

M Excuse me. Can you help me?
W Sure. What can I do for you?
M I want to _____ _____ _____, but I can't figure out where it is.
W May I see your ticket? [pause] You're on the wrong floor right now. Your seat is on the second floor.
M What? That can't be true. I _____ _____ _____ on the first floor.
W Well, the ticket says your seat is in row D _____ _____ _____ _____.
M Can you go to the ticket booth and make sure my ticket is right?
W _____

18 ◀ 마지막 말에 대한 응답

대화를 듣고, 여자의 마지막 말에 대한 남자의 응답으로 가장 적절한 것을 고르시오.

Man: _____

① I donated it to the library.
② Okay. I'll ask him and let you know.
③ Okay, don't forget to return the book.
④ Ethan doesn't have a library card.
⑤ I don't know much about fairytales.

W Hi, Jeremy. Do you still have the book I lent you six weeks ago?
M Umm… I thought I _____ _____ _____ _____ you already. What is it called?
W European Fairytales. It's one of my favorite books.
M Oh no. I think I _____ _____ _____ Ethan. I forgot that it was yours.
W Well, _____ _____ _____ _____ when I can get it back?
M _____

Man: _____

① You don't feel like talking, right?
② How did you do on your test?
③ I hope you learned your lesson.
④ What should I do to speak Spanish well?
⑤ I'd rather not swim today.

M Lauren, it's 11:00 p.m. Aren't you _____ _____ _____ _____ ?

W I'm afraid not, Dad. I _____ _____ _____ for my Spanish test. I didn't study for it at all today.

M What were you doing instead?

W I went to the pool with Amy. After that, we went shopping for a few hours.

M You _____ _____ _____ _____ and studied.

W Yeah, I realize that now.

M _____

Samantha: _____

① It rains too much here.
② I think one of the pipes is leaking.
③ I don't like the color of the wallpaper.
④ The apartment is flooded.
⑤ There is a stain on the door.

W Samantha just _____ _____ _____ _____ _____ . After living there for several days, she noticed that there was a _____ _____ _____ on her ceiling. When she came home from work the next day, she saw that _____ _____ _____ from the ceiling and landing on the floor. In this situation, what would Samantha most likely say to the owner?

Samantha _____

A

다음 영어 어휘나 표현의 뜻을 우리말로 쓰세요.

01 necessary

02 weed

03 babysit

04 feed

05 sore

06 garage

07 factory

08 check in

09 front

10 surface

11 dirt

12 familiar

13 astronaut

14 emergency exit

15 ceiling

16 housewarming party

B

우리말에 맞는 영어 어휘나 표현을 [보기]에서 찾아 쓰세요.

보기	directions	regular	stain	figure out	noticeboard
	install	leak	wrap	no later than	focus on

01 새다

02 길 안내

03 얼룩

04 포장하다, 싸다

05 게시판

06 일반적인, 보통의

07 늦어도 ~까지는

08 ~에 집중하다

09 ~을 이해하다[알아내다]

10 설치하다

점수   / 20문항

 일반 속도   빠른 속도

01 대화를 듣고, 여자가 만든 연을 고르시오.

①   ②   ③

④   ⑤

02 대화를 듣고, Fantastic Village에 관해 언급되지 않은 것을 고르시오.

① 출시 연도   ② 목표   ③ 추천 연령
④ 평점   ⑤ 용량

03 대화를 듣고, 남자가 여자에게 전화한 목적으로 가장 적절한 것을 고르시오.

① 약속 장소를 변경하려고
② 약속 시간을 변경하려고
③ 공연 시간을 물어보려고
④ 공연장에 가는 길을 물어보려고
⑤ 약속에 가지 못하는 것을 사과하려고

04 대화를 듣고, 두 사람이 영화를 보기로 한 시각을 고르시오.

① 9:00 a.m.   ② 11:00 a.m.   ③ 3:00 p.m.
④ 7:00 p.m.   ⑤ 9:00 p.m.

05 대화를 듣고, 남자의 심정으로 가장 적절한 것을 고르시오.

① upset   ② excited   ③ scared
④ jealous   ⑤ indifferent

06 다음 그림의 상황에 가장 적절한 대화를 고르시오.

①   ②   ③   ④   ⑤

07 대화를 듣고, 남자가 여자에게 부탁한 일로 가장 적절한 것을 고르시오.

① 명함 신청하기   ② 프린터 연결하기
③ 펜 빌려주기   ④ 사무용품 주문하기
⑤ 컴퓨터 설치하기

08 다음을 듣고, 항공편 지연에 관해 언급되지 않은 것을 고르시오.

① 지연 원인   ② 예상 지연 정도
③ 대체 항공편   ④ 상품권 사용 가능 장소
⑤ 상품권 수령 장소

09 다음을 듣고, 무엇에 관한 설명인지 고르시오.

① 호스   ② 정수기   ③ 물병
④ 스프링클러   ⑤ 식수대

10 다음을 듣고, 두 사람의 대화가 어색한 것을 고르시오.

①   ②   ③   ④   ⑤

11 대화를 듣고, 여자가 대화 직후에 할 일로 가장 적절한 것을 고르시오.

① 수강 신청하기   ② 이메일 보내기
③ 코딩 수업 참석하기   ④ 선생님과 면담하기
⑤ TV 프로그램 시청하기

12 다음 표를 보면서 대화를 듣고, 남자가 구입할 자전거를 고르시오.

	Bike	Price	Material	Lights
①	A	$200	Steel	○
②	B	$300	Aluminum	×
③	C	$400	Steel	×
④	D	$500	Aluminum	○
⑤	E	$600	Aluminum	×

13 대화를 듣고, 두 사람이 만나기로 한 요일을 고르시오.

① 월요일 ② 화요일 ③ 수요일
④ 목요일 ⑤ 금요일

14 대화를 듣고, 남자가 한 일로 가장 적절한 것을 고르시오.

① 이력서 쓰기 ② 봉사활동하기
③ 자격증 따기 ④ 인터뷰하기
⑤ 인턴 과정 수료하기

15 다음을 듣고, 방송의 목적으로 가장 적절한 것을 고르시오.

① 경기 장소 변경을 공지하려고
② 경기 취소를 안내하려고
③ 대설 주의보를 발령하려고
④ 무료 음료 서비스를 홍보하려고
⑤ 티켓 예매 방법을 설명하려고

16 대화를 듣고, 남자가 지불할 금액을 고르시오.

① $50 ② $75 ③ $80
④ $115 ⑤ $165

17 대화를 듣고, 남자의 마지막 말에 대한 여자의 응답으로 가장 적절한 것을 고르시오.

Woman: _____

① I can't. I always work on Wednesdays.
② Exercising is very good for your health.
③ Good idea. Then I'll see you on Sunday.
④ Can we meet somewhere else?
⑤ Badminton is a boring sport. What about playing soccer?

[18-19] 대화를 듣고, 여자의 마지막 말에 대한 남자의 응답으로 가장 적절한 것을 고르시오.

18 Man: _____

① What kind of flowers does she like?
② How long has she been in the hospital?
③ Do you need me to get him some medicine?
④ No problem. I'm sure she'll love these.
⑤ Okay. I'll drop them off at the hospital after band practice.

19 Man: _____

① There are 20 people in the cooking class.
② I've been to the community college once.
③ I like risotto more than lasagna.
④ I should have chosen Italian food.
⑤ Why don't we take the class together?

20 다음 상황 설명을 듣고, Monica가 고객 문의 담당자에게 할 말로 가장 적절한 것을 고르시오.

Monica: _____

① Do you have them in a larger size?
② I'd like to order another pair of blue boots.
③ Your rain boots got lost in the mail.
④ My rain boots should have arrived five days ago.
⑤ Your rain boots will be delivered within two days.

01 대화를 듣고, 여자가 구입할 컵을 고르시오.

02 대화를 듣고, 대형 마트에 관해 언급되지 <u>않은</u> 것을 고르시오.

① 판매 품목   ② 행사 진행 여부
③ 영업시간   ④ 반려견 출입 가능 여부
⑤ 개점 날짜

03 대화를 듣고, 여자가 남자에게 전화한 목적으로 가장 적절한 것을 고르시오.

① 수업 시간을 확인하려고
② 수업을 변경하려고
③ 미술 도구를 구입하려고
④ 수업 불참 소식을 알리려고
⑤ 수업을 등록하려고

04 대화를 듣고, 여자가 Bella를 만나기로 한 시각을 고르시오.

① 6:00 p.m.   ② 6:30 p.m.   ③ 7:00 p.m.
④ 7:30 p.m.   ⑤ 8:00 p.m.

05 대화를 듣고, 두 사람이 대화하는 장소로 가장 적절한 곳을 고르시오.

① 세탁소   ② 가구점   ③ 카페
④ 공연장   ⑤ 옷가게

06 다음 그림의 상황에 가장 적절한 대화를 고르시오.

①   ②   ③   ④   ⑤

07 대화를 듣고, 여자가 남자에게 부탁한 일로 가장 적절한 것을 고르시오.

① 이웃집에 연락하기   ② 음악 소리 낮추기
③ 영화표 예매하기   ④ 침실용 등 구입하기
⑤ 손전등 빌려주기

08 다음을 듣고, International Fair에 관해 언급되지 <u>않은</u> 것을 고르시오.

① 개최 날짜   ② 개최 장소
③ 입장권 가격   ④ 자원 봉사자 지원 방법
⑤ 자원 봉사자 업무

09 다음을 듣고, 무엇에 관한 설명인지 고르시오.

① 쇼핑 카트   ② 아이스박스   ③ 장바구니
④ 카시트   ⑤ 유모차

10 다음을 듣고, 두 사람의 대화가 <u>어색한</u> 것을 고르시오.

①   ②   ③   ④   ⑤

11 대화를 듣고, 여자가 대화 직후에 할 일로 가장 적절한 것을 고르시오.

① 신발 구입하기   ② 동물병원 가기
③ 댄스 수업 가기   ④ 개에게 줄 약 사러 가기
⑤ 신발 찾아보기

12 다음 농구 경기장 주차 안내도를 보면서 대화를 듣고, 두 사람이 주차할 구역을 고르시오.

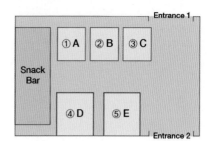

13 대화를 듣고, 여자가 탑승할 기차의 출발 시각을 고르시오.

① 3:00 p.m. ② 4:00 p.m. ③ 4:30 p.m.
④ 5:00 p.m. ⑤ 7:30 p.m.

14 대화를 듣고, 남자가 대화 직후에 할 일로 가장 적절한 것을 고르시오.

① 선물 사러 가기
② 할아버지 생신 잔치 참석하기
③ 피아노 연습하기
④ 공연 시간 변경하기
⑤ 할아버지께 전화 드리기

15 다음을 듣고, 방송의 목적으로 가장 적절한 것을 고르시오.

① 분실물 발생 시 해결 방법을 안내하려고
② 소지품 도난 신고 방법을 소개하려고
③ 분실물이 발생하지 않도록 주의를 부탁하려고
④ 지하철 기본 예절을 설명하려고
⑤ 지하철을 편안하게 이용하는 방법을 안내하려고

16 대화를 듣고, 여자가 지불할 금액을 고르시오.

① $40 ② $55 ③ $60
④ $70 ⑤ $85

17 대화를 듣고, 여자의 마지막 말에 대한 남자의 응답으로 가장 적절한 것을 고르시오.

Man: _____

① Your cat sleeps a lot.
② Cats are clean animals.
③ Don't worry. I can take care of it.
④ I hope you stay healthy in America.
⑤ Feel free to contact me if you leave.

[18-19] 대화를 듣고, 남자의 마지막 말에 대한 여자의 응답으로 가장 적절한 것을 고르시오.

18 Woman: _____

① We hope you enjoy the tour.
② You didn't give us enough notice.
③ You will receive your refund in a few days.
④ I advise you to cancel your reservation.
⑤ It takes about two hours to go to Damyang.

19 Woman: _____

① You can use this room for today, then.
② How long are you going to stay in a hotel?
③ It's only a five-minute walk from the station.
④ I'm really looking forward to hearing from you.
⑤ You can stay with my brother. He has a spare bedroom.

20 다음 상황 설명을 듣고, Tony가 음식점 주인에게 할 말로 가장 적절한 것을 고르시오.

Tony: _____

① I should have made a reservation today.
② How long do we have to wait for a table?
③ I'm very disappointed with the service here.
④ There's something wrong with my check.
⑤ Can I get some water, please?

MEMO

MEMO

지은이

NE능률 영어교육연구소

NE능률 영어교육연구소는 혁신적이며 효율적인 영어 교재를 개발하고
영어 학습의 질을 한 단계 높이고자 노력하는 NE능률의 연구조직입니다.

1316 Listening 〈Level 3〉

펴 낸 이	주민홍
펴 낸 곳	서울특별시 마포구 월드컵북로 396(상암동) 누리꿈스퀘어 비즈니스타워 10층
	㈜ NE능률 (우편번호 03925)
펴 낸 날	2024년 1월 5일 개정판 제1쇄 발행
	2024년 2월 15일 제2쇄
전 화	02 2014 7114
팩 스	02 3142 0356
홈페이지	www.neungyule.com
등록번호	제1-68호
I S B N	979-11-253-4292-2
정 가	14,000원

NE 능률

고객센터

교재 내용 문의 : contact.nebooks.co.kr (별도의 가입 절차 없이 작성 가능)
제품 구매, 교환, 불량, 반품 문의 : 02-2014-7114
☎ 전화문의는 본사 업무시간 중에만 가능합니다.

NE능률 교재 MAP

아래 교재 MAP을 참고하여 본인의 현재 혹은 목표 수준에 따라 교재를 선택하세요.
NE능률 교재들과 함께 영어실력을 쑥쑥~ 올려보세요!
MP3 등 교재 부가 학습 서비스 및 자세한 교재 정보는 www.nebooks.co.kr 에서 확인하세요.

듣기
말하기
쓰기

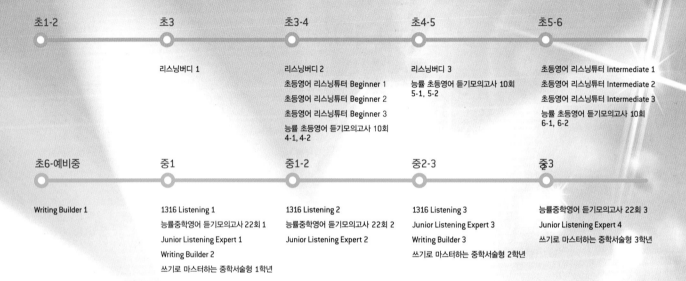

초1-2	초3	초3-4	초4-5	초5-6
	리스닝버디 1	리스닝버디 2 초등영어 리스닝튜터 Beginner 1 초등영어 리스닝튜터 Beginner 2 초등영어 리스닝튜터 Beginner 3 능률 초등영어 듣기모의고사 10회 4-1, 4-2	리스닝버디 3 능률 초등영어 듣기모의고사 10회 5-1, 5-2	초등영어 리스닝튜터 Intermediate 1 초등영어 리스닝튜터 Intermediate 2 초등영어 리스닝튜터 Intermediate 3 능률 초등영어 듣기모의고사 10회 6-1, 6-2

초6-예비중	중1	중1-2	중2-3	중3
Writing Builder 1	1316 Listening 1 능률중학영어 듣기모의고사 22회 1 Junior Listening Expert 1 Writing Builder 2 쓰기로 마스터하는 중학서술형 1학년	1316 Listening 2 능률중학영어 듣기모의고사 22회 2 Junior Listening Expert 2	1316 Listening 3 Junior Listening Expert 3 Writing Builder 3 쓰기로 마스터하는 중학서술형 2학년	능률중학영어 듣기모의고사 22회 3 Junior Listening Expert 4 쓰기로 마스터하는 중학서술형 3학년

중3-예비고	고1	고1-2	고2-3	고3
	TEPS BY STEP L+V Basic		TEPS BY STEP L+V 1	

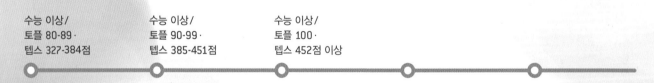

수능 이상/ 토플 80-89· 텝스 327-384점	수능 이상/ 토플 90-99· 텝스 385-451점	수능 이상/ 토플 100· 텝스 452점 이상		
TEPS BY STEP L+V 2 RADIX TOEFL Blue Label Listening 1 RADIX TOEFL Blue Label Listening 2	RADIX TOEFL Black Label Listening 1	TEPS BY STEP L+V 3 RADIX TOEFL Black Label Listening 2		

기초부터 실전까지 중학 듣기 완성

1316

1316 LISTENING

정답 및 해설

LEVEL
3

NE 능률

기초부터 실전까지 중학 듣기 완성

1316

1316 LISTENING

정답 및 해설

LEVEL
3

UNIT 1 그림 묘사·배치도

주요 어휘·표현 미리보기 p. 10

01 ⓒ tastes good
02 ⓑ on the subway
03 ⓔ used to be
04 ⓐ a better choice
05 ⓗ faces
06 ⓖ at the end of
07 ⓕ sit next to
08 ⓓ check it out

LISTENING PRACTICE

pp. 12-14

01 ③	02 ①	03 ②	04 ②	05 ④	06 ⑤
07 ⑤	08 ⑤	09 ③	10 ④	11 ⑤	12 ②

01 ③

M What do you think of this wallpaper?
W I like it. The pattern of pine trees is really nice.
M They also have wallpaper with stars. But I think stripes might be a better choice.
W Stars and stripes together?
M No, I like the one that just has stripes. I think I'm going to buy it.
W I prefer this one with wavy stripes. It would look great in your kitchen.
M I disagree. It gives me a headache. I'll stick with straight stripes.

남 이 벽지 어때?
여 마음에 들어. 소나무 무늬가 정말 멋지네.
남 별 무늬 벽지도 있어. 그런데 난 줄무늬가 더 좋은 선택 같아.
여 별이랑 줄무늬랑 같이 있는 거?
남 아니, 줄무늬만 있는 것이 좋아. 이걸 사야겠다.
여 난 이 물결 모양의 줄무늬가 더 좋은데. 너희 집 부엌에 잘 어울릴 거야.
남 난 반대야. 그 무늬 보니까 머리 아프다. 직선 줄무늬로 할래.

|어휘| wallpaper [명] 벽지 pattern [명] 무늬 pine tree 소나무 stripe [명] 줄무늬 choice [명] 선택 wavy [형] 물결 모양의 headache [명] 두통 stick with ~을 계속하다

02 ①

W Excuse me. I left my bag on the subway yesterday. Have you found it?
M Maybe. We found several bags yesterday. What does it look like?
W It's a black-and-white bag with two handles on top.
M How many pockets does it have on the front?
W It doesn't have any.
M Is your bag checkered?
W No. It is black with white dots.
M Aha! Here it is!

여 실례합니다. 제가 어제 지하철에 가방을 두고 내렸어요. 그걸 발견하셨나요?
남 아마도요. 어제 가방 몇 개를 발견했거든요. 그게 어떻게 생겼나요?
여 위에 손잡이가 두 개 달린 검은색과 흰색으로 된 가방이에요.
남 앞쪽에 주머니가 몇 개 있나요?
여 전혀 없어요.
남 가방이 체크무늬인가요?
여 아니요. 흰색 점이 있는 검은색 가방이에요.
남 아하! 여기 있습니다!

|어휘| several [형] 몇몇의 handle [명] 손잡이, 핸들 pocket [명] 주머니, 호주머니 on the front 앞쪽에 checkered [형] 체크무늬의

03 ②

M Where should we sit?
W Well, I don't want to sit near the front door.
M Okay. But that table over there is too close to the piano.
W Yes, someone will be playing it soon. It will be too noisy.
M How about over there, near the door to the kitchen?
W Okay, that looks perfect.
M Great. I just need to use the bathroom. Sit down, and I'll be right back.
W All right. I'll take a look at the menu while you're gone.

남 어디에 앉을까?
여 음, 앞문 근처에 앉고 싶지는 않아.
남 알겠어. 하지만 저기 있는 테이블은 피아노에 너무 가깝네.

여	응, 누군가 곧 피아노를 연주할 거야. 너무 시끄럽겠다.
남	저기 주방 문 근처는 어때?
여	그래, 딱 좋아 보이네.
남	좋아. 잠깐 화장실 좀 다녀와야겠다. 앉아있어, 금방 올게.
여	알았어. 네가 가 있는 동안 메뉴 좀 살펴보고 있을게.

|어휘| near 웹 ~에서 가까이   front door 앞문, 현관문, 정문
take a look at ~을 보다

04 ②

W	It's a perfect day for a picnic!
M	Yes, it is. Which side of the jogging path should we put the blanket on?
W	The playground is always noisy. Let's have our picnic on the other side.
M	Okay. We should have our picnic under a tree.
W	Yes. It will be cooler if we're not in the sun.
M	How about there?
W	It's too close to the soccer field. What if a ball lands on our blanket?
M	Good point. Let's go over there instead.
W	It looks perfect. The grass is soft, and the view is lovely.
M	And hopefully the food tastes good! This will be a great picnic.

여	피크닉 가기에 완벽한 날씨다!
남	응, 그러네. 조깅로 어느 쪽에 자리를 펼까?
여	놀이터는 항상 시끄러워. 반대편에서 피크닉을 하자.
남	좋아. 나무 밑에서 해야 해.
여	응. 햇빛 아래에 있지 않으면 더 시원할 거야.
남	저긴 어때?
여	축구장에 너무 가까워. 만약 공이 우리 자리에 떨어지면 어쩌려고?
남	좋은 지적이야. 대신 우리 저기로 가자.
여	딱 좋아 보이네. 잔디도 부드럽고 전망도 멋져.
남	바라건대 음식도 맛이 좋길! 멋진 피크닉이 될 거야.

|어휘| path 웹 길   blanket 웹 담요   soccer field 축구장
land 용 (땅·표면에) 내려앉다   instead 용 대신에   view 웹 전망
lovely 웹 사랑스러운, 멋진   hopefully 용 바라건대   taste 용 맛이 ~하다

05 ④

W	What do you think of this shirt? You should get it for your dad as a retirement present.
M	That's a good idea. But he doesn't really like shirts

without buttons.

W	Well, does he like patterned shirts or plain ones?
M	Actually, he likes striped shirts best.
W	How about this one?
M	Yes, it's nice, but do they have one with long sleeves?
W	Yes, but the color is different. Check it out.
M	Oh, yes. He'd love that one!

여	이 셔츠 어때? 너희 아버지 은퇴 선물로 이걸 사드리는 게 좋겠어.
남	좋은 생각이야. 하지만 아빠는 단추가 없는 셔츠를 그렇게 좋아하시지는 않아.
여	음, 무늬가 있는 걸 좋아하셔, 아니면 무늬 없는 걸 좋아하셔?
남	실은 줄무늬 셔츠를 가장 좋아하셔.
여	이건 어때?
남	응, 좋은데, 소매가 긴 게 있을까?
여	응, 하지만 색깔이 달라. 확인해 봐.
남	아, 그래. 아빠는 저걸 정말 좋아하실 거야!

|어휘| retirement 웹 은퇴   patterned 웹 무늬가 있는   plain
웹 무늬가 없는   sleeve 웹 소매   check out ~을 확인하다, ~을 점검하다

06 ⑤

W	Wow, look at all these tents!
M	A lot of people are camping this weekend! Which one is your brother's tent?
W	It's over there. It has black circles all over it.
M	Is it one of the triangular ones with a pointed top?
W	No, it is round. And the front zipper is open.
M	I see it. There's a picnic table behind it.
W	Yes. We all can sit there when we have dinner together.

여	우와, 이 모든 텐트를 좀 봐!
남	이번 주말에 많은 사람들이 캠핑을 하고 있네! 어떤 게 너희 오빠 텐트야?
여	저쪽에 있어. 텐트 전체에 검은색 동그라미가 그려져 있어.
남	위가 뾰족한 삼각형 모양 텐트 중 하나니?
여	아니, 둥근 모양이야. 그리고 앞에 있는 지퍼가 열려 있어.
남	보인다. 뒤에 피크닉 테이블이 있네.
여	응. 우리 다 같이 저녁 먹을 때 모두 저기에 앉을 수 있어.

|어휘| triangular 웹 삼각형의   pointed 웹 끝이 뾰족한

07 ⑤

M	This is my classroom for Chinese class, Mom. That's my teacher's desk at the front of the room.
W	Yes, I see. But where is your desk?

M It used to be in the middle of the room. But now it's in the back.
W Is it by the window?
M No, I don't like to sit by the window. It's too cold in the winter.
W That makes sense. Is it next to the bookshelf?
M Yes! And my best friend Carl sits next to me, in front of the map of the world.

남 엄마, 여기는 중국어 수업을 듣는 우리 교실이에요. 교실 앞쪽에 있는 저것은 우리 선생님 책상이에요.
여 응, 그렇구나. 그런데 네 책상은 어디 있니?
남 전에는 교실 한가운데에 있었어요. 그런데 지금은 뒤쪽에 있어요.
여 창가에 있니?
남 아니요, 저는 창가에 앉는 것을 좋아하지 않아요. 겨울에 너무 춥거든요.
여 그렇지. 책장 옆에 있니?
남 네! 그리고 제 단짝 Carl이 제 옆이자 세계 지도 앞쪽에 앉아요.

|어휘| at the front of ~의 앞부분에 used to-v 예전에는 ~이었다, ~하곤 했다 in the middle of ~의 중앙에 by the window 창가에 make sense 이해가 되다, 의미가 통하다 next to ~ 옆에 bookshelf [명] 책장

08 ⑤

M We're finally here.
W Right. Where should we park the car?
M Let's park close to the stadium.
W But what if someone hits a home run? The ball could hit my new car!
M I didn't think of that. Then let's park near the river. It will be a short walk to the stadium.
W But many cars will be leaving at the same time at the end of the game.
M That's true. So we should park near the parking lot entrance.
W Yes. Do you need to use the bathroom? There's one to the left of the entrance.
M No, that's okay. Let's just park on the other side.
W Sounds good.

남 드디어 도착했네.
여 그래. 우리 어디에 주차할까?
남 경기장 가까이에 주차하자.
여 하지만 누가 홈런을 치면 어쩌지? 공이 내 새 차를 칠 수도 있어!
남 그건 생각 못 했네. 그러면 강 부근에 주차하자. 경기장까지 걸어서 잠깐일 거야.
여 하지만 경기 종료 후에 많은 차가 동시에 떠나려고 할 거야.
남 맞네. 그러면 주차장 입구 부근에 주차해야겠다.
여 그래. 화장실 써야 하니? 입구 왼쪽에 화장실이 있는데.
남 아니, 괜찮아. 그냥 그 반대쪽에 주차하자.
여 그래.

|어휘| park [동] 주차하다 stadium [명] 경기장 home run 홈런 at the end of ~의 말에 parking lot 주차장 entrance [명] 입구, 문 to the left of ~의 왼쪽에

09 ③

W Officer! I saw the man who robbed the bank! He ran out and got into a van!
M Excellent. I need a description of him. What did he look like?
W He had black, curly hair.
M Did you see his face?
W No, I didn't. He was wearing a black mask over his face.
M Do you remember anything else?
W He was wearing blue jeans.
M Thank you for your help, ma'am.

여 경찰관님! 제가 은행을 턴 남자를 봤습니다! 뛰어나와서 밴을 탔어요!
남 잘하셨어요. 그 남자의 인상착의가 필요합니다. 어떻게 생겼던가요?
여 검은색 곱슬머리였어요.
남 그 남자의 얼굴을 보셨나요?
여 아니요, 못 봤어요. 얼굴에 검은색 마스크를 쓰고 있었거든요.
남 그 외에 기억나시는 것이 있나요?
여 청바지를 입고 있었어요.
남 도움 감사합니다.

|해설| 여자가 경찰에게 자신이 본 은행강도의 인상착의를 설명하고 있다. 검은색 곱슬머리와 마스크, 청바지라는 단서가 제공되었다.

|어휘| rob [동] 털다, 도둑질하다 description [명] 인상착의, 묘사 curly [형] 곱슬머리의

10 ④

W This is a really exciting tennis match. Which side are you cheering for?
M I'm cheering for the team that's winning.
W I'm cheering for the other team. My cousin is one of the players.
M Really? Which one is she?
W She's the one in the striped skirt.
M But they're both wearing striped skirts.

W Oh, right. She's the one <u>standing closer to</u> the net.

M I see her! She looks a lot like you!

여 정말 신나는 테니스 경기네. 너는 어느 편을 응원하고 있어?

남 이기고 있는 팀을 응원하고 있어.

여 나는 그 상대 팀을 응원하고 있는데. 내 사촌이 선수 중 한 명이거든.

남 정말? 누군데?

여 줄무늬 치마를 입은 선수야.

남 그런데 둘 다 줄무늬 치마를 입고 있잖아.

여 아, 그러네. 그녀는 네트 쪽에 더 가까이 서 있는 선수야.

남 그녀가 보여! 널 무척 닮았네!

|어휘| match ⓝ 경기, 시합   side ⓝ 편, 팀   cheer for ~을 응원하다   net ⓝ (테니스 경기 따위의) 네트

11 ⑤

W Where is <u>the best place</u> for the big vase?

M How about under the window?

W I'm going to put the fan there.

M How about putting the vase <u>next to the piano</u>?

W No, I don't think that's the right place.

M Why not? There's <u>plenty of space</u>.

W Yeah, but I'm going to put a bookshelf there.

M How about <u>on the table</u>? You can move the lamp somewhere else.

W That's a good idea! I'll put the lamp on the desk.

여 이 커다란 꽃병을 놓을 최적의 장소는 어디일까?

남 창문 밑 어때?

여 거기에는 선풍기를 둘 거야.

남 꽃병을 피아노 옆에 두는 건 어때?

여 아니, 거기는 적절한 장소가 아닌 것 같아.

남 왜 아니야? 공간이 많잖아.

여 응, 그런데 거기엔 책장을 둘 거야.

남 탁자 위는 어때? 등은 다른 곳으로 옮기면 되잖아.

여 좋은 생각이네! 등은 책상 위에 둘래.

|어휘| vase ⓝ 꽃병   fan ⓝ 선풍기, 부채   right ⓐ 알맞은   plenty of 많은   lamp ⓝ 램프, 등   somewhere ⓐ 어딘가에, 어디에서

12 ②

M Welcome to the Tropical Resort!

W Thank you! Do you have <u>any available rooms</u>?

M Yes. We have several rooms in the main building. We also have some rooms <u>near the beach</u>.

W I'd prefer to be in the main building.

M Certainly. We have rooms that <u>face the pool</u> and others that have a view of the mountain.

W Oh, I'd like to have a nice view of the mountain!

M Okay. If you <u>pay a little extra</u>, you can have a corner room. They're a bit bigger.

W No, a regular room is fine.

남 Tropical Resort에 오신 걸 환영합니다!

여 고맙습니다! 빈방 있나요?

남 네. 본관에 객실이 몇 개 있습니다. 해변 근처에도 몇 개가 있고요.

여 본관에 있는 것이 더 낫겠어요.

남 네. 풀장을 마주한 객실과 산이 보이는 객실이 있습니다.

여 아, 산의 멋진 광경을 보고 싶어요!

남 알겠습니다. 만약 비용을 조금 더 부담하시면, 모서리에 있는 객실을 얻으실 수 있습니다. 조금 더 넓어요.

여 아니요, 일반실이면 됩니다.

|어휘| available ⓐ 이용할 수 있는   main building 본관   face ⓥ ~을 향하다   extra ⓝ 추가되는 것   regular room 일반실

A

01	벽지	02	몇몇의
03	무늬	04	줄무늬
05	책장	06	담요
07	많은	08	꽃병
09	은퇴	10	소매
11	주차장	12	입구, 문
13	~을 응원하다	14	곱슬머리의
15	경기, 시합	16	털다, 도둑질하다

B

01	take a look at	02	plain
03	available	04	view
05	triangular	06	pointed
07	by the window	08	in the middle of
09	stick with	10	make sense

UNIT 2 언급되지 않은 내용

주요 어휘·표현 미리보기   p. 20

01	ⓕ participate in	02	ⓑ was founded

03 ⓗ graduate from
04 ⓓ took notes
05 ⓖ world-famous
06 ⓐ located on
07 ⓔ A variety of
08 ⓒ former

LISTENING PRACTICE

pp. 22-23

01 ③	02 ②	03 ①	04 ③	05 ②
06 ③	07 ④	08 ③	09 ③	10 ②

01 ③

M Excuse me, I'd like to buy a wallet for my mom.
W How wonderful! What type of wallet are you looking for?
M My mom usually carries a long wallet, so I want a long one.
W How about this wallet? It is designed by Victoria Lee.
M Oh, Victoria Lee? I know her. She's a world-famous designer.
W You're right. Also, it is on sale now, so it's just 100 dollars.
M Sounds like a good deal. What colors do you have?
W It comes in three colors: red, brown, and black.
M Then I'll take a brown one. I hope my mom will like it.

남 실례합니다, 엄마께 드릴 지갑을 사고 싶은데요.
여 정말 좋네요! 어떤 종류의 지갑을 찾고 계시나요?
남 저희 엄마는 주로 장지갑을 가지고 다니셔서, 장지갑을 원해요.
여 이 지갑은 어떠세요? 이건 Victoria Lee가 디자인한 거예요.
남 아, Victoria Lee라고요? 그 분 알아요. 세계적으로 유명한 디자이너잖아요.
여 맞아요. 또 지금 세일 중이어서 100달러밖에 안 해요.
남 괜찮은 가격인 것 같네요. 무슨 색상이 있나요?
여 빨간색, 갈색, 검은색 이렇게 세 가지 색상으로 나와요.
남 그럼 갈색 지갑으로 할게요. 엄마께서 좋아하시면 좋겠어요.

|어휘| world-famous [형] 세계적으로 유명한 deal [명] 거래

02 ②

W I heard you are participating in Walk across the Country.
M Right. I'm going to walk from one end of the country to the other.
W That's amazing. How long will it be?
M It's around 400 kilometers. We're planning to arrive in Seoul in 20 days.
W 400 kilometers in 20 days? I can't imagine walking such a long distance.
M I probably wouldn't be able to do it alone. But there are 200 other students, and we can help each other.
W True. How much is the participation fee?
M It's sponsored by several companies, so students don't need to pay any money.
W That's good. I hope you finish the walk without any problems.

여 네가 Walk across the Country에 참가한다고 들었어.
남 맞아. 우리나라의 한쪽 끝에서부터 다른 쪽 끝까지 걸을 예정이야.
여 대단하다. 거리가 얼마나 될까?
남 400킬로미터쯤이야. 서울에 20일 내에 도착하는 걸로 계획 중이야.
여 20일에 400킬로미터라고? 나는 그렇게 긴 거리를 걷는다는 걸 상상할 수도 없어.
남 아마 혼자는 할 수 없을 거야. 하지만 200명의 다른 학생들이 있어서, 우리는 서로를 도울 수 있어.
여 맞아. 참가비는 얼마야?
남 여러 회사들로부터 후원을 받기 때문에, 학생들은 돈을 낼 필요가 없어.
여 좋네. 네가 아무런 문제없이 그 도보 여행을 끝내기를 바랄게.

|어휘| participate in ~에 참가하다 walk [동] 걷다 [명] 걷기, 도보 여행 distance [명] 거리 participation [명] 참가, 참여 sponsor [동] 후원하다

03 ①

M Hey, Kate, have you ever seen the show called *Your Next Baker*?
W No, I haven't. When is it on?
M It is on Friday at 11:00 p.m. It started just two weeks ago.
W Oh, I see. Is it a competition for making creative desserts?
M Yep. There are 16 participants and the winner will receive 10,000 dollars.
W Sounds like fun.
M Also, Sandra Park hosts the show. She's really good at expressing how the desserts taste.
W Oh, I like her too. I'd like to watch the show the next time it airs.

남 얘, Kate, 〈Your Next Baker〉라는 프로그램 본 적 있니?
여 아니, 없어. 언제 하는 거야?
남 금요일 밤 11시에 해. 2주 전에 막 시작했어.

여 아, 그렇구나. 독창적인 디저트를 만드는 대회야?
남 응. 16명의 참가자가 나오고 우승자는 10,000달러를 받게 돼.
여 재미있겠다.
남 또 Sandra Park가 이 쇼를 진행해. 디저트가 어떤 맛인지를 정말 잘 표현해.
여 아, 나도 그녀가 좋아. 다음에 쇼가 방송될 때 보고 싶다.

|어휘| competition [명] 대회, 시합 participant [명] 참가자 receive [동] 받다 host [동] (TV · 라디오 프로그램을) 진행하다 express [동] 표현하다 air [동] 방송되다

04 ③

W Come to the Oceanview Resort! Located on sunny Panna Island, our resort features 15 double rooms and 5 single rooms. All of our rooms have air conditioning and ocean views. We also have a large swimming pool and one of the best restaurants on the island. There's a beautiful beach just minutes away. And you can walk to a popular museum and a traditional market. Make your reservation today!

여 Oceanview 리조트로 오세요! 화창한 Panna 섬에 있는 우리 리조트는 15개의 더블룸과 5개의 싱글룸이 있습니다. 모든 객실에는 에어컨이 있으며 바다 전망입니다. 대형 수영장과 섬에서 손꼽히는 음식점 중 한 곳도 있습니다. 단 몇 분 떨어진 곳에 아름다운 해변이 있고요. 그리고 인기 있는 박물관과 전통 시장에 걸어서 가실 수도 있습니다. 오늘 예약하세요!

|어휘| locate [동] 위치시키다 feature [동] 특별히 포함하다 air conditioning 에어컨 (장치)

05 ②

W Miller Memorial Hospital is the largest hospital in the New City area, with more than 1,000 rooms for patients. There are approximately 2,500 employees on the hospital's staff, including doctors and nurses. It was founded in 1931. At that time, it was located downtown. Later, it moved to its current location on Maple Street. It was named after Brian Miller, the former mayor of New City.

여 Miller Memorial 병원은 New City 지역에서 가장 큰 병원으로, 환자를 위한 1,000개 이상의 병실을 갖추고 있습니다. 의사와 간호사를 포함하여 병원 직원으로 대략 2,500명이 있습니다. 1931년에 병원이 설립되었는데요. 그 당시에는 시내에 위치했습니다. 나중에 Maple 거리에 있는 현재 위치로 옮겼습니다. 병원은 New City의 전 시장인 Brian Miller의 이름을 따서 명명되었습니다.

|어휘| patient [명] 환자 approximately [부] 대략 employee [명] 직원, 종업원 including [전] ~을 포함하여 found [동] 설립하다 downtown [부] 시내에 current [형] 현재의, 지금의 name after ~의 이름을 따서 명명하다 former [형] 이전의, 예전의 mayor [명] 시장, 구청장

06 ③

M Sally, have you decided on a topic for the research project?
W Yes. I want to write about a rising pianist, Eugene Williams.
M Eugene Williams?
W He's from Australia. He won first prize at the Chopin Competition when he was 16. He also won many awards in other competitions after that.
M Amazing. Why is his music so loved?
W His music has the power to make people happy. That's why many fans call him a ray of sunshine.
M I'm curious about his music now.
W He's going to have a recital this December in Korea. Why don't you go with me?
M Sounds great!

남 Sally, 너 연구 프로젝트를 위한 주제 정했니?
여 응. 나는 떠오르는 피아니스트인 Eugene Williams에 대해서 쓰고 싶어.
남 Eugene Williams라고?
여 호주 출신인데. 16살 때 쇼팽 콩쿠르에서 우승했어. 또 그 이후에 다른 대회에서도 많은 상을 받았어.
남 대단하다. 왜 그의 음악이 그렇게 사랑받는 거야?
여 그의 음악은 사람들을 행복하게 만드는 힘이 있어. 그게 바로 많은 팬들이 그를 한 줄기의 햇살이라고 부르는 이유지.
남 이제 그의 음악에 대해 궁금해졌어.
여 그는 이번 12월에 한국에서 연주회를 할 예정이야. 나랑 같이 가는 게 어때?
남 좋아!

|어휘| decide on ~을 결정하다 research [명] 연구, 조사 rising [형] 떠오르는, 신진의 award [명] 상 ray [명] 광선 curious [형] 궁금한 recital [명] 연주회

07 ④

W Look at this advertisement. Our city is going to start the City Garden Project.
M What is the City Garden Project?
W The city provides us with a piece of land, and then

we can plant flowers there.

M I see. It's like making our own garden! Where is the land located?

W It is located in Grand Park.

M Oh, it's close to my house. Are there any requirements to participate in the project?

W This project is only for teenagers. To apply for it, we should send an application via email.

M Okay. I want to plant roses and daisies. When is the deadline?

W It's next Monday, so we should apply soon.

여 이 광고를 봐. 우리 시에서 도시 정원 프로젝트를 시작할 예정이래.

남 도시 정원 프로젝트가 뭐야?

여 시에서 우리에게 땅 한 구획을 제공하고, 그런 다음 거기에 우리가 꽃을 심을 수 있는 거야.

남 알겠다. 우리만의 정원을 만드는 것 같은 거구나! 그 땅은 어디에 위치해 있어?

여 그랜드 파크 안에 위치하고 있어.

남 오, 우리집이랑 가깝네. 그 프로젝트에 참가하는 데 자격 조건이 있니?

여 이 프로젝트는 십 대들만을 위한 거야. 지원하려면, 이메일로 신청서를 보내야 해.

남 좋아. 나는 장미꽃과 데이지 꽃을 심고 싶어. 마감 일자가 언제니?

여 다음 주 월요일이니 빨리 지원해야 해.

|어휘| advertisement [명] 광고 provide [동] 제공하다 plant [동] 심다 requirement [명] 자격 요건, 요구 조건 application [명] 신청서 deadline [명] 기한, 마감 일자

08 ③

W Barrington National Park, the country's newest national park, attracts more than 200,000 visitors each year. It is located on a triangular piece of land next to beautiful Barrington Lake. A wide variety of wildlife can be found there, including elk, bears, and mountain lions. The park's visitor facilities include a parking lot, several hiking trails, and three campsites. You can find more information at the visitor center next to the main entrance or by visiting the national park website.

여 전국에서 가장 최근에 문을 연 Barrington 국립공원은 매년 200,000명 이상의 방문객을 끌어모으고 있습니다. 공원은 아름다운 Barrington 호수 옆 삼각지에 있습니다. 그곳에서는 엘크, 곰, 퓨마를 포함한 여러 야생동물을 찾아볼 수 있습니다. 공원의 방문객 편의시설로는 주차장, 등산로 몇 곳, 야영장 세 곳이 있습니다. 더 자세한 정보는 정문 옆 방문객 센터나 국립공원 홈페이지에 방문하셔서 알아보실 수 있습니다.

|어휘| attract [동] 끌다 triangular [형] 삼각형의 a variety of 여러 가지의 facility [명] 시설, 기관 hiking trail 등산로, 하이킹 코스 campsite [명] 야영지 main entrance 정문, 중앙 출입구

09 ③

M Littleton High School would like to introduce its newest teacher. Her name is Victoria Choi, and she'll be teaching English classes. Victoria graduated from Duke University with a degree in education in 2007. She worked at St. Mary's Middle School for seven years before joining our staff. Victoria now lives in Littleton with her husband and daughter. Welcome her to our school if you see her!

남 Littleton 고등학교에 새로 오신 선생님을 소개해드리려고 합니다. 성함은 Victoria Choi이시고, 영어를 가르치실 겁니다. Victoria 선생님은 2007년에 교육학 학사로 Duke 대학교를 졸업하셨습니다. 저희 직원으로 함께 하시기 전에, 7년 동안 St. Mary's 중학교에서 근무하셨습니다. Victoria 선생님은 현재 Littleton에서 남편과 딸과 함께 살고 계십니다. 선생님을 만나면 우리 학교에 오신 것을 환영해 주세요!

|어휘| introduce [동] 소개하다 graduate from ~을 졸업하다 degree [명] 학위

10 ②

W May I have your attention, please? This Friday, we will go on a field trip to Bulguksa. You must be at school by 8:30 a.m., and you have to wear your school uniform. I suggest you wear sneakers because we will walk a lot. Please bring a pen to take notes, as well as a lunch. We will return to school by 3:00 p.m. If it rains, the trip will be canceled, and we'll have classes as usual. Thank you.

여 주목해 주시겠어요? 이번 주 금요일에 우리는 불국사로 현장 학습을 갑니다. 반드시 오전 8시 30분까지 학교에 와야 하고, 교복을 착용해야 합니다. 많이 걸을 예정이므로 운동화를 신을 것을 권합니다. 점심뿐 아니라 메모할 펜도 챙겨 오세요. 우리는 학교에 오후 3시까지 돌아올 겁니다. 만약 비가 오면, 현장 학습은 취소되고, 평상시처럼 수업을 할 예정입니다. 감사합니다.

|어휘| field trip 현장 학습 school uniform 교복 sneakers [명] 운동화 take notes 메모하다, 기록하다 as well as ~뿐만 아니라 cancel [동] 취소하다 as usual 늘 그렇듯이, 평상시처럼

어휘·표현 다지기

p. 27

A

01 환자
02 에어컨 (장치)
03 시장, 구청장
04 대략
05 거리
06 직원, 종업원
07 운동화
08 시내에
09 연주회
10 현재의, 지금의
11 소개하다
12 떠오르는, 신진의
13 현장 학습
14 시설, 기관
15 교복
16 정문, 중앙 출입구

B

01 feature
02 participant
03 as usual
04 requirement
05 sponsor
06 degree
07 deadline
08 air
09 name after
10 as well as

UNIT 3 목적

주요 어휘·표현 미리보기

p. 28

01 ⓕ deal with
02 ⓒ at the last minute
03 ⓓ fully booked
04 ⓐ was supposed to
05 ⓔ hand over
06 ⓑ at least
07 ⓖ feel stressed
08 ⓗ come with

LISTENING PRACTICE

pp. 30-31

01 ③	02 ④	03 ①	04 ⑤	05 ②
06 ②	07 ③	08 ④	09 ①	10 ④

01 ③

[Telephone rings.]

W Dr. Hwang's clinic. May I help you?

M Yes. This is Dan Lee. I have an appointment in an hour.

W All right.

M Well, I was wondering if I could change the time. I lost my wallet, so I have to go to the lost and found office at the subway station.

W I see. What time would you like to come in?

M How about five o'clock?

W I'm sorry. We're fully booked at that time. How about 5:30?

M That's fine. Thank you.

[전화벨이 울린다.]

여 황 의원입니다. 도와드릴까요?

남 네. 저는 Dan Lee입니다. 한 시간 후에 예약이 있는데요.

여 맞습니다.

남 음, 시간을 바꿀 수 있는지 궁금해서요. 제가 지갑을 잃어버려서 지하철역 분실물 보관소에 가봐야 하거든요.

여 알겠습니다. 몇 시에 오길 원하세요?

남 5시 괜찮나요?

여 죄송합니다. 그 시간에는 예약이 다 찼네요. 5시 30분은 어떠세요?

남 좋습니다. 고맙습니다.

|어휘| clinic [명] 병원 appointment [명] 예약, 약속 wonder [동] 궁금하다 wallet [명] 지갑 lost and found office 분실물 보관소 fully booked 모두 예약된

02 ④

[Cell phone rings.]

M Hello?

W Hello, Mr. Phillips? This is Kate.

M Hi, Kate. We're supposed to meet in an hour, aren't we? Why are you calling?

W I'm sorry, but I can't make today's lesson. It's my father's birthday, so I have to go out to dinner with my family.

M I see. We can schedule an extra lesson for next week.

W Thank you for understanding. I'm sorry to cancel at the last minute.

M It's okay. Have a good time with your family.

[휴대전화벨이 울린다.]

남 여보세요?

여 안녕하세요, Phillips 선생님? 저 Kate예요.

남 안녕, Kate. 우리 한 시간 후에 만나기로 했지? 왜 전화했니?

여 죄송한데, 오늘 수업을 못 갈 것 같아요. 아버지 생신이라서, 가족들과 저녁 외식을 해야 해요.

남 그렇구나. 다음 주에 보강 수업을 잡으면 되겠다.

여 이해해 주셔서 감사해요. 임박하여 취소해서 죄송합니다.

남 괜찮아. 가족과 좋은 시간 보내렴.

|어휘| be supposed to-v ~하기로 예정되어 있다 make [동] (장

소·시간에) 겨우 맞춰 가다, (모임에) 가다 schedule [동] 일정을 잡다 extra [형] 추가의 cancel [동] 취소하다 at the last minute 마지막 순간에, 임박해서

03 ①

[Cell phone rings.]

W Hello?

M Hi, Hyejin. This is Seungmin.

W Hi, Seungmin. Are you calling about our Spanish homework?

M No. I'm calling about Sohyun. She was in a car accident yesterday.

W Oh no! I noticed she wasn't at school today, but I assumed she was sick. Is she okay?

M Yes, but she broke her leg. She's in the hospital.

W We should visit her!

M That's why I called. I'm going to the hospital tomorrow after soccer practice. Do you want to come with me?

W Sure. Where shall we meet?

M Let's meet at 3:00 in front of your house.

[휴대전화벨이 울린다.]

여 여보세요?

남 안녕, 혜진아. 나 승민이야.

여 안녕, 승민아. 스페인어 숙제 때문에 전화했니?

남 아니. 소현이 때문에 전화했어. 그 애가 어제 차 사고를 당했거든.

여 저런! 오늘 결석한 건 알아챘지만, 아픈가 보다 생각했는데. 괜찮은 거야?

남 응, 그런데 다리가 부러졌어. 병원에 입원해 있어.

여 우리 병문안 가야겠다!

남 그래서 전화했어. 나는 내일 축구 연습 후에 병원에 갈 거야. 같이 갈래?

여 응. 어디서 만날까?

남 너희 집 앞에서 3시에 보자.

|어휘| car accident 차 사고 notice [동] 알아채다, 눈치채다 assume [동] (사실로) 생각하다, 추정하다

04 ⑤

W Good morning, residents! This is an announcement from the apartment management office. Recently, new residents have moved into our building. So we would like to remind you about the rules for using the garbage area. You can only access the garbage area from Monday to Saturday. For large waste items such as desks, closets, and sofas, you have to submit a form to our office. You can find the form in the elevator. Please be considerate when taking out your trash. Thank you.

여 좋은 아침입니다, 주민 여러분! 아파트 관리실 공지입니다. 최근에 새로운 주민들이 아파트에 이사를 왔습니다. 그래서 쓰레기장 이용 규칙에 대해 상기시켜 드리려고 합니다. 월요일부터 토요일까지만 쓰레기장을 이용하실 수 있습니다. 책상, 옷장, 소파 등의 대형 폐기물의 경우에는, 저희 관리실로 양식을 제출하셔야 합니다. 양식은 엘리베이터 안에서 찾아보실 수 있습니다. 쓰레기 배출 시 배려 부탁드립니다. 감사합니다.

|어휘| resident [명] 주민 announcement [명] 안내, 공고 management office 관리실 recently [부] 최근에 remind [동] 상기시키다 rule [명] 규칙 garbage area 쓰레기장 access [동] 이용하다 waste [형] 쓸모가 없어진 submit [동] 제출하다 form [명] 양식, 신청서 considerate [형] 사려 깊은, 배려하는

05 ②

M Hello, passengers! It's raining heavily outside right now. It doesn't seem like it will stop raining soon. If you need an umbrella, you can buy one at the convenience store or the vending machine at the station. The convenience store is located at exit 1, and the vending machine is located right next to the ticket gate. You can also rent umbrellas at the station office on the second floor. However, you must hand over your ID and return the umbrella within three days. We hope everyone gets home safely. Thank you.

남 안녕하세요, 승객 여러분! 지금 밖에는 비가 많이 오고 있습니다. 금방 그칠 것 같지 않습니다. 우산이 필요하시면, 역 내 편의점이나 자판기에서 구입하실 수 있습니다. 편의점은 1번 출구에 위치해 있으며, 자판기는 개찰구 바로 옆에 위치해 있습니다. 또한, 2층에 있는 역 사무실에서 우산을 대여하실 수도 있습니다. 단, 신분증을 내셔야 하며, 우산을 3일 안에 반납해 주셔야 합니다. 모두 안전하게 귀가하시길 바랍니다. 감사합니다.

|어휘| passenger [명] 승객 heavily [부] 심하게 convenience store 편의점 vending machine 자판기 be located 위치해 있다 exit [명] 출구 ticket gate 개찰구 floor [명] 층 hand over ~을 건네다, ~을 내다 safely [부] 안전하게

06 ②

[Telephone rings.]

M Hello?

W Hi, Dad. It's Jinhee.

M Where are you? You were supposed to be home half an hour ago!

W Sorry. My car broke down. I'm at the auto repair shop on Oxford Avenue, near the library.

M I see. What's wrong with your car?

W I'm not sure, but I think it'll take some time to fix it. Could you pick me up?

M Okay. I'll be there in ten minutes.

[전화벨이 울린다.]

남 여보세요?

여 여보세요, 아빠. 저 진희예요.

남 너 어디니? 30분 전에 집에 와야 했잖니!

여 죄송해요. 제 차가 고장 났어요. 저 도서관 부근의 Oxford 가에 있는 자동차 정비소에 있어요.

남 알겠다. 차에 무슨 문제가 있는데?

여 잘 모르겠지만, 고치는 데 시간이 좀 걸릴 것 같아요. 저 좀 데리러 와 주실래요?

남 알겠다. 10분 후에 도착할 거다.

|어휘| break down (기계 · 차량이) 고장 나다 auto repair shop 자동차 정비소 fix [동] 고치다 pick up ~을 (차에) 태우러 가다

07 ③

[Telephone rings.]

W Thank you for calling Happy Hair. How may I help you?

M Hi, this is Carl. I had an appointment at eleven o'clock this morning.

W I remember. Don't you like your new haircut?

M Actually, I love it!

W Good! Then what can I do for you?

M I think I left my wallet at the salon. Can you please check and see if it's there?

W Of course. One moment, please. *[pause]* Someone left a green wallet here.

M Oh! That's mine!

[전화벨이 울린다.]

여 Happy Hair에 전화 주셔서 감사합니다. 어떻게 도와드릴까요?

남 안녕하세요, 저는 Carl입니다. 오늘 오전 11시에 예약이 있었는데요.

여 기억해요. 새로 자른 머리가 마음에 들지 않으신가요?

남 실은 정말 마음에 들어요!

여 다행이네요! 그럼 무엇을 도와드릴까요?

남 제가 미용실에 지갑을 두고 온 것 같아요. 그게 거기 있는지 한번 봐 주시겠어요?

여 물론이죠. 잠시만요. [잠시 후] 누군가가 여기에 초록색 지갑을 두고 갔네요.

남 아! 그거 제 거예요!

|어휘| haircut [명] 이발, 머리 모양 salon [명] 미용실

08 ④

[Cell phone rings.]

M Hello, Susan.

W Hi, Dan. I'm afraid I might be late for the meeting today.

M What is wrong?

W My flight to New York has been delayed due to bad weather conditions.

M Oh, I see. Then what time will you arrive?

W I will arrive around 2:00 p.m. So I need you to change the meeting time.

M I understand. I'll let the team know, and we'll adjust the schedule accordingly.

W Thank you for your understanding and help.

M No problem, Susan. Safe travels and see you soon.

[휴대전화벨이 울린다.]

남 여보세요, Susan.

여 안녕하세요, Dan. 저 오늘 회의에 늦을지도 모르겠어요.

남 무슨 일이에요?

여 제 뉴욕행 항공편이 악천후 때문에 지연되었어요.

남 아, 그렇군요. 그럼 몇 시에 도착해요?

여 오후 2시쯤 도착할 거예요. 그래서 회의 시간을 변경해줬으면 해요.

남 알겠어요. 팀에 알리고 그에 맞춰 일정을 조정할게요.

여 이해해주고 도와주어서 고마워요.

남 별말씀을요, Susan. 안전하게 여행하고 곧 봘게요.

|어휘| due to ~ 때문에 condition [명] 상태 adjust [동] 조정하다 accordingly [부] 그에 맞춰

09 ①

W Hello, students! I'm Ms. Smith, the school counselor. Sometimes you may feel worried or stressed. We want to remind you that counseling services are available at our school. We can help you with any personal, social, or academic issues that you may be facing. Everything will be kept secret and we won't share them with anyone else. You can schedule an appointment by phone, text, or email. Remember, it's okay to ask for help when you need it. Our counselors are here to support you. Thank you.

여 안녕하세요, 학생 여러분! 저는 학교 상담 교사인 Smith 선생님입니다. 때때로 여러분은 걱정스럽거나 스트레스를 받을 수도 있습니다. 우리 학교에서 상담 서비스를 이용할 수 있다는 것을 여러분에게 상기시키고 싶어요. 여러분이 직면하고 있을 수 있는 어떤 개인적, 사회적, 학업적 문제라도 도울 수 있어요. 모든 것은 비밀로 지켜지고 우리는 그것을 다른 누구와 공유하지 않을 것입니다. 전화나 문자, 이메일로 약속을 잡을 수 있어요. 기억하세요, 여러분이 도움이 필요할 때 도움을 요청해도 괜찮습니다. 우리 상담 교사들은 여러분을 지원하기 위해 여기 있어요. 감사합니다.

|어휘| counselor [명] 상담사 stressed [형] 스트레스를 받는 available [형] 이용할 수 있는 personal [형] 개인적인 social [형] 사회적인 academic [형] 학업의 issue [명] 문제 face [동] 마주하다, 직면하다 share [동] 공유하다 support [동] 지원하다, 후원하다

10 ④

M Hello, this is *Today's Health*! Many teenage listeners have asked about their various skin problems. Here are some tips for dealing with them. First, wash your face at least twice a day—once in the morning, and once before you go to bed. Second, use a gentle, oil-free cleanser. When you apply it, use your hands or a soft washcloth. Third, use sunscreen every day, even on cloudy days. It's important to protect your skin from the sun. Last, get enough sleep and eat a balanced diet. If you follow these tips, then you can keep your skin healthy!

남 안녕하세요, 〈오늘의 건강〉입니다! 많은 십 대 청취자분들께서 다양한 피부 문제에 대해 문의해 주셨는데요. 그 문제들을 해결할 수 있는 몇 가지 방법이 있습니다. 첫째, 하루에 최소한 두 번, 즉 아침에 한 번, 그리고 자기 전에 한 번, 세안하세요. 둘째, 순하고 유분기가 거의 없는 세안제를 사용하세요. 세안제를 바를 때는, 손이나 부드러운 수건을 이용하세요. 셋째, 흐린 날에도 매일 자외선 차단제를 쓰세요. 태양으로부터 피부를 보호하는 것이 중요합니다. 마지막으로, 충분한 수면을 취하고 균형 잡힌 식사를 하세요. 이 방법들을 따른다면, 피부를 건강하게 유지할 수 있을 거예요!

|어휘| teenage [형] 십 대의 deal with ~을 다루다[해결하다] at least 최소한 oil-free [형] 유분이 거의 없는 apply [동] 바르다 washcloth [명] 세안용 수건 sunscreen [명] 자외선 차단제 protect [동] 보호하다 balanced [형] 균형 잡힌

어휘·표현 다지기

p. 35

A

01 사려 깊은, 배려하는	02 병원
03 차 사고	04 관리실
05 상기시키다	06 자판기
07 사회적인	08 심하게
09 추가의	10 균형 잡힌
11 승객	12 편의점
13 십 대의	14 상태
15 제출하다	16 자동차 정비소

B

01 appointment	02 notice
03 resident	04 assume
05 schedule	06 apply
07 personal	08 form
09 access	10 accordingly

UNIT 4 숫자 정보

주요 어휘·표현 미리보기

p. 36

01 ⓕ get a discount	02 ⓔ per hour
03 ⓐ Would you like	04 ⓓ end
05 ⓑ attend	06 ⓖ speaker
07 ⓒ gain	08 ⓗ on sale

LISTENING PRACTICE

pp. 38-39

01 ③	02 ⑤	03 ④	04 ③	05 ⑤
06 ①	07 ②	08 ②	09 ④	10 ②

01 ③

M How much is a medium soda and a medium popcorn?

W A medium soda is $2, and a medium popcorn is $3. But there's a special offer.

M What is it?

W You can get a large soda and a large popcorn for the

same price as a medium.

M Great. I'll have that with caramel syrup.

W Okay. Caramel syrup is 50 cents extra. If you have a membership card, you get $1 off.

M I don't have one.

남 탄산음료 중간 사이즈와 팝콘 중간 사이즈는 얼마예요?

여 탄산음료 중간 사이즈는 2달러이고, 팝콘 중간 사이즈는 3달러입니다. 하지만 특별 할인이 있습니다.

남 뭔데요?

여 중간 사이즈와 똑같은 가격에 큰 사이즈의 탄산음료와 팝콘을 구매하실 수 있습니다.

남 좋네요. 캐러멜 시럽이랑 함께 그걸로 할게요.

여 네. 캐러멜 시럽은 50센트 별도 계산입니다. 멤버십 카드가 있으시면, 1달러를 할인받으실 수 있습니다.

남 그건 없어요.

|해설| 남자가 큰 사이즈의 탄산음료와 팝콘을 중간 사이즈 가격에 샀고, 거기에 50센트짜리 캐러멜 시럽을 추가했으므로 남자가 지불할 금액은 5.5달러이다.

|어휘| medium [형] (크기 등이) 중간의 soda [명] 탄산음료 special offer 특가 판매, 특별 할인 extra [형] 별도 계산의 off [부] 할인하여

02 ⑤

M Hi, Yuram. Do you have plans for tomorrow?

W Just a short meeting with some classmates.

M I'm going to Changdeokgung with my American friends. Do you want to come?

W You have American friends?

M Yes, I met them at summer camp.

W I'd love to join you. What time are you going?

M They have Korean class from ten o'clock until noon. After that, it'll take them an hour to get here.

W My meeting will be ending around then. Could you wait for me for thirty minutes?

M Sure. We'll wait at my house.

W Great!

남 안녕, 유람아. 내일 계획 있니?

여 그냥 반 친구 몇 명이랑 잠깐 만날 거야.

남 나는 미국인 친구들이랑 창덕궁에 가려고 해. 같이 갈래?

여 너 미국인 친구들이 있어?

남 응, 여름 캠프에서 그 애들을 만났어.

여 나도 함께하고 싶어. 몇 시에 갈 건데?

남 그 애들이 10시부터 정오까지 한국어 수업이 있거든. 그 후에 여기 도착하려면 한 시간 걸릴 거야.

여 내 모임이 그때쯤 끝날 거야. 나를 30분 기다려 줄 수 있어?

남 당연하지. 우리 집에서 기다릴게.

여 좋아!

|해설| 12시에 수업을 마친 미국인 친구들이 한 시간 걸려 남자 집에 도착한 뒤, 여자를 30분 동안 기다려야 하므로, 이들이 만날 시각은 오후 1시 30분이다.

|어휘| plan [명] 계획 classmate [명] 반 친구 join [동] 함께하다 end [동] 끝나다

03 ④

W Welcome to Smithfield Concert Hall. How can I help you?

M How much are your concert tickets?

W We have afternoon concerts and evening concerts. Which are you interested in?

M I'd like to attend an evening concert.

W All right. Tickets for our evening shows are $6 for adults and $4 for children.

M Okay. I'd like tickets for this evening's concert for two adults and one child.

W Certainly, sir. Here you are, and enjoy the concert.

여 Smithfield 콘서트장에 오신 것을 환영합니다. 무엇을 도와드릴까요?

남 콘서트 표가 얼마죠?

여 오후와 저녁 콘서트가 있습니다. 어떤 것에 관심 있으신가요?

남 저녁 콘서트를 가고 싶습니다.

여 알겠습니다. 저녁 콘서트 표 가격은 어른은 6달러, 어린이는 4달러입니다.

남 좋습니다. 오늘 저녁 콘서트로 어른 두 명과 어린이 한 명 표를 사겠습니다.

여 네, 손님. 여기 있습니다, 콘서트 재미있게 관람하시기 바랍니다.

|해설| 남자가 저녁 콘서트를 관람하기로 하였고, 6달러짜리 어른 표 2장, 4달러짜리 어린이 표 1장을 구매했으므로, 남자가 지불할 총 금액은 16달러이다.

|어휘| attend [동] 참석하다, 참여하다 adult [명] 성인, 어른 certainly [부] (질문에 대한 대답으로) 그럼, 물론이지

04 ③

W Hi, Paul. Long time no see. You look great. Have you been exercising?

M Yes. I ride my bicycle every day after school. Also, I've stopped eating fast food.

W Wow! How much weight did you lose?

M When I started in March, I weighed 80 kg. I lost 10 kg in six months.

W That's a lot.

M Unfortunately, I gained 2 kg this month.

W Don't worry. It's natural to gain back a little weight.

여 안녕, Paul. 오래간만이야. 멋있어 보인다. 운동하니?

남 응. 방과 후에 매일 자전거를 타. 그리고 패스트푸드 먹는 것도 그만두었어.

여 우와! 몸무게가 얼마나 줄어든 거야?

남 3월에 시작했을 때, 80kg이었거든. 6개월 동안 10kg이 줄었어.

여 많이 줄었네.

남 아쉽게도, 이번 달에 2kg 늘었어.

여 걱정하지 마. 몸무게가 다시 약간 느는 건 자연스러운 거야.

|해설| 남자가 80kg일 때 운동을 시작하여 6개월 동안 10kg이 줄었는데 이번 달에 2kg이 다시 늘었다고 했으므로 남자의 현재 몸무게는 72kg이다.

|어휘| exercise [동] 운동하다 ride a bicycle 자전거를 타다 weight [명] 체중, 몸무게 lose [동] 잃다, 줄다 weigh [동] 무게가 ~이다 unfortunately [부] 유감스럽게도, 불행히도 gain [동] 몸무게가 늘다 natural [형] 당연한, 자연스러운

05 ⑤

M May I take your order?

W Yes, please. I'd like a cheeseburger for myself and a chicken sandwich for my son.

M Would you like french fries with that?

W Yes, two orders of fries. And I'll have a coffee, and my son will have an orange juice.

M Okay, that's one cheeseburger, one chicken sandwich, one order of fries, one coffee, and one orange juice, right?

W No, two orders of fries.

M Okay.

남 주문하시겠어요?

여 네. 저는 치즈버거 하나 주시고, 제 아들은 치킨 샌드위치 하나 주세요.

남 프렌치프라이도 같이 하실 건가요?

여 네, 두 개 주세요. 그리고 저는 커피, 아들은 오렌지 주스 주세요.

남 네, 치즈버거 하나, 치킨 샌드위치 하나, 프렌치프라이 하나, 커피 한 잔, 오렌지 주스 한 잔, 맞습니까?

여 아니요, 프렌치프라이 두 개입니다.

남 알겠습니다.

|해설| 치즈버거는 3.5달러, 치킨 샌드위치는 4달러, 프렌치프라이 2개는 총 2달러, 커피와 오렌지 주스는 각각 1달러이므로, 여자가 지불할 총 금액은 11.5달러이다.

|어휘| take an order 주문을 받다 french fries 프렌치프라이, 감자튀김

06 ①

W Would you like to come to a lecture with me this evening? It'll be interesting.

M I'd like to go, but I'm not sure I can. What time does it start?

W It starts at 6:30. The speaker is a famous scientist. He studies global warming.

M It sounds great, but I have to pick up my mom at the airport at 9:00. How long will it be?

W It ends at 7:30.

M Okay. Then I can go.

여 오늘 저녁에 나랑 같이 강연 들으러 갈래? 재미있을 거야.

남 가고 싶은데, 갈 수 있을지 잘 모르겠어. 강연이 몇 시에 시작해?

여 6시 30분에 시작해. 연사가 유명한 과학자야. 지구 온난화를 연구하셔.

남 아주 좋은데, 9시에 공항에서 엄마를 모셔와야 해. 강연이 얼마나 오래 걸릴까?

여 7시 30분에 끝나.

남 좋아. 그러면 갈 수 있겠다.

|해설| 강연이 6시 30분에 시작해서 7시 30분에 끝난다고 했으므로, 1시간 동안 진행된다는 것을 알 수 있다.

|어휘| lecture [명] 강연, 강의 speaker [명] 연사, 발표자 global warming 지구 온난화

07 ②

W I'm finished using the internet. I'd like to pay now.

M All right. Which computer were you using?

W I was using number eight. It costs $1 per hour, doesn't it?

M Yes. You used the computer for five hours, right?

W No, I only used it for four hours. I started at eleven, and now it's three.

M That's right. I'm sorry.

W It's okay. I also have a coupon.

M Okay. Then you get a 10% discount.

여 인터넷 다 썼어요. 지금 계산하고 싶습니다.

남 알겠습니다. 어느 컴퓨터를 이용하고 계셨나요?

여 8번을 이용했어요. 시간당 1달러죠?

남 네. 5시간 동안 컴퓨터 이용하셨네요, 맞나요?

여 아니요, 4시간만 이용했어요. 11시에 쓰기 시작했는데, 지금 3시예요.

남 맞네요. 죄송합니다.
여 괜찮아요. 그리고 쿠폰도 있어요.
남 알겠습니다. 그러면 10% 할인을 받으실 수 있습니다.

|해설| 컴퓨터 이용료는 시간당 1달러이고, 여자는 4시간 동안 사용했는데 10% 할인 쿠폰이 있으므로, 여자가 지불할 총 금액은 3.6달러이다.

|어휘| pay [동] 지불하다, 계산하다 cost [동] (값이) ~이다[들다] per hour 시간당 discount [명] 할인

08 ②

W Can I help you?
M Yes. Does your spring sale include both books and magazines?
W No. Only our books are on sale. Magazines are still full price.
M And all of these books are 50% off?
W That's right. They're usually $10 each, but they're on sale for $5.
M I'll take these four books and these two magazines.
W Okay. The magazines are $4 each.
M Great.

여 도와드릴까요?
남 네. 봄 할인 판매에 책과 잡지 둘 다 포함되나요?
여 아닙니다. 책만 할인 판매 중입니다. 잡지는 여전히 제값입니다.
남 그러면 여기 있는 책 모두 50% 할인되나요?
여 맞습니다. 평상시에 권당 10달러인데 5달러에 할인 판매 중입니다.
남 책 네 권과 잡지 두 권을 사겠습니다.
여 알겠습니다. 잡지는 권당 4달러입니다.
남 좋네요.

|해설| 권당 5달러인 책 네 권과 권당 4달러인 잡지 두 권을 구매하기로 했으므로, 남자가 지불할 총 금액은 28달러이다.

|어휘| include [동] 포함하다 magazine [명] 잡지 on sale 할인 판매 중인 full price 전액, 제값 each [부] 각각, 한 개에

09 ④

[Cell phone rings.]
W Hey, Derek! Why don't we have lunch together this weekend?
M Hi, Emily. Sure! What day works for you?
W How about Saturday? I have a swimming lesson near your place on Saturdays. Let's meet after the lesson.
M What time does your lesson end?
W Around 2 p.m. I think we can meet at 2:30.
M I'm afraid that's too late. Most of the restaurants near here take their last orders at 2:30.
W Oh, I didn't know that. I can make it 15 minutes earlier then.
M Okay. That should give us enough time. See you then.
W Good. See you.

[휴대전화벨이 울린다.]
여 얘, Derek! 우리 이번 주말에 같이 점심 먹을까?
남 안녕, Emily. 좋지. 너는 어느 요일이 좋아?
여 토요일 어때? 토요일마다 너희 집 근처에서 수영 강습이 있거든. 강습 끝나고 만나자.
남 강습이 몇 시에 끝나?
여 오후 2시경에. 2시 30분에 만날 수 있을 것 같아.
남 그건 너무 늦는 것 같아. 이 근처 식당 대부분이 2시 30분에 마지막 주문을 받아.
여 아, 몰랐어. 그러면 15분 더 일찍 갈 수 있어.
남 좋아. 그럼 우린 시간이 충분할 거야. 그때 보자.
여 좋아. 안녕.

|해설| 2시 30분에 만나자는 여자의 제안에 남자는 너무 늦다고 말했고, 여자는 15분 더 일찍 만날 수 있다고 했으므로, 두 사람이 만날 시각은 2시 15분이다.

|어휘| make it 시간 맞춰 가다

10 ②

[Telephone rings.]
M Amy's Kitchen. May I help you?
W I'd like to make a reservation for five people at six o'clock this evening.
M I'm sorry. There are no tables for five available at that time. How about an hour later?
W We're going to a show at the theater next door. It ends at five, so that's too long to wait.
M Well, I can get you a table half an hour after your show ends.
W Thank you!

[전화벨이 울린다.]
남 Amy's Kitchen입니다. 무엇을 도와드릴까요?
여 오늘 저녁 6시에 5명 예약하고 싶어요.
남 죄송합니다. 그 시간에는 5명이 앉으실 수 있는 자리가 없습니다. 한 시간 뒤는 어떠세요?
여 저희가 바로 옆에 있는 극장에 공연을 보러 가거든요. 이게 5시에 끝나기 때문에, 기다리기에는 너무 오래네요.
남 음, 손님 공연이 끝나고 30분 후에 자리를 마련해 드릴 수 있겠네요.
여 감사합니다!

|해설| 공연이 끝나고 30분 후에 자리를 마련해 준다고 했는데, 공연은 5시에 끝나므로, 여자가 예약한 시각은 오후 5시 30분이다.

|어휘| make a reservation 예약하다   available ⓗ 이용 가능한   at that time 그때에(는)   later ⓤ 뒤에, 후에   next door 옆방[집]에   half an hour 30분

p. 43

어휘·표현 다지기

A

01 강연, 강의
02 성인, 어른
03 지구 온난화
04 자전거를 타다
05 함께하다
06 반 친구
07 포함하다
08 무게가 ~이다
09 탄산음료
10 옆방[집]에
11 잡지
12 전액, 제값
13 잃다, 줄다
14 운동하다
15 30분
16 뒤에, 후에

B

01 natural
02 medium
03 off
04 pay
05 take an order
06 certainly
07 special offer
08 cost
09 each
10 at that time

UNIT 5 | 심정·장소

주요 어휘·표현 미리보기

p. 44

01 ⓗ run out of
02 ⓐ do well
03 ⓖ making a mistake
04 ⓑ bring back
05 ⓓ won first prize
06 ⓒ in a few minutes
07 ⓔ around the corner
08 ⓕ have trouble

LISTENING PRACTICE

pp. 46-47

01 ⑤	02 ④	03 ④	04 ③	05 ④
06 ④	07 ②	08 ①	09 ⑤	10 ⑤

01 ⑤

W Hi! Long time no see! How have you been?
M I'm sorry, but do I know you?
W What? Come on, it's Stacey. Stacey Black. Don't you remember me?
M Stacey Black? Umm... I don't think I know you.
W I can't believe this. How could you forget me? We met at the Student Leaders' Camp in Seoul last year.
M Student Leaders' Camp? I've never been there before.
W Oh, my gosh! Aren't you Owen?
M No, I'm Harry, Harry Wilson.
W I'm so sorry. I thought you were my friend Owen. I've made a big mistake.
M That's fine. Don't worry about it.

여 안녕! 오랜만이야! 어떻게 지냈니?
남 죄송하지만, 저 아세요?
여 뭐라고? 왜 이래, 나 Stacey야. Stacey Black이라고. 나 기억 못 해?
남 Stacey Black이요? 음… 저는 당신을 모르는데요.
여 믿을 수가 없네. 어떻게 나를 잊을 수가 있어? 우리 작년에 서울에서 열린 학생 리더 캠프에서 만났잖아.
남 학생 리더 캠프요? 저는 전에 그곳에 간 적이 없어요.
여 오, 이럴 수가! 너 Owen 아니니?
남 아니요, 저는 Harry인데요, Harry Wilson이요.
여 정말 죄송합니다. 당신이 제 친구 Owen이라고 생각했어요. 제가 큰 실수를 했네요.
남 괜찮아요. 걱정하지 않으셔도 돼요.

|어휘| remember ⓥ 기억하다   forget ⓥ 잊다   make a mistake 실수하다   worry ⓥ 걱정하다   [문제] grateful ⓗ 고마워하는   excited ⓗ 신이 난   regretful ⓗ 후회하는   concerned ⓗ 걱정하는   embarrassed ⓗ 당황스러운

02 ④

M Mom, I'm home.
W Alex, you were supposed to be home by seven, but it's already nine o'clock.
M Well, I lost my bag. Unfortunately, my wallet was in the bag, so I couldn't take the bus.
W Oh no! Why didn't you call me?
M I couldn't use my phone because it ran out of battery. So I just walked home.
W I see. I was afraid something bad might have happened.
M I'm sorry for making you worry.
W No, it's okay. You got back home safely, so that's

enough.

남 엄마, 저 집에 왔어요.

여 Alex, 너 7시까지 집에 오기로 되어 있었는데, 이미 9시야.

남 그게, 가방을 잃어버렸어요. 안타깝게도 제 지갑이 가방 안에 있어서, 버스를 탈 수가 없었어요.

여 어머, 저런! 왜 엄마에게 전화 안 했니?

남 배터리가 없어서 휴대전화를 쓸 수가 없었어요. 그래서 그냥 집으로 걸어왔어요.

여 그랬구나. 뭔가 나쁜 일이 벌어졌나 걱정했단다.

남 걱정 끼쳐 드려서 죄송해요.

여 아니야, 괜찮아. 네가 무사히 집으로 돌아왔으니, 그걸로 충분하단다.

|해설| 연락 없이 집에 돌아오지 않던 아들이 무사히 집으로 돌아왔으므로 여자가 안도했음을 알 수 있다.

|어휘| be supposed to-v ~하기로 되어 있다 unfortunately ⓟ 불행히도, 안타깝게도 run out of ~이 없어지다 afraid ⓗ 두려운, 걱정하는 happen ⓥ 일어나다, 발생하다 safely ⓟ 무사히, 안전하게 **[문제]** relieved ⓗ 안도하는

03 ④

W I'm excited to see this musical! The show starts in a few minutes. We should hurry.

M Hmm… Wait a minute.

W What's wrong?

M Oh no! I think I left the tickets at home!

W Are you sure? Check your bag. What about your pockets?

M Nope, I can't find them. I put them on the table last night. They must still be there.

W Well, I guess we can't go to the show tonight then.

M You must be very angry at me.

W No. Everybody makes mistakes. Let's find something else fun to do!

여 이 뮤지컬을 보게 돼서 정말 신나! 공연이 몇 분 후에 시작할 거야. 서둘러야 해.

남 흠… 잠깐만.

여 무슨 일이야?

남 아 이런! 나 표를 집에 두고 온 것 같아!

여 정말이야? 가방을 확인해 봐. 주머니는?

남 아니, 못 찾겠어. 어젯밤에 탁자 위에 표를 두었거든. 아직 거기 있는 게 분명해.

여 음, 그러면 오늘 밤에 공연을 보러 갈 수 없겠는데.

남 나한테 엄청 화나겠구나.

여 아니. 누구나 실수하기 마련이지. 다른 재미있는 할 거를 찾아보자!

|어휘| in a few minutes 몇 분 후에 hurry ⓥ 서두르다 wait a minute 잠깐 기다리다 leave ⓥ 두고 오다 sure ⓗ 확실한 must ⓐ ~임에 틀림없다 else ⓗ 그 밖의, 다른 **[문제]** jealous ⓗ 부러워하는

04 ③

M Mina! I just heard the good news. I'm really jealous.

W Winning first prize was a great honor. It was hard work, but I earned it.

M You must have spent a lot of time on your essay.

W Yes, I stayed up late every night for two weeks.

M Well, congratulations! What did you write about?

W I wrote about my favorite book, *Me Before You*. It's a sad story, but you should read it.

남 미나야! 방금 좋은 소식을 들었어. 정말 부럽다.

여 일등 상을 타는 것은 대단한 영광이었어. 힘든 일이었지만, 내가 결국 얻어냈네.

남 과제물에 시간을 많이 썼겠다.

여 응, 2주 동안 매일 밤 늦게까지 자지 않았어.

남 음, 축하해! 뭐에 관해 썼니?

여 내가 아주 좋아하는 책 〈Me Before You〉에 관해 썼어. 슬픈 이야기이지만, 너도 꼭 읽어봐.

|어휘| win first prize 일등 상을 타다 honor ⓝ 명예, 영예 earn ⓥ 얻다, 받다 spend ⓥ (시간·돈을) 쓰다, 쏟다 essay ⓝ 과제물 stay up late 늦게까지 자지 않다

05 ④

W I'd like to go to Grand Central Station. Does the bus going there stop here?

M Yes. You should take bus number 71. But you've just missed it.

W How often does it come?

M It comes every 25 minutes.

W I see. But I need to be there in 20 minutes! Is there another bus that goes there?

M Not directly. I suggest you take the subway. The subway station is just around the corner.

W How long does it take by subway?

M It only takes 10 minutes. Grand Central Station is just four stops away.

여 Grand Central 역에 가고 싶은데요. 거기 가는 버스가 여기에 서나요?

남 네. 71번 버스를 타셔야 해요. 하지만 방금 놓치셨네요.

여 얼마나 자주 오나요?

남 25분마다 옵니다.
여 알겠습니다. 하지만 제가 20분 후에 거기 도착해야 하거든요! 거기 가는 다른 버스가 있나요?
남 곧장 가는 것은 없어요. 지하철 타시는 것을 추천해요. 길모퉁이만 돌면 지하철역이 있어요.
여 지하철로는 얼마나 걸리나요?
남 10분밖에 안 걸려요. Grand Central 역은 겨우 네 정거장 거리예요.

|해설| 지하철에 대한 언급이 있지만, 두 사람은 버스 정거장에서 대화하고 있다.

|어휘| miss [동] 놓치다 how often 얼마나 자주, 몇 번 directly [부] 곧장, 똑바로 suggest [동] 추천하다, 제안하다 around the corner 길모퉁이를 돈 곳에 stop [명] 정거장 away [부] 떨어져, 떨어진 곳에

06 ④

W Are you okay? You don't look well.
M I can't stop shaking.
W What's wrong? Are you cold?
M No. You don't remember? The Spanish speech contest is tonight. I really want to do well.
W Don't worry. Everything will be fine. You did great last year. Remember?
M I don't know, though. I'm sure I will make some mistakes.
W Don't think that way. You practiced a lot. I know you can win this contest.

여 너 괜찮아? 안색이 안 좋아 보인다.
남 떠는 걸 멈출 수가 없어.
여 무슨 일이야? 추워?
남 아니. 너 기억 안 나? 오늘 밤에 스페인어 웅변대회가 있잖아. 나 정말 잘하고 싶어.
여 걱정하지 마. 다 잘될 거야. 작년에 잘했잖아. 기억하지?
남 하지만 잘 모르겠어. 분명 실수를 좀 할 거야.
여 그렇게 생각하지 마. 많이 연습했잖아. 난 네가 이번 대회에서 우승할 수 있을 거란 걸 알아.

|해설| 웅변대회를 앞두고 떠는 걸 멈출 수 없다고 했으므로, 남자는 불안해하는 상태라는 것을 알 수 있다.

|어휘| shake [동] (추위 · 무서움 등으로) 떨다 do well 잘하다 though [부] 그렇지만, 하지만 practice [동] 연습하다 **[문제]** nervous [형] 불안해하는 thankful [형] 고맙게 생각하는

07 ②

[Cell phone rings.]
W Hello?
M Hello. Is this Mrs. Wilson?
W Yes, this is she.
M You were just in my taxi. You left your purse on the seat. Luckily, I found your number in it.
W Oh, I'm so glad you found it. I wasn't sure what to do.
M Well, I can bring it back to you. Let's meet at the spot where I dropped you off.
W That would be wonderful. I can't thank you enough.

[휴대전화벨이 울린다.]
여 여보세요?
남 안녕하세요. Wilson 부인이신가요?
여 네, 전데요.
남 손님께서 방금 제 택시에 타셨었는데요. 자리에 지갑을 두고 내리셨네요. 다행히 제가 그 안에서 손님 전화번호를 찾았고요.
여 오, 제 지갑을 찾아주셔서 정말 기쁘네요. 어떻게 해야 할지 몰랐거든요.
남 음, 제가 다시 가져다드릴 수 있어요. 손님을 내려드린 곳에서 만나죠.
여 그렇게 해 주시면 정말 좋죠. 대단히 고맙습니다.

|어휘| purse [명] 지갑 bring back ~을 다시 가져다주다, ~을 되돌려주다 spot [명] (특정한) 곳, 장소 drop off ~을 (탈것에서) 내려주다

08 ①

[Telephone rings.]
W Hello, AT Internet Services.
M Hi, I've been having trouble connecting to the internet all day.
W I'm sorry to hear that. Can I have your name and address?
M My name is Brian Kim, and my address is 100 Main Street.
W Let me check. *[pause]* It seems that there are some network problems in your area.
M Network problems again? I don't know why this happens so often.
W Repair work is already underway, so it should be okay within the next few hours.
M What? I couldn't work at all today. Now I have to wait even longer?
W I apologize again for the inconvenience.

[전화벨이 울린다.]

여 안녕하세요. AT 인터넷 서비스입니다.
남 안녕하세요. 온종일 인터넷 접속에 문제를 겪고 있어요.
여 유감이네요. 고객님의 성함과 주소를 알려주시겠어요?
남 제 이름은 Brian Kim이고, 주소는 Main가 100번지 Street입니다.
여 확인해 볼게요. [잠시 후] 고객님 지역에 네트워크 문제가 발생한 것 같습니다.
남 또 네크워크 문제라고요? 왜 이렇게 자주 이런 일이 일어나는지 모르겠군요.
여 수리 작업이 이미 진행 중이니, 몇 시간 내로 괜찮아질 거예요.
남 뭐라고요? 오늘 일을 전혀 못 했어요. 지금 훨씬 더 오래 기다려야 한다고요?
여 불편 드려 다시 한번 사과드립니다.

|해설| 인터넷 접속에 문제가 있는데 앞으로 몇 시간을 더 기다려야 한다는 답변을 들은 상황이므로, 남자는 짜증이 날 것임을 알 수 있다.

|어휘| have trouble v-ing ~하는 데 문제를 겪다 repair [명] 수리 underway [형] 진행 중인 apologize [동] 사과하다 inconvenience [명] 불편 **[문제]** delighted [형] 아주 기뻐하는

09 ⑤

W Look at all those boxes! Did you get a delivery?
M Yes. I got the clothes I ordered online.
W You must have ordered a lot.
M I did. Everything looked great and the prices were low, so I bought three pairs of pants and three shirts.
W I see. But why do you look so upset?
M The clothes don't look like the pictures. They're cheap and ugly.
W Really? I guess you have to be careful when you find good deals online.

여 저 상자들 좀 봐! 네가 배송받은 거니?
남 응. 온라인으로 주문한 옷을 받았어.
여 많이 주문했나 보다.
남 그랬지. 다 좋아 보이는데 가격도 싸길래, 바지 세 벌이랑 셔츠 세 장을 샀어.
여 그렇구나. 근데 왜 그렇게 속상해 보이는 거야?
남 옷이 사진과 달라. 싸구려에 볼품없어.
여 정말? 넌 온라인에서 좋은 가격의 물건을 발견했을 때 조심해야겠다.

|어휘| delivery [명] 배달(물) upset [형] 속상한 deal [명] 거래 **[문제]** relaxed [형] 느긋한 disappointed [형] 실망한

10 ⑤

M Good morning. How can I help you?
W I'm trying to decide between getting new glasses and switching to contact lenses.
M Have you ever worn contact lenses before?
W I tried them when I was a student, but they weren't comfortable.
M In that case, it's probably a better idea to continue wearing glasses.
W Okay. Can you show me some new styles?
M Sure. Here are some of our most popular frames.
W Wow! These look nice. My favorite movie actress has a similar pair.
M Why don't you try them on?
W Okay. *[pause]* Oh, they look good. I'll take them.

남 좋은 아침입니다. 무엇을 도와드릴까요?
여 새 안경을 맞추는 것과 콘택트렌즈로 바꾸는 것 사이에서 결정하려고 하고 있어요.
남 전에 콘택트렌즈를 껴보신 적이 있나요?
여 학생 때 껴보려고 했는데요, 편하지 않더라고요.
남 그렇다면 아마 계속 안경을 쓰시는 게 더 좋은 생각이겠어요.
여 알겠습니다. 새로운 안경 스타일 좀 보여 주실 수 있나요?
남 물론이죠. 여기 가장 인기 있는 안경테 몇 개가 있습니다.
여 우와! 이거 멋있어 보이네요. 제가 정말 좋아하는 영화배우가 비슷한 것을 쓰더라고요.
남 착용해보지 그러세요?
여 네. [잠시 후] 아, 좋아 보이네요. 이걸로 살게요.

|어휘| decide [동] 결정하다 switch to ~로 바꾸다 contact lense 콘택트렌즈 comfortable [형] 편한 probably [부] 아마 continue v-ing 계속 ~하다 frame [명] 안경테 similar [형] 비슷한

어휘·표현 다지기

p. 51

A

01 비슷한	02 떨어져, 떨어진 곳에
03 후회하는	04 추천하다, 제안하다
05 수리	06 불안해하는
07 아주 기뻐하는	08 편한
09 명예, 영예	10 잊다
11 결정하다	12 지갑
13 얻다, 받다	14 당황스러운
15 사과하다	16 계속 ~하다

B

01 leave	02 wait a minute

03 else
04 stay up late
05 directly
06 unfortunately
07 spot
08 switch to
09 inconvenience
10 drop off

UNIT 6 그림 상황에 적절한 대화 · 어색한 대화

주요 어휘·표현 미리보기

p. 52

01 ⓒ cool off
02 ⓑ got a perfect score
03 ⓓ wash the dishes
04 ⓔ wait in line
05 ⓕ Make sure
06 ⓐ ready to
07 ⓗ dying for
08 ⓖ scary

LISTENING PRACTICE

pp. 54-55

01 ③	02 ④	03 ①	04 ③	05 ⑤
06 ②	07 ③	08 ⑤	09 ②	

01 ③

① W Which camera do you recommend?
M That one on your right is 20% off this week.
② W My photo exhibition is next week. Would you like to come?
M Sure. I really like your photos of nature.
③ W Would you please take a picture of me?
M Sure. Go stand in front of the waterfall.
④ W Would you mind if I borrowed your phone?
M No, not at all. Here you are.
⑤ W How about going to the movies tomorrow?
M I can't. I'm going hiking in the woods.

① 여 어떤 카메라를 추천하시나요?
남 손님 오른쪽에 있는 저 카메라가 이번 주에 20% 할인됩니다.
② 여 다음 주에 제 사진전이 있어요. 와주시겠어요?
남 그럼요. 저는 당신의 자연 사진을 정말 좋아해요.
③ 여 제 사진 좀 찍어 주실래요?
남 네. 폭포 앞에 가서 서보세요.
④ 여 전화기 좀 빌릴 수 있을까요?
남 그럼요. 여기 있어요.
⑤ 여 내일 영화 보러 가는 게 어때요?
남 못 가겠어요. 저는 숲으로 하이킹을 갈 예정이에요.

|어휘| recommend [동] 추천하다 exhibition [명] 전시회, 전시 nature [명] 자연 in front of ~의 앞에 waterfall [명] 폭포 borrow [동] 빌리다 go hiking 하이킹을 가다 wood [명] 숲

02 ④

① M Can you bring me a glass of milk, Mom?
W Okay, but you need to start your homework soon.
② M I'm going to the library to study math.
W Okay. Can you return this book for me?
③ M Be careful. This tea is very hot.
W I won't drink it until it cools off.
④ M Oh, no. I spilled milk all over my textbook.
W Here! Clean it up with this towel.
⑤ M What happened? You look upset!
W I broke a glass while washing the dishes.

① 남 우유 한 잔 가져다주실 수 있어요, 엄마?
여 알았다. 하지만 곧 숙제를 시작해야 해.
② 남 저 수학 공부하러 도서관에 갈 거예요.
여 그래. 나 대신 이 책을 반납해 줄래?
③ 남 조심하세요. 이 차는 정말 뜨거워요.
여 차가 식으면 마셔야겠네.
④ 남 어이쿠, 이런. 교과서 전체에 우유를 쏟았어요.
여 여기! 이 수건으로 닦으렴.
⑤ 남 무슨 일 있었어요? 속상해 보여요!
여 설거지하다가 유리잔 하나를 깼어.

|어휘| return [동] (책을) 반납하다 cool off 식다 spill [동] 흘리다, 쏟다 textbook [명] 교과서 towel [명] 수건 upset [형] 속상한 break [동] 깨다 wash the dishes 설거지하다

03 ①

① W Do you have the time?
M Sure, I'm free now. What's up?
② W I am dying for a slice of pizza!
M That's just what I was thinking!
③ W Are there any more buses going to Seoul today?
M No. The last one just left a few minutes ago.
④ W How do you like your new middle school?
M I like it a lot. I've made many new friends.
⑤ W I've never seen such a strange film!
M I agree. I couldn't understand the story!

① 여 지금 몇 시야?
남 물론이지, 나 지금 시간 있어. 무슨 일이야?
② 여 피자 한 조각 먹고 싶어 죽겠어!
남 나도 딱 그 생각 하고 있었는데!

③ 여 오늘 서울행 버스가 더 있나요?
남 아니요. 막차가 몇 분 전에 막 떠났습니다.
④ 여 새로운 중학교는 어때?
남 아주 좋아. 새로운 친구를 많이 사귀었어.
⑤ 여 그렇게 이상한 영화는 본 적이 없어!
남 동의해. 줄거리를 이해할 수가 없었다니까!

|해설| ①의 Do you have the time?은 '지금 몇 시인가요?'라는 의미로, 현재 시각을 물어볼 때 쓰는 표현이다.

|어휘| be dying for ~하고 싶어 죽겠다 a slice of ~의 한 조각 make friends 친구를 사귀다 strange [형] 이상한 film [명] 영화

04 ③

① W We are out of milk and vegetables.
M Then let's go grocery shopping.
② W Would you like anything to drink?
M Yes, I'd like an orange juice, please.
③ W Did you bring the tickets with you?
M Yes, they're at home.
④ W I'm going to visit my sister this weekend.
M I hope you have fun together.
⑤ W How do I look in this blouse?
M You look wonderful!

① 여 우유랑 채소가 다 떨어졌어요.
남 그러면 식료품을 사러 갑시다.
② 여 마실 것 좀 드릴까요?
남 네, 오렌지 주스 주세요.
③ 여 너 표 가져 왔니?
남 응, 그건 집에 있어.
④ 여 난 이번 주말에 여동생 집을 방문할 예정이야.
남 함께 재미있게 보내길 바랄게.
⑤ 여 나 이 블라우스 입으니 어때?
남 멋져 보인다!

|어휘| be out of ~을 다 써서 떨어지다 go grocery shopping 식료품을 사러 가다 have fun 재미있게 보내다

05 ⑤

① M Can you help me fix this broken chair?
W Sure, I'd be happy to help you.
② M Did you enjoy the movie yesterday?
W Yes, I thought it was a wonderful film.
③ M Have you been waiting in line for a long time?
W No, I just arrived a few minutes ago.
④ M Let me carry that heavy chair for you.
W Oh, that's very nice of you.
⑤ M Excuse me, but is this seat taken?
W No, nobody is sitting there.

① 남 이 고장 난 의자 고치는 것을 도와줄래요?
여 그러죠, 기꺼이 도울게요.
② 남 어제 영화 좋았어요?
여 네, 훌륭한 영화라고 생각했어요.
③ 남 줄 서서 기다리신 지 오래되었나요?
여 아니요, 저 몇 분 전에 막 도착했어요.
④ 남 제가 대신 그 무거운 의자를 들어드릴게요.
여 아, 정말 친절하시네요.
⑤ 남 실례합니다만, 여기 자리 있나요?
여 아니요, 거기에 아무도 앉지 않아요.

|어휘| fix [동] 고치다 broken [형] 고장 난, 부서진 wait in line 줄 서서 기다리다 seat [명] 자리

06 ②

① M Did you see any tigers on your trip to India?
W Yes, I saw one or two in the jungle.
② M Does this zoo have any lions or tigers?
W Yes. All of our big cats are located over there.
③ M The tiger is one of Africa's most dangerous animals.
W Actually, it is only found in parts of Asia.
④ M This is going to be an excellent photograph.
W Make sure you include the little tiger in the picture.
⑤ M Look at this picture of a baby tiger!
W It's cute, but its mother looks pretty scary.

① 남 인도 여행에서 호랑이 봤어요?
여 네, 정글에서 한두 마리 봤어요.
② 남 이 동물원에 사자나 호랑이가 있나요?
여 네. 대형 고양잇과 동물은 모두 저쪽에 있습니다.
③ 남 호랑이는 아프리카에서 가장 위험한 동물 중 하나죠.
여 사실 호랑이는 아시아 일부 지역에서만 발견됩니다.
④ 남 이건 훌륭한 사진이 될 거예요.
여 사진에 반드시 저 새끼 호랑이가 나오게 찍어주세요.
⑤ 남 여기 새끼 호랑이 사진을 보세요!
여 귀엽네요, 하지만 어미 호랑이는 꽤 무서워 보여요.

|어휘| big cat (사자 · 호랑이 같은) 대형 고양잇과 동물 be located 있다, 위치하다 actually [부] 사실 make sure 반드시 ~하다 include [동] 포함하다 scary [형] 무서운

07 ③

① M Are you ready to order?

W Yes, thank you. I'd like shrimp fried rice.
② M I forgot my umbrella today.
W Here, we can share mine.
③ M You shouldn't bring such a big dog on the subway.
W I should've brought my dog.
④ M I got a perfect score on the math test.
W That's wonderful! I'm proud of you.
⑤ M What do you like to do in your free time?
W I play basketball with my friends.

① 남 주문하시겠어요?
여 네, 감사합니다. 새우볶음밥을 주문할게요.
② 남 오늘 우산 가져오는 걸 잊어버렸어요.
여 여기, 제 것을 함께 써요.
③ 남 지하철에 그렇게 큰 개를 데려오시면 안 됩니다.
여 제 개를 데려왔어야 했어요.
④ 남 저 수학 시험에서 만점 받았어요.
여 대단하다! 네가 자랑스럽구나.
⑤ 남 시간 날 때 뭐 하는 것을 좋아하니?
여 난 친구들이랑 농구를 해.

|해설| ③의 should have p.p.는 '(과거에) ~해야 했는데 (하지 않았다)'라는 의미로, 과거의 일에 대한 유감이나 후회를 나타낸다.

|어휘| be ready to-v ~할 준비가 되어 있다 shrimp [명] 새우 share [동] 함께 쓰다 perfect score 만점 be proud of ~을 자랑스러워하다 in free time 여가 시간에

08 ⑤

① W I wish I could lose weight more quickly.
M It would help if you exercised regularly.
② W I'm grateful for all the help you provided.
M We were glad to be of assistance.
③ W How was the concert you saw yesterday?
M Terrific. You should have joined us.
④ W My car has been breaking down a lot.
M Why don't you buy a new one?
⑤ W Do you know how to get to the highway?
M Yes, it was built more than 20 years ago.

① 여 살을 더 빨리 뺄 수 있다면 좋을 텐데.
남 규칙적으로 운동하면 도움이 될 거야.
② 여 여러분께서 주신 모든 도움에 대해 감사드립니다.
남 도움이 되었다니 저희가 기쁘네요.
③ 여 어제 본 콘서트 어땠어?
남 아주 좋았어. 너도 우리랑 같이 갔어야 했는데.
④ 여 내 차가 자주 고장 나고 있어.
남 새것을 사는 게 어때?
⑤ 여 고속도로에 어떻게 진입하는지 아세요?
남 네, 그것은 20년도 더 전에 지어졌어요.

|어휘| lose weight 살을 빼다 exercise [동] 운동하다 regularly [부] 규칙적으로 be grateful for ~에 감사하다 glad [형] 기쁜 assistance [명] 도움 terrific [형] 아주 좋은 break down 고장 나다 highway [명] 고속도로

09 ②

① M The traffic is terrible.
W Yeah, it's always like this during rush hour.
② M Excuse me. Do you mind if I sit here?
W Yes. The seat is empty.
③ M I'm thinking about getting a new laptop.
W Oh really? What kind are you considering?
④ M When is the deadline for this project?
W We should finish it by tomorrow.
⑤ M Do you want to go to the concert with me?
W I'm not sure. Who's performing?

① 남 교통 체증이 심하네요.
여 네, 혼잡 시간대는 항상 이래요.
② 남 실례합니다. 제가 여기 앉아도 될까요?
여 아니요. 이 자리는 비어 있어요.
③ 남 새 노트북 컴퓨터를 살까 생각 중이야.
여 오 정말? 어떤 종류를 생각하고 있어?
④ 남 이 과제는 기한이 언제야?
여 우리는 이걸 내일까지 끝내야 해.
⑤ 남 나와 콘서트에 가고 싶니?
여 모르겠어. 누가 공연해?

|해설| ②의 질문은 mind를 써서 여기 앉는 것을 꺼리는지 묻고 있으므로, Yes.라는 대답에 이어서 자리가 비어 있다고 말하는 것은 어색하다.

|어휘| traffic [명] 교통 체증 terrible [형] 심한 rush hour (출퇴근) 혼잡 시간대 empty [형] 비어 있는, 빈 laptop [명] 노트북 컴퓨터 consider [동] 고려하다 deadline [명] 기한, 마감 일자 project [명] 과제, 프로젝트 perform [동] 공연하다

어휘·표현 다지기 p. 59

A

01 고치다	02 아주 좋은
03 고려하다	04 폭포
05 식료품을 사러 가다	06 숲
07 친구를 사귀다	08 영화
09 살을 빼다	10 전시회, 전시
11 추천하다	12 고장 나다

13 하이킹을 가다
14 고속도로
15 재미있게 보내다
16 흘리다, 쏟다

B

01 upset
02 share
03 empty
04 a slice of
05 assistance
06 be grateful for
07 rush hour
08 return
09 regularly
10 nature

UNIT 7 부탁한 일

주요 어휘·표현 미리보기 p. 60

01 [g] lie down
02 [a] appreciate
03 [f] mind
04 [b] whole
05 [e] due
06 [c] seldom
07 [h] mostly
08 [d] relax

LISTENING PRACTICE pp. 62-63

01 ③	02 ④	03 ①	04 ②	05 ③
06 ①	07 ④	08 ③	09 ⑤	10 ④

01 ③

M What restaurant did you order this chicken from?
W Actually, I made it myself. Would you like some more?
M Yes, please! I can't stop eating it. It's delicious.
W Thanks. I got the recipe from my grandmother.
M Would you share it with me? I'd like to make it myself.
W I'd be happy to. I'll email it to you later.
M Thanks. I really appreciate it.

남 어느 식당에서 이 닭요리를 주문한 거야?
여 실은 내가 직접 만들었어. 더 먹을래?
남 응! 먹는 걸 멈출 수가 없네. 맛있어.
여 고마워. 할머니로부터 요리법을 받았어.
남 나에게도 그걸 공유해 주겠니? 나도 직접 만들고 싶어.
여 그렇게. 나중에 이메일로 보내줄게.
남 고마워. 정말 고마워.

|어휘| actually [부] 사실, 실은 recipe [명] 요리법, 레시피 share [동] 공유하다 email [동] 이메일을 보내다 later [부] 나중에 appreciate [동] 고마워하다

02 ④

W There's something wrong with my cell phone again.
M What happened this time?
W It deleted some of my saved phone numbers, including yours.
M You should get a new one. There are some great new models.
W I know, but they're too expensive. Can you just give me your number again?
M Sure. But you should at least get your phone repaired before it happens again.

여 내 휴대전화가 또 뭔가 잘못됐어.
남 이번에는 무슨 일이야?
여 네 번호를 포함해서 저장해 둔 전화번호 일부가 삭제됐어.
남 새 휴대전화를 사야겠네. 좋은 새 모델이 몇 개 있잖아.
여 알아, 하지만 그것들은 너무 비싸잖아. 그냥 네 번호 좀 다시 줄래?
남 그래. 하지만 그런 일이 또 생기기 전에 최소한 네 전화기를 수리 받아야겠다.

|어휘| wrong [형] 잘못된 delete [동] 삭제하다, 없애다 save [동] 저장하다 including [전] ~을 포함하여 expensive [형] 비싼 at least 적어도, 최소한 repair [동] 수리하다 happen [동] 발생하다

03 ①

M It's finally summer vacation! I'm going to relax and do nothing for a whole month.
W You'll get bored. You need to keep your brain active.
M I guess you're right. What are your plans? Are you taking a class?
W No, I'm going to relax too. But I'm also going to read some good books.
M Really? I like to read, but I seldom do.
W Why is that?
M I don't know any good authors. Do you think you could suggest a few?
W I'd be happy to. I know some perfect books for you.
M Excellent! Thanks, Michelle.

남 드디어 여름 방학이다! 한 달 내내 푹 쉬면서 아무것도 하지 않을 거야.

여 지루해질 텐데. 뇌를 계속 활성화해야 해.
남 네 말이 맞는 것 같아. 네 계획은 뭔데? 수업 들을 거야?
여 아니, 나도 푹 쉴 거야. 하지만 좋은 책도 좀 읽으려고 해.
남 정말? 나는 읽는 걸 좋아하지만, 좀처럼 안 읽어.
여 왜 그래?
남 괜찮은 작가를 모르겠어. 몇 명 추천해 줄 수 있겠니?
여 그럼. 너에게 딱 맞는 책을 몇 권 알아.
남 잘됐다! 고마워, Michelle.

|어휘| finally [부] 마침내, 드디어 summer vacation 여름 방학 relax [동] 푹 쉬다, 느긋이 쉬다 whole [형] 전체의 get bored 지루해지다 brain [명] 뇌 active [형] 활발한 plan [명] 계획 seldom [부] 좀처럼 ~ 않는 author [명] 작가 suggest [동] 추천하다, 제안하다

04 ②

W I can't believe I bought so much stuff. There were a lot of good sales.
M Wow, you have so many shopping bags! Let me carry a few for you.
W No, that's okay. They're not heavy. But can you get my cell phone? It's on the car seat.
M Sure, no problem. So, did you mostly buy clothes?
W Yes, and a pair of shoes. I'll show you everything later.
M All right. I'm looking forward to it.

여 내가 이렇게 많은 걸 샀다니 믿을 수 없네. 좋은 할인 판매 상품들이 많더라고.
남 우와, 쇼핑백이 정말 많아! 몇 개 좀 들어줄게.
여 아니, 괜찮아. 무겁지 않아. 그런데 내 휴대전화 좀 갖다줄래? 자동차 좌석에 있어.
남 물론이지. 그래, 주로 옷을 산 거니?
여 응, 그리고 신발 한 켤레도. 나중에 다 보여 줄게.
남 그래. 기대된다.

|어휘| stuff [명] 것, 물건 heavy [형] 무거운 mostly [부] 주로

05 ③

M Ellen, have you seen my glasses? I need my glasses!
W They're right there, on your desk.
M Oh! I can't find anything right now!
W Calm down, Justin. Are you all right?
M Yes. But I stayed up all night working on my report.
W Oh, that's right. It's due today. Did you finish it?
M Yes, but I still need to make copies. Would you mind doing that for me?
W Of course not. Why don't you lie down and rest for a while?
M Thank you, Ellen. That's a good idea.

남 Ellen, 내 안경 봤어요? 안경이 필요해요!
여 바로 저기, 당신 책상 위에 있잖아요.
남 아! 지금 아무것도 못 찾겠어요!
여 진정해요, Justin. 괜찮아요?
남 네. 하지만 보고서를 쓰느라 밤을 꼬박 새웠어요.
여 아, 맞네요. 오늘 마감일이죠. 끝냈나요?
남 네, 하지만 복사를 해야 해요. 나 대신 좀 해줄래요?
여 물론이죠. 누워서 잠깐 쉬는 게 어때요?
남 고마워요, Ellen. 좋은 생각이에요.

|어휘| calm down 진정하다 stay up all night 철야하다 work on ~에 노력을 들이다, 착수하다 due [형] ~하기로 되어 있는 make a copy 복사하다 mind [동] 언짢아하다, 상관하다 lie down 눕다 rest [동] 쉬다 for a while 잠시

06 ①

W We need some gas. I'm going to stop at that gas station up ahead.
M Oh, good idea. I really need to use the bathroom.
W It looks like they have a store. Could you get me a drink? I'm really thirsty.
M Sure. I'll get a snack for myself, too. Do you need some money for the gas?
W No, that's okay. You bought me lunch yesterday.
M That's right, I did. Okay, I'll be back in a few minutes.

여 휘발유가 필요해. 앞에 있는 저 주유소에서 세울게.
남 아, 좋은 생각이야. 난 꼭 화장실 가야 해.
여 상점도 있는 것 같네. 마실 것 좀 사다 줄 수 있어? 정말 목마르다.
남 물론이지. 내가 먹을 간식도 좀 사야겠다. 주유할 돈이 필요해?
여 아니, 괜찮아. 네가 어제 나한테 점심 사줬잖아.
남 맞아, 내가 그랬지. 알았어, 몇 분 후에 올게.

|어휘| gas [명] 휘발유 gas station 주유소 up ahead 그 앞쪽에 thirsty [형] 목이 마른 snack [명] 간식

07 ④

M Hanna, you took notes in yesterday's science class, didn't you?
W Of course I did. Didn't you? You didn't miss class. You sat right next to me.
M I took notes, but I lost my notebook. I think I left it on the bus.
W Oh, no! Did you check the lost and found office?

M Not yet. But can I borrow your notes for a short time? I just want to review them.

W Of course. You'll need that information for Friday's test.

남 Hanna, 어제 과학 수업시간에 필기했지?

여 당연히 했지. 넌 안 했니? 너도 수업 빠지지 않았잖아. 내 바로 옆에 앉았었고.

남 나도 필기했는데, 공책을 잃어버렸어. 버스에 그걸 두고 내린 것 같아.

여 어이쿠, 저런! 분실물 보관소 확인해 봤어?

남 아직 안 해봤어. 근데 잠시만 네 공책을 빌릴 수 있을까? 그냥 복습을 좀 할까 해서.

여 물론이지. 금요일 시험을 위해서는 그 자료가 필요할 거야.

|어휘| take notes 메모하다, 필기하다 miss [동] 놓치다, 빠지다 lost and found office 분실물 보관소 review [동] 복습하다 information [명] 정보, 자료

08 ③

M Welcome to my house, Maria! Come in!

W Thanks! What a lovely home! *[pause]* Oh! You have a dog…

M Yes. He's big, but he's very friendly. Don't be afraid.

W Sorry, but dogs make me nervous. Could you put him in the yard while I'm here?

M Oh, of course. He won't mind. He actually prefers playing in the backyard.

W I apologize. I'm sure he's well-behaved.

M It's my fault. I should have warned you about him. Anyway, have a seat!

남 우리 집에 온 걸 환영해, Maria! 들어와!

여 고마워! 정말 좋은 집이다! [잠시 후] 아! 너 개를 키우는구나…

남 응. 개가 크지만 아주 우호적이야. 겁내지 마.

여 미안하지만, 개가 있으면 내가 불안해서. 내가 여기 있는 동안 마당에 둘 수 있을까?

남 아, 물론이지. 개도 상관없을 거야. 사실 뒷마당에서 노는 것을 더 좋아해.

여 미안해. 개가 확실히 얌전하긴 하네.

남 내 잘못이야. 개에 대해서 예고했어야 했는데. 어쨌든 앉으렴!

|해설| 여자가 개가 있으면 불안하다며 개를 마당에 내보내달라고 부탁했다.

|어휘| friendly [형] 우호적인 afraid [형] 두려워하는, 겁내는 nervous [형] 불안한, 초조한 yard [명] 마당 prefer [동] 더 좋아하다 backyard [명] 뒷마당 apologize [동] 사과하다 well-behaved [형] 얌전한, 예의 바른 fault [명] 잘못, 책임 warn [동] 경고하다, 예고하다 have a seat 앉다, 착석하다

09 ⑤

M I really enjoyed listening to you sing at the party. You have such a beautiful voice.

W Thank you. Why didn't you sing along? It was fun.

M It looked fun. Unfortunately, I can't sing.

W Don't be silly. Everyone can sing!

M Yes, that's true. But I can't sing well. Can you teach me how?

W Sure, I'd be glad to give you lessons. It's easier than you think!

남 파티에서 네가 노래 부르는 것을 들어서 정말 좋았어. 목소리가 정말 아름답더라.

여 고마워. 왜 너는 따라 부르지 않았어? 재미있었는데.

남 재미있어 보였어. 안타깝지만 나는 노래를 못해서.

여 말도 안 돼. 모든 사람은 노래를 부를 수 있어!

남 응, 그렇지. 하지만 난 노래를 잘 부르지 못해. 어떻게 부르는지 가르쳐 줄 수 있니?

여 물론이지, 기꺼이 너한테 수업을 해 줄게. 생각보다 쉬워!

|어휘| voice [명] 목소리 sing along 노래를 따라 부르다 silly [형] 어리석은 true [형] 사실인 glad [형] 기꺼이 하려는

10 ④

M Do you need any help making dinner?

W No, it's just a simple meal. I'm making pasta and a salad.

M Are you making your own tomato sauce?

W No, I bought some at the store. But I can't get the jar open.

M It's because your hands are wet. Do you want a towel?

W No, but can you open the jar for me?

M Sure. I'm always happy to help you out.

남 저녁 만드는 데 도움이 필요하니?

여 아니, 그냥 간단한 식사인걸. 파스타랑 샐러드를 만들고 있어.

남 토마토소스를 직접 만들고 있는 거야?

여 아니, 가게에서 샀어. 그런데 병을 못 열겠네.

남 네 손이 젖어 있어서 그래. 수건 줄까?

여 아냐, 근데 네가 나 대신 병 좀 열어줄래?

남 그래. 널 돕는 건 항상 기뻐.

|어휘| meal [명] 식사 jar [명] (잼 등을 담는) 병 wet [형] 젖은 help out ~을 도와주다

어휘·표현 다지기

p. 67

A

01	요리법, 레시피	02	저장하다
03	삭제하다, 없애다	04	진정하다
05	어리석은	06	비싼
07	활발한	08	잘못, 책임
09	젖은	10	작가
11	지루해지다	12	복사하다
13	목이 마른	14	것, 물건
15	주유소	16	경고하다, 예고하다

B

01	miss	02	have a seat
03	friendly	04	up ahead
05	review	06	well-behaved
07	lost and found office	08	sing along
09	work on	10	help out

UNIT 8 주제/화제·직업

주요 어휘·표현 미리보기

p. 68

01	[f] depends on	02	[a] peel off
03	[g] motion	04	[b] is made of
05	[e] atmosphere	06	[h] is responsible for
07	[d] customer's needs	08	[c] overall

LISTENING PRACTICE

pp. 70-71

01 ⑤	02 ③	03 ④	04 ⑤	05 ②
06 ③	07 ②	08 ③	09 ④	10 ⑤

01 ⑤

W This is an electronic device that is popular nowadays. It looks like a smartphone, but it is larger. It has many of the same functions as a laptop. Instead of a keyboard and a mouse, however, it has a touchscreen. As it is easy to use, a lot of people own one. People like this because it is easy to carry around. It also allows them to connect wirelessly to the internet.

여 이것은 요즘 인기 있는 전자 기기입니다. 스마트폰처럼 생겼지만 더 큽니다. 이것은 노트북 컴퓨터와 같은 기능을 많이 가지고 있습니다. 하지만 키보드와 마우스 대신 터치스크린이 있습니다. 사용하기 용이하기 때문에, 많은 사람들이 이것을 가지고 있습니다. 사람들은 이것이 휴대하기 쉽기 때문에 좋아합니다. 또한 이것은 사람들이 인터넷에 무선으로 접속할 수 있게 합니다.

|어휘| electronic device 전자 기기 popular [형] 인기 있는 nowadays [부] 요즘에는 function [명] 기능 instead of ~ 대신에 own [동] 소유하다 carry around 들고 다니다, 휴대하다 allow [동] 가능하게 하다 connect [동] 연결하다, 접속하다 wirelessly [부] 무선으로

02 ③

W This is a team sport. It started in America, but it is now popular around the world. It is played on a field called a diamond. There are nine positions to play. The object of the game is to hit a white ball with a bat and then run around the bases. If a batter hits the ball over the wall on the far side of the field, it's called a home run.

여 이것은 단체 경기입니다. 미국에서 시작되었지만, 지금은 전 세계적으로 인기가 있습니다. 이것은 다이아몬드라고 불리는 경기장에서 진행됩니다. 선수의 자리는 9개입니다. 경기의 목적은 배트로 흰색 공을 치고 나서 베이스를 도는 것입니다. 타자가 공을 쳐서 경기장 먼 쪽 담을 넘기면 그것을 홈런이라고 부릅니다.

|해설| diamond, nine positions to play, to hit a white ball with a bat, base, a batter, home run 등은 야구와 관련 있는 표현이다.

|어휘| around the world 전 세계적으로 field [명] 경기장, 운동장 position [명] (팀 경기에서 선수의) 자리, 위치 object [명] 목적, 목표 hit [동] 치다, 때리다 base [명] (야구 등의) 베이스, -루 batter [명] 타자 far [형] 먼

03 ④

M This is a musical instrument in the string family. When you play it, you sit down and hold it between your legs. You also need a bow to play it. You move the bow across the strings with a smooth motion to create a sound. It is often used in classical music, and it has a deep and beautiful sound.

남 이것은 현악기류 악기입니다. 그것을 연주할 때, 앉아서 다리 사이에서 잡습니다. 또한, 이것을 연주하기 위해 활이 필요합니다. 소리를 내기 위해 부드러운 움직임으로 줄을 가로지르며 활을 움직입니다. 그것은 종종 클래식 음악에 사용되고, 깊고 아름다운 소리를 가지고 있습니다.

|어휘| musical instrument 악기 string [명] (악기의) 현[줄] hold [동] 잡다 bow [명] 활 motion [명] 움직임, 동작 create [동] 만들다

04 ⑤

W People who have this job work with animals, such as dogs, horses, birds, and dolphins. They study how animals behave and develop ways of training them. What they teach an animal depends on the owner's needs. For example, they might teach pets good behaviors and correct bad ones. Or, they might teach various tricks to animals for shows in zoos and aquariums.

여 이 직업을 가진 사람들은 개, 말, 새, 돌고래와 같은 동물들과 함께 일합니다. 그들은 동물이 어떻게 행동하는지 연구하고 그들을 훈련시키기는 방법을 개발합니다. 그들이 동물에게 가르치는 것은 주인의 요구에 달려 있습니다. 예를 들어, 그들은 반려동물에게 올바른 행동들을 가르치고 나쁜 행동들을 교정할 수도 있습니다. 아니면, 그들은 동물원과 수족관에서 쇼를 위해 동물들에게 다양한 묘기를 가르칠 수도 있습니다.

|어휘| behave [동] 행동하다 develop [동] 개발하다, 발전시키다 depend on ~에 달려 있다 need [명] 요구 correct [동] 바로잡다 trick [명] 묘기, 기술 aquarium [명] 수족관

05 ②

M People who have this job work to keep their clients safe. Their usual clients are well-known people, including singers, actors, and politicians. They stay close to their clients and escort them in their everyday life. They check their surroundings carefully to protect their clients. When something dangerous happens, they help their clients get out of the situation. To have this job, it is important to be healthy and strong, and you have to go through a lot of physical training.

남 이 직업을 가진 사람들은 의뢰인을 안전하게 지키기 위해 일합니다. 그들의 일반적인 의뢰인은 가수, 배우, 정치인을 포함한 잘 알려진 사람들입니다. 그들은 의뢰인 가까이에 머무르며 일상생활 속에서 의뢰인들을 호위합니다. 그들은 어떤 가능한 위험으로부터 의뢰인을 보호하기 위해 주변 환경을 면밀히 확인합니다. 무언가 위험한 일이 일어나면, 그들은 의뢰인이 그 상황에서 벗어날 수 있도록 돕습니다. 이 직업을 갖기 위해서는, 건강하고 힘이 센 것이 중요하고, 많은 신체 훈련을 거쳐야 합니다.

|어휘| client [명] 고객, 의뢰인 safe [형] 안전한 usual [형] 보통의, 일상의 well-known [형] 잘 알려진, 유명한 politician [명] 정치인 escort [동] 호위하다 surroundings [명] 주변 환경 go through ~을 거치다

06 ③

W This is a popular fruit that grows on trees. It is grown in many tropical countries around the world. It is usually long and yellow, and has soft, sweet white flesh inside. To eat it, you need to peel off the skin. It is a good source of vitamins and minerals. It is also great for making smoothies or baking into bread.

여 이것은 나무에서 자라는 인기 있는 과일입니다. 이것은 세계의 많은 열대 국가에서 자랍니다. 이것은 대개 길고 노랗고 안에 부드럽고 달콤한 하얀 과육을 가지고 있습니다. 이것을 먹기 위해서는 껍질을 벗겨야 합니다. 이것은 비타민과 미네랄의 좋은 공급원입니다. 이것은 또한 스무디를 만들기에 좋습니다.

|어휘| tropical [형] 열대의 flesh [명] (과일의) 과육 peel off ~을 벗기다 skin [명] 껍질 source [명] 공급원 mineral [명] 미네랄, 무기물

07 ②

M This is a tool for eating food. It has one handle and two or more points at the end of it. It is often made of metal, plastic, or wood. To use it, you just hold its handle and pick up food with its sharp points. You usually use it when you eat something like pasta or vegetables. But you don't use it for eating soup or ice cream. It is an important tool that is commonly found on dining tables around the world.

남 이것은 음식을 먹기 위한 도구입니다. 이것은 손잡이 하나와 끝에 두 개 이상의 뾰족한 끝이 있습니다. 이것은 대개 금속, 플라스틱 또는 나무로 만들어집니다. 이것을 사용하기 위해서는 손잡이를 잡고 날카롭고 뾰족한 끝으로 음식을 집으면 됩니다. 대개는 파스타나 채소 같은 것을 먹을 때 사용합니다. 하지만 수프나 아이스크림을 먹기 위해서는 사용하지 않습니다. 이것은 전 세계 식탁에서 흔히 찾아볼 수 있는 중요한 도구입니다.

|어휘| tool [명] 도구 handle [명] 손잡이 point [명] (사물의 뾰족한) 끝 be made of ~로 만들어지다 metal [명] 금속 pick up ~을 집다 sharp [형] 날카로운 commonly [부] 흔히

08 ③

W People who have this job work with airplanes. They are responsible for making sure that an airplane takes off, flies, and lands safely. Before takeoff, they check the weather and the airplane. During the flight, they communicate with air traffic control and the plane crew. They also make in-flight announcements for passengers. After landing, they do some paperwork and prepare for the next flight. Having this job requires a lot of training and experience, but it can be a very meaningful job.

여 이 직업을 가진 사람들은 비행기와 함께 일합니다. 그들은 비행기가 안전하게 이륙하고, 비행하고, 착륙하는 것을 확실히 하는 데 책임이 있습니다. 이륙 전에 그들은 날씨와 비행기를 확인합니다. 비행 중에는 항공 교통 관제소와 비행기 승무원들과 소통합니다. 그들은 또한 승객들을 위해 기내 방송을 합니다. 착륙 후에 그들은 서류 작업을 하고 다음 비행을 준비합니다. 이 직업을 갖는 것은 많은 훈련과 경험을 요구하지만, 매우 의미 있는 직업이 될 수 있습니다.

|어휘| be responsible for ~에 책임이 있다 take off 이륙하다 land [동] 착륙하다 takeoff [명] 이륙 flight [명] 비행 communicate [동] 의사소통하다 air traffic control 항공 교통 관제소 crew [명] 승무원 in-flight [형] 기내의 passenger [명] 승객 landing [명] 착륙 paperwork [명] 서류 작업 prepare for ~을 준비하다 require [동] 요구하다 meaningful [형] 의미 있는

09 ④

W People who have this job appear in special kinds of television shows. Together with one or more guests, they introduce a product to viewers during a live show. They try the product and explain its various features. They usually focus on showing its good points. They want viewers to make a phone call and purchase the product before the show ends. To do this job, people should have good public speaking skills and creative marketing strategies that attract customers.

여 이 직업을 가진 사람들은 특별한 종류의 TV 프로그램에 출연합니다. 한 명 이상의 게스트들과 함께, 그들은 생방송 프로그램 중에 시청자들에게 제품을 소개합니다. 그들은 그 제품을 써 보고 다양한 특징들을 설명합니다. 보통 그 제품의 장점을 보여주는 데 중점을 둡니다. 그들은 시청자들이 그 프로그램이 끝나기 전에 전화를 걸어 제품을 구입하기를 원합니다. 이 일을 하기 위해서, 사람들은 훌륭한 말솜씨와 고객을 끌어모으기 위한 창의적인 마케팅 전략이 있어야 합니다.

|어휘| appear [동] 출연하다 show [명] 프로그램 [동] 보여주다 introduce [동] 소개하다 product [명] 제품 viewer [명] 시청자 live [형] 생방송의 explain [동] 설명하다 feature [명] 특징 focus on ~에 집중하다 purchase [동] 구입하다 creative [형] 창의적인 strategy [명] 전략 attract [동] 끌어모으다 customer [명] 고객

10 ⑤

M People who have this job plan out indoor spaces in buildings. These spaces could be rooms in a house or larger spaces like hotel lobbies. Typically, they start by discussing the customer's needs, the budget, and the purpose of the space. Then, they decide on the overall design concept. This may include colors, materials, furniture, and even lighting. They consider every element of the space to create the atmosphere the customer wants. Their goal is to make the space both functional and beautiful.

남 이 직업을 가진 사람들은 건물 안의 실내 공간에 대해 세심히 계획을 세웁니다. 이 공간은 가정의 방일 수도 있고, 호텔 로비와 같은 더 큰 공간일 수도 있습니다. 일반적으로, 그들은 고객의 요구, 예산, 공간의 목적에 대해 논의하는 것으로 시작합니다. 그런 다음, 그들은 전체적인 디자인 콘셉트를 결정합니다. 여기에는 색상, 소재, 가구, 심지어 조명까지도 포함할 수 있습니다. 그들은 고객이 원하는 분위기를 만들어 내기 위해 공간의 모든 요소에 대해 고려합니다. 그들의 목표는 그 공간을 기능적이면서도 아름답도록 만드는 것입니다.

|어휘| indoor [형] 실내의 space [명] 공간 typically [부] 일반적으로 discuss [동] 논의하다 budget [명] 예산 overall [형] 종합적인, 전체의 material [명] 재료, 소재 lighting [명] 조명 element [명] 요소 atmosphere [명] 분위기 goal [명] 목표 functional [형] 기능적인

어휘·표현 다지기 p. 75

A

01 요소	02 무선으로
03 행동하다	04 기능
05 자리, 위치	06 열대의
07 흔히	08 이륙하다
09 출연하다	10 묘기, 기술
11 공급원	12 연결하다, 접속하다
13 요즘에는	14 치다, 때리다
15 전자 기기	16 일반적으로

B

01 surroundings	02 tool
03 own	04 go through
05 budget	06 pick up
07 in-flight	08 object
09 field	10 carry around

UNIT 9 할일·한일

주요 어휘·표현 미리보기 p. 76

01 [c] rest	02 [a] have a fever
03 [b] a big fan	04 [g] Put on
05 [h] a close game	06 [f] sign up
07 [d] absent from	08 [e] take the medicine

LISTENING PRACTICE pp. 78-79

01 ①	02 ④	03 ⑤	04 ⑤	05 ③
06 ①	07 ②	08 ③	09 ②	

01 ①

W What's that, William?
M It's an electric heater. I bought it on sale yesterday.
W Oh. Are you going to turn it on now?
M Yes. It's cold in here, isn't it?
W A little. But you're only wearing a T-shirt. Why don't you put on something warmer?
M All right. I have a sweater. I'll put it on instead.
W Great. Electric heaters use too much electricity.
M That's a good point.

여 그게 뭐야, William?
남 전열기야. 어제 할인할 때 샀어.
여 아. 지금 그걸 틀려고?
남 응. 여기 안에 춥지 않아?
여 약간. 그런데 넌 티셔츠만 입고 있잖아. 더 따뜻한 것을 입는 게 어때?
남 알았어. 나 스웨터 있는데. 그걸 대신 입어야겠다.
여 그래. 전열기는 전기를 너무 많이 소모해.
남 좋은 지적이야.

|어휘| electric heater 전열기, 전기난로 on sale 할인 중인 put on ~을 입다 electricity [명] 전기

02 ④

W What are you going to do after school?
M I'm going to buy some art supplies for a class.
W Why don't you buy them online? It's cheaper and more convenient.
M I've ordered books online before, but not art supplies. How long does it take?
W You can get your order the next day.
M That's great. Do you know any good sites?
W Yes, the website called Joe's Art Stuff is good.
M Oh, thanks. I'll do that at home after school.

여 방과 후에 뭐 할 거야?
남 수업에 필요한 미술용품 좀 살까 해.
여 온라인으로 사는 게 어때? 더 싸고 편리해.
남 전에 온라인으로 책을 주문한 적은 있지만, 미술용품은 해본 적 없어. 얼마나 걸려?
여 주문한 걸 바로 다음 날에 받을 수 있어.
남 그거 괜찮네. 좋은 사이트 아니?
여 응, Joe's Art Stuff라는 웹사이트가 괜찮아.
남 오, 고마워. 방과 후에 집에서 주문해야겠다.

|어휘| after school 방과 후에 art supplies 미술용품 cheap [형] (값이) 싼 convenient [형] 편리한

03 ⑤

M Hey, how have you been? Why were you absent from school yesterday?
W Well, do you remember that I went to the sea on Saturday?
M Of course, you said you were going swimming with Jessi.
W It was fun, but I started having a fever on Sunday.
M Oh, poor you! Did you go to the hospital yesterday?
W No, I just rested at home all day long.
M Are you feeling okay now?
W Yes, I feel much better today. Thanks.

남 안녕, 어떻게 지냈니? 어제 너 왜 학교에 결석했어?
여 그게, 토요일에 내가 바다에 갔던 거 기억하니?
남 물론이지, 너 Jessi랑 같이 수영하러 간다고 했잖아.
여 재미있었는데, 일요일에 열이 나기 시작했지.
남 저런, 안 됐다! 어제 병원에 갔니?
여 아니, 그냥 집에서 하루 종일 쉬었어.

남 지금은 괜찮은 거니?
여 그래, 오늘은 훨씬 나아. 고마워.

|어휘| be absent from ~에 결석하다 remember [동] 기억하다 have a fever 열이 나다 rest [동] 쉬다

04 ⑤

W Ryan, I heard you are a big fan of sports.
M Yes, I am. I love both playing sports and watching them on television.
W What sports do you like to play?
M I usually play soccer in my free time. I also enjoy playing basketball, tennis, and golf.
W Wow, you can play a variety of sports. That's amazing.
M Yesterday, I went to a stadium to watch a volleyball game for the first time.
W How was it? Did you enjoy it?
M It was incredible! It was a close game, so it was fun to watch.

여 Ryan, 네가 스포츠 열혈 팬이라고 들었어.
남 응, 맞아. 운동하는 거랑 텔레비전으로 보는 것 둘 다 정말 좋아해.
여 너는 어떤 운동을 하는 걸 좋아하니?
남 나는 보통 자유 시간에 축구를 해. 또 농구, 테니스, 골프도 즐겨해.
여 와, 너는 여러 가지 운동을 할 수 있구나. 대단하다.
남 어제는 처음으로 배구 경기를 보러 경기장에 갔었어.
여 어땠어? 재미있었니?
남 믿어지지 않을 정도였어! 막상막하의 경기여서, 보는 게 재미있었거든.

|어휘| big fan 열혈 팬, 골수 팬 free time 자유 시간 a variety of 여러 가지의 amazing [형] 놀라운 stadium [명] 경기장 volleyball [명] 배구 incredible [형] 믿어지지 않을 정도인 close [형] 막상막하의

05 ③

W Can you do me a favor, Martin?
M Sure. You don't look like you're feeling well.
W I'm not. So could you get me some ice cream at the supermarket?
M Oh, there's a full container in the refrigerator. Why do you want ice cream?
W My throat hurts. Eating ice cream makes it feel better.
M That's not good. You need to take some medicine. I'll get some at the pharmacy.
W No, it's okay. You don't have to.
M It's not a problem. I'll be back soon.

여 부탁 좀 들어줄래, Martin?
남 물론이지. 너 안 좋아 보여.
여 안 좋아. 그래서 그런데 슈퍼마켓에서 아이스크림 좀 사다 줄 수 있어?
남 아, 가득 들어 있는 용기가 냉장고에 있어. 왜 아이스크림을 원해?
여 목이 아파. 아이스크림을 먹으면 더 좋아지더라고.
남 그건 좋지 않아. 약을 먹어야 해. 내가 약국에서 사올게.
여 아니, 괜찮아. 그럴 필요 없어.
남 별거 아니야. 곧 돌아올게.

|어휘| do ~ a favor ~의 부탁을 들어주다 container [명] 그릇, 용기 refrigerator [명] 냉장고 throat [명] 목, 목구멍 hurt [동] 아프다 take medicine 약을 먹다 pharmacy [명] 약국

06 ①

W Hey, Ian. What do you usually do on Saturday afternoons?
M Well, I used to play soccer in the park. But it's too cold now.
W Then how about taking an art class with me?
M Oh, that sounds fun. Do you have one in mind?
W Yes, it starts next week. Today is the last day to sign up.
M Oh! Let's go sign up together right now!
W Actually, I've already signed up. And I have to go to my cello lesson now.
M Okay. Then I'll go alone. This is going to be fun.
W Yes. And we can have dinner together after our classes.
M That sounds great!

여 얘, Ian. 너 토요일 오후에는 보통 뭐 하니?
남 음, 공원에서 축구를 하곤 했어. 그런데 이젠 너무 춥네.
여 그러면 나랑 같이 미술 수업을 듣는 게 어때?
남 아, 재미있겠다. 생각하는 게 있니?
여 응, 다음 주에 시작해. 오늘이 등록하는 마지막 날이야.
남 아! 지금 당장 같이 등록하러 가자!
여 사실, 난 이미 등록했어. 그리고 지금은 첼로 수업에 가야 해.
남 알았어. 그러면 혼자 갈게. 재미있을 것 같다.
여 응. 그리고 수업이 끝나면 우리 같이 저녁을 먹을 수도 있겠다.
남 좋아!

|어휘| used to-v (과거에) ~하곤 했다, ~이었다 sign up 등록하다 already [부] 이미, 벌써 lesson [명] 수업 alone [부] 혼자서

07 ②

M How was your Christmas holiday? Did you <u>have a great time</u> with your grandparents?

W No, we couldn't visit their house.

M What happened?

W They live on Jeju Island, so we were going to <u>take a plane to get there.</u>

M Oh, I remember. You were so excited about going tangerine picking there.

W Right. But <u>due to the heavy snow,</u> all the flights were canceled during the holidays.

M No way! You must be very disappointed.

W Yes, my brother and I just played some board games at home.

M Well, at least you still had fun!

남 크리스마스 휴일 어떻게 보냈니? 조부모님과 즐거운 시간 보냈니?

여 아니, 조부모님댁을 방문하지 못했어.

남 무슨 일이 있었니?

여 제주도에 사셔서, 비행기를 타고 그곳에 갈 예정이었거든.

남 아, 기억 나. 거기에서 귤 따러 간다고 너 아주 신나했었잖아.

여 맞아. 그런데 폭설 때문에, 휴일 기간 동안 모든 항공편이 취소되었어.

남 말도 안 돼! 너 아주 실망했겠다.

여 응, 내 남동생이랑 나는 집에서 보드게임을 좀 했을 뿐이야.

남 뭐, 적어도 재미는 있었잖아!

|어휘| holiday 똉 휴일   tangerine 똉 귤   picking 똉 따기   due to ~ 때문에   cancel 똥 취소하다   isappointed 톙 실망한

08 ③

M Minji, look at this. There will be a K-pop dance contest in May.

W That's perfect for me. You know I'm a good dancer.

M Of course, I know. And the winner will <u>get a brand-new cell phone!</u>

W A cell phone? You know what? I <u>dropped my phone</u> a week ago and the screen cracked!

M Are you serious? And you weren't able to <u>get it fixed</u>?

W I went to a service center last Friday, but it was <u>too expensive to change</u> the screen.

M Oh, I see. Doesn't it cost about 200 dollars?

W Right. So I should just participate in the contest to get a new phone.

M I'm sure you can do it!

남 민지야, 이것 좀 봐. 5월에 케이팝 댄스 대회가 있을 거래.

여 그거 나한테 딱이네. 너 내가 춤 잘 추는 거 알잖아.

남 물론 알지. 그리고 우승자는 최신형 휴대전화를 받게 될 거래!

여 휴대전화라고? 그거 알아? 나 일주일 전에 내 휴대전화를 떨어뜨려서 화면에 금이 갔거든!

남 진짜로? 그리고 고치지 못한 거야?

여 지난 금요일에 수리 센터에 갔었는데, 화면을 교체하기엔 너무 비쌌어.

남 아, 그렇구나. 200달러 정도 들지 않아?

여 맞아. 그러니까 나는 새 휴대전화를 받기 위해 그 대회에 참가해야겠어.

남 너라면 분명 할 수 있을 거야!

|어휘| winner 똉 우승자, 승자   brand-new 톙 아주 새로운 drop 똥 떨어뜨리다   crack 똥 금이 가다   participate in ~에 참가하다

09 ②

W Taemin, what did you do last weekend?

M I met James to <u>discuss a trip</u> to New York this summer vacation.

W Are you going on a trip with him?

M No. James <u>is from</u> New York, so he helped me plan the trip.

W Oh, I see. Have you <u>finished planning your trip yet</u>?

M Almost. I'm going to visit an art museum, take a walk in Central Park, and go to a famous restaurant.

W Sounds great. <u>Don't forget to study</u> English before traveling.

M Of course. I'm taking an English class online these days.

여 태민아, 너 지난 주말에 뭐 했니?

남 이번 여름 방학에 갈 뉴욕 여행에 대해 의논하려고 James를 만났어.

여 걔랑 같이 여행 갈 거니?

남 아니. James가 뉴욕 출신이어서, 내가 여행 계획 짜는 걸 그 애가 도와주었어.

여 아, 그렇구나. 여행 계획 짜는 건 다 마쳤니?

남 거의. 미술관에 가고, 센트럴파크에서 산책하고, 유명 식당에 갈 거야.

여 그거 좋네. 여행 가기 전에 영어 공부하는 거 잊지 말고.

남 물론이지. 요즘 온라인으로 영어 수업 듣고 있어.

|어휘| go on a trip 여행 가다   take a class 수업을 듣다

A

01	목, 목구멍	02	편리한
03	우승자, 승자	04	수업을 듣다
05	~ 때문에	06	휴일
07	경기장	08	혼자서
09	전기	10	수업
11	자유 시간	12	약국
13	배구	14	취소하다
15	(값이) 싼	16	전열기, 전기난로

B

01	refrigerator	02	hurt
03	crack	04	brand-new
05	already	06	drop
07	disappointed	08	remember
09	container	10	do ~ a favor

UNIT 10 세부 정보 · 도표

주요 어휘·표현 미리보기 p. 84

01	ⓓ after school	02	ⓗ a trial class
03	ⓔ was sold out	04	ⓐ looking for
05	ⓒ go for	06	ⓑ make a reservation
07	ⓖ come soon	08	ⓕ looking forward to

LISTENING PRACTICE pp. 86-87

01 ④	02 ⑤	03 ④	04 ③	05 ⑤
06 ③	07 ①	08 ②	09 ④	

01 ④

W Hey, David! You love jazz, don't you?
M Yes, I absolutely do. Why do you ask?
W Well, the Seoul Jazz Festival is coming soon.
M Oh, that sounds like fun. When is it?
W It starts on June 4 and lasts for three days. Do you want to go with me?

M Yeah, I'd love to! But I'm not available on the first day.
W How about June 6?
M That day works for me.
W Let me check… Ah, the tickets for June 6 are already sold out.
M I guess we only have one option, then.
W Right. Let's buy tickets for June 5th.

여 얘, David! 너 재즈 좋아하지, 그렇지 않니?
남 응, 굉장히 좋아해. 왜 물어봐?
여 음, 서울 재즈 페스티벌이 곧 하거든.
남 오, 그거 재미있을 것 같아. 언제니?
여 6월 4일에 시작해서 3일 동안 지속돼. 나랑 같이 갈래?
남 응, 정말 그러고 싶어! 근데 나 첫날에는 시간이 없어.
여 6월 6일은 어때?
남 그날 괜찮아.
여 확인해 볼게… 아, 6월 6일 티켓은 이미 매진됐어.
남 그럼 우리에게는 하나의 선택권만 있는 것 같네.
여 맞아. 6월 5일 티켓을 사자.

|어휘| absolutely ⊕ 극도로, 굉장히 soon ⊕ 곧, 머지 않아 last ⑧ 지속되다 available ⑱ 시간이 있는 sold out 매진된 option ⑲ 선택(권)

02 ⑤

W Daniel, look at this advertisement. A newly-opened sports center is offering free trial classes.
M Sounds great. What class do you want to take?
W How about tennis? The trial class is this Thursday afternoon.
M Oh no. I have a dental appointment on Thursday.
W Umm, then we can take a golf class on Wednesday or a K-pop dance class on Friday.
M I love K-pop dances! Let's take that class. I'll show you my dancing skills.
W Okay, I look forward to it. See you on Friday!

여 Daniel, 이 광고 좀 봐. 새로 문을 연 스포츠 센터에서 무료 시범 수업을 해 준대.
남 그거 좋은데. 너는 어떤 수업 듣고 싶니?
여 테니스는 어때? 시범 수업은 이번 목요일 오후야.
남 아 이런. 목요일에는 치과 예약이 있어.
여 음, 그러면 수요일에 골프 수업을 듣거나 금요일에 케이팝 댄스 수업을 들을 수 있어.
남 나 케이팝 댄스 좋아해! 그 수업 듣자. 너에게 내 춤 실력을 보여줄게.
여 좋아, 고대하고 있을게. 금요일에 보자!

|어휘| advertisement [명] 광고 offer [동] 제공하다 trial class 시범 수업, 체험 수업 dental [형] 치과의 appointment [명] 예약, 약속 skill [명] 실력, 기술 look forward to ~을 고대하다

03 ④

M Are we going to study history together this week?
W Sure! How about tomorrow after school?
M Tomorrow is Tuesday. I have baseball practice on Tuesdays.
W Oh, I forgot that you play baseball.
M Is Thursday okay? Or do you work after school on Thursdays?
W No, it's fine. I only work on Wednesdays and Fridays.
M Great. I'll see you at the library.

남 우리 이번 주에 같이 역사 공부하는 거지?
여 물론이지! 내일 방과 후 어때?
남 내일 화요일이네. 나 화요일마다 야구 연습이 있어.
여 아, 네가 야구를 하는 것을 깜박했어.
남 목요일은 괜찮아? 아니면 목요일마다 방과 후에 일하니?
여 아니, 목요일 괜찮아. 나 수요일과 금요일에만 일해.
남 좋아. 도서관에서 보자.

|해설| 남자가 목요일에 보는 것을 제안하자 여자도 좋다고 했다.

|어휘| after school 방과 후에 practice [명] 연습

04 ③

[Cell phone rings.]
W Hello, this is Best Campers. How can I help you?
M Hi, I'd like to make a reservation for a campsite for next Saturday, July 5.
W Let me check. *[pause]* Sorry, we're fully booked on that day.
M How about July 4? I want to stay for one night.
W We have a few sites available on July 4. Would you like a tent camping site or a glamping one?
M This is our first time camping, so using a tent would be very challenging.
W Then glamping will be a better option. Do you need us to order any firewood?
M No, we'll bring our own supplies. Thanks.
W Okay, you're all set! See you next weekend.

[휴대전화벨이 울린다.]
여 안녕하세요, Best Campers입니다. 무엇을 도와드릴까요?
남 안녕하세요, 다음 주 토요일 7월 5일에 캠핑장을 예약하고 싶어요.
여 확인해 볼게요. [잠시 후] 죄송하지만, 그날은 예약이 꽉 찼어요.
남 7월 4일은 어떤가요? 하룻밤 머무르고 싶은데요.
여 7월 4일에는 이용 가능한 장소가 몇 군데 있네요. 텐트 캠핑하는 장소를 원하세요, 아니면 글램핑 장소를 원하세요?
남 이번이 첫 캠핑이라서요, 텐트를 이용하는 건 아주 어려울 것 같네요.
여 그러면 글램핑이 나은 선택일 겁니다. 저희가 장작을 주문해드려야 하나요?
남 아니요, 저희가 가지고 있는 걸 들고 갈게요. 감사합니다.
여 좋아요, 모두 다 됐습니다! 다음 주말에 뵐게요.

|어휘| make a reservation 예약하다 campsite [명] 캠핑장, 야영지 challenging [형] 어려운, 도전적인 firewood [명] 장작 supply [명] 비품, 준비물

05 ⑤

W Hi, how can I help you?
M Hello, I'd like to order some cupcakes for my party.
W How many cupcakes do you need? You can order them in a set of six.
M I need twelve cupcakes. What flavors do you have?
W You can choose chocolate or vanilla.
M Can I get half of them chocolate and half of them vanilla?
W Sure. Would you like any toppings on the cupcakes?
M No, I don't want any toppings.
W Okay. Thank you for your order.

여 안녕하세요, 무엇을 도와드릴까요?
남 안녕하세요, 파티를 위해 컵케이크를 좀 주문하고 싶은데요.
여 컵케이크가 몇 개 필요하세요? 6개 세트로 주문하실 수 있어요.
남 컵케이크 12개가 필요해요. 맛은 어떤 게 있나요?
여 초콜릿이나 바닐라 중에 고르실 수 있어요.
남 반은 초콜릿으로 반은 바닐라로 살 수 있나요?
여 물론이죠. 컵케이크 위에 토핑 원하시나요?
남 아니요. 토핑은 원하지 않아요.
여 알겠습니다. 주문 감사합니다.

|어휘| flavor [명] 맛 half [명] 절반 topping (음식 위에 얹는) 고명, 토핑 [문제] quantity [명] 양, 수량

06 ③

[Cell phone rings.]
M Hello?
W Hello. This is Galaxy Furniture Delivery Center. I'm calling for Mr. Brown.
M Speaking.

W Your bookcase order is ready now. Will you be home on April 10?
M April 10? Well, I'm not sure about my schedule that day. How about April 12 or 14?
W Wait a moment, please. *[pause]* We have a delivery slot available in the afternoon on April 12. Does that work for you?
M Yes, that's perfect. Thank you very much.

[휴대전화벨이 울린다.]
남 여보세요?
여 안녕하세요. Galaxy 가구 배달 센터입니다. Brown 씨에게 전화했어요.
남 접니다.
여 책장 주문이 이제 준비되었어요. 4월 10일에 댁에 계실까요?
남 4월 10일이요? 음, 그날 일정은 확실하지가 않아서요. 4월 12일이나 14일은 어떠세요?
여 잠시만 기다려 주세요. [잠시 후] 4월 12일 오후에 가능한 배달 시간이 있어요. 가능하세요?
남 네, 딱 좋아요. 감사합니다.

|어휘| delivery [명] 배달 bookcase [명] 책장 slot [명] 시간, 틈

07 ①

M Honey, how about taking a tourist train this weekend?
W A tourist train? Sounds interesting.
M We can choose our destination: the ocean or a mountain valley.
W I prefer the sea to the mountains. It'll be really amazing to travel along the coast.
M Absolutely. The Ocean Train runs twice a day, at 9:00 a.m. and 11:00 a.m.
W Is there a price difference?
M No, the price is the same: $50. There are two of us, so we have to pay $100 total.
W Let's leave and come back early.
M Yes, that sounds good to me. Let's make a reservation now.

남 여보, 이번 주말에 관광 열차를 타는 게 어때요?
여 관광 열차요? 재미있을 것 같네요.
남 우리는 목적지를 바다와 산속 계곡 중에서 고를 수 있어요.
여 난 산보다 바다가 더 좋아요. 해안을 따라 여행하면 정말 멋질 거예요.
남 그럼요. 바다 열차는 오전 9시와 11시, 하루에 두 번 운행해요.
여 가격 차이가 있나요?
남 아니요, 가격은 50달러로 동일해요. 우리는 두 명이니까, 총 100달러를 내야 해요.
여 일찍 떠났다가 돌아옵시다.
남 네, 그게 좋겠네요. 지금 예약합시다.

|어휘| destination [명] 목적지 ocean [명] 대양, 바다 valley [명] 계곡, 골짜기 prefer [동] 더 좋아하다 along [전] ~을 따라 coast [명] 해안 run [동] 운행하다 difference [명] 차이 **[문제]** departure [명] 출발

08 ②

W Steve, can you help me choose a new laptop?
M Sure. What is your budget?
W I'm saving money, and I'll have $1,500 to spend by next month.
M Okay, so your budget is $1,500. What will the laptop be mainly for?
W I'm planning to carry it around with me so I can do my homework.
M Then it shouldn't be too heavy. Hmm... A weight from 1 kg to 1.5 kg would be great.
W How about the screen size? Lightweight means a small-sized screen, doesn't it?
M Usually. But you can still get one with a 13-inch screen or with a 15-inch screen. The bigger one costs more, though.
W I think a 13-inch screen is fine. This one looks good! I'll buy it.

여 Steve, 내가 새 노트북 컴퓨터 고르는 거 도와줄 수 있니?
남 물론이지. 예산이 얼마인데?
여 지금 돈을 모으고 있고, 다음 달이면 쓸 수 있는 돈이 1,500달러일 거야.
남 좋아, 그러면 예산이 1,500달러구나. 노트북 컴퓨터는 주로 뭐 하는데 쓸 거야?
여 숙제할 수 있게 들고 다니려고 계획하고 있어.
남 그럼 너무 무거우면 안 되겠다. 음… 1kg에서 1.5kg 사이 무게가 좋을 것 같네.
여 화면 사이즈는 어때? 무게가 가볍다는 건 작은 사이즈의 화면이란 의미잖아, 그렇지 않니?
남 보통은. 하지만 13인치 화면이거나 15인치 화면인 걸 사도 돼. 하지만 더 큰 게 비용이 더 많이 들지.
여 13인치 화면이 좋을 것 같아. 이거 좋아 보이네! 이거 살래.

|어휘| budget [명] 예산 mainly [부] 주로 lightweight [명] 가벼움

09 ④

W Dad, I'm looking for key rings for my friends. Any

ideas?

M These animal-shaped ones look nice. Puppy-shaped or bunny-shaped ones should be a hit among girls.

W We were all born in the year of the rabbit, so I'll go for the bunny-shaped ones.

M Oh, good thinking. What about the color?

W Well, we used to love pink, but not anymore. Everybody will like the white ones, though.

M Okay. And you need to choose the size, too.

W I think small ones are better than big ones. They're easier to carry.

M I agree. Then let's order the small ones.

여 아빠, 저 친구들을 위한 열쇠고리를 찾고 있어요. 좋은 생각 있으세요?

남 이 동물 모양 열쇠고리들이 좋아 보이네. 강아지 모양이나 토끼 모양의 것들이 여자 아이들 사이에서 인기가 좋을 거야.

여 저희 모두 토끼해에 태어났으니까, 토끼 모양을 택할래요.

남 오, 좋은 생각이다. 색상은 어떻게 할래?

여 음, 우리는 핑크를 좋아했지만, 더 이상 아니에요. 하지만 모두 흰색 열쇠고리를 좋아할 거예요.

남 그래. 그리고 사이즈도 골라야 해.

여 저는 작은 것이 큰 것보다 나은 것 같아요. 가지고 다니기 더 쉬우니까요.

남 나도 그렇게 생각해. 그럼 작은 걸로 주문하자.

|어휘| look for ~을 찾다   be a hit 인기를 얻다, 히트를 치다 go for ~을 택하다

어휘·표현 다지기   p. 91

A

01 선택(권)   **02** 극도로, 굉장히
03 배달   **04** 캠핑장, 야영지
05 시간, 틈   **06** 가벼움
07 출발   **08** 계곡, 골짜기
09 맛   **10** 인기를 얻다, 히트를 치다
11 제공하다   **12** 실력, 기술
13 차이   **14** 어려운, 도전적인
15 연습   **16** 비품, 준비물

B

01 advertisement   **02** bookcase
03 firewood   **04** destination
05 half   **06** mainly
07 run   **08** prefer
09 coast   **10** quantity

주요 어휘·표현 미리보기   p. 92

01 ⓓ come in   **02** ⓔ motion sickness
03 ⓖ delayed   **04** ⓐ In fact
05 ⓕ out of stock   **06** ⓑ for dessert
07 ⓗ lately   **08** ⓒ gave me a ride

LISTENING PRACTICE   pp. 94-95

| **01** ③ | **02** ④ | **03** ④ | **04** ⑤ | **05** ⑤ |
| **06** ③ | **07** ① | **08** ② | | |

01 ③

W Good afternoon. How can I help you?

M Hello, I'm looking for a chair for my seven-year-old daughter.

W Okay. How about this pink one? It's one of the best-selling products in the store.

M I love its design, but do you have it in any other colors?

W It also comes in green, brown, and white.

M Then I'll take the white one. How much is it?

W It's $50. Do you want it to be delivered?

M No, I'll take it with me.

① It's on sale now.
② I'll pay by credit card.
④ Sure. When can I pick up my item?
⑤ Sorry, but we don't have a delivery service.

여 안녕하세요. 무엇을 도와드릴까요?

남 안녕하세요. 7살짜리 제 딸을 위한 의자를 찾고 있어요.

여 알겠습니다. 이 분홍색 의자는 어떠세요? 저희 가게에서 가장 많이 팔리는 제품 중 하나예요.

남 디자인은 마음에 드는데요, 다른 색상도 있나요?

여 초록색, 갈색, 그리고 흰색으로도 나와요.

남 그러면 흰색으로 할게요. 얼마죠?

여 50달러입니다. 배달받길 원하시나요?

남 아니요, 제가 가지고 갈게요.

① 지금 할인 판매 중입니다.
② 신용카드로 결제할게요.
④ 물론이죠. 언제 제 물건을 찾으러 오면 되나요?

⑤ 죄송하지만, 저희는 배달 서비스가 없습니다.

|어휘| best-selling [형] 가장 많이 팔리는 product [명] 제품 come in (상품 등이) 출시되다 deliver [동] 배달하다 [문제] credit card 신용카드

02 ④

M I heard that you're going to move to a new house soon.

W Right. I'm trying to organize my things, but there's one problem.

M What is it?

W I have so many things that I don't use anymore. But most of them are almost new, so I don't want to just throw them away.

M Here's a solution: Why don't you donate them to the nearby shelter?

W Are they taking donations?

M You should call the shelter first. They will let you know what they need.

W Oh, I see. Do you know their phone number?

M Wait a moment. I'll look it up on my phone.

① No, they don't have a website.
② You can call me anytime you want.
③ I can't believe you don't know my number.
⑤ No problem. I can help you move your items.

남 네가 곧 새집으로 이사한다고 들었어.

여 맞아. 물건을 정리하려고 하고 있는데, 한 가지 문제가 있어.

남 뭔데?

여 더 이상 사용하지 않는 것들이 정말 많이 있거든. 하지만 그것들 대부분이 거의 새것이라서, 그냥 버리고 싶지 않아.

남 해결책이 있어. 근처 쉼터에 기부하지 그래?

여 그들이 기부를 받니?

남 먼저 쉼터에 전화해야 해. 그들이 뭐가 필요한지 알려줄 거야.

여 아, 그렇구나. 전화번호 아니?

남 잠시만. 내 전화기에서 찾아볼게.

① 아니, 웹사이트는 없어.
② 네가 원할 때 언제든 내게 전화해도 돼.
③ 네가 내 번호를 모른다니 믿을 수가 없어.
⑤ 문제없어. 내가 네 물건 옮기는 걸 도와줄게.

|어휘| organize [동] 정리하다 throw away ~을 버리다 solution [명] 해결책 donate [동] 기부하다 nearby [형] 인근의, 가까운 곳의 shelter [명] 보호소, 쉼터 donation [명] 기부 [문제] look up ~을 찾아보다

03 ④

M Have you started your report for English class yet?

W Yes. In fact, I'm almost finished.

M Wow, you must have worked really hard!

W I guess so. English is my favorite subject, so it was kind of fun for me.

M That's good. And how long will it be when it's finished?

W It'll be about six pages long.

M I thought it only had to be three or four pages. That's too long!

W I think it's better if it's longer.

① I'd better start soon.
② Six hours is a lot of time.
③ I have lots of things to do.
⑤ But it's not for my English class.

남 영어 수업 보고서를 벌써 시작했니?

여 응. 사실은 거의 끝냈어.

남 와, 너 정말 열심히 했나 보다!

여 그런 셈이지. 영어는 내가 제일 좋아하는 과목이어서, 나한테는 약간 재미있었어.

남 잘됐네. 끝나면 분량이 얼마나 될 것 같아?

여 여섯 쪽 정도 될 거야.

남 난 서너 쪽만 되어야 한다고 생각했어. 그건 너무 긴데!

여 난 더 길면 더 좋다고 생각해.

① 난 곧 시작하는 게 좋겠어.
② 6시간은 많은 시간이야.
③ 난 할 일이 많아.
⑤ 하지만 그것은 내 영어 수업을 위한 것이 아니야.

|어휘| in fact 사실은 almost [부] 거의 hard [부] 열심히 kind of 약간, 어느 정도

04 ⑤

M Did you like the dinner?

W Yes, thank you. But I think I ate too much.

M Would you like a kiwi for dessert? They're really good.

W No, thanks. I'm so full.

M Oh, I see. Then maybe you can have one later.

W Actually, I think I have to go now.

M Can't you stay one more hour? My dad will give you a ride when he gets home.

W Thanks, but my brother is waiting for me.

① Sorry, I don't like fruit.

② I think I missed the last bus.
③ How can I get to the station?
④ It takes thirty minutes by subway.

남 저녁 괜찮았어?
여 응, 고마워. 근데 나 너무 많이 먹은 것 같아.
남 후식으로 키위 먹을래? 정말 맛있어.
여 아니, 괜찮아. 아주 배불러.
남 아, 그래. 그러면 이따 먹으면 되겠다.
여 실은 나 지금 가야 할 것 같아.
남 한 시간 더 있으면 안 돼? 우리 아빠가 집에 오시면 널 태워주실 거야.
여 고맙지만, 우리 오빠가 나를 기다리고 있어.

① 미안하지만, 난 과일을 안 좋아해.
② 내 생각에는 막차를 놓친 것 같아.
③ 역까지 어떻게 가야 하지?
④ 지하철로 30분 걸려.

|어휘| for dessert 후식으로 full [형] 배부른 stay [동] 있다, 머물다 give ~ a ride ~을 차로 태워주다 get home 집에 도착하다 **[문제]** miss [동] 놓치다 station [명] 역 wait for ~을 기다리다

05 ⑤

[Telephone rings.]
M Thank you for calling Riverside Bookstore. How can I help you?
W Hello. I ordered a book about a week ago, but it hasn't been delivered yet.
M I see. Can you tell me the order number? I'll check on it for you.
W Okay. It's SQ14732.
M Let me see. *[pause]* Oh, I'm really sorry. Your delivery has been delayed.
W Really? What's the problem?
M I'm afraid the book is temporarily out of stock.

① I can't seem to find your information.
② It was delivered to your home yesterday.
③ The book is very interesting and easy.
④ You must return the book in two weeks.

[전화벨이 울린다.]
남 Riverside 서점에 전화 주셔서 감사합니다. 무엇을 도와드릴까요?
여 안녕하세요. 제가 일주일 전에 책 한 권을 주문했는데, 아직 배송되지 않아서요.
남 알겠습니다. 주문 번호를 말씀해주시겠어요? 확인해 드리겠습니다.
여 네. SQ14732입니다.
남 확인해 보겠습니다. [잠시 후] 아, 정말 죄송합니다. 배송이 지연되었네요.
여 정말요? 뭐가 문제인가요?
남 유감스럽게도 그 책이 일시 품절 상태입니다.

① 고객님의 정보를 찾을 수 없는 듯하네요.
② 어제 고객님 댁으로 배송되었습니다.
③ 그 책은 아주 재미있고 쉽습니다.
④ 고객님께서는 그 책을 2주 안에 반납하셔야 합니다.

|어휘| delay [동] 지연시키다 **[문제]** information [명] 정보 return [동] 반납하다 temporarily [부] 일시적으로 out of stock 품절된, 재고가 없는

06 ③

W Hi, Patrick. Are you excited about the World Cup finals tomorrow?
M Of course. I can't believe our national team advanced to the finals! I'm sure they'll win. They've been playing very well lately.
W I agree. They have a good chance of winning even though they're playing Brazil.
M Where are you going to watch the game?
W At Seoul Plaza with some friends. How about you?
M I'm going to watch it at my house with my family.

① I was too busy studying to watch the game.
② I think Brazil has a better chance of winning.
④ I saw a soccer game with my classmates last year.
⑤ If I were you, I'd take the subway to City Hall station.

여 안녕, Patrick. 내일 월드컵 결승전 때문에 신나니?
남 물론이지. 우리 국가대표팀이 결승전에 진출한 게 믿기지 않아! 우리 팀이 분명 이길 거야. 최근에 경기를 아주 잘하고 있어.
여 동의해. 브라질과 겨루긴 해도 우리가 이길 충분한 가능성이 있어.
남 넌 어디서 경기를 볼 거야?
여 친구들 몇 명이랑 서울 광장에서. 넌?
남 집에서 가족과 함께 볼 거야.

① 공부하느라 너무 바빠서 경기를 못 봤어.
② 내 생각에는 브라질이 우승할 가능성이 더 높은 것 같아.
④ 난 작년에 반 친구들이랑 축구 경기를 봤어.
⑤ 내가 너라면, 지하철을 타고 시청역으로 갈 텐데.

|어휘| be excited about ~에 신이 나다 final [명] 결승전 national [형] 국가의 advance to ~에 진출하다 lately [부] 최근에 agree [동] 동의하다 chance [명] 가능성 **[문제]** classmate [명] 반 친구

07 ①

M Emily, don't forget that we're going to Busan next weekend!

W Of course I won't! I've never been to Busan, so I'm very excited.

M Me too. Do you want to go by car or train?

W I prefer going by train. I get motion sickness in cars.

M I see. Let's check the train schedule. *[pause]* There are trains leaving at eleven and two.

W The eleven o'clock train would be better. We can have lunch after arriving in Busan.

M That's a good idea. Do you have a seat preference?

W I'd like to sit by a window.

② The ticket price is 25,000 won.
③ Let me bring some snacks for you.
④ It will take two hours to get there.
⑤ I didn't know that you had motion sickness.

남 Emily, 다음 주말에 우리 부산 가는 거 잊지 마!

여 물론 잊지 않을 거야! 부산에 가본 적이 없어서 나 엄청 신나.

남 나도 그래. 너는 차로 가고 싶니 아니면 기차로 가고 싶니?

여 나는 기차로 가는 걸 더 좋아해. 차에서는 멀미를 하거든.

남 그렇구나. 열차 시간표를 확인해 보자. [잠시 후] 11시와 2시에 출발하는 기차가 있어.

여 11시 기차가 나을 것 같아. 부산에 도착한 후에 점심을 먹을 수 있어.

남 좋은 생각이야. 너는 선호하는 좌석이 있니?

여 나는 창가에 앉고 싶어.

② 티켓 가격은 2만 5천 원이야.
③ 내가 너를 위해 간식을 좀 가져올게.
④ 거기 도착하는 데 두 시간이 걸릴 거야.
⑤ 난 네가 멀미하는지 몰랐어.

|어휘| prefer [동] 더 좋아하다 motion sickness 멀미 preference [명] 선호(하는 것)

08 ②

M Christina, what's up? Why are you so busy these days?

W Well, I recently started working part-time.

M I didn't know that. Where are you working?

W I work at a Mexican restaurant in a shopping mall.

M Isn't that really tiring?

W A little bit. But I'm enjoying my work because I can have lots of Mexican food. It's really delicious.

M To be honest, I've never tried Mexican food before.

W Why don't you visit the restaurant while I'm working? I can recommend some dishes for you to try.

M Sounds great! When should I visit the restaurant?

W I work every Wednesday and Saturday.

① You can make a reservation online.
③ My favorite Mexican food is beef fajitas.
④ Why don't we cook Italian food instead?
⑤ The restaurant is located on the second floor.

남 Christina, 잘 지내니? 너 요새 왜 그렇게 바쁘니?

여 그게, 최근에 아르바이트 일을 시작했거든.

남 그건 몰랐네. 어디서 일해?

여 쇼핑몰 안에 있는 멕시코 음식점에서 일해.

남 일이 아주 피곤하지는 않니?

여 조금. 하지만 멕시코 음식을 많이 먹을 수 있어서 즐겁게 일하고 있어. 정말 맛있거든.

남 솔직히 말하면, 나는 멕시코 음식 한 번도 먹어본 적이 없어.

여 내가 일하고 있을 때 식당에 오는 거 어때? 네가 먹어볼 몇 가지 음식을 추천해줄 수 있어.

남 좋아! 내가 언제 식당을 방문해야 되니?

여 나는 수요일과 토요일마다 일해.

① 온라인으로 예약을 할 수 있어.
③ 내가 가장 좋아하는 멕시코 음식은 소고기 파히타야.
④ 대신 이탈리아 음식을 요리하는 게 어때?
⑤ 식당은 2층에 위치해 있어.

|어휘| recently [부] 최근에 tiring [형] 피곤하게 만드는 to be honest 솔직히 말하면 recommend [동] 추천하다 dish [명] 요리
[문제] be located 위치하다

어휘·표현 다지기 p. 99

A

01 정리하다	02 보호소, 쉼터
03 해결책	04 배부른
05 피곤하게 만드는	06 신용카드
07 동의하다	08 거의
09 열심히	10 역
11 가능성	12 ~을 기다리다
13 국가의	14 ~을 찾아보다
15 있다, 머물다	16 ~을 버리다

B

01 donate	02 nearby
03 temporarily	04 preference

05 final
06 best-selling
07 advance to
08 be excited about
09 recently
10 to be honest

UNIT 12 상황에 적절한 말

주요 어휘·표현 미리보기 p. 100

01 ⓔ make a plan
02 ⓓ have an idea
03 ⓗ take part in
04 ⓐ Not long after
05 ⓒ look back on
06 ⓖ get off
07 ⓕ dozed off
08 ⓑ encouraged

LISTENING PRACTICE pp. 102-103

01 ③	02 ③	03 ②	04 ④	05 ②
06 ⑤	07 ①	08 ⑤	09 ③	

01 ③

W Peter is sitting on a subway train to go to school. Yesterday, he was working on his homework until late at night. Feeling tired, he soon dozes off. After some time, he suddenly wakes up. He looks around, but he has no idea where he is. So he decides to ask the woman sitting next to him if she knows what the next station is. In this situation, what would Peter most likely say to the woman?

Peter Could you tell me what the next station is?

① May I sit here?
② Which station are you getting off at?
④ How long does it take to go to school by subway?
⑤ Can you give me a wake-up call tomorrow morning?

여 Peter는 학교에 가기 위해 지하철에 앉아 있다. 어제, 그는 늦은 밤까지 숙제를 하고 있었다. 피곤함을 느끼며, 그는 곧 잠이 든다. 시간이 조금 지난 후, 그는 갑자기 잠에서 깬다. 주위를 둘러보지만, 자신이 어디에 있는지 알 수가 없다. 그래서 그는 옆에 앉아 있는 여자에게 다음 역이 어디인지 아는지 묻기로 결심한다. 이 상황에서, Peter는 여자에게 뭐라고 말할까?

Peter 다음 역이 어디인지 말씀해 주실 수 있나요?

① 제가 여기 앉아도 될까요?
② 무슨 역에서 내리세요?
④ 학교까지 가는 데 지하철로 얼마나 걸리나요?
⑤ 내일 아침에 저에게 모닝콜을 해 주실 수 있나요?

|어휘| homework [명] 숙제 doze off 잠이 들다, 졸다 suddenly [부] 갑자기 situation [명] 상황 **[문제]** get off (탈것에서) 내리다

02 ③

W Mr. Wilson is a figure skating coach at Woori Middle School. Mina, one of his students, is taking part in the national competition for figure skating. She is a good figure skater, but she makes lots of mistakes during her performance and fails to win any prizes. Mina is very disappointed with the results. Mr. Wilson wants to encourage her by telling her that her performance will be better next time. In this situation, what would Mr. Wilson most likely say to Mina?

Mr. Wilson Mina, I'm sure you will do better next time.

① you should have practiced more.
② don't be afraid of making mistakes.
④ how about trying a new skating technique?
⑤ why don't you go skating with me tomorrow?

여 Wilson 선생님은 우리 중학교의 피겨스케이팅 코치이다. 그의 학생 중 한 명인 미나는 피겨스케이팅 전국 대회에 참가하고 있다. 그녀는 훌륭한 피겨스케이팅 선수이지만, 연기 중에 많은 실수를 하고 아무 상도 타지 못한다. 미나는 결과에 매우 실망한다. Wilson 선생님은 다음번에 그녀의 연기가 더 좋을 것이라고 말해서 그녀를 격려하고 싶다. 이 상황에서, Wilson 선생님은 미나에게 뭐라고 말할까?

Wilson 선생님 미나야, 나는 네가 다음번에 더 잘할 거라고 확신해.

① 너는 더 연습했어야 했어.
② 실수하는 것을 두려워하지 마.
④ 새로운 스케이팅 기술을 시도해보는 게 어떠니?
⑤ 내일 나와 스케이트 타러 가지 않을래?

|어휘| take part in ~에 참가하다 national [형] 전국적인, 국가의 competition [명] 대회 fail to-v ~하지 못하다 win a prize 상을 타다 be disappointed with ~에 실망하다 result [명] 결과 encourage [동] 격려하다, 용기를 북돋우다

03 ②

M Daniel plans to go to the sea tomorrow with his friend Colin. Daniel is an experienced surfer, and he will teach Colin how to surf. He checks to make sure he has all the items he will need. Now he thinks that he is fully prepared. While looking back on his last time surfing, he remembers that he got a terrible sunburn. So, he decides to call Colin to suggest that he apply sunscreen. In this situation, what would Daniel most likely say to Colin?

Daniel Colin, don't forget to put on sunscreen.

① how about learning first aid?
③ let's go surfing early in the morning.
④ the sun won't come out tomorrow.
⑤ why don't you wear a long-sleeved swimsuit?

남 Daniel은 친구인 Colin과 내일 바다에 갈 계획이다. Daniel은 숙련된 서퍼이고, Colin에게 서핑하는 법을 가르칠 것이다. 그는 필요할 모든 물품들이 있는지 확실히 하기 위해 확인한다. 이제 그는 충분히 준비되었다고 생각한다. 그는 마지막 서핑을 되짚어보다가, 햇볕에 심하게 탔다는 것이 기억난다. 그래서 그는 Colin에게 전화해서 자외선 차단제를 바르라고 제안하기로 결심한다. 이 상황에서, Daniel은 Colin에게 뭐라고 말할까?

Daniel Colin, 자외선 차단제 바르는 거 잊지 마.

① 응급처치를 배우는 게 어때?
③ 아침 일찍 서핑하러 가자.
④ 내일 해가 안 날 거야.
⑤ 긴 소매 수영복을 입는 게 어때?

|어휘| experienced 혱 숙련된, 경험이 많은   surfer 몡 서퍼, 파도타기를 하는 사람   surf 동 파도타기[서핑]를 하다   fully 児 충분히, 완전히   look back on ~을 되돌아보다   sunburn 몡 햇볕에 탐 [문제] first aid 응급처치   long-sleeved 혱 긴 소매의

04   ④

M Alice and Irene have been good friends since they were young. They trust each other, and there are no secrets between them. One day, Alice finds out that Irene told Alice's secret to their other friends. Alice is very annoyed. She doesn't want to end their friendship, but she worries it might happen again. So Alice wants to tell Irene never to talk about her secrets with others again. In this situation, what would Alice most likely say to Irene?

Alice Irene, don't share my secrets with anyone else again.

① I'm glad to be your friend.
② you should not lie to me.
③ why don't you stop talking for a while?
⑤ I can help you if you want to make new friends.

남 Alice와 Irene은 어릴 때부터 좋은 친구였다. 그들은 서로를 믿고,

그들 사이에는 비밀이 없다. 어느 날, Alice는 Irene이 Alice의 비밀을 다른 친구들에게 이야기했다는 것을 알게 된다. Alice는 아주 짜증이 난다. 친구 관계를 끝내고 싶지는 않지만, 이런 일이 다시 일어날지도 모른다는 것이 걱정이다. 그래서 Alice는 Irene에게 자신의 비밀을 다른 사람들과 절대 다시는 얘기하지 말라고 말하고 싶다. 이 상황에서, Alice는 Irene에게 뭐라고 말할까?

Alice Irene, 내 비밀을 다른 사람들과 다시는 공유하지 마.

① 네 친구여서 기뻐.
② 나에게 거짓말하면 안 돼.
③ 잠시만 말하는 걸 멈추는 게 어때?
⑤ 네가 새 친구를 사귀고 싶다면 내가 도와줄 수 있어.

|어휘| trust 동 신뢰하다   secret 몡 비밀   find out ~을 알게 되다   annoyed 혱 짜증이 난   friendship 몡 우정   worry 동 걱정하다   happen 동 일어나다, 발생하다   [문제] lie 동 거짓말하다 make a friend 친구를 사귀다

05   ②

W Ryan and his little brother are going to visit their grandfather. He lives in another city, so they will take the train there. When Ryan gets to the train station, his brother has an idea. There is a famous bakery near the train station that makes delicious apple pies. Their grandfather loves apple pie. So his brother suggests getting one for their grandfather. However, their train is leaving in five minutes. In this situation, what would Ryan most likely say to his brother?

Ryan There isn't enough time to do that.

① We can eat the pie on the train.
③ I think that is an excellent idea.
④ Why don't we bake one ourselves?
⑤ We need to visit our grandfather first.

여 Ryan과 그의 남동생은 할아버지 댁을 방문할 예정이다. 할아버지가 다른 도시에 살고 계셔서, 그들은 그곳에 기차를 타고 갈 것이다. Ryan이 기차역에 도착했을 때, 동생에게 좋은 생각이 난다. 기차역 부근에 맛있는 사과 파이를 만드는 유명 제과점이 있다. 할아버지는 사과 파이를 아주 좋아하신다. 그래서 동생은 할아버지를 위해 사과 파이 하나를 사 가자고 제안한다. 하지만 그들이 탈 기차가 5분 후에 떠날 것이다. 이 상황에서, Ryan은 남동생에게 뭐라고 말할까?

Ryan 그렇게 하기에 시간이 충분치 않아.

① 기차에서 파이를 먹으면 돼.
③ 그거 훌륭한 생각인 것 같아.
④ 우리가 직접 하나 굽는 게 어때?
⑤ 우리는 할아버지 댁을 먼저 방문해야 해.

|해설| 남동생이 사과 파이를 사 가자고 제안했으나, 5분 후에 기차가 떠나므로 그럴 수 없다는 식의 대답이 가장 적절하다.

|어휘| have an idea 좋은 생각이 나다 suggest [동] 제안하다
[문제] enough [형] 충분한 bake [동] (음식을) 굽다

06 ⑤

W Katie is on a trip with her best friend, Emily. It is nighttime, and after a great day of fun activities, Katie feels very tired. Not long after they lie on their beds, Emily starts playing games on her phone. Katie tries to fall asleep, but the light from Emily's phone is keeping her up. Katie would like to ask if Emily could stop using her phone. In this situation, what would Katie most likely say to Emily?

Katie Emily, could you turn off your cell phone, please?

① can I borrow your charger?
② do you know where my phone is?
③ what time do you usually go to bed?
④ what would you like to do tomorrow?

여 Katie는 가장 친한 친구인 Emily와 여행 중이다. 밤이 되고, 재미있는 활동들을 한 멋진 하루 후에, Katie는 매우 피곤하다. 그들이 침대에 누운 지 얼마 되지 않아, Emily가 휴대전화로 게임을 하기 시작한다. Katie는 잠들려고 노력하지만, Emily의 전화기에서 나오는 빛이 Katie를 잠자리에 들지 못하게 하고 있다. Katie는 Emily에게 휴대전화를 그만 사용하라고 부탁하고 싶다. 이 상황에서, Katie는 Emily에게 뭐라고 말할까?

Katie Emily, 네 휴대전화를 꺼줄 수 있니?

① 네 충전기를 빌릴 수 있을까?
② 내 전화기가 어디에 있는지 아니?
③ 너는 보통 몇 시에 잠자리에 드니?
④ 너 내일 뭘 하고 싶니?

|어휘| on a trip 여행 중인 nighttime [명] 야간, 밤 activity [명] 활동 not long after 오래지 않아 lie [동] 눕다 fall asleep 잠들다 light [명] 빛 keep ~ up ~을 잠자리에 들지 못하게 하다
[문제] charger [명] 충전기

07 ①

M Alex gets into an empty elevator on the first floor and presses the button for the ninth floor. On the next floor, a large group of people get on the elevator and stand in front of him. They are all going to the eleventh floor. When the elevator reaches the ninth floor, they don't notice that he is trying to get off. In this situation, what would Alex most likely say to the people?

Alex Excuse me. I need to get off.

② Can you tell me which floor we're on?
③ What can I do for you today?
④ That's right. It's on the ninth floor.
⑤ I'm sorry that I kept you waiting.

남 Alex는 1층에서 비어 있는 엘리베이터를 타고 9층 버튼을 누른다. 다음 층에서 큰 무리의 사람들이 엘리베이터에 타서 그 앞에 선다. 그들은 모두 11층에 간다. 엘리베이터가 9층에 이르렀을 때, 그들은 Alex가 내리려 하는 것을 알아차리지 못한다. 이 상황에서, Alex는 사람들에게 뭐라고 말할까?

Alex 실례합니다. 제가 내려야 해서요.

② 우리가 몇 층에 있는지 알려주시겠어요?
③ 오늘 무엇을 도와드릴까요?
④ 맞습니다. 그건 9층에 있습니다.
⑤ 기다리게 해서 미안합니다.

|어휘| empty [형] 비어 있는 press [동] 누르다 a group of 한 무리의 get on (탈것을) 타다 reach [동] 이르다, 도달하다 notice [동] 알아차리다

08 ⑤

M Bruce has an important English test tomorrow. So he made a plan to study with Jenny, one of his classmates tonight. She invited him to come to her house, and he agreed. But now she is calling Bruce to tell him there is a problem. Her brother's friends are at her house, and they are very noisy. However, Bruce's house is empty and quiet. In this situation, what would Bruce most likely say to Jenny?

Bruce Jenny, Why don't you come to my house instead?

① let's study for it tomorrow night.
② what time shall we meet today?
③ I'm sorry. I will try to be quieter.
④ I think we should study together.

남 Bruce는 내일 중요한 영어 시험이 있다. 그래서 반 친구 중 한 명인 Jenny와 오늘 밤에 같이 공부할 계획을 세웠다. 그녀가 Bruce를 자신의 집으로 초대했고, 그도 동의했다. 그런데 지금 그녀가 문제가 있다고 Bruce에게 말하려고 전화하고 있다. 그녀의 오빠 친구들이 집에 있는데 매우 시끄럽다는 것이다. 하지만 Bruce의 집은 비어 있는데다가 조용하기도 하다. 이 상황에서, Bruce는 Jenny에게 뭐라고 말할까?

Bruce Jenny, 대신 우리 집으로 오는 게 어때?

① 내일 저녁에 그것을 공부하자.
② 오늘 몇 시에 만날까?
③ 미안해. 내가 더 조용히 하도록 할게.
④ 우리 함께 공부해야 할 것 같아.

|어휘| important [형] 중요한　make a plan 계획을 짜다　invite [동] 초대하다　noisy [형] 시끄러운

09 ③

M Mason is in a new public library that opened just a few weeks ago. While looking around the library, he finds a series of books that he really wants to read. But only members can borrow books from the library. He would like to tell the librarian that he wants to become a member of the library. In this situation, what would Mason most likely say to the librarian?

Mason I'd like to sign up for a membership.

① What are the library hours?
② Could you help me find this book?
④ I forgot to bring my membership card.
⑤ How many days can I borrow a book for?

남 Mason은 몇 주 전에 막 문을 연 새로운 공립도서관에 있다. 도서관을 둘러보던 중에, 그가 정말로 읽고 싶은 책 시리즈를 발견한다. 하지만 회원만이 그 도서관에서 책을 빌릴 수 있다. 그는 도서관 사서에게 그가 도서관 회원이 되고 싶다고 말하고 싶다. 이 상황에서, Mason은 도서관 사서에게 뭐라고 말할까?

Mason 저는 회원 가입을 하고 싶어요.

① 도서관 (운영) 시간이 어떻게 되나요?
② 이 책 찾는 걸 도와주실 수 있을까요?
④ 회원 카드 가져오는 걸 깜박했어요.
⑤ 며칠 동안 책을 빌릴 수 있나요?

|어휘| public [형] 공공의　librarian [명] (도서관의) 사서　**[문제]** sign up for ~에 가입하다[등록하다]　membership [명] 회원

어휘·표현 다지기

p. 107

A

01 결과　**02** 누르다
03 (도서관의) 사서　**04** 상황
05 중요한　**06** 활동
07 신뢰하다　**08** 숙련된, 경험이 많은
09 응급처치　**10** 시끄러운
11 긴 소매의　**12** 충분한
13 공공의　**14** 초대하다
15 ~하지 못하다　**16** ~을 잠자리에 들지 못하게 하다

B

01 suddenly　**02** a group of
03 charger　**04** reach
05 get on　**06** annoyed
07 sunburn　**08** on a trip
09 friendship　**10** win a prize

실전 모의고사 1회

pp. 110-111

01 ⑤	02 ④	03 ④	04 ③	05 ②
06 ③	07 ③	08 ①	09 ④	10 ①
11 ②	12 ②	13 ①	14 ③	15 ④
16 ①	17 ⑤	18 ②	19 ⑤	20 ⑤

01 ⑤

W Which desk chair do you like, Kurt?
M I like the one with wheels. The chairs without wheels will scratch the floor.
W I agree. I like that one over there with the soft cushion seat.
M But that one doesn't have any arms. I think it would be uncomfortable.
W You're probably right. How about this chair? It has arms and a soft seat.
M I really like that one. Let's get it!

여 어느 책상 의자가 맘에 드니, Kurt?
남 바퀴 달린 의자가 맘에 들어. 바퀴 없는 의자는 바닥에 긁힌 자국을 낼 거야.
여 동감이야. 나는 저쪽에 있는 부드러운 쿠션 안장이 있는 저 의자가 좋아.
남 하지만 저것은 팔걸이가 없네. 불편할 것 같아.
여 네 말이 맞을 수도 있겠다. 이 의자는 어때? 팔걸이도 있고 안장도 부드러워.
남 그게 정말 맘에 드네. 그걸 사자!

|해설| 여자가 바퀴와 팔걸이가 있고 안장이 부드러운 쿠션으로 된 의자를 제안하자, 남자가 좋다고 했다.

|어휘| wheel [명] 바퀴 scratch [동] 긁다, 긁힌 자국을 내다 arm [명] (의자의) 팔걸이 uncomfortable [형] 불편한

02 ④

M Kate, did you see the poster for the Bloom Music Festival?
W No, I didn't. It sounds interesting. When will it be?
M On April 13th. Why don't you come with me?
W I'd love to. How much are the tickets for the festival?
M The tickets are usually twenty dollars, but they're only 10 dollars for teenagers like us.
W That's nice! Where is the event taking place?
M It will be held at Central Park.
W Wonderful! Then we can go there on foot. Who will be playing?
M Famous musicians like Thomas and Nathan will perform.
W Wow! I can't wait to see their show.

남 Kate, Bloom Music Festival 포스터 봤어?
여 아니, 못 봤어. 재미있겠다. 그건 언제 해?
남 4월 13일에. 나랑 함께 갈래?
여 그러고 싶어. 축제 티켓은 얼마야?
남 티켓은 보통 20달러인데 우리 같은 십 대는 10달러밖에 안 해.
여 좋다! 그 행사는 어디서 열려?
남 Central Park에서 열릴 거야.
여 훌륭해! 그러면 우리는 걸어서 그곳에 갈 수 있겠다. 누가 공연하니?
남 Thomas와 Nathan 같은 유명 음악인들이 공연할 거야.
여 와! 빨리 그들의 공연을 보고 싶어.

|어휘| festival [명] 축제 teenager [명] 십 대 take place 개최되다, 열리다 hold [동] 열다, 개최하다 musician [명] 음악가 perform [동] 공연하다, 연주하다 can't wait to-v 빨리 ~하고 싶다

03 ④

[Telephone rings.]
M Hello, Wallace Hotel. How may I help you?
W Good morning. This is Susan Collins in room 102. I'm checking out tomorrow.
M Yes, I remember. Should I call a taxi to pick you up?
W No, I'm going to take the shuttle bus. How often does it come?
M It comes every twenty minutes.
W I see. Thank you.

[전화벨이 울린다.]
남 안녕하세요, Wallace 호텔입니다. 무엇을 도와드릴까요?
여 좋은 아침입니다. 102호실의 Susan Collins입니다. 내일 퇴실할 예정인데요.
남 네, 기억합니다. 손님을 태울 택시를 부를까요?
여 아니요, 셔틀버스를 탈 거예요. 얼마나 자주 오나요?
남 20분마다 옵니다.
여 알겠습니다. 고맙습니다.

04 ③

W Excuse me. How much is this shirt?

M It was originally $25, but now it's on sale for $20.

W Oh! Do you have the same shirt in any other colors?

M Yes, it also comes in blue, white, red, and green.

W Okay. I'll take one green one and one blue one.

M Certainly. Would you also like some wool socks? They're $2 per pair.

W What a great price! I'll take two pairs.

여 실례합니다. 이 셔츠 얼마죠?

남 원래 25달러였는데, 지금은 20달러로 할인 판매 중입니다.

여 아! 같은 셔츠가 다른 색상으로도 있나요?

남 네, 파란색, 흰색, 빨간색, 초록색으로도 나옵니다.

여 그렇군요. 초록색 한 장과 파란색 한 장 살게요.

남 네. 모직 양말도 보시겠어요? 한 켤레에 2달러랍니다.

여 정말 좋은 가격이네요! 두 켤레 살게요.

05 ②

M Minji, what are you doing?

W Tickets to a K-pop concert are going on sale at two o'clock. I'm on standby.

M Oh, I see. Are they difficult to get?

W Of course. I've tried several times, but I've never succeeded.

M Really? Wow, it seems almost impossible.

W Right. Oh, I feel like my heart is racing.

M Calm down. Just click the button right away at two o'clock. I'm sure you'll get a ticket this time.

W Thanks. Oh my gosh, there are only five minutes left!

남 민지야, 뭐 하고 있니?

여 케이팝 콘서트 티켓이 2시에 판매될 거야. 난 대기하고 있어.

남 아, 그렇구나. 구하기 어렵니?

여 물론이지. 내가 여러 번 시도했었는데, 성공해본 적 없어.

남 진짜? 와, 거의 불가능한 것 같네.

여 맞아. 아, 심장이 빨리 뛰는 것 같아.

남 진정해. 2시 정각에 바로 버튼을 클릭하기만 해. 분명 이번에는 표를 구할 거야.

여 고마워. 어떻게 해, 5분밖에 안 남았어!

06 ③

① **W** Can I use this coupon to get a discount?

M No, I'm afraid not. It expired two days ago.

② **W** How much are these strawberries?

M They're on sale for $5.

③ **W** Where are the cookies? I can't find them.

M They're in aisle 12. I'll take you there.

④ **W** Do you like watermelons?

M Yes, they are my favorite fruit.

⑤ **W** A new grocery store opened last week.

M Really? I'll have to go there.

① 여 이 쿠폰을 써서 할인받을 수 있나요?

남 죄송하지만, 안 됩니다. 쿠폰이 이틀 전에 만료되었네요.

② 여 이 딸기는 얼마인가요?

남 5달러에 할인 판매 중입니다.

③ 여 쿠키가 어디 있나요? 찾을 수가 없네요.

남 12번 통로에 있습니다. 거기로 데려다 드릴게요.

④ 여 수박 좋아하시나요?

남 네, 제가 가장 좋아하는 과일이에요.

⑤ 여 지난주에 새 식료품점이 문을 열었어요.

남 정말요? 거기 가봐야겠네요.

07 ③

M Would you do me a favor, Susie?

W Sure. What can I do for you?

M Can you help me with my Spanish homework? I heard you lived in Spain when you were little.

W Okay. What's the assignment?

M I need to write an essay about Spanish culture.

W That should be easy. I'd be happy to help you.

M Thanks a lot. How about meeting at the library at 7:00 p.m.?

W That sounds good. I'll see you then.

남 부탁 좀 들어줄래, 수지야?
여 그래. 뭘 해줄까?
남 내 스페인어 숙제 좀 도와줄 수 있어? 네가 어렸을 때 스페인에서 살았다고 들었어.
여 좋아. 숙제가 뭔데?
남 스페인 문화에 관해 에세이를 써야 해.
여 쉬울 것 같네. 기꺼이 도와줄게.
남 정말 고마워. 저녁 7시에 도서관에서 만나는 게 어때?
여 괜찮아. 그때 보자.

|어휘| do ~ a favor ~의 부탁을 들어주다 assignment [명] 과제, 숙제 culture [명] 문화

08 ①

W Attention, parents and children! Our town is having an Easter egg hunt this Saturday, April 12. The event will be held at the Prairie Grove baseball field from 11:00 a.m. to 3:00 p.m. Children under the age of ten can participate in the egg hunt. They should bring a small basket for collecting eggs. After the egg hunt, refreshments will be served in the blue tent in the parking lot.

여 학부모님과 어린이 여러분께 알립니다! 우리 마을에서 이번 주 토요일 4월 12일에 부활절 달걀 찾기 행사가 있을 예정입니다. 이 행사는 오전 11시부터 오후 3시까지 Prairie Grove 야구장에서 열릴 것입니다. 10살 미만의 어린이들이면 달걀 찾기 행사에 참가할 수 있습니다. 어린이들은 달걀을 모을 작은 바구니를 가져와야 합니다. 달걀 찾기가 끝난 뒤에는, 주차장에 있는 파란색 천막에서 간단한 다과가 제공될 예정입니다.

|어휘| Easter egg hunt 부활절 달걀 찾기 collect [동] 모으다, 수집하다 refreshment [명] 다과 serve [동] 제공하다 parking lot 주차장

09 ④

M A person with this job checks people's dental health and provides any necessary treatment. People visit this person when there is something wrong with their teeth. They may need anything from a simple cleaning to a major surgery. To get this job, you have to have extensive medical knowledge about teeth and have a license.

남 이 직업을 가진 사람은 사람들의 치아 건강을 확인하고 필요한 처치를 제공합니다. 사람들은 자신의 치아에 이상이 생기면 이 사람을 찾아갑니다. 그들은 단순한 세척부터 큰 수술까지 필요할 수도 있습니다. 이 직업을 가지려면, 치아에 관한 폭넓은 의학 지식이 있어야 하며 면허가 있어야 합니다.

|어휘| dental [형] 치아의 health [명] 건강 provide [동] 제공하다 treatment [명] 치료, 처치 surgery [명] 수술 extensive [형] 광범위한 medical [형] 의학의 knowledge [명] 지식 license [명] 면허(증), 자격(증)

10 ①

① M How long does it take to finish your homework?
W I was on the bus for three hours.
② M This is the best meal I've had in a long time.
W Thanks. I'm glad you like it.
③ M I have a complaint about this shirt. It has a hole in it.
W I'm sorry about that. Let me get you a new one.
④ M I haven't seen you since last year. What have you been doing?
W I've been traveling.
⑤ M Why don't you join the dance club I belong to?
W I'll think about it.

① 남 숙제 끝내는 데 얼마나 걸려?
여 버스를 3시간 동안 타고 있었어.
② 남 오랜만에 먹어보는 최고의 식사네요.
여 고마워요. 좋다고 하시니 저도 기쁘네요.
③ 남 이 셔츠에 불만이 있습니다. 여기에 구멍이 하나 있어요.
여 죄송합니다. 새것을 가져다드리겠습니다.
④ 남 작년 이후로 너를 보지 못했네. 그동안 뭐하고 지냈어?
여 여행했었어.
⑤ 남 내가 속한 댄스 동아리에 가입하는 게 어때?
여 생각해볼게.

|어휘| meal [명] 식사 in a long time 오랜만에 complaint [명] 불만, 불평 belong to ~에 속하다

11 ②

W Hey! Turn off the TV! I'm doing my homework.
M Why? Tomorrow is Saturday. There's no school.
W Yes, but we're going to the beach this weekend. So I have to do my homework now.
M I thought we were going to visit our grandparents.
W No, that's next weekend.
M Oh! Then I need to cancel my plans for next Saturday.

여 얘! TV 좀 꺼! 나 숙제하고 있잖아.
남 왜? 내일 토요일이잖아. 학교 안 가는데.
여 맞아, 하지만 우리 이번 주말에 바닷가에 가잖아. 그래서 지금 숙제를 해야 해.

남 나는 우리가 조부모님 댁에 갈 거라고 생각했는데.

여 아니야. 그건 다음 주말이야.

남 아! 그러면 다음 주 토요일 내 계획을 취소해야겠네.

|해설| 남자는 이번 주말에 조부모님 댁을 방문할 거라고 착각하고 있었다. 두 사람의 일정은 바닷가에 가는 것이다.

|어휘| grandparent 몡 조부[모]   cancel 용 취소하다

12 ②

M Sally, what are you doing?

W Hi, Anthony. I'm trying to buy a book for my cousin.

M Let me help you. I have many cousins. How old is your cousin?

W He is fifteen years old.

M Then he won't like a fairy tale book. How about this book? It <u>won first place</u> in a competition.

W He doesn't seem to like essays. He <u>likes novels</u>.

M Then there are two options left. Which will you choose?

W I will buy the book that's <u>ranked higher</u>.

M Nice choice.

남 Sally, 뭐 하니?

여 안녕, Anthony. 사촌에게 줄 책을 사려는 중이야.

남 내가 도와줄게. 나는 사촌이 많거든. 네 사촌은 몇 살이니?

여 그 애는 15살이야.

남 그럼 동화책은 좋아하지 않겠네. 이 책은 어때? 대회에서 1위를 했어.

여 그 애는 에세이를 좋아하는 것 같지 않아. 소설을 좋아해.

남 그럼 두 개의 선택지가 남았네. 어떤 것을 고를래?

여 더 높은 순위를 차지한 책을 살래.

남 좋은 선택이야.

|어휘| fairy tale 동화   first place 1등   novel 몡 소설   rank 용 (등급 및 순위를) 차지하다

13 ①

W Trevor! Is that you?

M Molly! I haven't seen you in ages! What are you doing in Seoul?

W I'm <u>on a business trip</u>. I'll be here until next Monday.

M That's great! Are you free for lunch this weekend? Saturday <u>works for me</u>.

W No, I already have plans on that day. How about noon on Sunday?

M Sure. I have your phone number. I'll text you tonight <u>regarding the place</u>.

여 Trevor! 너 맞니?

남 Molly! 오랜만이야! 서울에서 뭐 하고 있어?

여 출장 중이야. 다음 주 월요일까지 여기 있을 거야.

남 잘됐다! 이번 주말 점심 때 시간 되니? 난 토요일이 괜찮은데.

여 아니, 그 날은 이미 계획이 있어. 일요일 정오는 어때?

남 좋아. 나 네 전화번호 있어. 장소에 관해서는 오늘 밤에 문자 보낼게.

|어휘| on a business trip 출장 중인   work 용 유효하게 작용하다 text 용 문자 메시지를 보내다   regarding 전 ~에 관해서

14 ③

M Good morning, Monica. Did you <u>have a good weekend</u>?

W Yes, Eric. I had a wonderful weekend.

M Oh, what did you do?

W Originally, I was going to go buy a new phone with my mom, but the cell phone store was closed.

M So you <u>couldn't change your phone</u>.

W Exactly. Instead, I went to the park with my mom and my dog.

M That sounds like fun. The <u>weather was nice</u> on the weekend.

W Right. I had a great time.

남 좋은 아침이야, Monica. 주말 잘 보냈니?

여 응, Eric. 멋진 주말을 보냈어.

남 오, 뭐 했는데?

여 원래는 엄마와 새로 전화기를 사러 가려고 했는데, 휴대전화 매장이 문을 닫았어.

남 그럼 전화기를 못 바꿨겠네.

여 응. 대신 엄마랑 개랑 함께 공원에 갔어.

남 재미있었겠다. 주말에 날씨가 좋았잖아.

여 맞아. 정말 좋은 시간을 보냈어.

|어휘| instead 변 대신에

15 ④

W Good afternoon, students! This is Principal Wilkins speaking. These days, the fine dust problem <u>is getting worse</u>. So I'd like to explain what you should do when the fine dust level is high. First, <u>close all classroom windows</u>. Second, turn on the air purifier in your classroom. Third, wash your hands frequently. Last, <u>wear a mask</u> when you are outside. Let's all follow these tips to stay healthy. Thank you.

여 안녕하세요, 학생 여러분! 저는 교장 Wilkins입니다. 요즘 미세 먼지 문제가 악화되고 있습니다. 그래서 미세 먼지 수치가 높을 때 여러분이 무엇을 해야 하는지 설명하려고 합니다. 첫째, 모든 교실 창문을 닫습니다. 둘째, 교실의 공기 정화기를 켭니다. 셋째, 손을 자주 씻으세요. 마지막으로, 실외에 있을 때 마스크를 착용하세요. 우리 모두 건강히 지내기 위해 이 조언을 따릅시다. 감사합니다.

|어휘| principal [명] 교장 fine dust 미세 먼지 explain [동] 설명하다 air purifier 공기 정화기 frequently [부] 자주 outside [부] 실외에 follow [동] 따르다

16 ①

W I think the cashier charged me too much for the shirt I just bought.
M Really? What does the receipt say?
W Well, it says that the shirt costs $50. But it was on sale.
M Oh. How much was it on sale for?
W It was 20% off, so it should have cost $40. I don't think the cashier knew it was on sale.
M You should go back and explain the situation.
W I will.

여 계산원이 내가 방금 산 셔츠에 너무 많이 청구한 것 같아.
남 정말? 영수증에 뭐라고 되어 있는데?
여 음, 셔츠가 50달러라고 되어 있어. 하지만 그건 할인 판매 중이었거든.
남 아. 얼마로 할인 중이었어?
여 20% 할인이었으니, 40달러였어야 해. 내 생각에는 계산원이 이게 할인 판매 중인지 모른 것 같아.
남 다시 가서 상황을 설명하는 게 좋겠네.
여 그러려고.

|해설| 50달러짜리 셔츠가 20% 할인되어 40달러로 계산됐어야 하는데, 계산원이 정상가 50달러를 청구했으므로, 여자는 10달러를 돌려받아야 한다.

|어휘| cashier [명] 계산원 charge [동] (돈을) 청구하다 receipt [명] 영수증 situation [명] 상황

17 ⑤

W Do you need some help? You look lost.
M Yes, I am. I'm trying to get to Dongdaemun, but I'm not sure which train to take.
W I'm sorry to tell you this, but the last train just left ten minutes ago.
M Oh no! What am I going to do now?
W You could take a night bus. It starts running at midnight.
M Okay. Can you tell me how to get to the bus station?

① No. I don't have a driver's license.
② I think I'll take an earlier train.
③ Dongdaemun is a great place to visit.
④ It takes about one hour to get there by train.

여 도움 필요하세요? 길을 잃으신 것 같네요.
남 네, 맞아요. 제가 동대문에 가려고 하는데, 어떤 열차를 타야 할지 잘 모르겠어요.
여 말씀드리기 유감스럽지만, 막차가 10분 전에 막 떠났습니다.
남 아, 이런! 그럼 제가 이제 뭘 해야 하죠?
여 심야버스를 타시면 됩니다. 자정에 운행을 시작해요.
남 알겠습니다. 버스 정류장에 어떻게 가는지 알려 주실 수 있나요?

① 아니요. 저는 운전면허증이 없어요.
② 더 이른 열차를 타야겠어요.
③ 동대문은 가볼 만한 멋진 곳이죠.
④ 열차로 거기 가는 데 한 시간 정도 걸립니다.

|어휘| lost [형] 길을 잃은 night bus 심야버스 run [동] 운행하다 midnight [명] 자정 **[문제]** driver's license 운전면허증

18 ②

M Hi. Are you Christine Smith?
W Yes, I am. Do I know you?
M No, but I am a big fan of your work. Your novels are wonderful.
W Thank you very much.
M I have one of your novels with me right now. Could you sign it for me?
W Sure. Do you have a pen?
M Yes. Here it is. Thank you. I want to be a novelist like you someday.
W I hope your dream comes true.

① I've written 15 novels.
③ I don't like the novel.
④ Oh, sorry. I don't have a pen.
⑤ I'm afraid I am not a novelist.

남 안녕하세요. Christine Smith 씨인가요?
여 네, 그런데요. 우리 아는 사이인가요?
남 아니요, 저는 작가님 작품의 열혈 팬입니다. 작가님의 소설은 훌륭해요.
여 정말 감사합니다.
남 지금 저한테 작가님 소설 중 한 권이 있어요. 제게 사인해주실 수 있나요?
여 그럼요. 펜 있으세요?
남 네. 여기 있습니다. 감사합니다. 저도 언젠가 작가님 같은 소설가가 되고 싶어요.
여 꿈이 이루어지길 바랄게요.

① 저는 15편의 소설을 썼습니다.
③ 저는 그 소설을 좋아하지 않아요.
④ 아, 죄송해요. 펜이 없네요.
⑤ 유감스럽게도 저는 소설가가 아닙니다.

|어휘| big fan 열혈 팬, 열성 팬 work [명] 작품 sign [동] 서명하다, 사인하다 novelist [명] 소설가 someday [부] 언젠가

19 ⑤

W James. You look happy. What's up?
M I am. Guess what happened.
W What? You must have some good news to tell me.
M I do! You're not going to believe it.
W Did you get an A on the math test?
M No, that's not it. Do you remember when I was practicing for the English speech contest?
W I sure do! Did you win a prize?
M Yes. I won first prize.
W Congratulations! I'm so proud of you.

① I'll keep my fingers crossed!
② Come on. I know you can do it.
③ I'm afraid I don't agree with you.
④ I promise you it won't happen again.

여 James. 기분 좋아 보인다. 무슨 일 있어?
남 기분 좋아. 무슨 일 있었는지 알아맞혀 봐.
여 뭔데? 나에게 말할 좋은 소식이 있나 보네.
남 있어! 믿기지 않을 거야.
여 수학 시험에서 A 받았니?
남 아니, 그건 아니야. 내가 영어 말하기 대회 연습하던 거 기억나니?
여 물론이지! 상 받았어?
남 응. 1등상을 탔어.
여 축하해! 네가 정말 자랑스럽다.

① 행운을 빌게!
② 왜 그래. 난 네가 그걸 할 수 있을 거라고 생각하는데.
③ 유감스럽지만 난 네 의견에 동의하지 않아.
④ 다시는 이런 일이 없을 거라고 너에게 약속할게.

|어휘| first prize 1등상 **[문제]** keep one's fingers crossed 행운을 빌다, 기도하다 promise [동] 약속하다 be proud of ~을 자랑스러워하다

20 ⑤

M Mary and her brother are spending a weekend together at home. Her brother plays the electric piano in a band, and he has been practicing for an upcoming concert. She understands that he needs to practice, but she is studying for a test. She can't concentrate on her work at all when his music is so loud. She wants him to turn the volume down. In this situation, what would Mary most likely say to her brother?
Mary Could you lower the volume on your electric piano?

① I don't want you to stop playing it.
② Good luck with your concert tomorrow.
③ Maybe you should play another instrument.
④ Could you please play the electric piano instead?

남 Mary와 오빠는 집에서 함께 주말을 보내고 있다. 오빠는 밴드에서 전자 피아노를 연주하는데, 다가오는 콘서트를 위해 연습하고 있다. 오빠가 연습해야 한다는 것은 이해하지만, 그녀는 시험공부를 하는 중이다. 그녀는 오빠의 연주가 너무 시끄러울 때 공부에 전혀 집중할 수가 없다. 그녀는 오빠가 음량을 좀 줄여주기를 원한다. 이 상황에서, Mary는 오빠에게 뭐라고 말할까?
Mary 전자 피아노 음량을 낮춰줄 수 있을까?

① 난 오빠가 연주를 그만두지 않으면 좋겠어.
② 내일 있을 콘서트에 행운을 빌어.
③ 아마 오빠가 다른 악기를 연주해야 할 것 같아.
④ 대신 전자 피아노를 연주해줄래?

|어휘| spend [동] 보내다 electric piano 전자 피아노 upcoming [형] 다가오는, 곧 있을 understand [동] 이해하다 concentrate on ~에 집중하다 loud [형] 시끄러운 turn down (소리를) 줄이다 volume [명] 음량 **[문제]** instrument [명] 악기 lower [동] 낮추다

어휘·표현 다지기

p. 119

01 바퀴	02 공연하다, 연주하다
03 불편한	04 과제, 숙제
05 만료되다	06 광범위한
07 (돈을) 청구하다	08 낮추다
09 면허(증), 자격(증)	10 개최되다, 열리다
11 자주	12 출장 중인
13 불만, 불평	14 원래, 본래
15 영수증	16 행운을 빌다, 기도하다

B

01 turn down	02 principal
03 aisle	04 concentrate on
05 explain	06 in a long time
07 text	08 treatment

09 regarding **10** upcoming

실전 모의고사 2회

pp. 120-121

01 ①	02 ④	03 ④	04 ⑤	05 ⑤
06 ②	07 ⑤	08 ③	09 ②	10 ③
11 ④	12 ①	13 ②	14 ④	15 ②
16 ④	17 ①	18 ④	19 ⑤	20 ⑤

01 ①

M Tiffany, this exercise will strengthen your stomach muscles.
W Oh, can you show me how to do it?
M Sure. First, stand up straight and spread your legs. There should be some space between your feet.
W Like this?
M Yes. Then spread your arms out to the sides.
W Okay. What's next?
M Balance on your left leg. Your right foot should be off the ground.
W I can already feel my muscles getting stronger!

남 Tiffany, 이 운동이 네 복근을 강화할 거야.
여 아, 그걸 어떻게 하는지 보여줄 수 있어?
남 그럼. 일단 똑바로 서서 다리를 벌려. 두 발 사이에 공간이 좀 있어야 해.
여 이렇게?
남 그렇지. 그 다음에 양쪽으로 팔을 벌려.
여 알았어. 다음은 뭐야?
남 왼쪽 다리로 균형을 잡아. 오른발은 땅에서 떨어져야 해.
여 벌써 근육이 더 강해지는 느낌이야!

|어휘| strengthen [동] 강화하다 stomach [명] 복부 muscle [명] 근육 spread [동] 벌리다, 펴다 balance [동] 균형을 잡다 off [전] ~에서 벗어나서[떨어져서]

02 ④

W Sam, do you have any special plans for this weekend?
M Yes, my history club will go on a field trip to the Global Museum on Saturday.
W I heard that the Global Museum is the largest museum in Korea.
M Right. It opened in 1920 and recently moved near City Hall.
W Interesting. Do you have to pay an entrance fee?
M No, it's free.
W That's great. How long is it open on Saturdays?
M The operating hours are from 9:00 a.m. to 5:00 p.m., so we'll have lots of time to look around.
W Nice! I hope you enjoy it!

여 Sam, 이번 주말에 특별한 계획 있니?
남 응, 역사 동아리에서 토요일에 Global 박물관으로 견학을 갈 거야.
여 Global 박물관이 한국에서 가장 규모가 큰 박물관이라고 들었어.
남 맞아. 1920년에 개관했고 최근에 시청 근처로 위치를 옮겼어.
여 흥미롭네. 입장료를 내야 하니?
남 아니, 무료야.
여 좋네. 토요일에는 얼마나 오래 열어?
남 운영 시간은 오전 9시부터 오후 5시까지라서, 둘러볼 시간이 많을 거야.
여 좋네! 재미있길 바라!

|어휘| field trip 견학 recently [부] 최근에 entrance fee 입장료 operating hour 운영 시간 lots of 많은 look around 둘러보다

03 ④

[Telephone rings.]
W Thank you for calling Happy Clinic. How may I help you?
M Hello, I'm going to be late for my four o'clock appointment today.
W What is your name?
M Jason Wilson. Can I come in at five thirty instead?
W Unfortunately, Dr. Herman won't be available then.
M Oh no. I really need to see him today.
W If it is urgent, I can get you an appointment at six with Dr. Thomas. Is that okay?
M Yes, Dr. Thomas would be fine.

[전화벨이 울린다.]
여 Happy Clinic에 전화 주셔서 감사합니다. 무엇을 도와드릴까요?
남 안녕하세요, 제가 오늘 4시 예약에 늦을 것 같아서요.
여 성함이 어떻게 되세요?
남 Jason Wilson입니다. 대신 5시 30분에 가도 될까요?
여 공교롭게도, 그때는 Herman 선생님이 시간이 없으시네요.
남 아, 안 되는데. 오늘 선생님을 정말 봬야 하거든요.
여 급하시면, 6시에 Thomas 선생님으로 예약해드릴 수는 있어요. 괜찮으신가요?
남 네, Thomas 선생님도 괜찮아요.

|어휘| appointment [명] 예약, 약속 unfortunately [부] 유감스럽게도, 공교롭게도 available [형] 시간이 있는 urgent [형] 긴급한

04 ⑤

[Cell phone rings.]

M Hey, Megan.

W Hi, James. I was thinking of going to the library tomorrow. Can you join me?

M Sure. I have to borrow some books. When are you going?

W I am thinking about going at 11:00 a.m. Would that be okay?

M Unfortunately, I have to take my brother to kindergarten at twelve o'clock. What about 1:00 p.m.?

W I'm having lunch with Linda at that time. Is 3:00 p.m. all right?

M Yeah, that will work. I'll meet you in front of the library.

[휴대전화벨이 울린다.]

남 안녕, Megan.

여 안녕, James. 나 내일 도서관에 갈까 생각 중이었어. 같이 갈래?

남 그럼. 나 책을 좀 빌려야 하거든. 언제 갈 거니?

여 오전 11시쯤 갈까 생각하고 있어. 괜찮을까?

남 유감스럽게도, 난 12시에 남동생을 유치원에 데려다줘야 해. 오후 1시는 어때?

여 나는 그 시간에 Linda와 점심을 먹을 거야. 오후 3시는 괜찮아?

남 그래, 그건 괜찮을 거야. 도서관 앞에서 보자.

|어휘| borrow [동] 빌리다 kindergarten [명] 유치원

05 ⑤

W Wow, these cars all look really nice.

M Look! That's the newest model. I saw advertisements for it on television.

W A superhero was driving this type of car in the new action movie I saw yesterday.

M That must be why everyone is taking pictures of it.

W I wish I could buy that car.

M You already have a really nice car.

W But my car is too old. I have to take it to the repair shop all the time to get it fixed.

여 와, 이 차들 모두 멋져 보인다.

남 봐! 저거 최신 모델이야. TV에서 저 차 광고 봤어.

여 어제 내가 본 새 액션 영화에서도 슈퍼 히어로가 이런 차종을 몰고 있더라.

남 그래서 모든 사람이 저 차 사진을 찍고 있겠지.

여 저 차를 살 수 있다면 좋을 텐데.

남 너 이미 정말 멋진 차가 있잖아.

여 하지만 내 차는 너무 오래됐어. 수리받으러 아주 자주 정비소에 가져가야 해.

|어휘| newest [형] 최신의 advertisement [명] 광고 repair shop 정비소 all the time 줄곧, 아주 자주

06 ②

① **M** How much is the entrance fee for the pool?
W It's $10.

② **M** Don't run by the pool! It's dangerous.
W I'm sorry. I won't do it again.

③ **M** Would you like to go to the pool today?
W Sure! That sounds like a great idea.

④ **M** Only people who are more than 150 cm tall can swim here.
W Oh, that's too bad. The pool looks really nice.

⑤ **M** You shouldn't swim right after you eat.
W Okay. I'll wait for thirty minutes, then.

① **남** 수영장 입장료가 얼마인가요?
여 10달러입니다.

② **남** 수영장 옆에서 뛰지 마세요! 위험합니다.
여 죄송해요. 다시는 안 그럴게요.

③ **남** 오늘 수영장 갈래요?
여 네! 좋은 생각이에요.

④ **남** 여기서는 키가 150cm 이상인 분만 수영하실 수 있습니다.
여 아, 아쉽네요. 수영장이 정말 좋아 보이는데 말이에요.

⑤ **남** 식사 직후에 수영하면 안 돼요.
여 알겠어요. 그러면 30분 동안 기다릴게요.

|어휘| pool [명] 수영장 dangerous [형] 위험한

07 ⑤

[Cell phone rings.]

W Hello?

M Hi, Heather. It's Jason.

W Hi, Jason. What's going on?

M Well, I need to ask a favor. I just realized that I left my science textbook at school.

W Did you? You'll need it to do our science homework this weekend. I can lend you my book when I'm finished with it tomorrow.

M I'd rather not wait until tomorrow. Could you send me pictures of the pages we should study?

W No problem. I'll send them right away.

M Thanks a lot, Heather!

[휴대전화벨이 울린다.]

여 여보세요?

남 안녕, Heather. 나 Jason이야.
여 안녕, Jason. 무슨 일이야?
남 그게, 부탁 좀 하려고. 내가 학교에 과학 교과서를 두고 왔다는 걸 방금 깨달았어.
여 그랬어? 이번 주말에 과학 숙제하려면 교과서가 필요할 텐데. 내가 내일 책 다 보면 내 것 빌려주면 되겠다.
남 내일까지 기다리고 싶진 않은데. 우리가 공부해야 하는 페이지 사진 좀 찍어서 보내줄래?
여 응. 바로 보내줄게.
남 정말 고마워, Heather!

|어휘| ask a favor 부탁하다 realize [동] 깨닫다 textbook [명] 교과서 lend [동] 빌려주다 would rather not ~하지 않겠다[하고 싶지 않다] right away 바로

08 ③

M At Hawaiian Surfboards, all of our surfboards are designed by the famous Hawaiian surfer Akamai Kalani. They are made out of special wood, so they are lighter, stronger, and more environmentally friendly than plastic boards. We mostly sell longboards, but we also have a small selection of shortboards. Our salespeople help customers find the perfect surfboard. So please stop by!

남 Hawaiian Surfboards에서는, 하와이 출신의 유명 서퍼 Akamai Kalani가 저희의 모든 서핑보드를 디자인합니다. 저희 서핑보드는 특수 목재로 제작되어, 플라스틱 보드보다 더 가볍고 튼튼하며 환경친화적입니다. 저희는 주로 긴 서핑보드를 판매하지만, 짧은 서핑보드도 소소하게 구비하고 있습니다. 저희 판매원들이 고객분들이 완벽한 서핑보드를 찾도록 도와드립니다. 그러니 들러주세요!

|어휘| environmentally friendly 환경친화적인 mostly [부] 주로 salespeople [명] 판매원 customer [명] 고객 stop by 들르다

09 ②

W You can sometimes see this during storms. It is a very bright light that flashes in the sky. It is often followed by a loud noise that sounds like an explosion. It can be dangerous because it is made of powerful electricity and sometimes hits the earth. Every year, many forest fires are started by this. If a person is hit by it, he or she can be killed or seriously injured.

여 폭풍이 칠 때 가끔 이것을 볼 수 있습니다. 이것은 하늘에서 번쩍이는 매우 밝은 빛입니다. 종종 이것 뒤에는 폭발 같은 소리가 나는 큰 소음이 뒤따릅니다. 이것은 강력한 전기로 만들어진데다 때때로 땅을 강타하기 때문에 위험할 수 있습니다. 매년 이것 때문에 많은 산불이 시작됩니다. 사람이 이것에 맞으면, 사망하거나 심각한 부상을 입을 수 있습니다.

|어휘| storm [명] 폭풍 flash [동] 번쩍이다 be followed by ~가 뒤따르다 explosion [명] 폭발 electricity [명] 전기 hit [동] 강타하다 earth [명] 땅 seriously [부] 심하게 injured [형] 부상을 입은

10 ③

① W Where can I find the milk and cheese?
M They're at the end of aisle 6.
② W Do you want some more cake?
M No, thanks. I'm full.
③ W Would you mind helping me with these bags?
M Yes, how may I help you?
④ W How do you like your meal?
M It's very good, thanks.
⑤ W How long will it take by bus?
M It'll take about five hours.

① 여 우유랑 치즈는 어디서 찾을 수 있을까요?
남 6번 통로 끝에 있습니다.
② 여 케이크 더 먹을래?
남 아니, 괜찮아. 배불러.
③ 여 이 가방 드는 걸 도와주시면 안 될까요?
남 안 됩니다. 무엇을 도와드릴까요?
④ 여 식사는 어떠세요?
남 매우 맛있어요. 고맙습니다.
⑤ 여 버스로 얼마나 걸릴까요?
남 5시간 정도 걸릴 거예요.

|해설| mind는 '~을 언짢아하다'라는 뜻으로, 'Yes'로 답하면 부탁을 거절하는 의미이기 때문에, 도와줄 의향이 있다면 'No' 등의 부정어로 답하는 것이 자연스럽다.

|어휘| full [형] 배가 부른 meal [명] 식사

11 ④

M There is going to be a free concert this Saturday.
W Wow! What time does it start?
M It starts at four.
W Really? I'd like to go. How can I get a ticket?
M You can get one online.
W I have a dentist appointment at four on Saturday. I'll reserve a ticket after I reschedule it.
M The tickets will be gone soon, so you should reserve one now. You can reschedule your appointment afterwards.

W Okay.

남 이번 토요일에 무료 콘서트가 열릴 거야.

여 와! 그거 몇 시에 시작하니?

남 4시에 시작해.

여 정말? 가고 싶다. 표는 어떻게 구할 수 있어?

남 온라인에서 구할 수 있어.

여 나 토요일 4시에 치과 예약이 있는데. 일정을 변경하고 나서 표를 예매해야겠다.

남 표가 곧 매진될 테니, 지금 예매해야 해. 네 예약은 그 뒤에 변경하면 되지.

여 알았어.

|어휘| reserve [동] 예약하다 reschedule [동] 일정을 변경하다 afterwards [부] 그 뒤에

12 ①

M This library is so big!

W It really is. Where is the computer room?

M It's over there. There are five sections. Which one do you want to sit in?

W Hmm. I don't want to sit by the entrance. There would be too many people walking by.

M I agree. What about section C?

W It's too noisy by the printer. I think section B would be better.

M But that's where the air conditioning is. I think it would be too cold.

W Okay. Let's sit in the section next to it instead.

남 이 도서관 정말 크다!

여 정말 그러네. 컴퓨터실은 어디지?

남 저기 있어. 다섯 구역이 있네. 어떤 구역에 앉고 싶니?

여 음. 출입구 옆에 앉고 싶진 않아. 지나다니는 사람이 너무 많을 거야.

남 내 생각도 그래. C 구역은 어때?

여 프린터 옆은 너무 시끄러워. B 구역이 더 좋을 것 같은데.

남 그런데 거기는 에어컨이 있는 곳이잖아. 너무 추울 것 같아.

여 알았어. 대신 그 옆에 있는 구역에 앉자.

|어휘| entrance [명] 출입구 air conditioning 에어컨

13 ②

W It's almost time to go to the concert. But let's have dinner before we leave. I'm starving.

M I'm not sure if we have time. When does the concert start?

W It starts at eight.

M We need to leave at least one hour before the concert starts. So we only have thirty minutes to eat now.

W That's not much time. Why don't we go to a fast-food restaurant?

M Oh, I don't like fast food. But I guess there's no other choice.

여 콘서트 갈 시간 거의 다 됐다. 그런데 출발하기 전에 저녁 먹자. 너무 배고파.

남 우리가 시간이 있을지 모르겠네. 콘서트 언제 시작하지?

여 8시에 시작해.

남 콘서트 시작하기 전에 적어도 한 시간 전에는 출발해야 해. 그러니까 우리는 지금 먹을 시간이 30분밖에 없는 거지.

여 시간이 별로 없네. 패스트푸드점에 가는 게 어때?

남 아, 난 패스트푸드를 좋아하지 않아. 하지만 다른 선택권이 없는 것 같아.

|어휘| starving [형] 몹시 배고픈 choice [명] 선택권

14 ④

M Mom, can I go to Ben's house now? We want to play computer games.

W Did you finish your homework?

M Yes, I finished it an hour ago, and I also put it in my backpack.

W What about your school uniform? Have you washed it yet?

M Oh, I forgot. It's still in the closet.

W You need to wash it before you go to Ben's house.

M Okay, Mom. I will.

남 엄마, 지금 Ben 집에 가도 돼요? 같이 컴퓨터 게임하고 싶어요.

여 숙제는 다 했어?

남 네, 한 시간 전에 끝냈고, 가방에 넣어두기도 했어요.

여 교복은? 벌써 세탁한 거니?

남 아, 잊어버렸어요. 아직 옷장 안에 있어요.

여 Ben 집에 가기 전에 세탁해야 한다.

남 네, 엄마. 그렇게 할게요.

|어휘| school uniform 교복 still [부] 아직 closet [명] 옷장, 벽장

15 ②

W Hello, students. This is Vice Principal Sarah Park. It is great to see all of the excitement for today's sports day. But please remember to stay with your class throughout the day. All of the events will be held at our school playground. If you need to leave the appointed area for any reason, you must get permission from your teacher. We want to put your safety first. Please cooperate so that we can all have a safe and fun day. Thank you.

여 안녕하세요, 학생 여러분. 저는 교감 Sarah Park입니다. 오늘 이 모든 체육대회의 신나는 일을 보게 되어 매우 좋습니다. 하지만 온종일 여러분의 학급과 함께 있을 것을 기억해 주십시오. 모든 행사는 학교 운동장에서 열릴 것입니다. 어떤 이유든 정해진 구역을 벗어나야 한다면, 선생님의 허락을 받아야 합니다. 여러분의 안전을 최우선으로 하려고 합니다. 모두가 안전하고 즐거운 날을 보낼 수 있도록 협조해 주십시오. 고맙습니다.

|어휘| vice principal 교감 excitement [명] 신나는 일 playground [명] 운동장 permission [명] 허락 appointed [형] 정해진 area [명] 지역, 구역 put ~ first ~을 가장 중시하다 safety [명] 안전 cooperate [동] 협조하다

16 ④

M Welcome to John's Hamburgers. How may I help you?

W Hello. I'd like to buy some chicken burger sets.

M Okay. The chicken burger set is seven dollars. How many would you like?

W I need two sets. And do you sell ice cream too?

M Yes, there is chocolate ice cream and vanilla ice cream. Chocolate is two dollars each and vanilla is one dollar each.

W Then please add one chocolate and one vanilla to my order.

M Okay. Do you need anything else?

W No. Here's my credit card.

M Okay. I'll call your number when the food is ready.

W Thank you.

남 John's Hamburgers입니다. 무엇을 도와드릴까요?

여 안녕하세요. 치킨버거 세트 주세요.

남 알겠습니다. 치킨버거 세트는 7달러입니다. 몇 개 원하시나요?

여 두 세트 필요해요. 그리고 아이스크림도 파나요?

남 네, 초콜릿 아이스크림과 바닐라 아이스크림이 있습니다. 초콜릿은 하나에 2달러이고 바닐라는 하나에 1달러입니다.

여 그럼 제 주문에 초콜릿 하나, 바닐라 하나 추가해 주세요.

남 네. 다른 필요하신 게 있나요?

여 아니요. 여기 제 신용카드입니다.

남 알겠습니다. 음식이 준비되면 번호를 불러드리겠습니다.

여 감사합니다.

|해설| 여자는 7달러짜리 치킨버거 세트 2개와 2달러짜리 초콜릿 아이스크림 1개, 1달러짜리 바닐라 아이스크림 1개를 주문했으므로, 17달러를 지불해야 한다.

|어휘| order [명] 주문 credit card 신용카드

17 ①

M Hey, are you busy?

W I'm fixing our computer right now. Why?

M Emily needs a ride home, but I need to go to the grocery store before it closes.

W When does it close?

M It closes at 5:00, and it's already four o'clock.

W How about picking up Emily after you buy groceries?

M That will be too late. I don't want her to wait at the school that long.

W Okay. Then I will pick Emily up.

② It is hard to fix a computer.
③ You should go shopping first.
④ We need some eggs from the grocery store.
⑤ The store is ten minutes away from here.

남 저기, 바빠요?

여 지금 컴퓨터 고치는 중이에요. 왜요?

남 Emily를 집으로 태워 와야 하는데, 식료품점이 닫기 전에 가야 해서요.

여 식료품점이 언제 닫는데요?

남 5시에 닫는데, 벌써 4시예요.

여 식료품을 사고 나서 Emily를 데려오는 건 어때요?

남 그건 너무 늦을 거예요. 그 애가 학교에서 그렇게 오래 기다리는 걸 원하지 않아요.

여 좋아요. 그럼 내가 Emily를 데리러 갈게요.

② 컴퓨터를 고치는 건 어려워요.
③ 당신은 장 보러 먼저 가야겠네요.
④ 식료품점에서 달걀이 좀 필요해요.
⑤ 상점은 여기서 10분 떨어져 있어요.

|해설| 남자는 식료품점에서 장 보기와 Emily를 데리러 가야 하는 일이 겹쳐 난감해하고 있으므로, 여자가 Emily를 데리러 가겠다고 하는 ①이 적절하다.

|어휘| busy [형] 바쁜 fix [동] 고치다

18 ④

M The food was delicious. Thanks for inviting me over for lunch.

W My pleasure. I'm glad you enjoyed it. Would you like some more?

M Thanks, but I'm full.

W Okay. But how about dessert? I have some apple pie

and some chocolate cake.

M Oh, I always have room for dessert!

W Which would you prefer?

M I'll have a piece of cake, please.

① Yes, I really enjoyed it.
② No, I didn't have any.
③ Thanks, that would be great.
⑤ I don't like sweet things.

남 음식 맛있었어요. 점심식사에 초대해 주셔서 감사합니다.

여 별말씀을요. 맛있게 드셨다니 제가 기쁘네요. 좀 더 드릴까요?

남 고맙지만, 배가 부르네요.

여 알겠습니다. 후식은 어떠세요? 사과 파이와 초콜릿 케이크가 있어요.

남 아, 항상 후식 배는 따로 있죠!

여 어떤 게 더 좋으세요?

남 케이크 한 조각 먹을게요.

① 네, 정말 맛있었습니다.
② 아니요, 저는 아무것도 안 먹었습니다.
③ 고마워요, 그러면 좋겠습니다.
⑤ 저는 단것을 좋아하지 않습니다.

|해설| 여자가 후식을 권하며 두 가지 중 어떤 게 더 좋은지 물었으므로, 하나를 택하여 답하는 응답이 적절하다.

|어휘| invite [동] 초대하다 room [명] 공간 prefer [동] 더 좋아하다

19 ⑤

M I don't think I've seen you before. Are you new here?

W Yes, I am. This is my first day at this school.

M Well, how do you like our school so far?

W So far, I really like it. Everyone seems very nice.

M That's great. But moving to a new school must be hard.

W It is. Actually, I'm a little homesick.

M Don't worry. I'm sure you'll make lots of friends soon.

① You are really outgoing.
② I haven't met them yet.
③ You will go to a new school next month.
④ You'd better go see a doctor as soon as possible.

남 너 전에 본 적 없는 것 같은데. 여기 새로 왔니?

여 응, 맞아. 오늘이 이 학교에서의 첫날이야.

남 음, 지금까지 우리 학교 어때?

여 지금까지는 정말 좋아. 모두 매우 친절한 것 같아.

남 잘됐다. 하지만 새 학교로의 전학은 분명 힘들 텐데.

여 그렇지. 실은, 약간 옛 생각이 나.

남 걱정하지 마. 곧 친구를 많이 사귈 거야.

① 넌 정말 외향적이구나.
② 아직 그 애들 못 만나봤어.
③ 너는 다음 달에 새 학교로 가게 될 거야.
④ 가능한 한 빨리 의사 선생님께 진찰을 받으러 가는 게 좋겠다.

|어휘| so far 지금까지 homesick [형] 향수병에 걸린 **[문제]** outgoing [형] 외향적인 as soon as possible 가능한 한 빨리 make a friend 친구를 사귀다

20 ⑤

W Mr. Smith and his wife plan to go camping this weekend. They have already prepared all of the food and supplies they need. Today, however, Mr. Smith found out that he needs to attend an important meeting this Saturday. He checked if the meeting could be moved to another day, but it was impossible to change the schedule. In this situation, what would Mr. Smith most likely say to his wife?

Mr. Smith I'm sorry, but we need to postpone our camping trip.

① It's hard to have meetings on the weekend.
② I'm excited to go camping this weekend.
③ I postponed the meeting to another day.
④ I think we should change the meeting date.

여 Smith 씨와 아내는 이번 주말에 캠핑을 갈 계획이다. 그들은 이미 필요한 음식과 용품을 모두 준비했다. 하지만 오늘 Smith 씨는 이번 주 토요일에 중요한 회의에 참석해야 한다는 것을 알게 되었다. 그는 회의를 다른 날로 옮길 수 있는지 확인했지만, 일정을 바꾸는 것은 불가능했다. 이 상황에서, Smith 씨는 아내에게 뭐라고 말할까?

Mr. Smith 미안하지만, 우리의 캠핑 여행을 미뤄야 해요.

① 주말에 회의를 하는 건 힘들어요.
② 이번 주말에 캠핑을 가서 신이 나요.
③ 회의를 다른 날로 미뤘어요.
④ 회의 날짜를 바꿔야 할 것 같아요.

|해설| Smith 씨는 주말 캠핑을 위해 회의 일정을 바꿔보려 했으나 불가능한 상황이므로, 아내에게 캠핑 일정을 미뤄야 한다고 말하는 ⑤가 가장 적절하다.

|어휘| plan [동] 계획하다 supply [명] 용품, 물품 find out ~을 알게 되다 attend [동] 참석하다 meeting [명] 회의 impossible [형] 불가능한 schedule [명] 일정 **[문제]** postpone [동] 미루다

어휘·표현 다지기

p. 129

A

01 부상을 입은
02 교과서
03 근육
04 가능한 한 빨리
05 많은
06 운영 시간
07 그 뒤에
08 협조하다
09 긴급한
10 옷장, 벽장
11 ~을 알게 되다
12 폭발
13 최신의
14 강화하다
15 미루다
16 외향적인

B

01 reserve
02 ask a favor
03 spread
04 starving
05 so far
06 entrance fee
07 realize
08 seriously
09 homesick
10 environmentally friendly

실전 모의고사 3회

pp. 130-131

01 ①	02 ④	03 ②	04 ②	05 ④
06 ⑤	07 ④	08 ⑤	09 ③	10 ③
11 ②	12 ⑤	13 ④	14 ②	15 ④
16 ①	17 ⑤	18 ④	19 ①	20 ③

01 ①

M Are you going to buy one of those shirts?
W I think so. I like this one. The neck is shaped like a V.
M But the sleeves are short. Won't you get cold?
W No, I'll wear it in the summer.
M It doesn't have a pocket on the chest. Is that okay?
W Yes, that isn't a problem. I'll buy this one!

남 저 셔츠 중에서 하나 사려고?
여 그럴 것 같아. 난 이게 좋아. 목 부분이 V자 모양이야.
남 하지만 소매가 짧은데. 춥지 않을까?
여 아니, 나 이거 여름에 입을 거야.
남 가슴 쪽에 주머니가 없네. 괜찮겠어?
여 응, 그건 문제가 아냐. 나 이거 살래!

|해설| 여자는 목이 V자 모양이고 반소매이며, 주머니가 없는 셔츠를 사려고 한다.

|어휘| shaped like ~의 모양을 한 sleeve [명] 소매 pocket [명] 주머니 chest [명] 가슴

02 ④

M Ann, did you hear about Junior Summer Camp for this summer?
W No. Can you tell me about it in detail?
M The camp is held in Mount Westwood and fosters student leadership.
W What activities can you do at the camp?
M You can do activities such as exploring the forest, setting traps, and grilling meat.
W That sounds great. How much is the participation fee?
M Eighty dollars a week.
W That's not that bad. How many people can apply for the camp?
M Only 20 people can participate, so we should apply quickly.

남 Ann, 너 이번 여름에 열리는 Junior Summer Camp에 대해 들었니?
여 아니. 그 캠프에 대해 상세하게 말해줄래?
남 그 캠프는 Westwood 산에서 열리는데 학생들의 리더십을 발전시킨대.
여 캠프에서는 어떤 활동들을 할 수 있니?
남 숲 탐험, 덫 놓기, 고기 굽기 같은 활동을 할 수 있어.
여 좋은 것 같다. 참가비는 얼마니?
남 일주일에 80달러야.
여 그렇게 나쁘지 않네. 캠프에 몇 명이 신청할 수 있니?
남 20명만 참여할 수 있어서, 우리 빨리 신청해야 해.

|어휘| in detail 상세하게 foster [동] 조성하다, 발전시키다 leadership [명] 리더십 explore [동] 탐사[탐험]하다 set [동] 설치하다 trap [명] 덫 grill [동] 불에 굽다 participation fee 참가비 apply [동] 신청하다, 지원하다

03 ②

[Telephone rings.]
W Hello?
M Hi. This is Jaeho. May I speak to Yunsu, please? He isn't answering his cell phone.
W Yunsu isn't here. He went skiing with his classmates.
M Oh, he must be busy skiing. When is he coming back?
W Tonight. Can I take a message?
M Yes, Yunsu and I were going to play badminton tomorrow, but I can't make it because I have to look after my sister.
W Okay. I'll let him know.
M Thanks. I'll send him a text message too.

[전화벨이 울린다.]

여 여보세요?

남 안녕하세요. 저 재호인데요. 윤수와 통화할 수 있을까요? 휴대전화를 받지 않네요.

여 윤수 없는데. 반 친구들이랑 스키 타러 갔단다.

남 아, 그럼 스키 타느라 바쁘겠네요. 언제 돌아오나요?

여 오늘 밤에. 메시지 남겨줄까?

남 네, 윤수랑 제가 내일 배드민턴을 치기로 했는데, 제가 여동생을 돌봐야 해서 못 갈 것 같아요.

여 알겠다. 윤수한테 전해줄게.

남 감사합니다. 제가 윤수에게 문자 메시지도 보낼게요.

|어휘| be busy v-ing ~하느라 바쁘다 take a message 메시지를 받다 make it (모임 등에) 가다[참석하다] look after ~을 돌보다

04 ②

W Welcome to Welton's Swimming Center. How may I help you?

M Hello. I'm here to sign up for a swimming class.

W Okay. Which level would you like to be in a beginner, intermediate, or advanced class?

M I want to be in an intermediate class.

W There are two intermediate classes. One starts at 4:30 and the other starts at 6:00.

M I'll have to take the class that starts at 4:30. I think the class at 6:00 will end too late.

W So you would like to register for the earlier class?

M Yes. Here's my credit card.

여 Welton's 수영 센터에 오신 것을 환영합니다. 무엇을 도와드릴까요?

남 안녕하세요. 수영 수업을 등록하려고 왔습니다.

여 네. 초급, 중급, 고급반 중에 어떤 레벨에 들어가길 원하시나요?

남 중급반 수업에 들어가길 원해요.

여 중급반 수업은 두 개가 있어요. 하나는 4시 30분에 시작하고 다른 하나는 6시에 시작해요.

남 4시 30분에 시작하는 수업을 들어야겠네요. 6시에 하는 수업은 너무 늦게 끝날 것 같아서요.

여 그럼 더 이른 시간 수업을 등록하시겠습니까?

남 네. 여기 제 신용카드입니다.

|어휘| sign up for ~을 등록하다 level [명] 수준, 레벨 beginner [명] 초보자 intermediate [형] 중급의 advanced [형] 상급의

05 ④

M How can I help you?

W Can you fill up my tank, please?

M Sure. Can you just move your car a little bit forward?

W Okay. *[pause]* How's that?

M Perfect. Is there anything else I can do for you?

W Well, can I get my car washed here for free?

M No. It costs $8. But you get a coupon for 50% off for filling up your tank.

남 무엇을 도와드릴까요?

여 기름을 가득 넣어주시겠어요?

남 알겠습니다. 차를 약간 앞으로 이동해 주시겠어요?

여 네. [잠시 후] 어떤가요?

남 좋습니다. 제가 더 해드릴 일이 있나요?

여 음, 여기서 무료로 세차할 수 있나요?

남 아니요. 세차는 8달러입니다. 하지만 기름을 넣으셔서 50% 할인 쿠폰을 받으십니다.

|어휘| fill up ~을 가득 채우다 forward [부] 앞으로

06 ⑤

① M Excuse me. How much is this desk?
W It's on sale this week for $50.

② M Is there a bank in this neighborhood?
W Yes. There's one next to the train station.

③ M I don't have much money these days.
W You can get a part-time job.

④ M We should get tickets to the concert.
W Is that a good idea? They're very expensive.

⑤ M I'd like to change $50 to Korean won.
W Certainly. May I see your ID card, please?

① 남 실례합니다. 이 책상 얼마인가요?
여 이번 주에 50달러로 할인 판매 중입니다.

② 남 이 인근에 은행이 있나요?
여 네. 기차역 옆에 있어요.

③ 남 나 요즘 돈이 별로 없어.
여 아르바이트를 구하면 되지.

④ 남 우리 콘서트 표 사야 해.
여 그게 좋은 생각일까? 표가 너무 비싼데.

⑤ 남 50달러를 원화로 환전하고 싶어요.
여 알겠습니다. 신분증 좀 보여 주시겠어요?

|어휘| neighborhood [명] 근처, 인근 these days 요즘 ID (card) 신분증

07 ④

M How are you feeling, Hillary?
W Terrible. My sunburn really hurts.
M I told you that you needed to put on more sunscreen.
W I know. You were right. Anyway, could you buy me a sandwich at the convenience store?
M Sure. Didn't you have lunch?
W No. There's no food in the house, and I don't want to go outside.
M Yes, you need to keep out of the sun. Wait there, and I'll be back soon.

남 몸 상태는 어때, Hillary?
여 형편없어. 햇볕에 탄 데가 정말 아파.
남 자외선 차단제를 더 발라야 한다고 했잖아.
여 그러니까. 네 말이 맞았어. 그건 그렇고, 편의점에서 샌드위치 좀 사다 줄 수 있어?
남 물론이지. 점심 안 먹었어?
여 응. 집에 먹을 게 없는데, 밖에 나가고 싶지 않네.
남 그래, 너는 햇빛을 피해야 해. 거기서 기다리고 있으면, 내가 금방 다녀올게.

|어휘| terrible [형] 끔찍한, 형편없는 sunburn [명] 햇볕으로 입은 화상 hurt [동] 아프다 sunscreen [명] 자외선 차단제 convenience store 편의점 keep out of (햇볕·한기 등을) 피하다

08 ⑤

W Good morning. This is a reminder about our school trip to Sokcho. We'll be leaving on July 8 and traveling to the beach by bus. The trip will last for three days and two nights. If you're interested in going on the trip, please pick up a permission form at the main office. The form must be signed by your parents and returned to the office. Thank you.

여 안녕하세요. 속초로의 수학여행에 관해 다시 알려드립니다. 우리는 7월 8일에 출발하여 해변까지 버스로 이동할 예정입니다. 여행은 2박 3일간 계속될 것입니다. 여행 가는 데 관심이 있으면, 본 교무실에서 허가서 양식을 가져가십시오. 양식은 부모님께 서명을 받아 교무실에 다시 제출해야 합니다. 감사합니다.

|어휘| reminder [명] 상기시키는 것 last [동] 지속되다 be interested in ~에 관심이 있다 permission [명] 허가 form [명] (문서의) 양식 sign [동] 사인하다, 서명하다 return [동] 돌려주다

09 ③

M This game is played by two or four people. They stand on either side of a big table. In the middle of the table, there's a net. Each player has a racket. The players hit a ball over the net with their rackets. The ball must bounce on the table. If a player doesn't hit the ball back over the net before it bounces twice, the other team gets a point.

남 이 경기는 두 명이나 네 명이 경기를 합니다. 선수들은 큰 테이블 양쪽에 섭니다. 테이블 중앙에는 네트가 있습니다. 각 선수는 라켓을 가지고 있습니다. 선수들은 라켓을 이용해 네트 너머로 공을 칩니다. 공은 반드시 테이블 위에 튀어야 합니다. 만약 공이 두 번 튀기 전에 선수가 네트 너머로 공을 받아치지 못하면, 상대편이 득점합니다.

|어휘| stand [동] 서다 net [명] 그물, 네트 racket [명] 라켓 bounce [동] 튀다 get a point 득점하다

10 ③

① **M** I'd like you to meet my mother tonight. Can you come to dinner?
W Sure. I'm looking forward to meeting her.
② **M** How do you get to school?
W I usually take the subway and then walk.
③ **M** Do you want some more pizza?
W Sure. Help yourself.
④ **M** Would you like to go out this evening?
W I'm afraid I can't. I'm busy.
⑤ **M** Where did you get that jacket?
W I don't know. My mother bought it for me.

① 남 오늘 밤에 네가 우리 어머니를 뵈면 좋겠어. 저녁 식사에 올 수 있니?
여 물론이지. 너희 어머니 뵙는 거 기대된다.
② 남 너는 학교에 어떻게 가니?
여 보통 지하철을 탄 다음에 걸어가.
③ 남 피자 더 먹을래?
여 물론이지. 마음껏 먹어.
④ 남 오늘 저녁에 외출할까?
여 미안하지만 안 될 것 같아. 바쁘거든.
⑤ 남 그 재킷 어디서 샀어?
여 모르겠어. 어머니께서 나에게 사주셨어.

|해설| 'Help yourself.'는 '마음껏 드세요.'라는 뜻이다.

|어휘| look forward to v-ing ~하기를 고대하다 go out 외출하다

11 ②

W Welcome to Kim's English Academy. How can I help you?

M I'd like to take an English conversation class.

W Have you ever taken a class here before?

M No. This will be my first class.

W Then you need to take a test so we can find the right level for you.

M Sure. Can I take it now?

W Yes. You can take it in this empty classroom.

M All right. How long will it take?

W About thirty minutes. After you finish, I'll tell you more about our classes.

여 Kim's 영어 학원에 오신 걸 환영합니다. 무엇을 도와드릴까요?

남 영어 회화 수업을 듣고 싶은데요.

여 전에 여기서 수업을 들으신 적 있나요?

남 아니요. 이번이 첫 수업입니다.

여 그러면 저희가 학생에게 맞는 수준을 알 수 있도록 시험을 보셔야 합니다.

남 알겠습니다. 지금 볼 수 있나요?

여 네. 이 빈 강의실에서 보시면 됩니다.

남 알겠습니다. 얼마나 걸릴까요?

여 30분 정도요. 마치신 후에, 저희 수업에 대해 더 말씀드리겠습니다.

|해설| 여자는 남자가 수업을 듣기 전에 시험을 먼저 봐야 한다고 했다.

|어휘| conversation [명] 회화, 대화 empty [형] 빈

12 ⑤

W Will the school flea market be held inside the gym this year?

M No. The weather will be nice, so I want to have it outside.

W How about on the playground?

M No, the playground is too busy. We could have it between the river and the playground.

W There's not enough space. And the parking lot will be full of cars.

M How about in front of the gym?

W That's a good idea. Let's have the flea market there.

M All right. I'll tell the principal.

여 올해 교내 벼룩시장은 체육관 내부에서 열리나요?

남 아니요. 날씨가 좋을 거라, 야외에서 했으면 해요.

여 운동장에서는 어떨까요?

남 안 돼요. 운동장은 너무 붐벼요. 강가와 운동장 사이에서 할 수도 있겠네요.

여 거기는 공간이 넉넉하지 않아요. 그리고 주차장은 차들로 가득 차 있겠죠.

남 체육관 앞은 어때요?

여 좋은 생각이네요. 거기에서 벼룩시장을 합시다.

남 알겠습니다. 제가 교장 선생님께 말씀드릴게요.

|어휘| flea market 벼룩시장 inside [전] ~의 안[내부]에서 playground [명] 운동장, 놀이터 enough [형] 충분한 space [명] 공간 parking lot 주차장 principal [명] 교장

13 ④

W Welcome to Seoul! It's been such a long time since I saw you! When did you get here?

M Two days ago, on July 8.

W I see. Do you have time to meet for dinner? I know a restaurant that makes great hamburgers.

M Sure. But I have business meetings on July 11 and 14.

W Are you free the day after your first meeting?

M I am. Let's have dinner then!

여 서울에 온 것을 환영해! 정말 오랜만에 만나네! 여기에 언제 왔어?

남 이틀 전 7월 8일에.

여 그렇구나. 만나서 저녁 먹을 시간 있어? 맛있는 햄버거 만드는 음식점 아는데.

남 물론이지. 그런데 나 7월 11일과 14일에는 업무 회의가 있어.

여 첫 번째 회의 다음 날에는 한가하니?

남 응. 그때 저녁 먹자!

|해설| 두 사람은 남자의 첫 번째 회의 다음 날인 7월 12일에 만나기로 했다.

|어휘| business meeting 업무 회의

14 ②

M Hello, Carol. Did you have a good vacation?

W Hi, Darrin. I had a productive one.

M Really? Did you finish a lot of work at home?

W No, not really. But I learned to cook this vacation.

M What type of cuisine did you learn to cook?

W I learned to cook Western dishes such as pasta and pizza.

M You must have worked very hard. I should try to learn to cook too.

W You should. It's easier and more fun than you think.

남 안녕하세요, Carol. 휴가 잘 보내셨나요?

여 안녕하세요, Darrin. 저는 건설적인 휴가를 보냈어요.

남 정말요? 집에서 많은 일을 끝내셨나요?
여 아뇨, 그건 아니에요. 하지만 이번 휴가 때 요리를 배웠어요.
남 어떤 종류의 요리하는 걸 배우셨나요?
여 파스타나 피자 같은 양식 요리하는 것을 배웠어요.
남 정말 열심히 하셨겠네요. 저도 나중에 요리를 배워봐야겠어요.
여 꼭 배워보세요. 생각보다 더 쉽고 재밌답니다.

|어휘| vacation [명] 방학, 휴가 productive [형] 생산적인, 건설적인 cuisine [명] 요리, 요리법 Western dishes 서양 요리, 양식

15 ④

W Ladies and gentlemen, welcome to our Sunflower Circus. We promise to show you the best performance you've ever seen. Please remember that you have to follow these rules when you watch the performance. First, never stand up during the performance. There are flying acts in our performance, so it can be dangerous. Second, taking pictures and videos is not allowed. We ask you to turn off your cell phone before the performance starts. If you follow these rules, everyone will be able to enjoy the performance. Thank you.

여 신사 숙녀 여러분, 저희 해바라기 서커스에 오신 것을 환영합니다. 저희는 여러분이 여태껏 보신 중 최고의 공연을 보여드릴 것을 약속합니다. 공연을 관람하실 때 이 규칙들을 따라야 한다는 점을 기억해 주십시오. 첫째, 공연 중에 절대 자리에서 일어나지 마십시오. 공연에 날아다니는 연기가 있기 때문에, 위험할 수 있습니다. 둘째, 사진 및 동영상 촬영은 허용되지 않습니다. 공연 시작 전 휴대전화 전원을 꺼주실 것을 요청드립니다. 이 규칙들을 지켜주신다면, 모두가 공연을 즐기실 수 있을 것입니다. 감사합니다.

|어휘| circus [명] 서커스 promise [동] 약속하다 performance [명] 공연 remember [동] 기억하다 follow [동] 따르다 rule [명] 규칙 dangerous [형] 위험한 allow [동] 허락하다

16 ①

M Can I help you?
W Yes. How much is this guitar?
M That one is $400. But it's on sale for $300. It's one of our best guitars.
W Do you have anything cheaper?
M This one is $250. It's perfect for beginners.
W I'll take it. And how much is a pack of strings?
M It's $25. But the guitar comes with extra strings.
W Oh. Then I don't need to buy more. Great!

남 도와드릴까요?
여 네. 이 기타 얼마예요?
남 그건 400달러입니다. 그런데 300달러로 할인 판매 중입니다. 저희가 가진 최고의 기타 중 하나예요.
여 더 싼 것 있나요?
남 이 기타는 250달러예요. 초보자들에게 제격이죠.
여 그걸로 살게요. 그리고 기타 줄 한 묶음은 얼마죠?
남 25달러입니다. 그런데 그 기타에는 여분의 줄이 딸려 있어요.
여 아. 그러면 더 살 필요가 없군요. 잘됐네요!

|해설| 여자는 250달러짜리 기타를 골랐는데 기타 줄은 살 필요가 없다고 했으므로, 250달러를 지불하면 된다.

|어휘| pack [명] 묶음, 꾸러미 string [명] 줄 come with ~이 딸려 있다 extra [형] 여분의

17 ⑤

W Parker, what are you doing on your smartphone?
M I'm looking for my dad's birthday present, but I can't find anything good.
W Let me help you. What price range do you have in mind?
M I'm thinking between twenty and forty dollars.
W Then how about an electric shaver?
M That's a great idea, but he recently bought one.
W Hmm… What about a fountain pen? He'd be able to use it at work.
M It would be too expensive to get a nice one. Can you think of something else?

① A fountain pen is what I really need at school.
② It's very hard to recommend something for you.
③ You have to choose your father's present today.
④ That's a good idea! I will buy a shaver for him.

여 Parker, 스마트폰으로 뭘 하고 있니?
남 아빠 생신 선물을 보고 있는데, 좋은 걸 고를 수가 없네.
여 내가 도와줄게. 어느 가격대를 생각하고 있니?
남 20달러에서 40달러 사이로 생각하고 있어.
여 그렇다면 전기 면도기 어때?
남 정말 좋은 생각이지만, 아버지는 최근에 하나 사셨어.
여 음… 만년필은 어때? 일하실 때 사용할 수 있으실 거야.
남 좋은 걸 사려면 너무 비쌀 거야. 다른 것을 생각해볼 수 있겠어?

① 만년필은 내가 학교에서 정말 필요한 거야.
② 너에게 뭔가를 추천하는 것은 정말 어려워.
③ 너는 오늘 너희 아버지 선물을 골라야 해.
④ 그거 좋은 생각이야! 면도기를 사드릴래.

|해설| 여자가 남자에게 아버지 생신 선물을 추천하는 상황이다. 전기 면도기에 이어 만년필을 추천했으므로, 추천을 받아들이거나 다른 것을 추천해 달라는 말이 이어지는 것이 가장 적절하다.

|어휘| price rage 가격대 have in mind ~을 생각하다[염두에 두다] electric shaver 전기 면도기 fountain pen 만년필

18 ④

M Hi, I'm Sam Jones with NC Insurance Company.
W Hi. What can I do for you?
M Well, I'd like to know if you have any life insurance.
W No, I don't. But I don't want to buy any either.
M What will your family do if something happens to you? Everyone has to think about that.
W My husband has excellent life insurance.
M But you should have some too. Our company has the nation's most trusted life insurance.
W Sorry, I'm really not interested.

① I already have one.
② I highly recommend it.
③ Did you make a reservation?
⑤ He's not at home. Can I take a message?

남 안녕하세요. NC 보험사의 Sam Jones입니다.
여 안녕하세요. 무엇을 도와드릴까요?
남 음, 생명보험을 가지고 계신가 해서요.
여 아니요, 없어요. 그런데 들고 싶지도 않아요.
남 고객님께 무슨 일이 생기면 가족분들은 어떻게 할까요? 모든 사람이 그걸 생각해 봐야 해요.
여 제 남편이 아주 괜찮은 생명보험이 있어요.
남 하지만 고객님도 있으셔야죠. 저희 회사에는 우리나라에서 가장 신뢰받는 생명보험이 있습니다.
여 죄송합니다. 정말 관심 없습니다.

① 저는 이미 하나 있어요.
② 그걸 아주 추천합니다.
③ 예약하셨나요?
⑤ 그는 집에 없어요. 메시지 남기시겠어요?

|어휘| insurance [명] 보험 trusted [형] 신뢰받는 [문제] highly [부] 매우, 크게 make a reservation 예약하다

19 ①

W Hi, Jihun. Are you going to Hyejin's birthday party tonight?
M Yes, I am. I'm really looking forward to it. Did you get her a present yet?
W Yes, I stopped by the mall after school yesterday and bought her a scarf. What about you?
M Not yet. I'm not sure what she would like.
W Whenever I see her, she's always reading a book. Maybe you could buy her a new novel.
M Do you know what genre she likes?
W She seems to like mystery novels.

② I think that she is really kind.
③ Yes, she is a great writer.
④ I forgot that it is Hyejin's birthday.
⑤ I can't make it to the party tonight.

여 안녕, 지훈아. 오늘 밤에 혜진이 생일 파티에 갈 거야?
남 응, 갈 거야. 파티 정말 기대된다. 너 벌써 혜진이 선물 샀어?
여 응, 어제 학교 끝나고 쇼핑몰에 잠시 들러서 그 애에게 스카프를 사 줬어. 너는?
남 아직. 그 애가 뭘 좋아할지 모르겠어.
여 내가 그 애를 볼 때마다 그 애는 늘 책을 읽고 있더라. 아마도 그 애에게 새 소설을 사 주면 될 것 같아.
남 그 애가 무슨 장르를 좋아하는지 아니?
여 그 애는 추리소설을 좋아하는 것 같아.

② 그 애는 정말 친절한 것 같아.
③ 응, 그녀는 훌륭한 작가야.
④ 나는 그날이 혜진이의 생일인 걸 잊었어.
⑤ 나는 오늘 밤에 파티에 갈 수 없어.

|어휘| stop by ~에 잠시 들르다 whenever [접] ~할 때마다

20 ③

M Carrie is going to the lake for one night next week. She asks Peter if he can join her. He wants to, but he has classes on Monday and Wednesday. Also, his cousin's birthday party is on Friday, so he's only free on Tuesday and Thursday. He asks Carrie when she is going. She says she plans to leave on Friday morning. In this situation, what would Peter most likely say to Carrie?
Peter Oh, I have to go to a birthday party on Friday.

① I'm fine, and you?
② Sorry, I have a class on that day.
④ Great! Can you pick me up on Friday morning?
⑤ Why don't we go on Wednesday instead?

남 Carrie는 다음 주에 1박으로 호수에 간다. Carrie는 Peter에게 함께 갈 수 있는지 묻는다. 그는 가고 싶지만, 월요일과 수요일에 수업이 있다. 또한, 그의 사촌의 생일 파티가 금요일에 있어서, 화요일과 목요일에만 한가하다. 그는 Carrie에게 언제 갈 예정인지 묻는다. Carrie는 금요일 아침에 떠날 계획이라고 말한다. 이 상황에서, Peter는 Carrie에게 뭐라고 말할까?
Peter 아, 나 금요일에는 생일 파티에 가야 해.

① 난 잘 지내, 너는?

② 미안, 그날에는 수업이 있어.
④ 잘됐다! 금요일 아침에 나 데리러 와줄 수 있어?
⑤ 우리 대신 수요일에 가는 것은 어때?

|어휘| free [형] 한가한 plan [동] 계획하다

어휘·표현 다지기

p. 139

A

01	운동장, 놀이터	02	회화, 대화
03	공간	04	상세하게
05	허락하다	06	상급의
07	신뢰받는	08	득점하다
09	자외선 차단제	10	허가
11	요즘	12	벼룩시장
13	생산적인, 건설적인	14	보험
15	초보자	16	~을 돌보다

B

01	reminder	02	forward
03	make it	04	highly
05	last	06	neighborhood
07	string	08	bounce
09	fill up	10	have in mind

실전 모의고사 4회

pp. 140-141

01 ①	02 ④	03 ③	04 ⑤	05 ⑤
06 ②	07 ③	08 ④	09 ③	10 ①
11 ③	12 ③	13 ②	14 ①	15 ②
16 ④	17 ⑤	18 ①	19 ⑤	20 ②

01 ①

M Hello, I'm looking for some macarons for my daughter.
W Okay. We have several options. What about our animal-shaped macarons?
M Well, I don't like the chocolate bear macarons, but the rabbit ones are cute.
W Oh, actually someone has already reserved those to be picked up later.
M That's too bad. What about the macarons decorated with ribbons?
W Those are our most popular ones. It's $20 for a box of six.
M I'll take it!

남 안녕하세요, 제 딸에게 줄 마카롱을 좀 찾고 있는데요.
여 알겠습니다. 손님이 선택하실 만한 것들이 몇 가지 있어요. 저희 동물 모양 마카롱은 어떠세요?
남 음, 초콜릿 곰 모양 마카롱은 마음에 들지 않지만, 토끼 모양 마카롱은 귀엽네요.
여 아, 사실 어떤 분이 나중에 가져가겠다고 그것들을 이미 예약하셨어요.
남 정말 아쉽네요. 리본으로 장식된 마카롱은 어떤가요?
여 그건 저희 가게에서 가장 인기 있는 마카롱인데요. 6개가 들어 있는 한 상자에 20달러예요.
남 그걸로 할게요!

|어휘| several [형] (몇)몇의 reserve [동] 예약하다 decorate [동] 장식하다

02 ④

M Good morning, Megan. Did you have a good weekend?
W Hi, Tyler. I did! I went to my favorite writer's book signing.
M Really? Who did you go to see?
W I saw Andy Lee. He is a famous writer who wrote the bestseller *HOPE*.
M What do you like about him?
W He grew up in a poor family, but he wasn't discouraged. He expresses his journey through life beautifully in his book.
M That's amazing. Did he major in literature in college?
W No, he majored in psychology. He said he has a hobby of reading books related to psychology.
M He sounds cool. I should try reading one of his books.

남 좋은 아침이야, Megan. 좋은 주말 보냈니?
여 안녕, Tyler. 응! 내가 가장 좋아하는 작가의 책 사인회에 다녀왔어.
남 정말? 누구를 보러 갔는데?
여 Andy Lee를 봤어. 그는 〈HOPE〉라는 베스트셀러를 쓴 유명 작가야.
남 그의 어떤 점이 좋아?
여 그는 가난한 집안에서 자랐지만 낙담하지 않았어. 그는 책에서 그의 인생 여정을 아름답게 표현해.
남 놀랍다. 그는 대학에서 문학을 전공했니?
여 아니, 심리학을 전공했어. 그는 심리학 관련 책을 읽는 취미가 있다고 했어.
남 멋지다. 나도 그의 책 한 권 읽어볼래.

|어휘| book signing 책 사인회 discourage [동] 낙담시키다 journey [명] 여행, 여정 beautifully [부] 아름답게 major in ~을 전공하다 literature [명] 문학 college [명] 대학 psychology [명] 심리학 related to ~와 관련된

03 ③

[Cell phone rings.]

M Hello?

W Hi, Michael, this is Julie. Is everything all right? I've tried calling you several times this morning.

M Sorry, I just turned on my phone.

W Were you sleeping?

M No, I was watching a movie at the theater this morning.

W Oh, I see. I was just hoping you could tell me what the English assignment is.

M You have to write a two-page essay on your favorite celebrity.

W Okay. Thanks, Michael.

[휴대전화벨이 울린다.]

남 여보세요?

여 안녕, Michael, 나 Julie야. 괜찮은 거야? 오늘 아침에 너한테 여러 번 전화하려고 했는데.

남 미안, 방금 전화기를 켰어.

여 자고 있었니?

남 아니, 오늘 아침에 극장에서 영화 보고 있었어.

여 아, 그랬구나. 영어 과제가 뭔지 네가 알려줄 수 있을까 해서.

남 네가 제일 좋아하는 유명인에 관한 두 쪽짜리 에세이를 써야 해.

여 그렇구나. 고마워, Michael.

|어휘| turn on (전원을) 켜다 assignment [명] 과제 celebrity [명] 유명인

04 ⑤

[Telephone rings.]

M Hello, this is Tom's Kitchen. How may I help you?

W Hello. I'd like to make a reservation. Is there a separate room for meetings?

M Yes, there is. How many people is the reservation for?

W Thirteen people. I'd like to make the reservation for October 15. What times are available?

M Two, five, and seven are available.

W We're going to have dinner, so two o'clock is too early.

M Then would you like to make a reservation for the latest time?

W Yes. Please make the reservation for Anne Hoult.

[전화벨이 울린다.]

남 안녕하세요, Tom's Kitchen입니다. 무엇을 도와드릴까요?

여 안녕하세요. 예약을 하고 싶은데요. 모임을 위한 분리된 룸이 있나요?

남 네, 있습니다. 몇 분 예약인가요?

여 13명입니다. 10월 15일로 예약하고 싶은데요. 몇 시가 가능한가요?

남 2시, 5시, 7시가 가능합니다.

여 저희는 저녁을 먹을 거라, 2시는 너무 이르네요.

남 그럼 가장 늦은 시간으로 예약하시겠습니까?

여 네. Anne Hoult로 예약해 주세요.

|어휘| reservation [명] 예약 separate [형] 분리된 available [형] 이용 가능한 latest [형] 가장 늦은, 맨 뒤의

05 ⑤

[Cell phone rings.]

W Hello?

M Marie, I have some bad news. I missed my flight.

W What? You usually get to the airport so early.

M I was three hours early. To pass the time, I looked around the duty free shops.

W So you didn't go to the gate on time?

M That's right. I was too busy looking at new bags and sunglasses.

W Didn't they call your name over the loudspeaker?

M I don't know. I was listening to music on my earphones.

[휴대전화벨이 울린다.]

여 여보세요?

남 Marie, 안 좋은 소식이 있어. 나 항공편을 놓쳤어.

여 뭐라고? 너 보통 공항에 무척 일찍 가잖아.

남 세 시간 일찍 왔었어. 시간을 보내려고 면세점을 둘러봤지.

여 그래서 제시간에 탑승구에 못 간 거야?

남 맞아. 새 가방과 선글라스를 보느라 너무 바빴어.

여 스피커로 네 이름을 부르지 않았어?

남 모르겠어. 나는 이어폰으로 음악을 듣고 있었거든.

|해설| 남자가 항공편을 놓친 이유를 말하고 있는 데서 당황한 심정을 읽을 수 있다.

|어휘| miss [동] 놓치다 flight [명] 항공편 pass [동] (시간을) 보내다 look around 둘러보다 duty free shop 면세점 gate [명] 탑승구 on time 제시간에 be busy v-ing ~하느라 바쁘다 loudspeaker [명] 스피커, 확성기 [문제] satisfied [형] 만족한 relieved [형] 안도하는

06 ②

① **M** Excuse me! You dropped your wallet.
W Oh, thank you very much.
② **M** You're over your credit limit.
W Oh, am I? I guess I'll pay in cash.
③ **M** Do I have to pay a late fee?
W No, you don't have to.
④ **M** Are you hungry? Let's get dinner!
W I'm starving. How about burgers?
⑤ **M** I don't have any money right now. Can you lend me some?
W Sure, how much do you need?

① **남** 실례합니다! 지갑을 떨어뜨리셨어요.
여 아, 정말 고맙습니다.
② **남** 신용카드 한도액을 초과하셨네요.
여 아, 그런가요? 현금으로 내야겠네요.
③ **남** 연체료를 내야 하나요?
여 아니요, 그러실 필요 없습니다.
④ **남** 배고프세요? 저녁 먹읍시다!
여 배고파 죽을 지경이에요. 버거 어때요?
⑤ **남** 지금 돈이 하나도 없어요. 좀 빌려주실 수 있나요?
여 물론이죠. 얼마나 필요하세요?

|어휘| drop [동] 떨어뜨리다 wallet [명] 지갑 credit limit 신용 한도, 신용카드 한도액 pay in cash 현금으로 내다 late fee 연체료 starving [형] 몹시 배고픈 lend [동] 빌려주다

07 ③

[Cell phone rings.]
W Hello?
M Hi, Laura. This is Adam. Where are you?
W I'm almost there. The next stop is Sinchon station. What about you?
M I'm actually running late. Could you go to the restaurant and wait in line?
W Okay. I heard that people have to wait in line for at least forty minutes on weekends.
M All right. Then I should be there by the time you get a table.

[휴대전화벨이 울린다.]
여 여보세요?
남 안녕, Laura. 나 Adam이야. 어디니?
여 거의 다 왔어. 다음 정거장이 신촌역이야. 넌?
남 난 사실 늦을 것 같아. 음식점 가서 줄 서서 기다릴 수 있어?
여 알겠어. 주말에는 적어도 40분은 줄 서서 기다려야 한다더라.
남 맞아. 그러면 난 네가 테이블에 자리 잡을 때까지는 도착할 거야.

|해설| 남자는 자신이 늦는다고 하며 여자에게 먼저 음식점에 가서 줄 서 기다리라고 부탁하고 있다.

|어휘| wait in line 줄을 서서 기다리다 at least 적어도, 최소한 by the time ~할 때까지

08 ④

W Attention, everyone. Pinewood College is having a networking event next Saturday, October 4 from 12:00 to 6:00 p.m. The event is open to current students and recent graduates. The purpose of this event is to help current and former students build professional relationships with employers. We will start the afternoon by having lunch in the cafeteria. After that, you will have time to talk with various business professionals. Please dress professionally.

여 주목해 주시기 바랍니다, 여러분. Pinewood 대학교는 10월 4일 다음 주 토요일 오후 12시부터 6시까지 교류 행사가 있습니다. 이 행사에는 재학생과 최근 졸업생들이 참여할 수 있습니다. 이 행사의 목적은 재학생들과 졸업생들이 고용주들과 전문적인 관계를 맺도록 돕는 것입니다. 우리는 구내식당에서 점심을 먹으면서 오후를 시작할 것입니다. 그 후에, 여러 업계 전문가들과 이야기를 나눌 시간을 가질 것입니다. 정장 차림으로 오시기 바랍니다.

|어휘| networking [명] 네트워킹, 교류 open to ~에게 열려 있는, ~가 참여할 수 있는 current [형] 현재의 graduate [명] 대학 졸업생[졸업자] purpose [명] 목적 former [형] 이전의 professional [형] 전문적인 [명] 전문가 relationship [명] 관계 employer [명] 고용주 cafeteria [명] 구내식당

09 ③

M People who have this job work in museums. They study ancient books or objects. They have usually graduated from a university with a history degree and have extensive knowledge of ancient things. They not only introduce artifacts to people, but also plan and manage exhibitions in museums.

남 이 직업을 가진 사람들은 박물관에서 일합니다. 그들은 고서나 고대 물건을 연구합니다. 그들은 보통 대학에서 역사학 학위로 졸업하며, 고대 물건에 관한 폭넓은 지식을 갖고 있습니다. 그들은 사람들에게 공예품을 소개할 뿐만 아니라, 박물관에서 전시를 계획하고 관리합니다.

|어휘| ancient [형] 고대의 object [명] 물건 graduate from ~을 졸업하다 university [명] 대학 history [명] 역사(학) degree [명] 학위 extensive [형] 폭넓은 knowledge [명] 지식 introduce

동 소개하다　artifact 명 공예품　plan 동 계획하다　manage 동 관리하다　exhibition 명 전시(회)

10 ①

① W　How did you like the musical?
　 M　We went there by subway.
② W　Please slow down. This is a school zone.
　 M　Oh, is it? I didn't see the sign.
③ W　You're not allowed to chew gum during class.
　 M　Okay. I'm sorry I broke the rules.
④ W　This newspaper review says the movie is great.
　 M　Let's go see it.
⑤ W　When do I have to hand in my report?
　 M　By this Friday.

① 여　뮤지컬 어땠어?
　 남　우리는 지하철로 그곳에 갔어.
② 여　속도를 늦추세요. 여기는 어린이 보호구역이에요.
　 남　아, 그래요? 표지판을 못 봤네요.
③ 여　수업 중에 껌을 씹는 건 안 된단다.
　 남　알겠습니다. 규칙을 어겨서 죄송해요.
④ 여　이 신문 논평에서 말하길 그 영화가 정말 좋대.
　 남　그거 보러 가자.
⑤ 여　보고서를 언제 제출해야 하나요?
　 남　이번 주 금요일까지요.

|해설| ①에서 여자가 뮤지컬이 어땠는지 묻고 있으므로, 남자는 뮤지컬을 본 소감을 말하는 것이 자연스럽다.

|어휘| slow down 속도를 늦추다　sign 명 표지판　allow 동 허락하다, 허용하다　chew 동 씹다　break a rule 규칙을 어기다　review 명 논평　hand in ~을 제출하다　report 명 보고서

11 ③

M　Molly, is there something wrong with your foot?
W　Yes, it really hurts. I think it's swollen.
M　Can you take off your skates? [pause] Wow, they're way too small.
W　I know. They're my sister's. She let me borrow them because I lost mine.
M　You shouldn't wear these. Please go to the rental shop and rent a bigger pair.
W　Okay. Where is the shop?
M　Over there!

남　Molly, 너 발에 무슨 문제 있니?
여　응, 정말 아파. 내 생각엔 부은 것 같아.
남　스케이트화를 벗어 볼래? [잠시 후] 와, 스케이트화가 너무 작네.

여　맞아. 내 여동생 것이거든. 내가 내 스케이트화를 잃어버려서 동생이 스케이트화를 빌려줬어.
남　이건 신으면 안 돼. 대여점에 가서 더 큰 걸 빌리렴.
여　알았어. 대여점이 어디니?
남　저기!

|어휘| swollen 형 부은　take off ~을 벗다　rental shop 대여점

12 ③

M　Hey, Julie. I'm looking for a new phone, but it's hard to choose one.
W　Let me help you. Is there anything inconvenient about your current phone?
M　Yes. My phone is too heavy for me.
W　I see. Then you want a light one.
M　Right. I want my new cell phone to be under 200 g.
W　Good thinking. Weight is an important factor in choosing a cell phone.
M　Also, my phone color is too dark right now. I want to get a lighter one this time.
W　Sounds good. Now what about the phone's storage space?
M　I like taking pictures, so I hope it has a large amount of storage.
W　Then I think this cell phone would be best for you.
M　It looks great! I'll take it.

남　안녕, Julie. 새 휴대전화를 찾아보고 있는데, 고르는 게 어렵네.
여　내가 도와줄게. 현재 휴대전화를 사용하면서 불편한 것이 있니?
남　응. 내 휴대전화는 나에게 너무 무거워.
여　알겠어. 그럼 가벼운 걸 원하겠네.
남　응. 새 휴대전화는 200g 이하면 좋겠어.
여　좋은 생각이야. 무게는 휴대전화를 선택할 때 중요한 요소지.
남　그리고 지금 내 휴대전화 색상은 너무 어두워. 이번에는 더 밝은 색을 사고 싶어.
여　좋아. 자, 휴대전화 저장 공간은?
남　사진 찍는 걸 좋아해서, 저장 용량이 크면 좋겠어.
여　그럼 이 휴대전화가 너에게 제일 좋을 것 같아.
남　좋아 보여! 그걸로 살래.

|어휘| choose 동 선택하다　inconvenient 형 불편한　heavy 형 무거운　light 형 가벼운; 밝은　weight 명 무게　factor 명 요소　dark 형 어두운　storage 명 저장　space 명 공간　amount 명 양

13 ②

W　The musical starts at 6:00 p.m., doesn't it?

M Yes. Do you want to meet at the concert hall?

W How about having dinner before the show?

M That's a good idea. What do you want to eat?

W I want to eat Mexican food.

M Sounds great. Then shall we meet at 5:00 p.m.?

W Isn't that too late? How about 4:00 p.m. instead?

M That would be too early. Let's meet at 4:30 p.m.

W Okay. See you then!

여 뮤지컬이 오후 6시에 시작하지?

남 응. 공연장에서 만날래?

여 공연 전에 저녁 먹는 게 어때?

남 좋은 생각이야. 뭐 먹을래?

여 멕시코 음식을 먹고 싶어.

남 좋아. 그럼 오후 5시에 만날까?

여 그건 너무 늦지 않아? 대신 오후 4시는 어때?

남 그건 너무 일러. 4시 30분에 만나자.

여 좋아. 그때 보자!

|어휘| concert hall 공연장   Mexican 휑 멕시코의

14 ①

W Michael, you look sad. What's the matter?

M Hi, Emily. My mom is sick.

W I'm so sorry. Do you know what's wrong?

M She has the flu. I should do something for her.

W Why don't you get her some medicine?

M She got medicine from the hospital yesterday.

W Then why don't you help her with housework?

M Great idea! I think she'd really appreciate that.

여 Michael, 슬퍼 보인다. 무슨 일 있니?

남 안녕, Emily. 엄마가 아프셔.

여 정말 유감이야. 뭐 때문인지 아니?

남 독감에 걸리셨어. 엄마를 위해서 뭔가를 해야겠어.

여 약을 사다 드리는 게 어때?

남 약은 어제 병원에서 받으셨어.

여 그럼 집안일을 도와드리는 게 어때?

남 좋은 생각이야! 엄마가 그걸 정말 고마워하실 것 같아.

|어휘| flu 휑 독감   medicine 휑 약   housework 휑 집안일
appreciate 통 고마워하다

15 ②

M May I have your attention, please? This is your principal, Mr. James. Unfortunately, last week, a student was injured while crossing a crosswalk. Running across the street without checking the crossing light was the cause of the accident. I strongly recommend that you check the light before crossing a crosswalk. Also, wait for at least three seconds once the signal changes. This simple act will protect you from danger. Our teachers will also do their best to keep you safe. Thank you.

남 주목해 주시겠습니까? 저는 교장 James입니다. 유감스럽게도, 지난주에 한 학생이 횡단보도를 건너다가 다쳤습니다. 신호등을 확인하지 않고 달려 길을 건넌 것이 사고의 원인이었습니다. 횡단보도를 건너기 전에 신호등을 확인할 것을 강경하게 권고합니다. 또한 신호가 바뀌면 최소 3초는 기다리십시오. 이 간단한 행동이 여러분을 위험으로부터 지켜줄 것입니다. 교사들도 여러분의 안전을 지키기 위해 최선을 다할 것입니다. 감사합니다.

|어휘| attention 휑 주의, 주목   injure 통 부상을 입히다
cross 통 건너다   crosswalk 휑 횡단보도   crossing light 신호
등   cause 휑 원인   accident 휑 사고   strongly 튀 강경하게
recommend 통 권고하다   second 휑 초   signal 휑 신호   act
휑 행동   protect 통 보호하다   danger 휑 위험

16 ④

W I'd like to have some clothes dry-cleaned.

M Okay. What do you have?

W I have two dresses and a pair of pants. How much will that be?

M It's $5 for each dress and $3 for the pants.

W Okay. But can you shorten these pants by 2 cm?

M I can do that. It'll cost $5 extra.

W Oh, really? That's expensive.

M The pants are made of an unusual fabric. That will make it more difficult.

W All right. I'll come back next weekend to pick them up.

여 옷 몇 벌을 드라이클리닝하고 싶은데요.

남 알겠습니다. 무엇을 가져오셨나요?

여 원피스 두 벌과 바지 한 벌이요. 비용이 얼마나 들까요?

남 원피스는 각 5달러이고 바지는 3달러입니다.

여 알겠습니다. 그런데 이 바지를 2센티미터 줄여주실 수 있나요?

남 가능합니다. 5달러가 추가될 거예요.

여 아, 정말요? 비싸네요.

남 이 바지는 흔치 않은 천으로 만들어졌어요. 그것 때문에 줄이는 게 더 어려울 거예요.

여 알겠습니다. 다음 주말에 옷 가지러 다시 오겠습니다.

|해설| 원피스는 드라이클리닝 비용이 각 5달러인데 두 벌을 맡겼으므로 10달러이고, 바지는 한 벌로 3달러이다. 그런데 바지를 줄이는 비용 5달러가 추가되므로 여자가 지불할 총 금액은 18달러이다.

|어휘| shorten [동] 줄이다, 짧게 하다 unusual [형] 흔치 않은 fabric [명] 천, 직물

17 ⑤

M Hannah, which after-school class did you sign up for?
W I signed up for the theater class. How about you?
M I did too! I thought I would be alone in the theater class, so I'm glad you'll be there.
W I'm glad too. So, what do we have to bring on the first day of class?
M We need to bring our notebooks and something to write with.
W Is that all we have to bring?
M Yes. But don't forget to wear comfortable clothes.

① The drama teacher is a great person.
② You shouldn't bring a bicycle to school.
③ Theater class will help you a lot in your career.
④ I'm thinking about changing my after-school class.

남 Hannah, 어떤 방과후 수업을 신청했니?
여 연극반을 신청했어. 너는?
남 나도! 연극반에 혼자일 줄 알았는데, 너가 있어서 기뻐.
여 나도 기뻐. 그럼 수업 첫째 날 뭘 가져가야 할까?
남 공책과 필기구를 좀 가져가면 돼.
여 가져가야 하는 게 그게 전부니?
남 응. 하지만 편안한 복장을 입는 걸 잊지 마.

① 연극 선생님은 훌륭한 분이셔.
② 학교에 자전거를 가져와서는 안 돼.
③ 연극 수업은 너의 진로에 많은 도움이 될 거야.
④ 방과후 수업을 바꿀까 생각 중이야.

|해설| 남자가 연극반 수업 첫째 날에 필요한 물건들을 말해주고 여자가 그것만 가져가면 되는지 물었으므로, 준비물에 관해 말하는 ⑤가 가장 적절하다.

|어휘| after-school class 방과후 수업 theater [명] 극장, 연극 alone [형] 혼자, 다른 사람 없이 glad [형] 기쁜 bring [동] 가져오다 [문제] career [명] 진로 comfortable [형] 편안한

18 ①

M Hello, are the tickets available for the gallery's new exhibition?
W Yes. How many tickets would you like?
M Just one, please. How much are the tickets?
W The weekend price is $15 for adults.
M Is there a discount for students?
W Yes, the ticket price for students is $10. But you need to show a current student ID to get the discount.
M I have my student ID card right here.
W Great. That will be $10.

② Okay, you need a new ID card now.
③ Can I see your driver's license, please?
④ It is unfair for students to get a discount.
⑤ Sorry, but children under the age of six can't go inside.

남 안녕하세요, 미술관의 새 전시회 표를 살 수 있나요?
여 네. 몇 장 원하시나요?
남 한 장만 주세요. 표가 얼마죠?
여 성인 주말 요금은 15달러입니다.
남 학생 할인이 있나요?
여 네, 학생 표 가격은 10달러입니다. 하지만 할인을 받기 위해서는 현 학생증을 보여 주셔야 합니다.
남 여기 제 학생증이 있습니다.
여 네. 10달러입니다.

② 알겠습니다. 이제 새 신분증이 필요하겠네요.
③ 운전면허증을 볼 수 있을까요?
④ 학생이 할인을 받는 것은 부당해요.
⑤ 죄송하지만, 6세 미만의 아이는 들어갈 수 없습니다.

|어휘| student ID 학생증 [문제] driver's license 운전면허증 unfair [형] 불공정한

19 ⑤

M Thanks for taking me to the movies.
W It's my pleasure. The movie was exciting, wasn't it?
M I guess so...
W What's wrong? Didn't you like it?
M It was a little too scary for me.
W I see. You must not like horror movies very much.
M No, I don't. I prefer funny and heart-warming movies such as romantic comedies and animated movies.
W Okay, next time we'll see a different kind of movie.

① Great! I like horror movies best.
② I heard that movie is really good.
③ Okay, let's watch this movie again.
④ Sorry. I can't go to the movies tonight.

남 영화관에 데려가 줘서 고마워.
여 천만에. 영화가 흥미진진했지?
남 그런 것 같은데…
여 뭐가 안 좋았어? 영화가 별로였니?
남 나한테는 좀 무서웠어.

여 그랬구나. 네가 공포 영화를 그렇게 좋아하지는 않나 보다.
남 응, 좋아하지 않아. 나는 로맨틱 코미디나 애니메이션처럼 재미있고 마음이 따뜻해지는 영화를 더 좋아해.
여 그래, 다음에는 다른 종류의 영화를 보자.

① 잘됐다! 나는 공포 영화가 제일 좋아.
② 그 영화가 정말 좋다고 들었어.
③ 그래, 이 영화 다시 보자.
④ 미안해. 나 오늘 밤에 영화 보러 못 가.

|해설| 남자가 공포 영화가 아닌 로맨틱 코미디나 애니메이션처럼 재미있고 마음이 따뜻해지는 영화를 좋아한다고 했으므로, 그에 대한 여자의 대답으로 다음에는 다른 영화를 보자고 하는 것이 적절하다.

|어휘| horror movie 공포 영화 heart-warming [형] 마음이 따뜻해지는 animated movie 애니메이션 영화, 만화영화

20 ②

M Amanda bought a pair of hiking shoes as a present for her brother, but he is not interested in hiking anymore. He recently started playing golf, so he asked Amanda to return the shoes and buy him some golf clothes instead. In this situation, what would Amanda most likely say to the clerk at the shoe store?
Amanda Can I get a refund, please?

① I would like to sign up for golf lessons.
③ Which golf shoes do you recommend?
④ Do you have these shoes in a larger size?
⑤ These shoes are damaged. Can I get a new pair?

남 Amanda는 오빠에게 선물로 등산화 한 켤레를 사주었으나, 오빠는 등산에 더 이상 흥미를 보이지 않는다. 그는 최근에 골프를 치기 시작해서, Amanda에게 신발을 반품하고 대신 골프복을 사달라고 부탁했다. 이 상황에서, Amanda는 신발 가게 점원에게 뭐라고 말할까?
Amanda 환불받을 수 있을까요?

① 골프 수업을 등록하고 싶습니다.
③ 어느 골프화를 추천해주시겠어요?
④ 이 신발로 더 큰 치수 있나요?
⑤ 이 신발에 하자가 있어요. 새것을 받을 수 있을까요?

|해설| 남편이 Amanda에게 등산화를 반품하고 골프복을 사달라고 부탁했으므로, 신발 가게 점원에게 환불받을 수 있는지 묻는 것이 가장 적절하다.

|어휘| hiking shoes 등산화, 하이킹 신발 clerk [명] 점원, 직원
[문제] get a refund 환불받다

어휘·표현 다지기

p. 149

A

01	제시간에	02	연체료
03	불공정한	04	여행, 여정
05	흔치 않은	06	놓치다
07	장식하다	08	부은
09	문학	10	만족한
11	유명인	12	씹다
13	낙담시키다	14	점원, 직원
15	분리된	16	줄이다, 짧게 하다

B

01	lend	02	look around
03	be busy v-ing	04	break a rule
05	relieved	06	weight
07	sign	08	hand in
09	career	10	related to

실전 모의고사 5회

pp.150-151

01 ④	02 ⑤	03 ②	04 ①	05 ⑤
06 ②	07 ③	08 ②	09 ④	10 ⑤
11 ⑤	12 ④	13 ⑤	14 ⑤	15 ④
16 ③	17 ①	18 ③	19 ①	20 ②

01 ④

M What are you doing?
W I'm picking out a new smartphone case online. What do you think of this one?
M It's okay. I like the big heart in the middle.
W Yes. And there's a bird flying in front of the heart.
M What does it say underneath the heart?
W It says "Always Free." So, do you like it?
M Yes. I think it's cute.
W Okay. I'll buy this one!

남 뭐 하고 있어?
여 온라인에서 새 스마트폰 케이스를 고르고 있어. 이거 어때?
남 괜찮네. 가운데에 있는 커다란 하트가 마음에 들어.
여 응. 그리고 하트 앞에 날고 있는 새가 있어.
남 하트 밑에 뭐라고 쓰여 있는 거야?
여 "Always Free"라고 쓰여 있네. 그래서 마음에 드니?
남 응. 귀여운 것 같아.

여 좋아. 이걸 살래!

|어휘| pick out (여러 개 중에서 신중히) 고르다 in the middle 가운데에 say [동] ~라고 쓰여 있다 underneath [전] ~ 밑에

02 ⑤

W John, what are you doing this Saturday?
M Nothing special. Why?
W My school club is holding a bazaar to help neighbors in need. Why don't you come?
M I should. What time does it start?
W It starts at 9:00 a.m. and closes at 5:00 p.m.
M Sounds good. Where will it be held?
W We decided to do it at the school gym.
M How many booths will there be?
W We have enough room for about fifty booths in the gym. There will be a lot of stuff to look at!
M Great! I'll see you on Saturday.

여 John, 이번 주 토요일에 뭐 하니?
남 별다른 계획은 없어. 왜?
여 내 학교 동아리에서 어려움에 처한 이웃을 돕기 위해 바자회를 열거든. 오는 게 어때?
남 그래야겠다. 언제 시작해?
여 오전 9시에 시작해서 오후 5시에 닫아.
남 좋네. 어디에서 열리니?
여 학교 체육관에서 열기로 결정했어.
남 부스가 몇 개나 있을까?
여 체육관에 50개 정도의 부스를 위한 공간이 있어. 볼 물건이 많을 거야!
남 좋다! 토요일에 보자.

|어휘| hold [동] 열다, 개최하다 bazaar [명] 바자회 neighbor [명] 이웃 in need 어려움에 처한 decide [동] 결정하다

03 ②

[Telephone rings.]
W Go Travel. Can I help you?
M Yes, I'd like to check my reservation. My name is Eric Roberts.
W Let's see... You have a reservation for the 8:00 p.m. flight to Tokyo on Friday.
M That's right. Will a meal be served on that flight?
W Yes, a full dinner will be served. And you're checking just one bag?
M Yes. Do I have a window seat?
W Yes. And you've already paid, so your reservation is all set.

[전화벨이 울린다.]
여 Go Travel입니다. 도와드릴까요?
남 네, 제 예약 사항을 확인하려고요. 제 이름은 Eric Roberts입니다.
여 확인해보죠… 금요일 저녁 8시 도쿄행 항공편을 예약하셨네요.
남 맞습니다. 항공편에 식사가 제공되나요?
여 네, 정찬이 제공됩니다. 그리고 가방은 한 개만 부치시나요?
남 네. 저 창가 자리인가요?
여 네. 그리고 이미 결제를 하셨으니, 예약이 모두 확정되셨습니다.

|해설| 남자가 예약 사항을 확인하려고 전화해서 기내식 제공 여부, 좌석 위치 등을 묻고 있다.

|어휘| meal [명] 식사 full dinner 정찬 (모든 코스가 다 제공되는 저녁) check [동] (비행기를 탈 때 수화물을) 부치다 be all set 준비가 되어 있다

04 ①

W Let's go see the fireworks show at Central Park tonight!
M Sure! What time does it start?
W It starts at 7:00 p.m.
M Okay. It will take about forty-five minutes to drive there. So let's leave an hour before the show starts.
W Well, there will be lots of traffic today because of the show. Two hours would be better.
M All right. Or we could take the subway. It only takes thirty minutes.
W The subway will be too crowded. Let's drive there.

여 오늘 밤에 센트럴파크에서 열리는 불꽃놀이를 보러 가자!
남 좋아! 몇 시에 시작하지?
여 저녁 7시에 시작해.
남 알았어. 거기에 운전해서 가는 데 45분 정도 걸릴 거야. 그러니까 행사 시작하기 한 시간 전에 출발하자.
여 음, 불꽃놀이 때문에 오늘 교통량이 많을 거야. 두 시간 전이 더 좋을 거야.
남 알았어. 아니면 우리 지하철을 타도 돼. 30분밖에 안 걸려.
여 지하철은 너무 붐빌 거야. 거기 운전해서 가자.

|해설| 불꽃놀이는 저녁 7시에 시작하는데 여자가 시작하기 두 시간 전에 출발하여 운전해서 가자고 했으므로, 두 사람은 5시에 출발할 것이다.

|어휘| crowded [형] 붐비는

05 ⑤

W Hello. Can I help you with something?

M Yes. I'm looking for a briefcase. I think I left it on the bus this morning.

W I see. Well, we have several briefcases. Is this one yours?

M No, mine is brown with a black stripe down the center.

W Hmm, let's see... I think this might be it.

M Yes, that's it!

W Great. Here you go. Please take a look inside to see if everything is there.

M Oh, everything is here! This is very important to me. Thank you.

여 안녕하세요. 무엇을 도와드릴까요?

남 네. 저는 서류 가방을 찾고 있어요. 오늘 아침에 버스에 놓고 내린 것 같아요.

여 알겠습니다. 음, 서류 가방이 몇 개 있네요. 이것이 손님 건가요?

남 아니요, 제 것은 하단 중앙에 검은색 줄무늬가 있는 갈색 거예요.

여 흠, 어디 봅시다… 이게 그것 같네요.

남 네, 바로 그거예요!

여 잘됐네요. 여기 있습니다. 물건이 다 있는지 안을 한번 보세요.

남 아, 다 여기 있네요! 이건 저에게 아주 중요하거든요. 고맙습니다.

|해설| 남자가 서류 가방을 버스에 놓고 내렸다고 하자 여자가 여러 서류 가방 중에서 남자의 것을 찾아주고 있으므로, 두 사람이 대화하는 장소는 분실물 보관소가 가장 적절하다.

|어휘| briefcase [명] 서류 가방 stripe [명] 줄무늬 take a look ~을 (한번) 보다

06 ②

① **W** Excuse me, sir. Where can I find tomato sauce?
M Our tomato sauce is in aisle three.

② **W** Which of these do you prefer?
M Let's get the one on the right. It's cheaper.

③ **W** We need to buy some food for dinner.
M Why don't we go to the supermarket?

④ **W** Look what I bought at the store this morning!
M Oh, great! That's my favorite snack.

⑤ **W** Can you carry my shopping bags for me?
M Sure. I'd be happy to help you.

① 여 실례합니다. 토마토소스를 어디에서 찾을 수 있죠?
남 토마토소스는 3번 통로에 있습니다.

② 여 이것들 중에서 뭐가 더 좋아?
남 오른쪽에 있는 걸 사자. 그게 더 싸네.

③ 여 저녁거리를 좀 사야 해.
남 우리 슈퍼마켓에 가는 게 어때?

④ 여 오늘 아침에 내가 가게에서 사 온 것을 봐!
남 오, 좋다! 저건 내가 제일 좋아하는 간식이야.

⑤ 여 내 쇼핑백 좀 들어줄 수 있니?
남 그럼. 기꺼이 도와줄게.

|어휘| carry [동] 나르다, 들고 있다

07 ③

W What are you doing, Ronald?

M It's my turn to clean the classroom this week.

W Would you like some help?

M Well, I've already swept the floor. Could you empty the trash can?

W Sure! No problem.

M Thanks a lot. I just need to erase the whiteboard, and then I'll be finished!

W Great. Then we can walk home together.

여 뭐 하니, Ronald?

남 이번 주에 내가 교실을 청소할 차례야.

여 좀 도와줄까?

남 음, 내가 이미 바닥은 쓸었어. 쓰레기통 좀 비워줄 수 있어?

여 그럼! 문제없어.

남 정말 고마워. 이제 화이트보드만 지우고 나면 끝날 거야!

여 잘됐네. 그럼 우리 집에 같이 걸어갈 수 있겠다.

|어휘| turn [명] 차례 sweep [동] (바닥을 빗자루 등으로) 쓸다, 청소하다 floor [명] 바닥 empty [동] 비우다 trash can 쓰레기통 erase [동] 지우다

08 ②

M Roosevelt Middle School will hold its annual Sports Day on Friday, May 3. It will take place on the school soccer field. Games will include soccer, badminton, baseball, and more. First-year and second-year students should wear red T-shirts, while third-year students should wear blue T-shirts. It's supposed to be warm and sunny on Friday, so be sure to bring plenty of water.

남 Roosevelt 중학교에서 5월 3일 금요일에 연례 체육대회를 개최합니다. 학교 축구장에서 개최될 예정입니다. 축구, 배드민턴, 야구와 기타 경기를 포함할 것입니다. 1학년과 2학년 학생들은 빨간색 티셔츠를 입어야 하는 데 반해, 3학년 학생들은 파란색 티셔츠를 입어야 합니다. 금요일에는 날씨가 따뜻하고 화창할 것이므로, 반드시 물을 많이 가져오시기 바랍니다.

|어휘| annual [형] 연례의 take place 개최되다 include [동] 포함하다 while [접] ~인데 반하여 be supposed to-v ~하기로 되어 있다, ~할 예정이다 be sure to-v 반드시 ~하다 plenty of 많은

09 ④

W You can find these in romantic restaurants. People light them. They create a special light that makes the dinner feel special. They are found in many shapes, sizes, and colors. Some even have special smells. Traditionally, they were used to light rooms. These days, they are usually found on birthday cakes. The number of these on a birthday cake often shows the age of the birthday person.

여 이것은 낭만적인 식당에서 찾을 수 있습니다. 사람들은 이것에 불을 붙입니다. 이것은 저녁 식사를 특별하게 느껴지게 하는 특별한 빛을 만듭니다. 많은 형태, 크기, 색깔을 찾아볼 수 있습니다. 심지어 어떤 것은 특별한 향도 있습니다. 전통적으로 이것은 방을 밝히는 데 쓰였습니다. 요즘에는 보통 생일 케이크 위에서 찾아볼 수 있습니다. 생일 케이크 위의 이것의 개수는 보통 생일을 맞은 사람의 나이를 나타냅니다.

|어휘| romantic [형] 낭만적인, 로맨틱한 light [동] 불을 붙이다, 밝히다 [명] 빛 traditionally [부] 전통적으로 age [명] 나이

10 ⑤

① **M** I'm not feeling well.
W Is there anything I can do to help?
② **M** I can't believe that you broke my Bluetooth speakers!
W I owe you an apology.
③ **M** It was the best game I've ever seen!
W I couldn't agree more.
④ **M** Wow! Look at all those clouds. I think it's about to rain.
W Yes, it looks like it will.
⑤ **M** Can you guess how old I am?
W I haven't seen you in ages.

① **남** 몸 상태가 좋지 않아.
여 내가 도와줄 게 있을까?
② **남** 네가 내 블루투스 스피커를 고장 내다니 믿을 수가 없어!
여 정말 미안해.
③ **남** 그건 내가 본 최고의 게임이었어!
여 그 말에 완전히 동의해.
④ **남** 와! 저 구름 봐. 비가 막 올 것 같아.
여 응, 그럴 것 같네.
⑤ **남** 내가 몇 살인지 맞혀볼래?
여 오랫동안 널 보지 못했어.

|해설| 자신의 나이를 맞혀보라는 질문에 오랫동안 보지 못했다는 대답은 어색하다.

|어휘| feel well 건강 상태가 좋다 owe ~ an apology ~에게 사과할 것이 있다 be about to-v 막 ~하려고 하다 in ages 오랫동안

11 ⑤

M This research project is very difficult.
W It's about endangered animals, isn't it?
M Yes. I already found information in the library and went to a few zoos.
W Why did you go to the zoos?
M I took photos of animals for the presentation. Now I need to write descriptions of them.
W What will you do after that?
M Nothing. After that, I'll be finished. I'm going to start now.
W Good luck!

남 이 연구 과제 정말 어렵네.
여 멸종 위기에 처한 동물에 관한 거지?
남 응. 이미 도서관에서 자료는 찾았고 동물원도 몇 군데 갔었어.
여 동물원에는 왜 갔어?
남 발표를 위해서 동물 사진을 찍었거든. 이제 그 사진들에 관한 설명을 써야 해.
여 그 후에는 뭘 할 건데?
남 아무것도 없어. 그러고 나면 끝나. 지금 시작할 거야.
여 잘해봐!

|어휘| research [명] 연구 project [명] 과제 endangered [형] (동식물이) 멸종 위기에 처한 take a photo of ~의 사진을 찍다 description [명] 기술, 설명

12 ④

M I need to buy a rice cooker. Can you help me choose one?
W Sure! I'd be happy to help.
M Here's a list of rice cookers.
W Okay. How much money can you spend?
M I can only spend $100 or less.
W That's enough. Do you need a medium or large rice cooker?
M Actually, I want a small one. I don't have much space

in my kitchen.
W All right. And does the color matter?
M Any color is fine, except red.
W In that case, you should buy this one!

남 나 밥솥을 사야 해. 고르는 것을 도와줄 수 있니?
여 물론이지! 얼마든지 도와줄게.
남 여기 밥솥 목록이 있어.
여 알겠어. 돈을 얼마나 쓸 수 있어?
남 100달러 이하로만 쓸 수 있어.
여 그거면 충분해. 중형이나 대형 밥솥이 필요하니?
남 사실 나는 작은 것을 원해. 부엌에 공간이 많지 않거든.
여 그렇구나. 색깔이 중요하니?
남 빨간색을 제외하고는 어떤 색깔이든 좋아.
여 그렇다면 넌 이걸 사야겠다!

|해설| 남자는 100달러 이하의 소형 밥솥을 원하며, 빨간색을 제외하면 어떤 색깔이든 괜찮다고 했다.

|어휘| rice cooker 밥솥 list [명] 목록 spend [동] (돈 · 시간 등을) 쓰다 matter [동] 중요하다, 문제 되다 except [전] ~을 제외하고

13 ⑤

M Hi, Chloe. Are we still going to meet on Wednesday night?
W Oh, I forgot all about that! I have a soccer game that night.
M That's okay. How about meeting on Tuesday instead?
W I have class on Tuesdays and Thursdays.
M And I have to work on Friday night. How about Saturday then?
W That's fine with me. I'll see you then!

남 안녕, Chloe. 우리 수요일 저녁에 만나는 거 맞지?
여 아, 그걸 완전히 잊어버리고 있었네! 나 그날 밤에 축구 경기가 있는데.
남 괜찮아. 대신 화요일에 만나는 건 어때?
여 난 매주 화요일과 목요일에 수업이 있어.
남 난 금요일 밤에 일해야 해. 그럼 토요일은 어때?
여 그건 괜찮아. 그때 보자!

|어휘| be fine with ~에게 괜찮다, ~은 좋다

14 ⑤

W Hello, Mr. Park. My name is Amy, and I am in charge of this construction project.
M Nice to meet you, Amy.
W Did you visit our construction site this morning?
M No. I went to check out the building supplies this morning.
W I see. Then do you have any time in the afternoon?
M I have a meeting in the afternoon, but I can postpone it to another day. Let's visit the construction site.
W All right. Meet me here at one o'clock.

여 Park 씨, 안녕하세요. 저는 이 건설 사업을 맡은 Amy라고 합니다.
남 만나서 반갑습니다, Amy 씨.
여 오늘 오전에 저희 건설 현장을 방문해 보셨나요?
남 아니요. 오늘 오전에는 건축 자재를 확인하러 갔었습니다.
여 그렇군요. 그럼 오후에 시간 있으신가요?
남 오후에 회의가 하나 있지만, 다른 날로 미룰 수 있습니다. 건설 현장을 방문해 보도록 하죠.
여 좋습니다. 여기서 1시에 저와 만나시죠.

|어휘| in charge of ~을 맡아서[담당해서] construction [명] 건설 site [명] 장소, 현장 building supplies 건축 자재 postpone [동] 연기하다, 미루다

15 ④

M Good afternoon, listeners. This is James, the manager of our community center. I'd like to tell you about our new community contest, Pawsitively Fantastic Pets. This is a big contest that anyone can participate in. It will be held in our center and the prize is $100. The person who has the best performance with their pet will win the prize. If you are interested in this contest, please visit our website.

남 안녕하세요, 청취자 여러분. 지역 사회 센터의 관리자 James입니다. 저는 여러분에게 새로운 지역 사회 대회인 Pawsitively Fantastic Pets에 대해 말씀드리려고 합니다. 이 대회는 누구나 참여할 수 있는 큰 대회입니다. 대회는 우리 센터에서 열릴 것이고 상금은 100달러입니다. 반려동물과 최고의 공연을 하는 사람이 상금을 탈 것입니다. 이 대회에 관심이 있으시다면, 저희 웹사이트를 방문해 주세요.

|어휘| community [명] 지역 사회 prize [명] 상금

16 ③

W Hello. I'd like to buy a purse.
M Okay. Do you prefer large purses or small ones?
W I'm looking for a large one.
M How about this one? It's $100.
W That's too expensive. Can I get a discount?
M No. I'm sorry. It's a new item, so I can't give you a

discount.

W That's too bad.

M This one is on sale. It's also $100, but it's 30% off. If you buy it today, I'll take an additional 10% off.

W I can get 40% off? I'll take it.

여 안녕하세요. 지갑을 사고 싶어요.

남 알겠습니다. 큰 지갑을 선호하시나요, 아니면 작은 지갑을 선호하시나요?

여 큰 것을 찾고 있어요.

남 이건 어떠세요? 100달러입니다.

여 너무 비싸네요. 할인을 받을 수 있나요?

남 아니요. 죄송합니다. 이게 신상품이어서 할인해 드릴 수가 없네요.

여 아쉽네요.

남 이건 할인 판매 중입니다. 이것도 100달러이지만, 30% 할인됩니다. 오늘 사신다면, 추가로 10% 할인해 드리겠습니다.

여 40%를 할인받을 수 있다고요? 그걸로 할게요.

|어휘| purse [명] 지갑 new item 신상품 give a discount 할인해 주다 additional [형] 추가의

17 ①

W I won't be at work on Monday. I'm going to Hawaii for a week.

M You've been there before, haven't you? Why do you like it so much?

W Because I really like beaches and warm weather.

M That's a good reason. But there are lots of other places with beautiful beaches.

W Yes, but my sister's family lives in Hawaii. So I don't have to pay for a hotel when I go there.

M You're lucky to have relatives who live there!

② You should have reserved a hotel room earlier.
③ I think you'd like Hawaii if you ever went there.
④ That's too bad, but you can visit your sister next time.
⑤ You should tell them that you want some time alone.

여 나 월요일에 회사에 없을 거야. 일주일 동안 하와이 가려고.

남 거기 전에 가본 적 있지 않아? 거기를 왜 그렇게 좋아해?

여 해변과 따뜻한 날씨를 정말 좋아하기 때문이야.

남 좋은 이유네. 하지만 아름다운 해변이 있는 곳은 많은 걸.

여 그렇지. 하지만 우리 여동생 가족이 하와이에 살거든. 그래서 그곳에 가면 호텔 비용을 지불할 필요가 없어.

남 거기 사는 친척이 있다니 행운이네!

② 넌 호텔 객실을 더 일찍 예약했어야 했어.
③ 너도 하와이에 가게 된다면 그곳을 좋아할 거야.
④ 안됐다. 하지만 다음번에 여동생을 방문할 수 있을 거야.
⑤ 네가 혼자 있는 시간을 좀 원한다고 그들에게 말해야 해.

|어휘| [문제] relative [명] 친척, 친지

18 ③

M This is my new dog, Ralph. He's a three-month-old poodle.

W Oh! He's so cute! Where did you get him?

M He didn't have a home, so I adopted him.

W That's great. I want to get a dog too.

M Then why don't you get one? There are many dogs that need homes.

W I'd love to, but there's just one problem.

M What is it?

W My parents won't let me.

① I'll adopt one next month.
② I got my dog from my cousin.
④ I really enjoy taking care of my dog.
⑤ Ralph needs to find a good home.

남 얘는 내 새로운 개, Ralph야. 3개월 된 푸들이야.

여 아! 엄청 귀엽다! 어디서 났어?

남 유기견이어서 내가 입양했어.

여 좋다. 나도 개 키우고 싶어.

남 그럼 한 마리 키우는 게 어때? 집을 필요로 하는 개가 많아.

여 그러고 싶지만, 문제가 딱 하나 있어.

남 뭔데?

여 부모님께서 허락하지 않으실 거야.

① 나는 다음 달에 한 마리 입양할 거야.
② 나는 사촌으로부터 개를 얻었어.
④ 나는 개를 돌보는 것이 정말 즐거워.
⑤ Ralph는 좋은 가정을 찾아야 해.

|어휘| adopt [동] 입양하다 [문제] let [동] 허락하다

19 ①

W Hi, Peter. What did you do yesterday?

M My classmates and I went to our teacher's wedding. I saw Eunjae there.

W Really? What was she doing there? She doesn't go to your school, does she?

M No, she doesn't. Actually, I hadn't seen her for a long time.

W So why was she there?

M The man my teacher was marrying is her cousin!

W It's a small world, isn't it?

② I was really happy to see her.

③ Congratulations! You did a good job.
④ There were about 150 people at the wedding.
⑤ They were the most beautiful couple.

여 안녕, Peter. 어제 뭐 했니?
남 반 친구들이랑 우리 선생님 결혼식에 갔었어. 거기서 은재를 봤어.
여 정말? 은재가 거기서 뭐 하고 있었는데? 그 애는 너희 학교를 다니지 않잖아?
남 응, 안 다니지. 실은 오랫동안 은재를 본 적이 없었어.
여 그래서 은재는 왜 거기에 있었던 건데?
남 우리 선생님과 결혼하신 남자분이 은재의 사촌이야!
여 세상 정말 좁다, 그렇지 않니?

② 난 그 애를 보게 되어 정말 좋았어.
③ 축하해! 잘했어.
④ 결혼식에는 약 150여 명이 있었어.
⑤ 그들은 가장 아름다운 부부였어.

[해설] 한동안 보지 못했던 친구를 선생님 결혼식에서 보게 되었다는 말에 세상이 정말 좁다고 답하는 것이 자연스럽다.

[어휘] marry [동] 결혼하다

20 ②

W Tony drives to work every day. One day, he accidentally locks his keys in his car. He has an extra key, but it's on his desk at home. He knows his sister Olivia is home. He really wants her to bring the spare key to his office so he can drive home. He picks up his phone and calls her. In this situation, what would Tony most likely say to Olivia?
Tony Olivia, would you bring my spare car key to me?

① can you give me a ride to my office?
③ don't worry. I'll bring your key to you soon.
④ I'll pick you up at your office.
⑤ you need to be careful when you drive.

여 Tony는 매일 차로 출근한다. 하루는 그가 실수로 차에 열쇠를 두고 문을 잠갔다. 그에게는 여분의 열쇠가 있긴 하지만 그것은 집 책상 위에 있다. 그는 여동생 Olivia가 집에 있다는 것을 알고 있다. 그는 여동생이 자신의 사무실로 여분의 열쇠를 가져와서 그가 집에 운전해서 돌아갈 수 있기를 바란다. 그는 전화기를 들고 그녀에게 전화를 한다. 이 상황에서, Tony는 Olivia에게 뭐라고 말할까?
Tony Olivia, 내 여분의 차 열쇠를 가져와 줄 수 있니?

① 내 사무실까지 태워줄 수 있어?
③ 걱정하지 마. 내가 곧 너에게 네 열쇠를 가져다줄게.
④ 내가 네 사무실에 너를 태우러 갈게.
⑤ 운전할 때는 조심해야 해.

[어휘] accidentally [부] 우연히, 뜻하지 않게 lock [동] 잠그다 spare key 여분의 열쇠, 스페어 키 [문제] careful [형] 조심하는

어휘·표현 다지기 p. 159

A

01 건설	02 붐비는
03 바자회	04 쓰레기통
05 이웃	06 추가의
07 ~ 밑에	08 나르다, 들고 있다
09 쓸다, 청소하다	10 친척, 친지
11 ~을 맡아서[담당해서]	12 할인해 주다
13 ~을 제외하고	14 기술, 설명
15 입양하다	16 연례의

B

01 in need	02 accidentally
03 in ages	04 pick out
05 briefcase	06 be about to-v
07 be all set	08 be sure to-v
09 matter	10 endangered

실전 모의고사 6회 pp. 160-161

01 ③	02 ④	03 ①	04 ②	05 ①
06 ④	07 ④	08 ④	09 ③	10 ②
11 ④	12 ①	13 ⑤	14 ③	15 ③
16 ④	17 ③	18 ②	19 ③	20 ②

01 ③

M Hey, Bonnie. Did you make this poster yourself?
W Yes, I designed this for the school play. Its title is *Long Time No See*.
M I like that you put the title at the top.
W Me too. I also put a clock in the bottom left corner.
M That's great. Why didn't you add "Goodland High School" under the title?
W I didn't think it was necessary. Instead, I put the ticket price under the title.
M I see. The tickets are five dollars?
W Yes, they are. You should come!

남 안녕, Bonnie. 네가 이 포스터 직접 만들었니?

여 응, 내가 교내 연극을 위해 디자인했어. 연극 제목은 〈Long Time No See〉야.
남 네가 제목을 맨 위에 넣은 것이 마음에 들어.
여 나도 그래. 왼쪽 하단 모퉁이에 시계도 하나 넣었어.
남 그거 멋지다. 왜 제목 아래에 'Goodland 고등학교'를 넣지 않았니?
여 그게 필요할 것 같지 않았어. 대신 제목 아래에 표 가격을 넣었어.
남 그렇구나. 표가 5달러니?
여 응, 맞아. 너 와야 해!

|어휘| corner [명] 모퉁이 necessary [형] 필요한

02 ④

W Good morning. This is the Fantastic Hotel.
M Hello. My name is Lucas Barton, and I'd like to check in.
W All right. This is the room key. Also, our hotel offers a storage service for valuables, so please let us know if you need to use it.
M Thank you. Where is the exercise facility in the hotel?
W It's on the 2nd floor. If you want to use the swimming pool, it is located on the 9th floor.
M Thank you. Is my checkout time eleven o'clock?
W Yes, that's right. Enjoy your stay!

여 좋은 아침입니다. Fantastic Hotel입니다.
남 안녕하세요. 저는 Lucas Barton이고, 체크인하려고요.
여 네. 여기 방 키입니다. 그리고 저희 호텔은 귀중품 보관 서비스를 제공하고 있으니, 이용하시려면 말씀해 주십시오.
남 감사합니다. 호텔에 운동 시설은 어디에 있나요?
여 2층에 있습니다. 수영장을 이용하고 싶으시면, 9층에 위치해 있습니다.
남 감사합니다. 체크아웃 시간이 11시인가요?
여 네, 맞습니다. 좋은 시간 보내십시오!

|어휘| check in 체크인하다 offer [동] 제공하다 storage [명] 보관 valuables [명] 귀중품 facility [명] 시설 be located 위치하다

03 ①

[Cell phone rings.]
W Hello?
M Hi, Cindy.
W Hi, Mr. Johnson. I'm just feeding Jason now.
M Good. I have to stay at the office late today. I still have a lot of work to do.
W Oh, I'm sorry to hear that.
M If you're free this evening, could you babysit Jason a little longer? My wife also has to work late.
W Sure, no problem. How long do you need me to stay?
M For two or three more hours. Is that okay?
W That's fine.

[휴대전화벨이 울린다.]
여 여보세요?
남 안녕하세요, Cindy.
여 네, Johnson 씨. 지금 막 Jason에게 밥을 먹이는 중이에요.
남 좋아요. 제가 오늘 사무실에 늦게까지 있어야 해요. 아직 할 일이 많아서요.
여 아, 안타깝네요.
남 오늘 저녁에 시간 여유 있으시면, Jason을 조금 더 봐 주실 수 있나요? 아내도 늦게까지 일해야 해서요.
여 물론이죠, 문제없어요. 제가 얼마나 오래 있어야 할까요?
남 두세 시간 더요. 괜찮으신가요?
여 괜찮아요.

|어휘| feed [동] 밥을 먹이다 babysit [동] 아이를 봐 주다

04 ②

W Oliver, I'm really looking forward to our trip.
M Me too. It's been a long time since we traveled abroad. What time is our flight?
W It's at nine thirty in the morning.
M Then shall we meet at the bus stop at seven o'clock?
W I think that's too late. We have to arrive at the airport at least three hours in advance.
M Then should we meet at the bus stop at six o'clock?
W Okay. Are you going to shop at the airport?
M No. I don't have anything to buy.
W Then I'll see you in front of the bus stop.

여 Oliver, 우리 여행 정말 기대된다.
남 나도 그래. 우리 해외로 여행한 지 오래됐지. 우리 항공편이 몇 시지?
여 오전 9시 30분이야.
남 그럼 7시에 버스 정류장에서 만날까?
여 그건 너무 늦을 것 같아. 우리는 적어도 3시간 미리 공항에 도착해야 해.
남 그럼 버스 정류장에서 6시에 만나면 될까?
여 그래. 공항에서 쇼핑할 거니?
남 아니. 나는 살 거 없어.
여 그럼 버스 정류장 앞에서 보자.

|어휘| look forward to ~을 기대하다 abroad [부] 해외로 in advance 미리, 전부터

05 ①

W How may I help you?
M I would like to get some flowers for my wife for our 10th wedding anniversary.
W Okay. Which ones would you like?
M Do you have any pink roses? My wife carried a bouquet of them at our wedding. Pink is her favorite.
W I'm afraid not. We only have red ones now.
M Hmm… Then can you wrap them in pink paper?
W No problem! We have many different kinds of pink paper.

여 무엇을 도와드릴까요?
남 결혼 10주년 기념일이라 아내에게 꽃을 좀 사주고 싶어요.
여 알겠습니다. 어떤 걸로 하시겠어요?
남 분홍색 장미 있나요? 아내가 결혼식에서 그 꽃으로 된 부케를 들었거든요. 분홍색은 아내가 제일 좋아하는 색이에요.
여 유감스럽게도 없네요. 지금 빨간색 장미만 있어요.
남 음… 그러면 그걸 분홍색 종이로 포장해주실 수 있나요?
여 그럼요! 저희는 많은 종류의 분홍색 종이가 있어요.

|어휘| wedding anniversary 결혼기념일 bouquet [명] 부케, 꽃다발 wrap [동] 포장하다, 싸다 kind [명] 종류

06 ④

① **M** What's wrong, Sally?
W I have a sore throat and a fever.
② **M** Can you tell me how to get to the post office?
W It's five minutes from here. I'll show you the way.
③ **M** What a big box!
W We need two more boxes to pack all those clothes.
④ **M** Do you need help carrying that? It looks heavy.
W Thank you! That would be great.
⑤ **M** Which size box would you like?
W The largest one, please.

① 남 무슨 일이야, Sally?
여 목이 아프고 열도 나.
② 남 우체국에 어떻게 가는지 알려주실 수 있나요?
여 여기서 5분 거리예요. 제가 길을 알려드릴게요.
③ 남 상자가 정말 크네!
여 우리가 저 옷들을 다 싸려면 상자가 두 개 더 필요해.
④ 남 그거 옮기는 데 도움 필요하니? 무거워 보여.
여 고마워! 그래 주면 좋을 것 같아.
⑤ 남 어떤 크기의 상자로 하시겠어요?
여 가장 큰 것으로 주세요.

|어휘| sore [형] 아픈 throat [명] 목, 목구멍 fever [명] 열 pack [동] (짐을) 싸다, 꾸리다

07 ④

W Hi, Frank! I heard that you're moving next month.
M I am! The apartment I found is much closer to my office.
W That's great! Are you going to have a housewarming party?
M I'm not sure. I'm just focusing on packing right now.
W Oh, I see. Do you have a lot to do?
M Yes. If you're not busy this weekend, could you help me pack?
W Sure!

여 안녕, Frank! 너 다음 달에 이사한다고 들었어.
남 응! 내가 찾은 아파트가 우리 사무실과 훨씬 더 가까워.
여 잘됐다! 집들이할 거야?
남 잘 모르겠어. 지금 당장은 그냥 짐 싸는 데 집중하고 있어.
여 아, 그렇구나. 짐 쌀 거 많아?
남 응. 이번 주말에 바쁘지 않으면, 내가 짐 싸는 걸 도와줄 수 있니?
여 물론이지!

|어휘| move [동] 이사하다 office [명] 사무실 housewarming party 집들이 focus on ~에 집중하다

08 ④

M Good morning, students. Don't forget that our class field trip is on Friday, March 4. We will visit a jellybean factory. The CEO of the company will give us a tour, and she will also teach us how to make jellybeans. The cost of the trip is $50. Please ask your parents to sign this form. I would like it back by this Wednesday.

남 좋은 아침입니다, 학생 여러분. 우리 학급 견학이 3월 4일 금요일에 있다는 것을 잊지 마세요. 우리는 젤리과자 공장에 갈 예정입니다. 그 회사 대표님께서 우리에게 견학을 시켜주시고 젤리과자 만드는 방법도 알려주실 겁니다. 견학 비용은 50달러입니다. 부모님께 이 양식에 서명해달라고 말씀드리세요. 이번 주 수요일까지는 양식을 제출하기 바랍니다.

|어휘| field trip 견학, 현장 학습 factory [명] 공장 cost [명] 비용 sign [동] 서명하다, 사인하다 form [명] 양식

09 ③

W You can find this in your house. It stands upright and is pushed across the floor. It sucks up small pieces of food and dirt, so it helps keep the floor clean. It can be used on almost any kind of surface, from hardwood to carpet. It can even clean hard-to-reach areas like corners!

여 여러분은 이것을 집에서 찾아볼 수 있습니다. 이것을 똑바로 세워서 바닥에 밉니다. 이것은 작은 음식 조각과 먼지를 빨아들여서, 바닥을 깨끗하게 유지하는 데 도움을 줍니다. 이것은 원목부터 카펫까지 거의 모든 종류의 표면에 이용할 수 있습니다. 이것은 모퉁이처럼 닿기 어려운 부분까지도 청소할 수 있습니다!

|어휘| upright ㈜ 똑바로 suck up ~을 빨아올리다 piece ㈐ 조각 dirt ㈐ 먼지 surface ㈐ 표면 hardwood ㈐ 원목 carpet ㈐ 카펫 area ㈐ 구역, 부분

10 ②

① M What do you want to be when you grow up?
　 W I'm interested in space, so I want to be an astronaut.
② M When did you get up this morning?
　 W I will get up no later than 7:00 a.m.
③ M Are you afraid of spiders?
　 W I was afraid of them when I was younger, but not anymore.
④ M I love your new dress!
　 W Thank you for noticing!
⑤ M What's the matter?
　 W I lost my favorite cap on the subway this morning.

① 남 너는 커서 뭐가 되고 싶니?
　 여 나는 우주에 관심이 있어서, 우주비행사가 되고 싶어.
② 남 오늘 아침에 몇 시에 일어났니?
　 여 나는 늦어도 7시까지는 일어날 거야.
③ 남 너 거미 무서워하니?
　 여 어렸을 때는 무서워했는데 더는 아니야.
④ 남 네 새 원피스 예쁘다!
　 여 알아봐 줘서 고마워!
⑤ 남 무슨 일 있니?
　 여 오늘 아침에 지하철에서 내가 정말 좋아하는 모자를 잃어버렸어.

|어휘| space ㈐ 우주 astronaut ㈐ 우주비행사 no later than 늦어도 ~까지는 be afraid of ~을 두려워하다[무서워하다] notice ㈌ 알아채다

11 ④

M What is Mr. Grey doing? Why is he working in the sun in this hot weather?

W Hmm… I think he is pulling weeds out of his garden.
M It looks like it will take a long time to weed the garden. I'll go over there and ask him if he needs help.
W Good idea!
M Do you have a hat?
W Yes. It's in the garage. I'll go find it now.

남 Grey 씨가 뭘 하시는 거지? 왜 이렇게 더운 날씨에 햇빛 아래에서 일하고 계시지?
여 음… 정원에 있는 잡초를 뽑고 계신 것 같아.
남 정원의 잡초를 뽑는 건 시간이 오래 걸릴 것 같은데. 내가 저쪽에 가서 도움이 필요하신지 여쭤볼게.
여 좋은 생각이야!
남 모자 있니?
여 응. 차고에 있어. 내가 지금 가서 찾아볼게.

|해설| 모자 있냐는 남자의 질문에 찾아보겠다고 답했으므로, 여자는 모자를 찾으러 차고에 갈 것이다.

|어휘| pull out ~을 뽑다 weed ㈐ 잡초 ㈌ 잡초를 뽑다 garage ㈐ 차고

12 ①

M I'm here to check in.
W Okay. We have three window seats and two aisle seats left.
M I would like a window seat.
W Two of them are in the back. Is that okay?
M No, I don't like sitting in the back. Where is the other window seat?
W It's in the middle, but it's next to the emergency exit.
M I don't want to sit next to an emergency exit. Where are the two aisle seats?
W One is on the left side of the plane in the middle. The other one is on the right side near the front.
M I prefer the front.

남 탑승 수속을 하러 왔습니다.
여 네. 창가 쪽 좌석 세 곳과 통로 쪽 좌석 두 곳이 남아 있습니다.
남 창가 쪽 좌석으로 하고 싶어요.
여 그중 두 곳은 뒤쪽입니다. 괜찮으세요?
남 아니요, 뒤쪽에 앉는 것은 싫습니다. 다른 창가 쪽 좌석은 어디인가요?
여 그건 중간에 있긴 한데, 비상구 옆이에요.
남 비상구 옆자리도 앉고 싶지 않네요. 통로 쪽 좌석 두 곳은 어디에 있나요?
여 하나는 비행기 좌측 중앙에 있습니다. 다른 하나는 우측 앞쪽 근처에 있고요.

남 앞이 더 좋겠네요.

|어휘| check in 탑승 수속을 하다 aisle [명] 통로 emergency exit 비상구 front [명] 앞면, 앞쪽

13 ⑤

M Hey Subin, how do you like my smile? I just got my teeth cleaned at the dentist.

W Hi, Josh. It looks good! I should go to the dentist too. It's been more than a year since I've been to one.

M More than a year? You need to get your teeth checked more often than that.

W I know, but I'm always so busy.

M Even though you're busy, you still need to take care of yourself. I recommend going to my dentist. *[pause]* How about going on the afternoon of the thirteenth? That's the earliest you can make a reservation for.

W I have a meeting on the afternoon of the thirteenth. How about the seventeenth?

M The clinic is fully booked then. Would a week from the seventeenth work?

W Yes. I'll make a reservation right now.

남 안녕, 수빈아, 나 웃는 거 어때? 치과에서 치아 스케일링을 받았어.

여 안녕, Josh. 좋아 보여! 나도 치과에 가야 하는데. 치과에 간 지 1년이 넘었어.

남 1년이 넘었다고? 그보다 더 자주 치아 검진을 받아야 해.

여 아는데, 늘 정말 바빠.

남 바쁘더라도 몸을 관리해야지. 우리 치과에 가는 걸 추천해. [잠시 후] 13일 오후에 가는 게 어때? 그때가 예약할 수 있는 가장 빠른 거야.

여 13일 오후에는 회의가 있어. 17일은 어때?

남 그때는 병원 예약이 꽉 찼어. 17일에서 일주일 뒤는 괜찮을까?

여 응. 지금 예약할게.

|어휘| get one's teeth cleaned 치아를 세척하다[스케일링을 받다] recommend [동] 추천하다 clinic [명] 병원 fully booked 모두 예약된

14 ③

W Do you know where we are? Nothing looks familiar to me.

M I thought we were close to the hotel, but I don't see it.

W Maybe we should call the front desk and ask for directions.

M That's a good idea, but I don't know the number.

W Well, there's a taxi over there.

M Oh! I will go ask the driver for directions.

여 우리가 어디에 있는지 알아? 익숙해 보이는 것이 하나도 없어.

남 우리가 호텔 근처에 있다고 생각했는데, 호텔이 안 보이네.

여 아마 호텔 안내 데스크에 전화해서 길을 물어봐야 할 것 같아.

남 좋은 생각이긴 한데, 난 번호를 모르는 걸.

여 음, 저기 택시가 있다.

남 아! 내가 가서 택시 기사님께 길을 여쭤볼게.

|어휘| familiar [형] 익숙한 front desk 안내 데스크 directions [명] 길 안내

15 ③

M Good afternoon, residents. I'm Mike Wilson, the resident representative. Recently, people who do not live in our apartment building have been frequently entering the building. To solve this problem, we would like to install a locked gate at the front of the building. Starting next week, all residents should use a phone application to enter the apartment. I will post the name of the app on the noticeboard of the apartment. Thank you.

남 좋은 오후입니다, 주민 여러분. 저는 주민 대표 Mike Wilson입니다. 최근 우리 아파트에 살지 않는 사람들이 건물에 들어오는 일이 잦아지고 있습니다. 이 문제를 해결하기 위해, 건물 앞쪽에 차단문을 설치하려고 합니다. 다음 주부터, 모든 주민들은 아파트에 들어오려면 휴대전화 앱을 이용하셔야 합니다. 앱 이름은 아파트 게시판에 게시하겠습니다. 감사합니다.

|어휘| resident [명] 주민 representative [명] 대표(자) enter [동] 들어오다[가다] solve [동] 해결하다 install [동] 설치하다 application [명] 애플리케이션, 앱 noticeboard [명] 게시판

16 ④

W I'd like to rent bikes for four people. I'm here with my husband and kids.

M Okay. We have regular bikes and two-seater bikes.

W How much is it to rent a regular bike?

M It's $5 for thirty minutes and $10 for an hour.

W Okay. I'd like to rent two regular bikes for an hour for my kids.

M Sure. Would you and your husband like a two-seater bike? They're $7 for thirty minutes and $11 for an hour.

W Yes. I would like to rent one for an hour.

여 네 사람이 이용할 자전거를 빌리고 싶은데요. 제 남편이랑 아이들과 함께 왔어요.
남 알겠습니다. 일반 자전거와 2인용 자전거가 있어요.
여 일반 자전거를 빌리는 건 얼마인가요?
남 30분에 5달러이고, 한 시간에는 10달러입니다.
여 그렇군요. 아이들이 이용할 일반 자전거 두 대를 한 시간 동안 빌리고 싶어요.
남 그러시죠. 손님하고 남편분은 2인용 자전거로 하시겠어요? 그건 30분에 7달러이고, 한 시간에 11달러예요.
여 네. 그걸로 한 시간 빌릴게요.

|해설| 여자는 한 시간 동안 일반 자전거 두 대($20)와 2인용 자전거 한 대($11)를 빌리기로 했다.

|어휘| rent [동] 빌리다 regular [형] 일반적인, 보통의

17 ③

M Excuse me. Can you help me?
W Sure. What can I do for you?
M I want to find my seat, but I can't figure out where it is.
W May I see your ticket? *[pause]* You're on the wrong floor right now. Your seat is on the second floor.
M What? That can't be true. I reserved a seat on the first floor.
W Well, the ticket says your seat is in row D on the second floor.
M Can you go to the ticket booth and make sure my ticket is right?
W Yes. Please wait here for a moment while I go check.

① All right. I'll call a taxi for you. It can seat four people.
② No, this ticket is not available. Can you pick another one?
④ Yes, the performance will start in a minute. You can enter now.
⑤ No. Cancellation on the day of the performance is not possible.

남 저기요. 저 좀 도와주시겠어요?
여 네. 무엇을 도와드릴까요?
남 제 자리를 찾고 싶은데요, 어디인지 알 수가 없네요.
여 티켓을 봐도 될까요? [잠시 후] 지금 다른 층에 계시네요. 고객님 자리는 2층에 있습니다.
남 네? 그럴 리가 없어요. 저는 1층에 있는 자리를 예매했는데요.
여 글쎄요, 티켓에는 고객님 자리가 2층 D열이라고 되어 있네요.
남 매표소에 가서 제 티켓이 맞는지 확인해 주시겠어요?
여 네. 제가 가서 확인하는 동안 여기서 잠시 기다려주세요.

① 알겠습니다. 택시를 불러드리겠습니다. 4인이 앉으실 수 있어요.
② 아니요, 이 티켓은 사용하실 수 없습니다. 다른 것을 고르시겠어요?
④ 네, 공연이 곧 시작할 거예요. 지금 들어가시면 됩니다.
⑤ 아니요. 공연 당일 취소는 불가능합니다.

|해설| 남자가 자신이 예매한 자리와 표가 다르다며 매표소에 가서 확인해 달라고 요청했으므로, 확인할 동안 잠시 기다려 달라고 말하는 ③이 가장 적절하다.

|어휘| figure out ~을 이해하다[알아내다] floor [명] 층 ticket booth 매표소 **[문제]** available [형] 이용 가능한 for a moment 잠시 cancellation [명] 취소

18 ②

W Hi, Jeremy. Do you still have the book I lent you six weeks ago?
M Umm… I thought I gave it back to you already. What is it called?
W *European Fairytales*. It's one of my favorite books.
M Oh no. I think I lent it to Ethan. I forgot that it was yours.
W Well, can you ask him when I can get it back?
M Okay. I'll ask him and let you know.

① I donated it to the library.
③ Okay, don't forget to return the book.
④ Ethan doesn't have a library card.
⑤ I don't know much about fairytales.

여 안녕, Jeremy. 너 내가 6주 전에 빌려줬던 책 아직 가지고 있니?
남 음… 내가 너에게 이미 돌려줬다고 생각했는데. 그거 제목이 뭐지?
여 〈유럽의 동화들〉이야. 내가 정말 좋아하는 책 중 하나지.
남 아, 저런. 내가 그거 Ethan에게 빌려준 것 같아. 그게 네 것이라는 걸 깜박했어.
여 음, 내가 언제 돌려받을 수 있을지 그 애한테 물어봐 줄 수 있니?
남 알겠어. Ethan에게 물어보고 알려줄게.

① 그거 내가 도서관에 기증했어.
③ 알겠어, 책 반납하는 것 잊지 마.
④ Ethan은 대출증을 가지고 있지 않아.
⑤ 나는 동화에 대해 잘 몰라.

|어휘| lend [동] 빌려주다 fairytale [명] 동화 **[문제]** donate [동] 기증하다

19 ③

M Lauren, it's 11:00 p.m. Aren't you going to bed soon?
W I'm afraid not, Dad. I need to study for my Spanish test. I didn't study for it at all today.

M What were you doing instead?
W I went to the pool with Amy. After that, we went shopping for a few hours.
M You should have stayed home and studied.
W Yeah, I realize that now.
M I hope you learned your lesson.

① You don't feel like talking, right?
② How did you do on your test?
④ What should I do to speak Spanish well?
⑤ I'd rather not swim today.

남 Lauren, 밤 11시다. 곧 자러 안 가니?
여 못 잘 것 같아요, 아빠. 스페인어 시험공부 해야 해요. 오늘 공부를 전혀 안 했어요.
남 그럼 뭐 하고 있었는데?
여 Amy랑 수영장에 갔었어요. 그 후에 몇 시간 동안 쇼핑을 했고요.
남 넌 집에 남아서 공부를 했어야지.
여 네, 이제 깨달았어요.
남 네가 교훈을 얻었길 바란다.

① 너는 말하고 싶지 않은 거야, 맞지?
② 시험 어떻게 봤니?
④ 스페인어를 잘하기 위해서는 어떻게 해야 하니?
⑤ 오늘은 수영을 안 하는 게 낫겠어.

|어휘| stay [동] 머물다 realize [동] 깨닫다 **[문제]** feel like v-ing ~하고 싶다 lesson [명] 교훈 would rather not ~하지 않는 게 낫겠다

20 ②

W Samantha just moved into a new apartment. After living there for several days, she noticed that there was a small water stain on her ceiling. When she came home from work the next day, she saw that water was dripping from the ceiling and landing on the floor. In this situation, what would Samantha most likely say to the owner?
Samantha I think one of the pipes is leaking.

① It rains too much here.
③ I don't like the color of the wallpaper.
④ The apartment is flooded.
⑤ There is a stain on the door.

여 Samantha는 새 아파트에 막 이사 왔다. 며칠간 그곳에 산 뒤에, 그녀는 천장에 작은 물 얼룩이 있는 것을 발견했다. 다음 날 일을 마치고 집에 왔을 때, 그녀는 천장에서 물이 뚝뚝 흘러 바닥에 떨어지는 것을 보았다. 이 상황에서, Samantha는 집주인에게 뭐라고 말할까?
Samantha 배관 중 하나가 새는 것 같아요.

① 이곳은 비가 너무 많이 와요.
③ 벽지 색이 마음에 들지 않아요.
④ 아파트가 침수되었어요.
⑤ 문에 얼룩이 있어요.

|해설| 집 천장에서 물이 새는 상황이므로, Samantha는 집주인에게 그와 관련된 건의나 요청 사항을 말할 것이다.

|어휘| stain [명] 얼룩 ceiling [명] 천장 drip [동] 방울방울[뚝뚝] 흐르다 land [동] (땅 · 표면에) 내려앉다 owner [명] 주인, 소유자 **[문제]** leak [동] 새다 wallpaper [명] 벽지 flood [동] 물에 잠기게 하다

어휘 · 표현 다지기

p. 169

A

01	필요한	02	잡초, 잡초를 뽑다
03	아이를 봐 주다	04	밥을 먹이다
05	아픈	06	차고
07	공장	08	체크인하다, 탑승 수속을 하다
09	앞면, 앞쪽	10	표면
11	먼지	12	익숙한
13	우주비행사	14	비상구
15	천장	16	집들이

B

01	leak	02	directions
03	stain	04	wrap
05	noticeboard	06	regular
07	no later than	08	focus on
09	figure out	10	install

시험 직전 모의고사 1회

pp. 170 - 171

01 ①	02 ⑤	03 ②	04 ③	05 ①
06 ①	07 ④	08 ③	09 ⑤	10 ③
11 ②	12 ①	13 ③	14 ①	15 ②
16 ④	17 ①	18 ④	19 ⑤	20 ④

01 ①

M I love your kite, Carrie! Did you make it yourself?
W I did! I made it out of paper and bamboo. Do you like its diamond shape?

M Definitely. I think it'll fly high in the sky. What did you paint on it?
W I painted a dragon. Do you think I should add one more tail to the kite?
M No, it looks nice with three tails. Four would be too many.
W Yeah, you're right. I can't wait to fly it!

남 네 연 정말 마음에 든다, Carrie! 네가 직접 만든 거야?
여 응! 종이랑 대나무로 만들었어. 마름모 모양이 마음에 드니?
남 그렇고말고. 하늘 높이 날 것 같아. 연에 무엇을 그린 거야?
여 용을 그렸어. 연에 꼬리를 하나 더 더해야 할까?
남 아니, 꼬리 세 개가 보기 좋아. 네 개는 너무 많을 거야.
여 그래, 네 말이 맞아. 빨리 이거 날려보고 싶다!

|어휘| kite [명] 연 bamboo [명] 대나무 diamond [명] 마름모꼴 shape [명] 모양 definitely [부] 그렇고말고 dragon [명] 용 add [동] 더하다 tail [명] 꼬리 can't wait to-v 빨리 ~하고 싶다

02 ⑤

W Andy, what are you doing?
M I'm playing a game called *Fantastic Village*. It is the latest game released in 2023.
W Really? What kind of game is it?
M It's a game where you make your own village. The goal of the game is to make a village that everyone is satisfied with.
W It looks interesting. Is there an age recommendation for the game?
M Yes. This game is made for ages 7 and up.
W What is the rating of the game?
M One website rated it 4.7 out of 5.
W That's very high. I'll download it when I get home.

여 Andy, 뭐 하니?
남 나는 〈Fantastic Village〉라는 게임을 하고 있어. 2023년에 출시된 최신 게임이야.
여 정말? 어떤 게임인데?
남 마을을 만드는 게임이야. 모두가 만족하는 마을을 만드는 게 게임의 목표야.
여 재미있어 보인다. 게임에 추천 연령이 있니?
남 응. 7세 이상 연령을 위해 만들어졌어.
여 그 게임의 평점이 얼마나 되니?
남 한 웹사이트에서 5점 만점에 4.7점으로 평가했어.
여 아주 높네. 집에 가서 다운로드해야겠다.

|어휘| village [명] 마을 latest [형] 최신의 release [동] 출시하다 goal [명] 목표 be satisfied with ~에 만족하다 recommendation [명] 추천 rating [명] 평가, 평점, 등급 rate [동] 평가하다

03 ②

[Cell phone rings.]
W Hello?
M Hi, Laura. This is Adam. Are you on your way to the concert hall?
W I'm waiting for you in a café next to the concert hall.
M I'm actually running late. So... Could we meet at six fifty instead?
W But the show starts at six thirty, remember? We are not allowed to enter once it begins.
M Oh no! I thought the show started later.
W Please try your best to get here in time.

[휴대전화벨이 울린다.]
여 여보세요?
남 안녕, Laura. 나 Adam이야. 콘서트장 가는 길이니?
여 콘서트장 옆에 있는 카페에서 너 기다리고 있어.
남 실은 나 늦을 것 같아. 그래서… 우리 대신에 6시 50분에 만나도 될까?
여 하지만 공연이 6시 30분에 시작하잖아, 기억하지? 공연이 일단 시작되면 입장이 허용되지 않아.
남 아, 이런! 공연이 더 늦게 시작하는 줄 알았어.
여 시간 맞춰 여기 올 수 있게 최선을 다해봐.

|어휘| on one's way to ~로 가는 길에 actually [부] 실은 remember [동] 기억하다 be allowed to-v ~하는 것이 허용되다 enter [동] 들어가다 once [접] 일단 ~하면 show [명] 공연 try one's best 최선을 다하다

04 ③

M Hi, Sophia. Have you heard about the new movie called *The Car*?
W Yeah. I heard it's amazing. I'm definitely going to see it.
M Then why don't we go see it together this Sunday?
W Sounds great. Let me check the movie times. *[pause]* Sunday at nine or eleven a.m. looks fine.
M I have a piano lesson in the morning, so the evening works for me.
W I have an appointment in the evening. I'll look for another movie theater. *[pause]* How about Sunday at three o'clock?
M All right. Let's meet in front of the movie theater.

남 안녕, Sophia. 〈The car〉라는 새로 개봉한 영화에 대해 들어봤

니?

여 응. 굉장하다고 들었어. 그 영화를 꼭 볼 거야.

남 그럼 이번 주 일요일에 함께 보러 가는 게 어때?

여 좋아. 내가 영화 시간을 확인해볼게. [잠시 후] 일요일 오전 9시나 11시가 괜찮아 보이네.

남 나는 아침에 피아노 레슨이 있어서, 저녁 시간이 괜찮아.

여 저녁에는 내가 약속이 있어. 내가 다른 영화관을 찾아볼게. [잠시 후] 일요일 3시는 어때?

남 좋아. 영화관 앞에서 만나자.

|어휘| amazing [형] 놀라운 definitely [부] 분명히, 꼭 appointment [명] 약속 in front of ~ 앞에서 movie theater 영화관

05 ①

M I can't believe this!

W What is it? Did something happen?

M I just picked up my favorite scarf from the dry cleaner's.

W The light blue one you spilled grape juice on?

M Yes, that one. I paid full price, but the stain is still there!

W No way!

M That's not all. I also noticed that there is a small tear in it.

W That's terrible. The dry cleaner's must have damaged it.

남 믿을 수가 없어!

여 뭔데? 무슨 일 있니?

남 나 방금 세탁소에서 내가 제일 좋아하는 목도리를 찾아왔거든.

여 네가 포도 주스를 쏟았던 하늘색 목도리 말이지?

남 응, 그거야. 전액 지불했는데, 얼룩이 여전히 있어!

여 말도 안 돼!

남 그게 다가 아니야. 작게 찢어진 부분이 있는 것도 발견했어.

여 심하다. 세탁소에서 훼손한 게 분명해.

|어휘| happen [동] 일어나다, 발생하다 pick up (어디에서) ~을 찾아오다 dry cleaner's 세탁소 spill [동] (액체 등을) 흘리다, 쏟다 pay [동] 지불하다 notice [동] 알아채다 tear [명] 찢어진 데[곳] terrible [형] 끔찍한, 심한 damage [동] 훼손하다

06 ①

① M I'm going to take out the trash now.

W Make sure you separate the recyclable materials first.

② M Look at this place! It's terrible.

W I agree. People shouldn't throw trash on the ground.

③ M What are some ways to reduce the amount of garbage we produce?

W We can use fewer disposable products.

④ M Honey, did you throw away my favorite sweater?

W Yes, I did. It had a big hole in it.

⑤ M Are you okay, dear? You look tired.

W I am. The garbage truck woke me up at six o'clock this morning.

① 남 나 지금 쓰레기 버리러 갈 거야.

여 먼저 재활용이 가능한 소재들을 분리하도록 해.

② 남 이곳 봐! 심하다.

여 맞아. 사람들이 바닥에 쓰레기를 버리면 안 되는데.

③ 남 우리가 만들어내는 쓰레기의 양을 줄이는 방법에는 무엇이 있을까?

여 일회용품을 더 적게 쓰면 돼.

④ 남 여보, 내가 제일 좋아하는 스웨터 버렸어요?

여 네, 버렸어요. 큰 구멍이 났던데요.

⑤ 남 얘야, 너 괜찮니? 피곤해 보인다.

여 피곤해요. 오늘 아침 6시에 쓰레기 차 때문에 깼거든요.

|어휘| trash [명] 쓰레기 separate [동] 분리하다, 분리되다 recyclable [형] 재활용할 수 있는 material [명] 물질, 소재 throw [동] 버리다 ground [명] 땅 reduce [동] 줄이다 amount [명] 양 garbage [명] 쓰레기 produce [동] 만들어내다 disposable product 일회용품 hole [명] 구멍

07 ④

W Here are your business cards, Sean. How is your first day at work going?

M Wow, thank you so much. Everything is going really well so far.

W That's good! Did you connect your printer already?

M Yes, I just did. Oh, could you order some office supplies for me? I need a couple of pens and some notebooks.

W Of course. I'll let you know once they arrive.

M I appreciate it, Tiffany.

여 여기 명함이에요, Sean. 출근 첫날은 어떤가요?

남 와, 정말 감사합니다. 지금까지는 모든 것이 정말 순조로워요.

여 좋네요! 벌써 프린터를 연결했나요?

남 네, 방금 했습니다. 아, 제 사무용품 좀 주문해주실 수 있나요? 펜 두세 자루와 노트 몇 권이 필요해서요.

여 물론이죠. 도착하면 알려드릴게요.

남 감사합니다, Tiffany.

|어휘| business card 명함　so far 지금까지　connect [동] 연결하다　office supplies 사무용품　a couple of 두서너 개의　arrive [동] 도착하다　appreciate [동] 고마워하다

08 ③

M Hello, passengers of Flight 25. We're sorry to inform you that there is a mechanical problem with the airplane. Our aircraft mechanics are working on it right now. Unfortunately, the flight will be delayed until early tomorrow morning. As an apology, we are offering all passengers a $100 gift certificate. You can use it in the airport gift shop, restaurants, and cafés. Please stop by the ticket counter to pick up your certificate. Again, I'm very sorry for the inconvenience.

남 안녕하세요, 25 항공편 승객 여러분. 항공기에 기계적인 결함이 있음을 알려드리게 되어 죄송합니다. 저희 항공기 정비사가 현재 작업을 하고 있습니다. 유감스럽게도, 항공편은 내일 이른 아침까지 지연되겠습니다. 사과의 뜻으로, 모든 승객분들께 100달러짜리 상품권을 제공해 드릴 예정입니다. 상품권은 공항 기념품점, 음식점, 그리고 커피 전문점에서 사용하실 수 있습니다. 매표구에 들러서 상품권을 받아가시기 바랍니다. 다시 한번 불편을 끼쳐드려 대단히 죄송합니다.

|어휘| passenger [명] 승객　inform [동] 알리다　mechanical [형] 기계적인　aircraft [명] 항공기　mechanic [명] 정비공　delay [동] 지연시키다　apology [명] 사과, 사죄　offer [동] 제공하다　gift certificate 상품권　stop by ~에 들르다　ticket counter 매표구　inconvenience [명] 불편

09 ⑤

W This is found in public places. People use it inside and outside, and it is usually made out of steel. People use this when they're thirsty. Clean tap water comes out of this. To use it, people bend down and drink the water. They don't have to use a cup or glass.

여 이것은 공공장소에서 찾아볼 수 있습니다. 사람들은 이것을 실내외에서 이용하며, 대개는 강철로 만들어집니다. 사람들은 목이 마를 때 이것을 이용합니다. 이것에서 깨끗한 수돗물이 나옵니다. 이것을 이용하기 위해서, 사람들은 몸을 숙이고 물을 마십니다. 컵이나 유리잔은 쓸 필요가 없습니다.

|어휘| public place 공공장소　steel [명] 강철　thirsty [형] 목이 마른　tap water 수돗물　bend down (몸을) 숙이다

10 ③

① **M** Do you play any musical instruments?
W Yes, I play the violin and the piano.
② **M** Would you like some strawberries?
W No, thank you. I'm allergic to them.
③ **M** What time is the boxing match tomorrow?
W It takes about two and a half hours.
④ **M** Can I watch TV now?
W No, you need to brush your teeth first.
⑤ **M** Diane, you said you were going to wash the dishes.
W Sorry, Dad. I'll wash them right now.

① **남** 너 악기 연주하니?
여 응, 나는 바이올린이랑 피아노를 연주해.
② **남** 딸기 좀 먹을래?
여 아니, 괜찮아. 나 딸기에 알레르기가 있어.
③ **남** 내일 권투 시합이 몇 시니?
여 그건 2시간 30분 정도 걸려.
④ **남** 지금 TV 봐도 돼요?
여 아니, 양치부터 해야지.
⑤ **남** Diane, 너 설거지하겠다고 했잖니.
여 죄송해요, 아빠. 지금 당장 할게요.

|어휘| musical instrument 악기　be allergic to ~에 알레르기가 있다　match [명] 경기, 시합　brush one's teeth 양치질을 하다　wash the dishes 설거지하다

11 ②

M Hi, Denise. Have you signed up for summer school yet?
W Not yet. I'm still deciding on what classes to take. Have you?
M Yeah. I'm taking American History and Health Science.
W Those sound like good classes. I'll probably take Basic Coding. I want to learn how to make computer programs.
M Oh, that class might be full by now. I think you should send an email to the teacher and ask if you can still sign up.
W I'll do that right now. Thanks for the suggestion.

남 안녕, Denise. 여름 학교 등록했니?
여 아직 안 했어. 어떤 수업을 들을지 아직도 정하는 중이야. 너는 했어?
남 응. 나는 미국사랑 건강학을 들을 거야.
여 좋은 수업일 것 같아. 나는 아마 기초 코딩을 들을 것 같아. 컴퓨터 프로그램을 어떻게 만드는지 배우고 싶어.

남 아, 그 수업은 지금쯤 꽉 찼을 텐데. 선생님께 이메일을 보내서 네가 아직 등록할 수 있는지 여쭤봐야 할 것 같아.

여 지금 당장 할게. 제안 고마워.

12 ①

M Grace, can you help me choose a bike?

W Sure. Is there a price range you want to stay within?

M Yeah. I don't want it to be over $500.

W All right. What about the material? Which do you like better, steel or aluminum?

M Steel is much stronger than aluminum. I want my bike to be strong.

W There are two options left. Do you need lights on your bike?

M Well, I think it's better to have lights.

W Then this will be the best option for you.

남 Grace, 내가 자전거 고르는 걸 도와줄 수 있니?

여 그럼. 벗어나고 싶지 않은 가격대가 있니?

남 응. 500달러가 넘지 않으면 좋겠어.

여 좋아. 소재는 어때? 강철과 알루미늄 중에 어떤 게 더 좋니?

남 강철이 알루미늄보다 훨씬 더 튼튼해. 나는 자전거가 튼튼하면 좋겠어.

여 두 가지 선택지가 남네. 자전거에 등이 필요하니?

남 글쎄. 등이 있는 게 더 좋을 것 같아.

여 그럼 너한테는 이게 최선의 선택이겠네.

|해설| 남자는 500달러가 넘지 않고, 강철 소재이며 등이 있는 게 좋다고 했다.

13 ③

W Chris, I think we need to set a time to practice for the talent show.

M Okay. I'm not available today because I have to go to the dentist.

W How about the day after tomorrow?

M Wednesday? I have a drum lesson on Wednesday. How about Thursday?

W I have an appointment on Thursday. When does the drum lesson end?

M It ends at five.

W Then let's meet after the drum lesson.

M All right. I'll see you then.

여 Chris, 우리 장기자랑 연습 시간을 정해야 할 것 같아.

남 좋아. 오늘은 치과에 가야 해서 시간이 없어.

여 모레는 어때?

남 수요일? 수요일에는 드럼 레슨이 있어. 목요일은 어때?

여 목요일에는 내가 약속이 있어. 드럼 레슨이 언제 끝나?

남 5시에 끝나.

여 그럼 드럼 레슨 후에 만나자.

남 알겠어. 그때 보자.

14 ①

W Joshua, what are you doing?

M Hi, Gabrielle. I'm looking for volunteer work.

W Why are you looking for volunteer work?

M I'm applying for an internship at the LM Company soon.

W LM is a big company. Good luck. What have you prepared so far?

M I've only written my resume, but there isn't much on it. So I'm going to do some volunteer work.

W You should also check to see if there are any certificates you can get that can improve your resume.

M Right. I'll look into that. Thank you.

여 Joshua, 뭐 하고 있니?

남 안녕, Gabrielle. 자원봉사 활동을 찾고 있어.

여 자원봉사 활동을 왜 찾니?

남 곧 LM사 인턴직에 지원할 거야.

여 LM은 큰 회사잖아. 잘 해봐. 지금까지 어떤 것을 준비했니?

남 이력서밖에 못 썼는데, 거기에 쓸 게 많이 없어. 그래서 자원봉사 활동을 좀 해보려고.

여 네 이력서를 더욱 좋게 할 수 있는 취득 가능한 자격증이 있는지 알아보는 것도 좋겠다.

남 맞아. 살펴볼게. 고마워.

15 ②

M Ladies and gentlemen, may I have your attention, please? The game scheduled for today has been canceled due to too much snow. We sincerely apologize for the sudden cancellation of the game. Ticket refunds will be available on the right side of the ticket office, or you can rebook tickets for a different date. We promise a better response to changes in weather in the future. All ticket holders will be provided with a free drink on their next visit to the stadium. Thank you.

남 신사 숙녀 여러분, 주목해 주시겠습니까? 눈이 너무 많이 오는 관계로 오늘로 예정된 경기는 취소되었습니다. 갑작스러운 경기 취소에 대해 진심으로 사과드립니다. 티켓 환불은 매표소 오른쪽에서 가능하며, 혹은 다른 날짜의 티켓으로 다시 예약하실 수 있습니다. 앞으로는 기후 변화에 더 나은 대응을 약속드립니다. 표 구매자는 다음에 경기장에 방문 시 무료 음료 한 잔을 제공받으시게 됩니다. 감사합니다.

|어휘| schedule [동] 예정하다 cancel [동] 취소하다 due to ~ 때문에 sincerely [부] 진심으로 apologize [동] 사과하다 sudden [형] 갑작스러운 cancellation [명] 취소 refund [명] 환불 rebook [동] 다시 예약하다 promise [동] 약속하다 response [명] 대응 ticket holder 표 구매자 provide [동] 제공하다 stadium [명] 경기장

16 ④

M Hello. How much does it cost to rent a guitar for a month?

W The acoustic guitars are $50 per month, and the electric guitars are $75 per month.

M I'd like to rent an acoustic guitar.

W Okay. If you rent it for two months, I will take $20 off the price.

M Oh, that's great! I'll rent it for two months, then. I also want to get this guitar stand.

W Sure. It's $35. I'll add it to your bill.

남 안녕하세요. 한 달 동안 기타를 빌리는 데 비용이 얼마나 드나요?

여 통기타는 한 달에 50달러이고, 전자 기타는 한 달에 75달러입니다.

남 통기타를 빌리고 싶어요.

여 알겠습니다. 두 달 동안 빌리신다면, 비용에서 20달러를 할인해 드릴게요.

남 아, 그거 좋네요! 그럼 두 달 동안 빌릴게요. 그리고 이 기타 지지대도 사고 싶어요.

여 알겠습니다. 그건 35달러예요. 계산서에 추가하겠습니다.

|해설| 남자는 통기타를 두 달치 빌리는 비용인 100달러에서 20달러의 할인을 받았는데, 추가로 35달러짜리 기타 지지대도 사겠다고 했으므로 남자가 지불할 총 금액은 115달러이다.

|어휘| cost [동] 비용이 들다 rent [동] 빌리다 acoustic guitar 통기타 per [전] ~당 electric guitar 전자 기타 stand [명] 지지대 bill [명] 계산서

17 ①

M Ashley! It's been a long time since we've last met.

W How have you been, Anthony? You look incredible.

M Yeah, I've been working out these days.

W Good for you. I think I should exercise too.

M You should! You can get energy from exercising. What is your favorite sport?

W I like playing badminton the most.

M Then how about playing badminton with me every Wednesday?

W I can't. I always work on Wendnesdays.

② Exercising is very good for your health.
③ Good idea. Then I'll see you on Sunday.
④ Can we meet somewhere else?
⑤ Badminton is a boring sport. What about playing soccer?

남 Ashley! 우리 마지막으로 본 이후로 오랜만이다.

여 어떻게 지냈니, Anthony? 너 굉장해 보인다.

남 응, 요즘 운동하거든.

여 정말 잘됐다. 나도 운동을 해야 할 것 같아.

남 그래야지! 운동을 하면 활력을 얻을 수 있어. 가장 좋아하는 운동이 뭐니?

여 배드민턴 치는 것을 제일 좋아해.

남 그럼 나와 매주 수요일마다 배드민턴 칠래?

여 안 돼. 나는 수요일마다 늘 일해.

② 운동은 건강에 매우 좋아.
③ 좋은 생각이야. 그럼 일요일에 봐.
④ 다른 장소에서 만나도 될까?
⑤ 배드민턴은 따분한 운동이야. 축구를 하는 건 어때?

|해설| 남자가 수요일마다 함께 배드민턴을 치자고 제안했으므로, 제안을 받아들이기에 불가능하다고 말하는 대답이 가장 적절하다.

|어휘| incredible [형] 굉장한 work out 운동하다 these days 요즘 exercise [동] 운동하다

18 ④

W Paul, can you visit your grandmother in the hospital

after school today?

M I can't, Mom. I have band practice. Can I go tomorrow instead?

W I promised her that I would see her today, but your brother is sick. I'd like someone else to keep her company this afternoon.

M Okay. I can skip band practice today. Should I bring her something?

W There are some flowers on the table. Please take those with you when you go.

M No problem. I'm sure she'll love these.

① What kind of flowers does she like?
② How long has she been in the hospital?
③ Do you need me to get him some medicine?
⑤ Okay. I'll drop them off at the hospital after band practice.

여 Paul, 오늘 방과 후에 할머니 병문안 갈 수 있니?
남 못 가요, 엄마. 저 밴드 연습이 있어요. 대신 내일 가도 될까요?
여 내가 할머니께 오늘 뵙겠다고 약속드렸는데, 네 남동생이 아프단다. 오후에 다른 누군가가 할머니 곁에 있어 드리면 좋겠는데.
남 알겠어요. 제가 오늘 밴드 연습을 빠지면 돼요. 할머니께 뭐 좀 가져다드려야 할까요?
여 탁자 위에 꽃이 있어. 갈 때 그것을 가져가렴.
남 문제없어요. 할머니께서 분명히 이 꽃을 좋아하실 거예요.

① 할머니는 어떤 꽃을 좋아하세요?
② 할머니는 병원에 입원하신 지 얼마나 되신 건가요?
③ 그 애에게 약을 좀 가져다줄까요?
⑤ 알겠어요. 밴드 연습 끝나고 병원에 그걸 두고 올게요.

|어휘| practice [명] 연습 keep ~ company ~의 곁에 있어 주다 [문제] drop off ~을 갖다 두다

19 ⑤

W What are you doing today, Gordon?

M I'm taking an Italian cooking class at a community college near my house.

W Wow, that's great. What are you going to make?

M We will learn how to make risotto and lasagna.

W Will you get to take some home with you?

M I don't think so. I heard that everyone just eats it there.

W Oh, okay. Maybe you can teach me how to make Italian food sometime!

M Why don't we take the class together?

① There are 20 people in the cooking class.
② I've been to the community college once.
③ I like risotto more than lasagna.
④ I should have chosen Italian food.

여 오늘 뭐 하니, Gordon?
남 우리 집 근처에 있는 지역 전문대학에서 이탈리아 요리 수업을 들을 거야.
여 와, 멋지다. 뭘 만들 건데?
남 우리는 리소토와 라자냐를 만드는 방법을 배울 거야.
여 집에도 좀 가져가게 되니?
남 안 그럴 것 같아. 모든 사람이 그냥 거기서 먹는다고 들었어.
여 아, 그렇구나. 아마도 언젠가 네가 나한테 이탈리아 음식 만드는 법을 가르쳐줄 수 있겠다!
남 우리 수업 같이 듣는 게 어때?

① 요리 수업에 수강생이 스무 명 있어.
② 나는 지역 전문대학에 한 번 가봤어.
③ 나는 라자냐보다 리소토를 더 좋아해.
④ 나는 이탈리아 음식을 선택해야 했어.

|어휘| community college 지역 전문대학 sometime [부] 언젠가

20 ④

W Monica ordered a pair of blue rain boots from her favorite store. The confirmation email she received said that they would be delivered in two days. Unfortunately, a week has passed and she still hasn't gotten them. She wants to call the customer service number and explain the situation. In this situation, what would Monica most likely say to them?

Monica My rain boots should have arrived five days ago.

① Do you have them in a larger size?
② I'd like to order another pair of blue boots.
③ Your rain boots got lost in the mail.
⑤ Your rain boots will be delivered within two days.

여 Monica는 그녀가 가장 좋아하는 가게에서 파란색 장화 한 켤레를 주문했다. 그녀가 받은 (구매) 확인 메일에는 장화가 이틀 뒤에 배송될 것이라고 쓰여 있었다. 유감스럽게도, 일주일이 지났는데도 그녀는 아직 장화를 받지 못했다. 그녀는 고객 서비스 번호로 전화해서 이 상황을 설명하고 싶어 한다. 이 상황에서, Monica는 그들에게 뭐라고 말할까?
Monica 제 장화는 5일 전에 배송되어야 했어요.

① 이걸로 더 큰 치수 있나요?
② 저는 파란색 장화를 한 켤레 더 주문하고 싶습니다.
③ 배송 중에 고객님의 장화가 분실되었네요.
⑤ 고객님의 장화는 이틀 내로 배송될 예정입니다.

|해설| 배송 예정일이 지났는데도 주문한 물건을 받지 못한 상황이다.

|어휘| rain boot 장화   confirmation 몡 확인   receive 통 받다
deliver 통 배달하다   pass 통 지나가다   customer service 고
객 서비스   explain 통 설명하다

시험 직전 모의고사 2회   pp. 172-173

01 ①	02 ③	03 ②	04 ⑤	05 ⑤
06 ④	07 ④	08 ②	09 ①	10 ④
11 ④	12 ②	13 ③	14 ⑤	15 ①
16 ②	17 ③	18 ②	19 ⑤	20 ③

01 ①

M   Sarah! I didn't expect to see you here.

W   I'm here to buy a birthday present for my friend. I'm going to get her this coffee cup.

M   That's a great idea. I like that it has two handles.

W   Me too. It will be easier for her to pick it up. It comes in several patterns. How about this one with polka dots?

M   It's cute but that one with zebra stripes is my favorite.

W   My friend loves animals. I'll get that one.

M   I hope she likes it!

남   Sarah! 우리가 여기서 만날 거라고 예상하지 못했어!

여   난 여기에 친구 선물 사러 왔어. 그 애한테 이 커피잔을 사줄 거야.

남   좋은 생각이다. 손잡이가 두 개인 게 마음에 들어.

여   나도 그래. 친구가 들기도 더 쉬울 거야. 여러 가지 무늬로 나오는 구나. 이 물방울무늬는 어때?

남   귀엽긴 한데, 얼룩말 줄무늬가 있는 게 가장 마음에 들어.

여   친구가 동물을 정말 좋아하거든. 저걸 사야지.

남   그 애가 마음에 들어 하길 바랄게!

|어휘| expect 통 예상하다, 기대하다   handle 몡 손잡이
pick up ~을 들어 올리다   pattern 몡 무늬   polka dot 물방울
무늬   stripe 몡 줄무늬

02 ③

M   Kristen, did you hear the news? There will be a big mart in our town at the end of this month!

W   Really? What will they sell there?

M   They will sell daily necessities, food, and even clothes.

W   That's amazing. Will there be any sales events when it opens?

M   I believe so! I heard they're offering a 20% discount on all purchases in their opening week.

W   That's perfect. Can I take my dog to the mart? I want to go shopping with my dog.

M   It says that the mart allows dogs to enter.

W   That's great. What's the exact opening date?

M   It's June 30th. Let's go shopping together on the opening day.

남   Kristen, 너 그 소식 들었니? 이번 달 말에 우리 동네에 대형 마트 가 생길 거야!

여   정말? 거기에선 뭘 팔 거래?

남   생필품, 음식 그리고 심지어는 옷도 팔 거야.

여   놀랍다. 개점하면 할인 행사가 있을까?

남   그럴 것 같아! 개점하는 주에는 모든 구매품에 대해 20% 할인을 제공한다고 들었어.

여   완벽하다. 마트에 개를 데려가도 될까? 개와 함께 쇼핑하고 싶어.

남   그 마트는 개의 출입을 허용한다고 써 있어.

여   잘됐다. 정확한 개점 날짜는 언제야?

남   6월 30일이야. 개점하는 날 같이 쇼핑 가자.

|어휘| daily necessity 생필품   allow 통 허락하다   exact 혱
정확한

03 ②

[Telephone rings.]

M   Hello, thank you for calling Derek's Art Studio.

W   Hello. This is Lily Potter.

M   Hello, Ms. Potter. Are you calling to enroll in a class?

W   No. Actually, I enrolled in a drawing class a few weeks ago.

M   Let me see... That's right. Your first class starts next Monday at 4:00 p.m.

W   Yes, but I changed my mind. Could I take the oil painting class instead?

M   Hmm. The class is on Tuesdays at 2:00 p.m. Is that okay?

W   Yes, that's fine.

[전화벨이 울린다.]

남   안녕하세요, Derek's Art Studio에 전화 주셔서 감사합니다.

여   안녕하세요. 저는 Lily Potter인데요.

남   안녕하세요, Potter 씨. 수업 등록하려고 전화 주셨나요?

여   아니요. 실은 몇 주 전에 소묘 수업에 등록했어요.

남   한번 볼게요… 맞네요. 첫 수업이 다음 주 월요일 오후 4시에 시작 하네요.

여   네, 그런데 마음이 바뀌었어요. 대신 유화 수업을 들을 수 있나요?

남   음. 그 수업은 매주 화요일 오후 2시에 있습니다. 괜찮으세요?

여   네, 괜찮습니다.

|어휘| enroll in ~에 등록하다 oil painting 유화

04 ⑤

W Oh no! What time is it?
M It's 7:30 p.m. Why?
W I'm late. I'm sorry, but I have to go.
M Do you have to go right now? We still have work to do.
W I'm sorry, but I have to meet Bella in half an hour.
M Can't you just ask Bella to come here?
W That's not possible. I'm going to go eat at her house.
M Then let's meet again tomorrow.

여 이런! 지금 몇 시야?
남 오후 7시 30분이야. 왜?
여 나 늦었어. 미안하지만, 가야겠어.
남 지금 당장 가야 하니? 우리 아직 할 일이 남았잖아.
여 미안하지만, 나는 30분 뒤에 Bella를 만나야 해.
남 그냥 Bella에게 여기로 오라고 부탁하면 안 될까?
여 안 돼. 나는 그 애의 집에 가서 식사를 하기로 했거든.
남 그럼 우리는 내일 다시 만나자.

|어휘| half an hour 30분 possible [형] 가능한

05 ⑤

W Hello. Can I help you with anything?
M Yes. I would like to get a new coat for my wife, but I'm not sure where to start.
W What kind of coat would she like? We have trench coats, winter coats, and fur coats.
M She asked for a new trench coat.
W Okay. What color would she like? We have beige, khaki, and navy blue.
M A khaki one, please.

여 안녕하세요. 도와드릴까요?
남 네. 아내를 위해서 새 코트를 사고 싶은데, 어디서부터 시작해야 할지 모르겠어요.
여 아내분이 어떤 종류의 코트를 좋아하실까요? 저희는 트렌치코트, 겨울 코트, 털 코트가 있는데요.
남 아내가 새 트렌치코트를 부탁했어요.
여 알겠습니다. 아내분께서 어떤 색상을 좋아하시나요? 저희는 베이지색, 카키색, 감청색이 있습니다.
남 카키색으로 주세요.

|어휘| fur [명] 털, 모피

06 ④

① M What's wrong?
W I don't feel well. I have a stomachache.
② M Can I borrow an umbrella?
W I wish I could lend one to you, but I don't have an extra one.
③ M How much is this umbrella?
W It's $16.
④ M Don't forget your umbrella! It's raining outside.
W Thanks, Dad!
⑤ M What are you doing after school today?
W I was planning to go to the park, but it's raining.

① 남 무슨 일이야?
여 몸이 안 좋아요. 배가 아파요.
② 남 우산 좀 빌릴 수 있을까?
여 저도 빌려드리고 싶지만, 여분의 우산이 없어요.
③ 남 이 우산 얼마예요?
여 16달러입니다.
④ 남 우산 챙기는 것 잊지 마! 밖에 비 오고 있어.
여 고마워요, 아빠!
⑤ 남 오늘 방과 후에 뭐 하니?
여 공원에 갈 계획이었는데, 비가 오네요.

|어휘| stomachache [명] 복통 borrow [동] 빌리다 lend [동] 빌려주다 extra [형] 여분의 outside [부] 밖에

07 ④

M Tracy, you look so tired.
W Yeah, Dad. I didn't sleep very well last night.
M Were our neighbors playing loud music again? I can ask them to be quiet.
W No, it wasn't them. I watched a scary movie a few days ago, and I've been having nightmares ever since.
M That's not good. Maybe you need to sleep with the lights on.
W But that would be too bright. Could you buy me a bedroom lamp?
M Oh, sure. Let's get one at the store this afternoon.

남 Tracy, 너 정말 피곤해 보이는구나.
여 네, 아빠. 어젯밤에 잠을 잘 못 잤어요.
남 이웃들이 또 시끄러운 음악을 틀었니? 내가 조용히 해달라고 부탁할 수 있는데.
여 아니요, 이웃 때문이 아니었어요. 제가 며칠 전에 무서운 영화를 봤는데, 그 이후로 악몽을 꾸고 있어요.
남 그거 안됐구나. 아마 불을 켜 놓고 자야 할지도 모르겠네.

여　하지만 그건 너무 밝을 거예요. 침실용 등을 사주실 수 있나요?
남　아, 물론이지. 오늘 오후에 매장에서 하나 사자.

|어휘| loud 휑 시끄러운　scary 휑 무서운　nightmare 몡 악몽
bright 휑 밝은　lamp 몡 등, 램프

08 ②

M　Hello, students. This is Principal Cooper speaking. I'd like to remind you that the International Fair is on May 7. You can purchase tickets at the door thirty minutes before the fair begins. Tickets are $5 for students and $7 for parents and teachers. And if any of you would like to volunteer, tell your homeroom teacher by tomorrow. We need volunteer staff members to guide the international students.

남　안녕하세요, 학생 여러분. 교장 Cooper입니다. 5월 7일에 국제 박람회가 있다는 것을 다시 한번 알려드리려고 합니다. 여러분은 박람회 시작 30분 전에 입구에서 표를 구입할 수 있습니다. 학생 표는 5달러이며, 학부모님과 선생님 표는 7달러입니다. 그리고 여러분 중에서 자원봉사를 하고 싶은 학생이 있다면, 내일까지 담임 교사에게 이야기하세요. 국제 학생들을 안내할 자원봉사 진행 요원이 필요합니다.

|어휘| principal 몡 교장　remind 동 다시 한번 알려주다
international 휑 국제적인　fair 몡 박람회　purchase 동 구입하다　volunteer 동 자원봉사하다 몡 자원봉사　homeroom teacher 담임 교사　guide 동 안내하다

09 ①

W　You can find this in a grocery store. You use it to transport groceries to the checkout counter. When you're shopping, you put the things you want to buy in it. It is made out of steel, and it has four rubber wheels on the bottom and a plastic handle for steering. It also usually has a seat for a child to sit in.

여　여러분은 이것을 식료품점에서 찾아볼 수 있습니다. 여러분은 식료품을 계산대로 옮기기 위해서 이것을 사용합니다. 쇼핑할 때, 여러분은 사고 싶은 것을 이것 안에 넣습니다. 이것은 철로 만들어졌고, 아래쪽에는 4개의 고무바퀴가 있으며 조종을 위한 플라스틱 손잡이도 있습니다. 보통 이것은 아이가 앉을 수 있는 자리도 있습니다.

|어휘| grocery store 식료품점　transport 동 옮기다
checkout counter 계산대　rubber 몡 고무　wheel 몡 바퀴
bottom 몡 아래　steer 동 조종하다

10 ④

① M　What is your cat's name?
　 W　Her name is Tabitha.
② M　Can I try this on?
　 W　Sure. The fitting room is over there.
③ M　What do you like to do in your free time?
　 W　I like to go camping.
④ M　Can you fix my laptop? The screen is cracked.
　 W　There's a free Wi-Fi zone in the lobby. Here is the password.
⑤ M　Shall we meet tomorrow morning to work on our project?
　 W　Sorry, but I have another appointment then.

① 남　네 고양이 이름이 뭐니?
　 여　Tabitha야.
② 남　이거 입어봐도 되나요?
　 여　물론이죠. 탈의실은 저쪽에 있습니다.
③ 남　쉴 때 뭐 하는 걸 좋아해?
　 여　나는 캠핑 가는 걸 좋아해.
④ 남　제 노트북 컴퓨터를 수리해 주실 수 있나요? 화면에 금이 갔어요.
　 여　로비에 무료 와이파이 존이 있습니다. 여기 비밀번호입니다.
⑤ 남　우리 내일 아침에 과제 작업하러 만날까?
　 여　미안하지만, 그때 다른 약속이 있어.

|어휘| try on ~을 입어보다　fitting room 탈의실　fix 동 수리하다　screen 몡 화면　cracked 휑 깨진, 금이 간　lobby 몡 로비
password 몡 비밀번호

11 ④

M　Hi, Julie. How was your dance class?
W　It was okay. I was fifteen minutes late because I couldn't find my tap shoes.
M　Oh no. Did you find them?
W　Yes, I did. My dog had them. He ate some of the leather.
M　That's terrible! I hope your dog is okay. Does he need to go to the vet?
W　My mom took him there this morning. Now I have to get him some medicine.
M　I'm sure he will get better soon.

남　안녕, Julie. 댄스 수업은 어땠니?
여　괜찮았어. 내 탭 슈즈를 못 찾아서 15분 지각했어.
남　아, 이런. 그거 찾았니?
여　응, 찾았어. 우리 개가 가지고 있었어. 가죽을 조금 먹었더라고.
남　큰일이네! 네 개가 괜찮았으면 좋겠다. 동물병원에 가야 하니?
여　엄마가 오늘 아침에 거기 데리고 가셨어. 지금은 개에게 약을 좀

사줘야 해.
남 곧 나을 거라 믿어.

|어휘| tap shoes 탭 슈즈 leather [명] 가죽 vet [명] 수의사 medicine [명] 약 get better 호전되다

12 ②

W I can't wait to go to my first basketball game!
M Where do you think we should park?
W What about one of the spots in front of the snack bar?
M But then we would have to walk really far to get to the entrance.
W That's true. What about section E? It is close to entrance 2.
M Actually, our seats are closer to entrance 1.
W Oh! Then section C would be better.
M But those are handicapped spots. Let's park in the section next to it. We could walk to both entrance 1 and the snack bar.

여 빨리 내 첫 농구 경기를 보러 가고 싶다!
남 우리 어디에 주차해야 할까?
여 매점 앞에 있는 자리 중 한 곳은 어때?
남 하지만 그럼 출입구에 가기 위해 정말 멀리 걸어야 할 거야.
여 맞네. E 구역은 어때? 거긴 2번 출입구와 가까운데.
남 사실, 우리 자리는 1번 출입구에 더 가까워.
여 아! 그러면 C 구역이 더 좋겠다.
남 하지만 거긴 장애인 주차 공간이잖아. 그 옆에 있는 구역에 주차하자. 1번 출입구와 매점 두 곳에 모두 걸어갈 수 있을 거야.

|어휘| park [동] 주차하다 spot [명] 장소 entrance [명] (출)입구 section [명] 구역 handicapped spot 장애인 주차 공간

13 ③

M Good afternoon. How may I help you?
W Hi. I'd like to buy a train ticket to Busan.
M All right. What time would you like to depart?
W Any time before five would be best. I have to arrive in Busan by 7:30 p.m.
M We have a 3:00 p.m. train and a 4:30 p.m. train. Which one would you like?
W The later train would be better. I'd like a ticket for that one, please.
M Here's your ticket. Have a nice trip.

남 좋은 오후입니다. 무엇을 도와드릴까요?
여 안녕하세요. 부산으로 가는 기차표를 구매하고 싶습니다.
남 알겠습니다. 몇 시에 출발하기를 원하시나요?
여 5시 이전 아무 시간이나 좋습니다. 저녁 7시 30분까지는 부산에 도착해야 하거든요.
남 오후 3시 기차와 4시 30분 기차가 있습니다. 어떤 것을 하시겠습니까?
여 더 늦은 기차가 나을 것 같아요. 그 기차로 표 한 장 주세요.
남 여기 티켓 있습니다. 좋은 여행 되십시오.

|해설| 여자는 5시 이전 출발하는 오후 3시 기차와 4시 30분 기차 중에 더 늦은 기차를 타기로 했다.

|어휘| depart [동] 출발하다 arrive [동] 도착하다

14 ⑤

W Hi, Brandon. Did you buy a present for Grandpa's 90th birthday party yet?
M Yes, I bought something a few days ago. But I just realized that I can't go to the party.
W Oh no! Why not?
M I have a piano recital at the same time. It was supposed to be next week, but the date changed.
W I see. Grandpa is going to be disappointed. You should call him and apologize.
M Okay, Mom. I will call him now and say I'm sorry.

여 안녕, Brandon. 할아버지의 구순 잔치 선물은 샀니?
남 네, 며칠 전에 샀어요. 그런데 제가 파티에 갈 수 없다는 걸 방금 깨달았어요.
여 아, 이런! 왜 못 가니?
남 같은 시간에 피아노 연주회가 있어요. 다음 주 예정이었는데, 날짜가 바뀌었어요.
여 알겠다. 할아버지께서 실망하실 텐데. 전화해서 죄송하다고 말씀드려야겠네.
남 네, 엄마. 지금 할아버지께 전화해서 죄송하다고 할게요.

|어휘| realize [동] 깨닫다 recital [명] 연주회 be supposed to-v ~하기로 되어 있다 disappointed [형] 실망한

15 ①

M Good morning, ladies and gentlemen. I'm Steven, stationmaster at Greenville station. Recently, many lost and found items have been brought to our station. If you have lost something at the station, please visit the lost and found center in the station's office. However, if you have lost something on the subway, please call the line management center, as there is nothing we can do to help in such situations. Thank you for listening to this important announcement.

남 좋은 아침입니다, 신사 숙녀 여러분. 저는 Greenville역의 역장 Steven입니다. 최근에 우리 역에 분실물이 많이 들어오고 있습니다. 역에서 물건을 잃어버리셨다면, 역 사무실에 있는 분실물 센터를 방문해 주십시오. 하지만 지하철 안에서 물건을 잃어버리셨다면, 그런 상황에서는 저희가 도와드릴 수 있는 것이 없으니, 해당 노선 관리 센터에 전화하십시오. 중요 알림을 들어주셔서 감사합니다.

|어휘| stationmaster [명] 역장 station [명] 역 recently [부] 최근에 lost and found item 분실물 management center 관리소 situation [명] 상황 announcement [명] 알림

16 ②

W I would like to buy two tickets for the baseball game on Saturday.
M Okay. Where would you like to sit?
W How much are the seats in the middle section of the infield?
M They are $45 each. The seats in the outfield are $30 each.
W I would like two tickets in the outfield, please.
M Sure. Do you have any coupons?
W Yes, I have a coupon for $5 off a full-price ticket.
M Great. I'll subtract that from your total.

여 토요일 야구 경기 표 두 장을 사고 싶어요.
남 알겠습니다. 어디에 앉고 싶으신가요?
여 내야 중앙 구역 자리는 얼마인가요?
남 각 45달러입니다. 외야 좌석은 각 30달러이고요.
여 외야 좌석 표 두 장 주세요.
남 네. 쿠폰 있으신가요?
여 네, 전체 표 값에서 5달러 할인되는 쿠폰이 있어요.
남 잘됐네요. 총액에서 그만큼 빼드릴게요.

|어휘| infield [명] (야구 등의 운동 경기에서의) 내야 outfield [명] 외야 full-price 총 매매가의, 제값의 subtract [동] 빼다, 공제하다 total [명] 총액

17 ③

M Chloe, is it true that you are going to study abroad next month?
W Hey, Jaden. Yeah, it's true.
M You didn't tell me! Where are you going?
W I'm going to Florida, USA.
M Wow, I heard it's very hot there. You should bring a lot of light clothes.
W I will. But I'm worried about who to leave my cat with while I'm away.
M Don't worry. I can take care of it.

① Your cat sleeps a lot.
② Cats are clean animals.
④ I hope you stay healthy in America.
⑤ Feel free to contact me if you leave.

남 Chloe, 네가 다음 달에 외국에 공부하러 갈 거라는 게 사실이니?
여 안녕, Jaden. 응, 사실이야.
남 나한테 말하지 않았잖아! 어디로 가니?
여 미국 플로리다로 가.
남 와, 거긴 아주 덥다고 들었는데. 얇은 옷을 많이 가져가야겠네.
여 그래야지. 그런데 내가 떠나 있는 동안 내 고양이를 누구에게 맡겨야 할지 걱정이야.
남 걱정하지 마. 내가 돌볼 수 있어.

① 네 고양이는 잠을 많이 자는구나.
② 고양이는 깨끗한 동물이야.
④ 네가 미국에서 건강하게 지내기를 바랄게.
⑤ 떠나면 나한테 마음껏 연락해.

|해설| 여자는 미국으로 공부하러 가는데 자신의 고양이를 맡길 곳이 없어 걱정이라고 했으므로, 남자가 고양이를 돌볼 수 있다고 말하는 ③이 가장 적절하다.

|어휘| abroad [부] 외국에, 해외에 be worried about ~에 대해 걱정하다 [문제] take care of ~을 돌보다 stay [동] (어떤 상태에) 머무르다, ~인 채로 있다 feel free to-v 마음껏 ~하다 contact [동] 연락하다

18 ②

[Telephone rings.]
W Hello, this is Great City Tours. How may I help you?
M Hi, this is Joe Merdler. I made a reservation for three people for a tour of Damyang on Saturday.
W Yes. Would you like to change your reservation?
M I want to cancel it, actually. My family and I are planning to go somewhere else on Saturday.
W Oh, I see. Unfortunately, I cannot give you a refund.
M What? Why not?
W You didn't give us enough notice.

① We hope you enjoy the tour.
③ You will receive your refund in a few days.
④ I advise you to cancel your reservation.
⑤ It takes about two hours to go to Damyang.

[전화벨이 울린다.]
여 안녕하세요, Great City Tours입니다. 무엇을 도와드릴까요?
남 안녕하세요, 저는 Joe Merdler입니다. 토요일에 담양 여행 세 사람 예약했었는데요.

여 네. 예약을 변경하시겠습니까?

남 실은 취소하고 싶어서요. 토요일에 가족들과 다른 곳을 가려고 계획 중이거든요.

여 아, 알겠습니다. 유감스럽게도 환불해드릴 수는 없겠네요.

남 네? 왜 안 되는 거죠?

여 저희에게 충분히 미리 알리지 않으셨습니다.

① 즐거운 여행 하시길 바랍니다.
③ 며칠 후에 환불받으실 수 있을 겁니다.
④ 예약 취소를 권해드립니다.
⑤ 담양에 가는 데 2시간 정도 걸립니다.

|어휘| make a reservation 예약하다 plan to-v ~할 계획이다 give a refund 환불해주다 **[문제]** notice [명] (미리) 알림, 통지 receive [동] 받다 advise [동] 충고하다, 권고하다

19 ⑤

[Cell phone rings.]

W Hello?

M Hi, Susan! How have you been?

W Hey, Bob! It's so great to hear from you. I'm doing well. How are you?

M I'm great! I'm planning to visit Baltimore next week.

W Oh, really? We should meet for lunch when you're in town!

M Actually, I was hoping that you could help me find a place to stay. I can't afford a hotel right now.

W You can stay with my brother. He has a spare bedroom.

① You can use this room for today, then.
② How long are you going to stay in a hotel?
③ It's only a five-minute walk from the station.
④ I'm really looking forward to hearing from you.

[휴대전화벨이 울린다.]

여 여보세요?

남 안녕, Susan! 어떻게 지냈어?

여 안녕, Bob! 목소리 들어서 정말 좋다. 난 잘 지내고 있어. 너는 어때?

남 잘 지내! 다음 주에 볼티모어에 가려고 계획 중이야.

여 아, 정말? 네가 동네에 오면 만나서 같이 점심 먹어야겠다!

남 실은 숙소 찾는 걸 네가 도와줬으면 해. 지금 당장 호텔에 묵을 형편이 안 되거든.

여 내 남동생하고 지내면 되겠다. 그 애한테 남는 방이 있어.

① 그럼 너는 오늘 이 방을 쓰면 돼.
② 호텔에 얼마나 오래 묵을 건데?
③ 그곳은 역에서 겨우 도보 5분 거리야.
④ 네 소식을 듣게 되기를 정말 고대하고 있어.

|어휘| afford [동] ~할 여유[형편]가 되다 **[문제]** spare [형] 남는

20 ③

W Tony and his family went to the grand opening of a new restaurant. They made a reservation for 7:00 p.m., but there weren't any tables available when they arrived. After waiting for forty minutes, they were finally seated. The waiter who served them was rude, and he forgot to give them water. After Tony received the check, the owner of the restaurant asked him how the meal was. In this situation, what would Tony most likely say to the owner?

Tony I'm very disappointed with the service here.

① I should have made a reservation today.
② How long do we have to wait for a table?
④ There's something wrong with my check.
⑤ Can I get some water, please?

여 Tony와 그의 가족은 새로 생긴 음식점의 개업식에 갔다. 그들은 오후 7시로 예약을 했지만, 그들이 도착했을 때 앉을 수 있는 테이블이 하나도 없었다. 40분을 기다린 끝에, 그들은 마침내 자리에 앉았다. 그들에게 서비스를 제공한 종업원은 무례했고, 물을 가져다주는 것도 잊었다. Tony가 계산서를 받은 후에, 음식점 주인이 그에게 식사가 어땠는지 물었다. 이 상황에서, Tony는 주인에게 뭐라고 말할까?

Tony 저는 이곳의 서비스에 매우 실망했어요.

① 오늘 예약을 해야 했어요.
② 자리에 앉으려면 얼마나 오래 기다려야 하나요?
④ 제 계산서가 뭔가 잘못됐어요.
⑤ 물 좀 가져다주실래요?

|해설| Tony는 새로 개업한 식당에서 만족스러운 서비스를 받지 못했으므로, 서비스에 대한 실망감을 말하는 ③이 가장 적절하다.

|어휘| grand opening 개업식 finally [부] 마침내 be seated 앉다 serve [동] 서비스를 제공하다 rude [형] 무례한 check [명] 계산서 owner [명] 주인

MEMO

MEMO

MEMO

MEMO

MEMO

기초부터 실전까지 중학 듣기 완성

1316
LISTENING LEVEL 3